ARTHUR WOODY

And The Legend Of The Barefoot Ranger

Also by Duncan Dobie

Dawn of American Deer Hunting, a Photographic Odyssey of Deer Hunting History (2015)

Trophy Whitetails with Pat & Nicole Reeve (2013)

Legendary Whitetails III, Stories and Photos of 40 More of the Greatest Bucks of All Time (2012)

Hunting Mature Whitetails the Lakosky Way (2011)

Whitetail Dawn (2006)

Producing Power Bucks (2002)

The Back to Nature Handbook (1998)

If You've Ever Seen a Rhinoceros Charge… (1992)

White Tales and Other Hunting Stories (1989)

Georgia's Greatest Whitetails (1986)

ARTHUR WOODY
And The Legend Of The Barefoot Ranger

The Man Who Brought Deer Back to the North Georgia Mountains

By Duncan Dobie

Bucksnort Publishing
Marietta, Georgia
2016

Published by Bucksnort Publishing, Ltd.
Marietta, Georgia

For information, please write:

The Donning Company Publishers
731 S. Brunswick
Brookfield, MO 64628

Lex Cavanah, General Manager
Nathan Stufflebean, Production Supervisor
Rick Boley, Graphic Designer
Katie Gardner, Marketing and Project Coordinator
Lynn Walton, Project Director

Library of Congress Cataloging-in-Publication Data

Names: Dobie, Duncan, author.
Title: Arthur Woody and the legend of the barefoot ranger : the man who brought deer back to the north Georgia mountains / by Duncan Dobie.
Description: First edition. | Marietta, Georgia : Bucksnort Publishing, 2016.
Identifiers: LCCN 2016049853 | ISBN 9780615866314
Subjects: LCSH: Woody, Arthur, 1884-1946. | Forest rangers--Georgia--Biography. | Chattahoochee National Forest (Ga.) | Forests and forestry--Georgia--History--20th century. | Wildlife conservation--Georgia--History--20th century. | Forest conservation--Georgia--History--20th century.
Classification: LCC SD129.W66 D63 2016 | DDC 333.7509758/272--dc23
LC record available at https://lccn.loc.gov/2016049853

First Edition

Printed in the United States of America at Walsworth

Dedication

For Jean White McNey and Charlie Elliott –

This book would not have been possible to write without the help of two key individuals – Jean White McNey, Arthur Woody's beloved granddaughter, and my dear friend, Charlie Elliott, who passed away in 2000 at the age of 94. Jean lived with her grandparents during a time which happened to coincide with the years that saw Ranger Woody reach his greatest fame in the outside world. Sadly, Jean also witnessed the rapid decline of her much cherished "Papa" due to his failing health in 1945. Seeing this once energetic and robust man succumb to a debilitating illness beyond anyone's control was not an easy thing to live through – for Jean or her family. I owe Jean so much for sharing with me so much of her personal life and love for her grandfather.

Jean also shared with me her one-of-a-kind scrapbook filled with photos, letters and old newspaper clippings about her larger-than-life grandfather. She was attending North Georgia College in Dahlonega when her grandfather passed away. Shortly after that sad event she had the amazing insight to collect and put together a priceless collection of stories and photos about Ranger Woody. Without access to the photos and stories that she so willingly shared with me, this book would have never gotten off the ground. What's more, an important piece of history would have been lost forever.

When I first started working on this book, I had no idea that my old friend Charlie Elliott would play such a large or important role in its creation. I knew Charlie well back in the late 1980s and early 1990s. I visited him a number of times at his home in Covington, Georgia, after he retired from an extraordinary writing career that spanned many decades. Charlie's office was a veritable museum filled with books, magazines and other memorabilia collected over a lifetime of hunting, fishing and pursuing the various conservation projects with which he had been so deeply involved from a very young age, not to mention his 40 years of being the Southeastern field editor for Outdoor Life magazine. It was always an adventure to visit with Charlie. Today that one-of-a-kind office has been reconstructed and preserved just as it was at the Charlie Elliott Wildlife Center (located about 40 miles east of Atlanta), not far from his longtime home in Covington.

I wrote several magazine stories about Charlie in the late 1980s, and I considered him to be a true mentor to me in my own outdoor writing career. Although I interviewed him several times about his relationship with Ranger Woody, I had no idea he had written so extensively about the Ranger until I started digging up story after story that he had written in various magazines and newspapers during the 1930s and '40s.

Much like Ranger Woody, Charlie was a larger-than-life figure in his own right. He was involved in many of the same historical conservation initiatives that took place during the Ranger Woody era, and much like Ranger Woody, he had his finger in just about every conservation pie. His personal contributions and achievements during his long and productive life are nothing short of amazing. Truly a book should be written about his life and times as well.

It was late in Charlie's life only a few years before his death when I asked him about his relationship with Ranger Woody. Unfortunately, his health was in decline and he was not physically able to tell me a great deal. I got several good stories right from the "horse's mouth," stories that he frequently told, but I had waited too long to tap into the vast resources that were stored away in the recesses of his amazing mind. However, he graciously gave me permission to reprint any or all of the wealth of material he had written about Ranger Woody, much of which I knew nothing about.

Later on, while researching some old magazine stories at the University of Georgia Library in Athens, I soon discovered not one, but numerous magazine articles that Charlie had written about the Ranger in the late 1930s and throughout the '40s.

With the added help of Jean's scrapbook, which also contained a number of newspaper articles and columns that Charlie had penned, I was treated to a storehouse of written accounts about the famous forest ranger. Charlie also wrote several heartfelt tributes to the Ranger after his death and served as a pallbearer at his funeral. All of these stories were eloquently written with love and respect for the man in a way that only a great Southern writer like Charlie could have put down on paper. How lucky I was to locate those stories and use them in this book!

I think Charlie would be very proud to know that I have borrowed many of his own words to describe the man he knew and loved so well. Charlie always wrote about Ranger Woody in a professional, objective way, but reading between the lines you can feel the great respect and love he had for this man. Somehow, I have to feel that he is looking down and smiling from that great trout stream in the sky that he and Ranger Woody no doubt share today. Few individuals left such an important imprint on so many facets of conservation and wildlife management in Georgia during the 1930s and '40s as did Charlie Elliott and his mentor Ranger Arthur Woody!

Because of Jean McNey and Charlie Elliott, two incredible human beings, I will never be able to refer to this book as *my* book. It will always be *our* book. I just thank my lucky stars for Jean and Charlie!

Table of Contents

SECTION THREE –

Legacy

Harry L. Rossoll
Ole Man o' the Mountains
Ranger Woody
Chattahoochee National Forest
Nov 10, 1941
Outdoor Georgia
December, 1941

Foreword

By Jean McNey

Looking around today and seeing so many people whose priorities apparently are getting power, position and money, I am increasingly grateful for the lessons my grandfather, Ranger Arthur Woody (Papa to me), taught me when I lived with him for ten of the most formative years of my life. He did not lecture. He did not preach. His priorities were made unquestionably clear, however, by his actions. He valued everything about the place where he was born and lived all his life.

He cared for every person, rich or poor, young or old. Frequently he provided money for shoes and food for the needy and lent money to those in temporary need. Because he thought every youngster should have access to a high school education, he bought and gave to the county land for a high school building site, and had the stone for the building's exterior quarried near the dam of his lake. He cared about the spiritual welfare of his family and neighbors and therefore helped to build a new church building.

He loved the mountains, the trees on them, and the animals that inhabited them. Consequently he worked to preserve and, when needed, to replenish and restore them. He understood that he functioned best where his roots were – like a hardwood tree whose taproot goes deep into the soil to get the nutrients that give it strength.

These and other principles like them were indelibly etched into my brain as I watched him work, rode with him, fished with him, and always learned from him. I share these reminiscences so that the readers of this book will understand the depths of my gratitude to its author, Duncan Dobie, who has labored long and hard to capture the essence of this man, not simply to review facts and repeat legends that have been embellished considerably since my grandfather's death in 1946.

Jean McNey
Suches, Georgia
April 2016

Introduction –
Arthur Woody, Always Looking Out for His People

"In the annals of wildlife management in North America, there are few success stories as great as that of the white-tailed deer."

White-Tailed Deer: Ecology and Management
R.E. and T.R. McCabe
Stackpole Books, Harrisburg, PA, 1984

In November 2015, my wife and I spent two weeks in Rhode Island. Since it is possible to drive all the way across the smallest state in the Union in just over an hour's time, we spent considerable time wandering from one end of the state to the other exploring historic areas. Driving down Interstate 95, I couldn't help but notice the numerous game management areas peppering the countryside run by the state Department of Environmental Management (DEM). Whenever we passed near one of these wildlife areas, a big smile crossed my face and my thoughts immediately turned to the North Georgia mountains and Ranger Arthur Woody. Nearly 100 years ago, his vision for his beloved mountain region in the early 1920s made wildlife management areas like those scattered across Rhode Island (and every other state) in this great nation the success stories they are today.

For all practical purposes, Ranger Arthur Woody had two driving motivations in life: 1) to help restore the forests, and fish and wildlife species living in those forests, whose populations had been so devastated during the late 1800s; and 2) to lend a helping hand to his fellow mountaineers who had also been severely devastated through years of hard economic times. His mission was not only to bring back the wildlife, but once that task had been achieved, he wanted to share it with the world. He displayed a life-long inclination for helping his fellow man. He gave freely of his money and resources – often spontaneously without any thought of ever being repaid or receiving anything in return.

During the nearly three decades of what is frequently referred to as "the Ranger Woody Regime," Arthur Woody wielded considerable power in the mountain region, especially in his local community of Suches. One might be tempted to ask: Why would a man who had attained a significant degree of financial success as well as a prominent position in his community want to reach out to others during his entire adult life to the degree in which he did? Why would he be inclined to share his wealth with the community at large? And why would he work so hard and devote his life's energies to attain his goals when he could have taken it easy?

There are several possible answers. First, Arthur Woody was a man of his times. As such, it was the mountain way to help others in need. Even though he was an only child (something quite unusual for a mountain family at that time in history), he grew up watching his parents (especially his mother) take in, and in some cases raise, a number of orphan children. Apparently this deep sense of reaching out to others whenever possible was instilled in him at an early age.

The timeless words of Charlie Elliott come to mind here:

> "Woody's influence and kindliness reached beyond the boundaries of the forest. Legend are the stories of a helping hand he gave to his neighbors in need. His generosity was always so matter of fact, so casual that many times it did not dawn on one until later what a fine deed the Ranger had done."

Beyond his upbringing, beyond the legendary façade of being a man's man and refusing to take orders from anyone, Arthur Woody had a heart of gold. He truly cared about his fellow man. Although numerous stories have survived about his incredible generosity, little has been written about his motivation for willingly sharing his wealth with others or why he used his own resources to restore deer and trout to the mountain region. After reading many of those stories and talking to people who knew him well, I think it is safe to say that once he had attained a certain degree of financial independence and success in his life, Arthur Woody felt that it was his Christian obligation to share his wealth with others. This he selflessly did throughout his life. He was a driven man.

That rare form of generosity possessed by Ranger Woody spilled over into his professional life again and again. He adamantly believed that any type of "government property" was actually owned by all Americans. Therefore, the vast wealth contained in the federally owned national forests should be shared by the people whenever possible. That included everything from cutting trees for firewood and boards with which to build a house or a barn to enjoying and utilizing the fish and wildlife resources. It also included the use of material property owned and used by the Forest Service – tools and various types of heavy equipment like tractors and bulldozers (more on that later). In essence, anything owned by the federal government belonged to the people, and as long as he had anything to say about the matter, he intended to do everything he could to allow the people to benefit from the government's great wealth. Sometimes this philosophy got him into hot water with his supervisors.

As a Forest Ranger, he believed with all his heart that the people, especially the *local* people, should be the first to benefit from the government's vast wealth. Certainly one of his primary motivations for improving roads in and around Suches, and across mountain gaps, was to help his people climb out of the 19th century; he helped make this happen so that they could benefit from modern technology, and travel from one place to another in modern vehicles without making it the ordeal it had always been.

Ranger Woody worked tirelessly to see that the local people got their little piece of the government pie whenever possible. And to him, this didn't mean in the form of government handouts. He detested people who were looking for handouts. Fortunately, that concept was rare in the mountain region during the early 1900s. Mountaineers were typically a proud, determined people, and the last thing they wanted was a handout from the government. But hard times made things tough, especially during those long Depression years, and plenty of situations arose where people needed help through no fault of their own.

It's hard to believe that it's been just over 100 years since Ranger Arthur Woody began his amazing, 30-plus-year career with the U.S. Forest Service in the North Georgia mountains. In some ways, ancient history has a way of seeming so recent, and recent history sometimes seems so ancient. When you walk the woods of Sosebee Cove or stand on the edge of Woody Lake and gaze out at the sparkling water, you can feel the Ranger's presence; and it seems as though it all happened just last week.

I never knew Ranger Woody, but I grew up with him. I knew him in my heart. He died seven months before I was born, but I heard many stories about him while I was growing up. As a teenager back in the mid-1960s, I cut my teeth hunting grouse and deer on national forest land near Vogel State Park and trout fishing in many of the streams Ranger Woody had stocked with his beloved "speckled trout." I no doubt walked some of the same trails that Ranger Woody had often walked. He kept popping up in my life over and over again, and finally, like so many people before me, I was taken in under his magical spell. Some day, I promised myself, I would write a book about this man. I thank my lucky stars and the Good Lord above that I am finally able to realize that longtime dream. This book has been a work in progress for many years.

I wanted to portray Ranger Arthur Woody as the high energy, larger-than-life individual that he was. I hope I have been successful in that endeavor. Even though I never knew him personally, this book reflects many of my own instincts and intuitions about him. I have tried very hard to be accurate and factually correct. Since Ranger Woody lived during a very historic time, I have also tried to document many of those historic events that occurred during his 30-plus-year tenure. Any mistakes or omissions belong to me alone. Whenever you write a book about a certain subject, people automatically consider you to be an expert on that subject. I am far from being an expert on Arthur Woody. But I have learned a great deal about him, and I hope I can share some of those fascinating facts with you. Chronicling what is known about his life has been an amazing journey!

And finally, because Ranger Woody was a legend in his own time, many of the stories written about him and his many achievements have been greatly exaggerated. In some cases, they've been embellished to the point of being totally untrue. I refer to some of these stories as the "Woody Myth" and I have tried to separate fact from fiction wherever possible. Sometimes that is a hard thing to do.

In closing, I'd just like to say that you will find some repetition regarding various facts in many of the chapters. I found this to be necessary for the sake of congruity in each chapter. Because the Ranger was such a colorful character in life, I hope this repetition will only bring a smile to your face for a second time.

As the quote at the beginning of this introduction so aptly implies, there are few success conservation stories in North America as great as that of the white-tailed deer. And one of the greatest in American history was initiated and carried forward by Ranger Arthur Woody in the North Georgia mountains. So please sit back, relax and prepare yourself for an incredible and fascinating journey. I don't think you'll be disappointed!

God bless America!

Duncan Dobie
Marietta, Georgia
August 2016

William Arthur Woody was born on April 1, 1884 in a log cabin very similar to this 19th century mountain cabin. (This photo was found in Ranger Woody's safe, so it no doubt has some local significance.) Perhaps it was serendipity that a man with such joy and goodness in his heart would be born on April Fool's Day. All his life, Arthur Woody loved to laugh and play practical jokes on those closest to him. Photo courtesy of Dr. Ed Woody.

A view from Woody Gap looking south into the Yohoola Valley where the Woody family first homesteaded in the early 1840s. Photo circa 1940. Courtesy of Jean McNey.

SECTION ONE –

Mountain Days and Mountain Ways

Being the most recognizable photo of Arthur Woody ever taken, this classic picture of the ranger was made in1940 by iconic Atlanta Constitution photographer Kenneth Rogers. Rogers took numerous photos of Ranger Woody during the early 1940s. This photo has appeared in nearly every story written about Ranger Woody during the last 40 years. Photo courtesy of Jean McNey.

PROLOGUE – An Idea Whose Time Had Come

"Do what needs to be done and get permission later."

Ranger Arthur Woody

It was a simple idea that had been stewing in his mind for quite some time – just over 30 years to be exact. Even though it was a simple idea at its core, it would ultimately have a profound impact on the people of North Georgia, the state and the entire country.

"Ya' gotta start somewhere," the Ranger more-than-likely mused in his boisterous manner. "Ain't nothin' gonna happen 'less we at least give 'er a try."

The Ranger's instincts were usually right on the money and he knew the timing was right for taking this definitive action. Being an "action" person all his life, he was finally ready to begin implementing his plan.

Many of the legends about Arthur Woody are larger than life; that is, more "tall tale" than truth or, what I like to refer to as the "Woody Myth." In this case however, the legend is fairly accurate, with a few small exceptions. According to that legend, at some point during the summer of 1927, probably in June or July, then 43-year-old Arthur Woody reportedly loaded his family into a brand-new 1926 Dodge Brothers sedan and headed for the wilds of North Carolina. His destination was the Pisgah National Forest just south of Asheville, roughly just over 100 miles as the crow flies from his Union County home in Suches. It was probably a good six- or seven-hour journey at best by car over some very poor mountain roads, roads that were mostly unpaved. His reason for making such a trip was to collect and bring home five long-legged, frisky whitetail fawns.

Had he been making the trip a few short years earlier, he would have been using a horse and wagon and it would have taken several days of hard travel. But times had changed drastically over the past two decades in the mountain region. Now those newfangled automobiles had taken over the entire lower world and aeroplanes were beginning to rule the sky. Only a month or so earlier, a relatively unknown American aviator named Charlie Lindbergh had flown his single-engine monoplane named "The Spirit of St. Louis" all the way across the Atlantic Ocean on a non-stop flight from New York to Paris. Young Charlie's daddy had been a prominent congressman from Minnesota for 10 years, and the energetic son had a hankering to make a name for himself as well. This amazing feat made world-wide headlines and Charlie Lindbergh got his wish. Like it or not, he became as an enduring American icon for the rest of his life and his name became a household word.

Few people in Ranger Arthur Woody's isolated community probably even noticed his Dodge Brothers sedan leaving Suches that day, but he too had embarked on a historical journey that would ultimately have far reaching effects. And even though it would be 13 more years before the results of what he was about to do would be fully realized, he too would become an American icon. Perhaps not as famous as Charlie Lindbergh, mind you, but Arthur Woody would go on to become one of the most famous forest rangers of the 20th century!

By 1927, the Ranger's immediate family consisted of his devoted wife June and three grown children – Walter, 25, his oldest son; Clyne, 22, his youngest son; and Mae or "Mae Bird" as he often called her, 20, his only daughter. Both sons worked with the Forest Service in various capacities, often helping their father with one or more of his never-ending conservation or civic projects. He usually had five or six projects going on all over Union County at any given time. Walter was married and raising a family of his own. Following a long tradition of Woody women, Mae taught school in Union County.

Even though the story that has been told many times over the past 75 years tells us the Ranger "loaded his entire family" in the car that day for the trip to North Carolina, that part of the story is unlikely. Always supportive of her "you-never-know-what-he's-going-to-do-next" husband, it would have been very unusual for June to have left home for an entire day to make a trip of that nature. Chances are she stayed home to hold down the fort. And Mae no doubt was teaching school that day.

That leaves the two boys – Walter and Clyne. Since Walter and Clyne frequently helped their father, it makes sense that one or both of the boys might have gone on the trip. But according to Lou Nichols, Clyne's daughter, Clyne never said anything to his family in later years about traveling to North Carolina on that historic day. If he had gone along he probably would have mentioned it because the family frequently talked about Ranger Woody's deer program in later years. Common sense tells us that the Ranger must have known he would have his hands full bringing home a carload of tiny, bleating, whitetail fawns, and it stands to reason that at least one other person probably went along to help. And although we really don't really know for certain who that person was, it may well have been Walter.

If you had been present when that shiny new sedan pulled out of the Woody driveway on that historic day, you might not have been overly impressed with the man behind the wheel if you didn't know who he was – at least, not initially. You would have been confronted with a rosy-cheeked man in his mid-40s dressed in dark, wrinkled work clothes who seemed to wear a perpetual smile always cloaked in a bit of mischief. He was a man who talked and acted much like any other typical, hard-working, mountain native. In other words, a typical mountain hillbilly (today we commonly use the term "redneck" or "country hick" instead of hillbilly. Mountain natives seldom used any of these terms. They simply referred to themselves as "mountain men").

But first impressions can be deceiving. Behind those all-knowing deep-blue eyes and that burly, 6-foot frame sat an extraordinary, self-made character of a man who possessed an endless amount of God-given talent and ability. He had the drive and ambition to make things happen. He also possessed his own flavor of stubborn determination that usually paved the way for taking on just about any preposterous scheme he might have up his sleeve at any given moment. There were often many such endeavors going on at once, and failure was seldom part of the equation. The negative concept of "it can't be done" was not part of his psyche.

On this special day, the Ranger was on a mission. Because of the way things turned out, you might say that it was one of the most important missions of his life. It had been roughly 32 years since an unforgettable childhood incident – one that had a far-reaching impact on his life – had taken place. It was still as fresh in his memory as if it had happened yesterday....

Fannin County, 1895
The Last Deer

Legend tells us that in the fall of 1895, a 10-year-old mountain boy named Arthur Woody witnessed his father kill what was said to be the last white-tailed deer to ever walk a steep ridge in the North Georgia Mountains during the late 1800s. The deer was reported to be a large buck, with a handsome rack. Young Arthur's father, Abraham Lincoln Woody, or Abe as he was known, reportedly shot the deer while he and a group of companions were hunting with a pack of dogs in what is now present-day Fannin County.

Watching his notorious father shoot this deer was a life-altering event for young Arthur. Years later, after he had grown up and gained a reasonable amount of notoriety in his own right, he would immortalize the story by telling a number of people that he wholeheartedly believed it was the *last* deer ever taken in the North Georgia region. The story soon became a local folk legend, fuelled by the fact that as the young mountain boy grew older, he began to nurture a dream that he also shared with several people: to one day bring back the beautiful and majestic white-tailed deer that had once been so plentiful in his beloved mountains.

As young girls, neither of Ranger Woody's granddaughters – Jean White McNey, daughter of Mae Woody, or Lou Nichols, daughter of Clyne Woody – ever remembered hearing any stories about how their grandfather had vowed to bring deer back to the region. But in a 1939 article in *American Forestry* magazine, Ranger Woody was quoted as saying he had always nurtured a desire to someday have a hand in bringing deer back to his sacred mountains. Ranger Woody also told certain friends and co-workers that he felt a personal obligation to try to achieve this dream since his father had been responsible for shooting the last living deer. Having attained a reasonable degree of success and independence by 1927, he had finally reached a point in his career where he could take the necessary steps to begin making that lifelong dream a reality.

Had young Arthur's father actually killed the last living deer in the region as legend claims? Certainly the deer had to be *one* of the last deer ever seen in the area during the 19th century. So the story has merit. Without question, stories like this make for great folk legends, but can we really be sure?

In his classic book, *Whose Woods These Are, the Story of the National Forests,* published in 1962, author Michael Frome posed the question below to an unnamed "friend" who had known Ranger Woody well. At the time, Frome had traveled to Dahlonega, Georgia, to gather research material for his book.

Hunting was a cherished tradition in the southern Appalachians during the late 1800s. It was not uncommon for a man to take off with his sons or companions for a day or two and go a-huntin' with his muzzle-loading shotgun or long-barrelled mountain rifle and a pack of dependable dogs. Photo circa 1890, from the Duncan Dobie collection.

This "unnamed" friend apparently proved to be a good source of "Woody" information.

> "But how can you be sure that was the *last* deer of all?" Frome asked the man. "Because," the man answered, "Woody told me so."
>
> In other words, if Woody said it was true, you could take it to the bank.

Later on, during his adult life, Ranger Woody had a favorite saying: "There are three things in life I really love: my gun, my dog and my wife." As a 10-year-old boy who loved guns and hunting, being in the woods became a way of life at an early age. Arthur Woody certainly would have wanted to tag along with his father and the other men of the community on any kind of hunt if the opportunity availed itself, but especially a deer hunt! So it's entirely likely that he did witness a deer being killed. However, there are no shortages of other family stories from Union and Fannin counties about various family members killing the last deer in the mountain region as well. All of these stories probably have some foundation. By 1895, deer were quite scarce in Union, Fannin, Lumpkin and White counties. By 1900, they were virtually gone from the mountain region.

In those days, mountain hunters typically used large packs of dogs and often hunted at night with the use of fire torches. By today's standards, it was anything but sporting, but mountaineers had been using this method of hunting since the first settlers came to the region in the early 1840s. Once the dogs were on a hot trail, the deer really didn't have much of a chance. After becoming exhausted from trying to elude the dogs for many miles, deer being chased would often seek bodies of water as a last resort. Here, with nowhere to go, they were vulnerable to hunter's bullets.

The dogs would eventually hem up their prey, and the hunters following would quickly dispatch any deer that were present. The idea of incorporating anything close to today's concept of "ethical sportsmanship" was as foreign to these men as refraining from taking a good slug of moonshine at a Saturday night church social. After all, these men were meat hunters. In fact, trapping deer with large iron bear traps was also a common practice in the southern Appalachians in the late 1800s. Deer hunting served a utilitarian purpose. Although it was definitely a much-anticipated form of recreation for these hard-working mountain men (and boys like Arthur Woody), who seldom had time for any type of serious recreation, securing meat was the primary objective. For many decades venison was a much-loved staple among mountain folk. Nothing ever went to waste. Sadly, deer meat became a rare commodity around 1900.

Ironically, Ranger Woody probably saw few, if any, deer running wild in the mountains from 1895 to 1927. He might have stolen a rare glimpse of a surviving straggler from time to time during his extensive wanderings, but for the most part, there were no deer left to see.

Serving as District Ranger in his later life over many thousands of acres of North Georgia forestland was not an easy job. In fact, it was much more than a job. It was a seven-day-a-week way of life. It required long hours of hard work day and night and the pay was minimal. But the position did carry a certain amount of prestige. Fortunately, by most local pre-Depression-era standards, the Ranger was fairly well-off financially. By 1927, he had done well buying and selling land, and this success gave him a certain amount of financial security. Now he was about to embark on perhaps his greatest adventure. He was planning on going headlong into the deer-raising business!

The obvious question one has to ask is: Why was he doing this on his own account instead of in conjunction with his employer? Had he even discussed his plan with his Forest Service superiors? Did he have their blessings? Certainly he would have wanted the Forest Service to know about and support this project because it would prove to be a substantial undertaking. In fact, it would end up being one of the most significant actions of his entire career.

Ads like this one for Dodge Brothers automobiles were quite popular in 1927 when Ranger Arthur Woody drove from Suches to the Pisgah Game Refuge in North Carolina in his brand-new Dodge sedan to buy a carload of fawns for his deer herd of the future. Courtesy Dodge Motor Corporation, from the Duncan Dobie collection.

Had the Forest Service told him there was no money available for such an endeavor? Is this why he acted on his own? Or was he simply too impatient to wade through all of the government red tape he typically had to undergo (yes, even in those days) to begin a formal restocking program? This may well have been the case. It's likely that his superiors supported the idea, but since resources were so limited, he simply did what he so often was prone to do – he took matters into his own hands. It certainly wouldn't be the first time and it would not be the last. Ten years earlier he had done the same thing when he began reestablishing native brook trout and introducing for the first time rainbow and brown trout (from out West) into Georgia mountain streams. All we know for certain is that something motivated him during the summer of 1927 to get this project underway because it was long overdue. And he did.

"Do what needs to be done and get permission later." That was the Ranger's modus operandi.

The Pisgah Game Reserve

Unlike the North Georgia region where deer had been wiped out by hungry settlers and pioneers by the late 1800s, whitetails were still fairly plentiful in parts of western North Carolina in the early 1900s because they had been protected. The wealthy Vanderbilt family of New York had amassed a huge fortune from railroads, shipping and other businesses during the "Gilded Age" (a period beginning in the early 1870s and ending around the turn of the century). Among its many assets, the family had accumulated vast tracts of mountain land in western North Carolina. (Biltmore Estate near Ashville still bears witness to the Vanderbilt dynasty. At the time it was constructed, Biltmore Estate was the largest and most expensive "house" ever built in the U.S.)

After the Weeks Act was passed in 1911, the Vanderbilt family sold a 90,000-acre tract to the federal government that became the basis for the Pisgah National Forest (today encompassing just over 500,000 acres). Both the Vanderbilt tract in North Carolina and the 31,000-acre Gennett tract in North Georgia, which became Ranger Woody's Rock Creek/Blue Ridge Refuge (eventually reaching 40,000 acres in size), were the first two large tracts bought in the Eastern U.S. under the Weeks Act to be put into the national forest system.

The 10,000-acre Pisgah National Game Preserve was created by an act of the North Carolina legislature, an act of congress and presidential proclamation in 1916. Whitetails had been protected on Vanderbilt lands for many years during the early part of the 20th century. By 1927, park officials were dealing with an over-population of deer in some areas, and some were captured and used for restocking in other areas. Others were sold to out-of-state wildlife officials like Ranger Woody for that same purpose.

So Ranger Woody drove to the Pisgah Game Reserve in North Carolina and purchased five young fawns with his own money. Reportedly, the fawns cost him $20 apiece. One hundred dollars was a lot of money in 1927, but the Ranger was no doubt thrilled with his purchase. It was the purchase of a lifetime! “Best money I ever spent!” he probably mused with a broad smile on more than one occasion years later. The deer were so young they had to be bottle fed for several weeks.

Precious Cargo

Having been an avid outdoorsman as well as a tough mountaineer all of his life, Ranger Woody had hunted and fished for just about every creature that walked, crawled, flew or swam in his beloved mountains. But contrary to several written accounts, he had never hunted or killed a single deer in his life. After all, by the time he was old enough to become a deer hunter, whitetails were absent from the entire mountain region.

Ranger Woody’s five little whitetail fawns quickly captured his heart as well as the hearts of everyone in Suches. It wasn’t long before these beautiful and graceful creatures, known fondly as “the five friendly fiends of Suches,” struck a chord deep within the Ranger’s soul. They melted his heart. He would never be the same again. Although he was a lifelong hunter who had a passion for matching wits with wild turkeys and squirrels, and to a lesser degree rabbits, quail and grouse (usually referred to as “pheasants” in the mountain region) for table fare, and perhaps an occasional wild hog here and there, from that time on he would never be able to draw a bead on what he considered to be God’s most beautiful creation – the majestic white-tailed deer.

He became more determined than ever to see his dream come to full fruition. As soon as they were old enough to fend for themselves, sometime in 1928, under the Ranger’s watchful and protective eye, the five deer were released into his beloved Rock Creek Refuge (later to become Blue Ridge Wildlife Management Area). From this meager beginning, North Georgia’s deer herd of the future was spawned.

Two-year-old Dick Woody, the Ranger's grandson (Walter's son), born in 1925, bottle feeds several fawns in the special pen built next to the Woody house as his grandfather looks on. These fawns may well be three of the original "five friendly fiends," purchased by Ranger Woody in 1927. If not, they likely came from the second group of fawns purchased by the Ranger in 1928. Photo courtesy of Jean McNey.

Ranger Woody made several more trips to the Pisgah Reserve over the next few years (1928 and 1929) and purchased several deer each trip. It didn't take long before the Forest Service got involved (just as it had done with Ranger Woody's trout stocking program). By the early 1930s, the Forest Service stepped up the deer program and bought several dozen more whitetails from the Pisgah Reserve. Some of the deer were adult animals that had been live-trapped; others were young fawns that had been caught in early summer. Most of the deer were kept in pens and released in the refuge under the careful guidance of Ranger Woody or his trusted assistants as soon as they were deemed old enough to survive in the wild. Many of the deer he knew by name, and for years they would come up to him in the woods and beg for a treat. Woe to the man who ever plotted to harm one of Ranger Woody's precious deer. His methods of protecting his flock and dealing with poachers became legendary. By the mid-1930s, things were going so well at Rock Creek that plans were made by the Forest Service to release deer in other mountain game reserves as well.

By 1940, in the span of just 13 short years, the 60- to 80-odd deer that had been the foundation for the Ranger's fledgling deer herd at Rock Creek Refuge had increased substantially. The herd in and around the refuge had now grown to an estimated 2,000 animals. It had taken four and a half decades to turn a lifelong dream into a reality, but Ranger Woody had finally made good on his longtime promise! "Granddaddy" Abe, his formidable father, having been at rest peacefully in his grave for the past 8 years, would have been right proud of his boy!

Ranger Woody astride one of his beloved horses. He loved to ride through his mountain paradise. He spent much time working on horseback in areas inaccessible by automobile, even in later years. The photo was taken by famed Atlanta Constitution photographer Kenneth Rogers around 1940. Photo courtesy of Jean McNey.

CHAPTER 1
An American Original

"We should look at forests as a source of good as well as wood."

Arthur Woody

William Arthur Woody was probably the most famous forest ranger who ever refused to wear a uniform. He became a legendary figure in Georgia during the first half of the 20th century. During the late 1930s and early '40s, he became a much-loved statewide and national celebrity. In the decades following his death in 1946, his fame grew to larger-than-life status. Today, in the minds of many, he is a much-loved folk hero and legendary figure in the mountain region of North Georgia.

And why not? Certainly his unparalleled accomplishments and his uncommon generosity put him in a class by himself. He earned his legendary fame every step of the way through hard work. But being larger-than-life often makes it difficult to separate fact from fiction. Because of his status and the many achievements that took place while he served as custodian over a huge block of reclaimed mountain forestland, it's tempting to sing his praises and embellish his life even more than his legendary status has already done. In truth, though, the man really did lead a remarkable life. Yes, he was human, and yes, he certainly had plenty of faults. But he lived during a unique time in American history in the early days of forest and wildlife conservation in the southern Appalachians. Without question, he helped forge many of the historic events that occurred during those remarkable years.

While it is true that much embellishment has taken place about the exploits of Ranger Arthur Woody in the 70 years since his death, posterity has provided us with a rich treasure-trove of published accounts that help tell his amazing story. Documented accounts from the past have a way of opening our eyes and filtering out some of the exaggerations, thus giving us a truer glimpse of what type of person he really was. And what better way is there to accurately tell a man's story and gain insight than to study firsthand accounts written by those who knew him best and worked with him side-by-side during his lifetime?

The following story is but one of many published accounts written about a man who was truly an American original. It appeared in the *Journal of Forestry* magazine in April 1946. (In print since 1902, The *Journal of Forestry* magazine has long been the official publication of the Society of American Foresters.) Ironically, this story was published two months before Ranger Woody's death on June 10, 1946.

WE PRESENT
William Arthur Woody: "The Ranger"

In the Blue Ridge Mountains of North Georgia – a few hundred feet from the main divide and near a cold, bubbling mountain spring – lays a pile of weather-worn boards. Here, on April 1, 1884, when nature was reawakening with all the vibrant music and breathtaking color characteristic of that rugged mountain country, Arthur Woody was born. The gray boards were part of his first home, the hub of a 250,000 acre tract of timberland which he loved from the start, from which he has consistently refused to let anyone or anything lure him, and in which his later dramatic and useful activities have added up to a lifetime of public service.

As a boy, Woody tramped, hunted and fished every ridge, cove and creek within horse-riding distance, unconsciously laying an excellent foundation for the career he was destined to follow. During his early years he put in many long, arduous hours driving cattle to Atlanta (with his father), 90 miles to the south. From those 10-day trips came a solid appreciation of the value of forests to people, an enviable ability to drive a good bargain, and a sense of humor rarely excelled in forestry ranks. According to Woody, he is now wearing his seventh set of toenails; the other six were worn out on drives.

At the age of 16, after exhausting the school facilities available in his immediate vicinity, Arthur Woody attended North Georgia College, in the small gold-mining town of Dahlonega. Within a year he had filled his academic life in this fine institution, which his great grandfather helped to found, and where his two sons and several of his grandchildren subsequently attended.

For two years Woody helped his father run cattle, in the mountains. Then on October 1, 1912, he worked his first day for the U.S. Forest Service – as an ax man on a baseline (survey) crew. Later he ran a compass on land-acquisition work and May 1, 1915, saw him sworn in as the newly appointed forest guard, protector against fire and trespass, on an embryo national forest which he helped establish. Upon passing the ranger's examination, Woody became on July 1, 1918, the first forest ranger of the Blue Ridge District of the Georgia National Forest. Ranger Woody served faithfully for 30 years, 4 months and 29 days, until his retirement on September 30, 1945.

"We should look at forests as a source of good as well as wood." This simple philosophy, expressed in his own words, governed the activities of the "The Ranger," as he is known throughout the state of Georgia, during his long tenure as a timberland manager.

A staunch advocate of bettering the welfare of his mountain friends and neighbors, Ranger Woody has worked constantly for improved schools, churches, roads, medical care and recreation. Rich and poor alike have beaten a path to the door of this veritable "Scattergood Baines." Governors, judges, congressmen, preachers, lawyers, merchants, doctors, college professors, students and a host of other people in all walks of life have found refreshment in his humor, enlightenment through his down to earth logic, and, in time of need, financial assistance. Youngsters, in particular, instinctively take to him and he to them.

(Scattergood Baines was the lead character in a popular 1941 Hollywood film starring Guy Kibbee. Much like Ranger Woody, Baines was portrayed as a shrewd, homespun, common-sense pillar of the community who, because of his down-home wisdom, found himself drawn into all types of controversial community events. He wasn't afraid to take on the most powerful men in town. The film was so popular that five sequels were made. Scattergood Baines was described as "the best loved, most cussed at, and by all odds the fattest man in the modern, bustling fictitious New England town of Cold River.")

As a homespun philosopher, Woody is rated "tops." Consider this one incident. Upon returning home with his telephone dispatcher one afternoon, the ranger met two attorneys from the county seat who had availed themselves of the fine fishing afforded by the little lake which nestles behind his home, a crystal-clear body of water built, stocked and maintained by the Ranger himself. Each lawyer carried an imposing string of fish, and with but a casual "Hello, Ranger," and a passing comment on their luck, they got into their car and drove off.

The dispatcher waxed indignant. "Say, Ranger, aren't those two men the ones who are prosecuting that land case you're a defendant in?"

"That's right, Jimmy. They are."

"Well, good gravy, man, why do you let them fish in your lake after what they're trying to do to you?"

Ranger Woody smiled. "Remember what the Good Book says, Jimmy. *Do good for evil.*" Never one to carry a bible under his own arm or to shout its contents, Arthur Woody nevertheless has always heeded its admonitions.

(The "little" lake behind Ranger Woody's house – Woody Lake – built by the Ranger in the mid-1930s, was then about 80 acres in size. It became well-known for producing trophy largemouth bass, some in the 14- to 15-pound range. Today the lake is considerably smaller in size due to heavy siltation.)

To his more intimate friends Woody is known as "the Kingfish." Under this dual designation he effectively administered one of the largest and most active ranger districts in the United States. Since he defines an "expert" as "an average boy away from home," Woody's methods were not always in strict accord with what the experts considered orthodox methodology. Nevertheless, outstanding achievement resulted from his work in fire prevention, timber management, and game restoration and protection. The secret of his success may be found in his ability to think out the problem at hand and arrive at the best solution – before referring to the rules, policies and regulations to determine the limitations under which he could act. Then too, because he never overlooked or failed to appraise local reaction to any forest program or policy, Woody always managed to pick the right man for the right job.

In his work with "up-and-coming" foresters, Ranger Woody was at his best. Many "young bucks" have come under his wing, worked and learned awhile, and then passed on to more responsible positions, singularly blessed as a result of their association with "the Kingfish."

Ranger Woody has never been one to display great emotionalism. But underneath his large frame – as his host of friends can testify – beats a large heart filled to overflowing with a sensitivity to the beauties of nature and all her works, and with an abounding love for his family. In full sincerity, he has often remarked: "Yessir! There are three things in this life of mine that I love – my gun, my dog and my wife!" However, his two sons, one daughter and six grandchildren, all living, have come in for a full measure of attention, guidance, and affection. His sons are both employed in Forest Service work and his daughter is a teacher in the new school recently built near his house.

No story about Ranger Woody can be complete without at least mention of this school in the heart of the Blue Ridge District, which represents for Ranger Woody the culmination of a dream that has been constantly on his mind for years. The school, accommodating all grades including high school, is built from the finest granite available from Woody's own quarry, its lumber was sawed in Woody's mill, and it rests on land donated by Woody for the purpose. A large auditorium, dining room and transportation facilities make up-to-date education possible for the children of his mountain friends.

(Dedicated in November 1940, Woody Gap School opened in January 1941, at mid-term. The school consolidated five remote schools scattered across Union County, three of which were being held in small churches and two of which were held in one-room school houses. See Chapter 8 for more details.)

Space will not permit the full telling of all those romantic and colorful stories for which Ranger Woody is most famous. It will suffice for now, we think, that as Arthur Woody, alias "the Ranger," alias "the Kingfish," turns over his forest-green pickup and fire tools to his more youthful successor and takes down his rifle and calls his dog, we present: Woody the forester, public servant, philanthropist, humanitarian, educator, game lover and above all, Woody the Man.

Yes, a pile of weather-worn boards marks the spot in the Blue Ridge Mountains of North Georgia where Arthur Woody was born, 62 years ago. But long after those boards become a part of the soil surrounding the cold, bubbling mountain spring – for many, many years in the future, Ranger Woody's influence, guidance, and force will live in the homes of countless people in the forest and elsewhere who have experienced the generosity of spirit, and who will long enjoy the fruits of his activity.

William W. Bergoffen
Milton M. Bryan
Donald E. Clark

A Heartfelt Tribute to a Beloved Mentor and Friend

The above story was written by three U.S. Forest Service employees who worked under Ranger Woody in North Georgia at various times during the late 1930s and early 1940s. The account is extremely telling in several ways. There is no question that the three co-authors loved their mentor in a very special way.

After interning with Ranger Woody in North Georgia, all three men moved on to "more responsible positions" as mentioned in the story, and each enjoyed long, distinguished careers with the U.S. Forest Service. William W. "Bill" Bergoffen spent most of his later career at Forest Service headquarters in Washington, D.C. In 1976, the year he retired, he wrote *100 Years of Federal Forestry*, an annotated pictorial history of the U. S. Forest Service.

Milton M. Bryan, who also spent the majority of his career in Washington D.C., worked for the Forest Service for 40 years before retiring in 1972. He died in 2000 at the age of 90. Bryan wrote extensively about Forest Service history and took many historic photos, including some at Camp Woody, the famous Civilian Conservation Corps camp in Suches, Georgia, run by Ranger Woody's son, Walter. Donald E. Clark later became a Regional Forester in Denver, Colorado, where he spent most of his career.

Arthur Woody was a mentor to countless young foresters coming up through the ranks, but he obviously had a profound impact on the lives of the three men mentioned above. Each man no doubt loved Ranger Woody in his own way, but of the three, Bill Bergoffen, who is mentioned a number of times throughout this book, developed a deep friendship with and especial fondness for the Ranger. Because of his love for Ranger Woody, it is highly probable that most if not all of the above article was written by his hand. As a young forester, Bergoffen served in the North Georgia Mountains early in his career under Ranger Woody as a junior ranger for 14 months during the mid 1930s.

100 Years Of Federal Forestry

United States Department of Agriculture
Forest Service

Agriculture Information Bulletin No. 402

Bill Bergoffen, who had worked under Ranger Woody as a budding forester in the 1930s and grew to adore him, went on to enjoy a very successful career with the U.S. Forest Service in Washington D.C. In 1978, the year he retired, he authored 100 Years of Federal Forestry. *Duncan Dobie photo.*

For many of those months, Bergoffen rented an upstairs bedroom in the Woody home and lived with the Woody family – June, the Ranger's wife, Mae, his daughter and Ned and Jean, Mae's two children. Bergoffen got to know the family on an intimate basis and he came to know and love the Ranger much like a surrogate son. You can feel the deep sense of love and respect he had for his mentor in his prophetic words that were written from the heart. At the time the article was published, all three men knew that Ranger Woody's health was rapidly deteriorating and they were deeply concerned. They were obviously saddened at his sudden but necessary retirement seven months earlier due to declining health, and they must have known that his days were numbered.

Despite the fact that this story was written by three very credible eye-witnesses to history who knew Ranger Woody well while he was alive, several of the "facts" stated in the story should be clarified. (Apparently the "Woody Myth" was alive and well even in those days!) The third paragraph refers to Ranger Woody attending North Georgia College at age 16. This subject will be discussed in more detail in Chapter 5, but it's likely that the sum total of Ranger Woody's education ended at some point while he was in the fifth grade. There is good evidence to support this.

With the distinction of being the most famous forest ranger who ever refused to wear a uniform, a then vibrant Ranger Arthur Ranger Woody (far right, with hat in hand and sleeves rolled up), poses with a group of Forest Service officials. His daily uniform usually consisted of wrinkled work clothes or loose overalls. Photo circa mid-1930s, courtesy of Jean McNey.

Life in the North Georgia Mountains in the late 1880s was much different than it is today. Children were needed to work on the farm, especially boys. Families were by necessity large with eight to 10 children (or more), and as soon as they were old enough and strong enough to put in a good day's work, boys often bid farewell to school and spent their days working on the farm. A "good day's work" at the turn of the 20th century often meant working from "dark to dark" – that is, well before daylight in the mornings to well after dark in the evenings. Typical chores for a boy might include milking cows early in the morning, tending to the hogs and feeding the chickens. The balance of the day might be spent tending to the free ranging cattle that roamed the hills or working in the fields as young Arthur no doubt did. A family's very survival depended upon being able to put food on the table, and farm work was considered much more important than any very basic schooling in a one-room schoolhouse that a boy might receive. Everyone worked, and everyone was expected to do his or her part.

When I think about the importance of this principle 100 years ago, I am reminded of a scene from the Pulitzer Prize winning book *The Yearling* by Marjorie Kinnan Rawlings. After young Jody's beloved yearling fawn has destroyed much of the family's annual food crop by decimating the corn field, Penny, Jody's father, tells his son that the deer has to be destroyed:

> "Penny said, 'Jody, all's been done was possible. I'm sorry. I can't never tell you, how sorry. But we cain't have our year's crops destroyed. We cain't all go hongry. Take the yearlin' out in the woods and tie him and shoot him.'"

Powerful words indeed, "We cain't all go hungry." By the way, this quote is very meaningful to this book. In 1942, after *The Yearling* and *Cross Creek* were published and became best sellers, Marjorie Kinnan Rawlings made a special trip to the North Georgia Mountains from her home in Florida to meet Ranger Woody. (See Chapter 5 for details.)

It is doubtful that Ranger Woody ever attended North Georgia College even for a day. However, numerous stories have been written and rewritten over the years stating that he attended college for an indefinite period of time – anywhere from several days to several months – because his grandfather, John Wesley Woody II, postmaster at Dahlonega in the early 1870s, was one of the co-founders of the school.

Since a great many of the people Ranger Woody served with in the Forest Service over the years were college graduates with degrees in forestry (many from some of the country's top colleges like Harvard and Yale), the Ranger was probably content to allow people to believe he had actually received more schooling than the facts bore out. Although it's doubtful that he ever deliberately falsified his educational record to any co-workers, it would be in perfect keeping with the Ranger's prankish character to allow certain exaggerations about his education to perpetuate, especially since he was often in the presence of highly educated men (many of whom he detested because of their pomp and self-importance). And if he did allow this and other exaggerations to perpetuate, he probably did so with a sly grin!

A thoughtful Ranger Woody poses beside his truck in this April 1937 photo. By this time in his career, he had already made great strides in restocking deer in his beloved Rock Creek Refuge and native brook trout back in the streams (as well as non-native rainbow trout and brown trout). He was well on his way toward becoming an iconic figure in the North Georgia mountains. Photo courtesy of Jean McNey.

The fourth paragraph in the Bergoffen story states that Ranger Woody worked with his father running cattle in the mountains for "two years." Although very little is known about the Ranger's early days, that is, from young boyhood to young adulthood, he more than likely worked with his father doing farm chores and cattle work (as mentioned above) for quite a few years before taking a job with the U.S. Forest Service in 1912.

The Ranger would have been 28 years old in 1912. During his boyhood and young adulthood, he reportedly spent as much time as he could hunting, fishing and roaming and exploring the mountains near his home. He loved being in the woods more than anything else, but he also had certain responsibilities that he was expected to meet. From what is known, he usually carried out those responsibilities and his daily chores to his father's satisfaction.

Ranger Woody married around 1900 at the age of 16 or 17. By 1912 when he was 28 years old, he had a wife and three children to support; and although he often stated in later life that he always had a decided dislike for farm work of any kind, he probably spent those early years doing the very farm work he detested, since his options for doing anything else were limited.

On the other hand, there is no question that young Arthur Woody was a man who would never be content to live a life of mediocrity. He "dreamed big" and it was only a matter of time before he would 'bust out" of the normal mountain mold and make his mark in the world. It just so happened that a number of historic events were taking place in North Georgia during the early 1900s, and William Arthur Woody found himself right smack-dab in the middle of them! Fate had big plans for him. He couldn't have been born at a better time!

Since very few photos survive of the "Barefoot Ranger" in his stocking feet, could this be how he earned his famous nickname? Holding two small trout in front of the primitive fish-rearing structure that he built next to Woody Lake behind his house, Ranger Woody later constructed some larger and more elaborate fish-rearing pools along Rock Creek inside Rock Creek Refuge. Photo circa early-1920s, courtesy of Jean McNey.

CHAPTER 2

The Legend of the Barefoot Ranger

"It's a fascinating cosmic coincidence that throughout history the right people seem to come along at just the right time to effect major change."

Forever Green, the History and Hope of the American Forest,
by Chuck Leavell, 2001

Ranger Arthur Woody of Suches, Georgia, came along at precisely the right time – a time in history when the North Georgia mountains were in a sad and neglected state. He was a gift to the people of the mountains and to the badly depleted natural resources that were once so plentiful in the region.

By 1910, much of the vast virgin timber was gone from the southern Appalachians. Most of the once prolific fish and wildlife resources had disappeared as well. Ever since the Cherokees had been pushed out of their sacred mountain homeland in the late 1830s, the region had been shamelessly exploited; first with the gold exploration that initiated the removal of the Indians in the first place, and later with the destruction and virtual annihilation of the virgin forests. After many of the trees were gone, it was inevitable that the once plentiful fish and wildlife would disappear at an alarming rate as well. Unchecked erosion and forest fires added to the calamity and also took a heavy toll in a variety of ways.

As if all of that were not bad enough, the Civil War reared its ugly head a few decades after the gold rush, causing untold human suffering in the region by dividing families during the war years and creating havoc through the widespread lawlessness that took place during those turbulent times; both during the war years in the early 1860s and during the bitter "reconstruction" period that followed. The Woody family was no exception. Some of Arthur Woody's descendents were so distraught after the Civil War ended they left Georgia and traveled west, never to return and never to see their families again.

Ironically, many of the adverse events that took place in the North Georgia mountains from the 1830s to the early 1900s were caused by outside influences. That is, the mountain folk who originally settled the area after the Cherokee Land Lottery of 1832 had little to do with the vast exploitation of their region. True, many of the original settlers came to this part of Georgia because they were drawn by the lure of gold, but those who stayed after the initial gold rush craze had peaked were determined to try to eke out a simple life by farming and living off the land. All they wanted was to be left alone so that they could quietly go about their business.

It was never an easy life. You had to be tough to be a mountaineer. And even though most of these early settlers and pioneers seemed to struggle just to make ends meet, the vast majority never considered themselves to be poor or

The "Barefoot Ranger" in action! Sitting with June in front of the hearth churning butter, the Ranger often shed his shoes or work boots as quickly as possible after a long day afield. Note the wood-burning stove in the background, used before electricity came to Suches in the late 1930s. Photo circa 1935, courtesy of Jean McNey.

less privileged than anyone else. Mountain people loved their secluded way of life. By outside standards, most families never had much, but they got by and that was enough for them. What's more, they always managed to find enough extra food or whatever else was needed to share with a neighbor in need. That was the mountain way.

Arthur William Woody of Suches, Georgia, was one of those tough, determined mountain people. He was a one-of-a-kind character. Widely known today as "the Barefoot Ranger," folk legend tells us that he often refused to wear shoes. Unless, of course, it was during the dead of winter when temperatures fell below freezing or when he was traversing a rough, rocky mountain trail. Otherwise, the legend says, he was perfectly content to traipse around his beloved mountains the way God had made him – barefooted. After all, he had grown up in the late 1800s during the horse-and-wagon days. Like most mountain boys, he seldom wore shoes of any type during the golden, warm-weather days of his youth. Today, some 70 years after his death, practically every piece of printed material you read about Arthur Woody fondly refers to him as the "Barefoot Ranger." But where did the "Barefoot Ranger" legend come from?

A Legend is Born

"He hated to wear shoes worse than anything," Charlie Elliott (1905-2000) was quoted as saying many times in the years following Arthur Woody's death in 1946. Charlie was a long-time friend of the Ranger and he should have known. Having studied forestry at the University of Georgia for three years in the early 1920s, Charlie later served a stint with the Georgia Department of Forestry. Later still he worked for the National Park Service. In 1937, he was named Director of the newly organized Georgia State Parks Department. Within a year, he was appointed Commissioner of Natural Resources for the state of Georgia. Much of his work during those years in the late 1920s and throughout the '30s found him in Union County building parks and trails. He stayed in very close contact with his friend and mentor, Ranger Woody. He often ate dinner with the Woody family and sometimes stayed the night.

The two men probably met for the first time in the mid 1920s while Charlie was an assistant district forester with the state of Georgia. They had much in common. Both men were passionate about their work in forestry and conservation, and they hit it off at once. Charlie knew right away that Arthur Woody was a unique individual. The two men remained good friends right up until the Ranger's death. Like Ranger Woody, Charlie was an American original in his own right. His list of accomplishments during his long and productive career in forestry and conservation is nothing short of extraordinary.

Among other things, Charlie helped develop Vogel State Park and helped layout that portion of the Appalachian Trail that traverses Union County across Blood Mountain. Reportedly, he also helped develop the Joyce Kilmer Memorial Forest in North Carolina (a 3,800-acre stand of virgin timber established in 1936 in memory of Joyce Kilmer, a beloved poet and journalist killed in France during World War I. Kilmer is best-known for his enormously popular 1913 poem "Trees" which has long been considered a national treasure).

Charlie should have been a very credible witness to the "Barefoot Ranger" folk legend, since he was an eyewitness to many historical events that occurred in Ranger Woody's domain during the time period from roughly 1928 to 1946 known as the "Ranger Woody Regime."

An avid turkey hunter and trout fisherman just like Ranger Woody, Charlie spent considerable time hunting and fishing in the area, often in the company of the Ranger or other Forest Service friends. Charlie went on to become director of the Georgia Game and Fish Commission in 1943. His first turkey hunt took place in the mountains of Union County during the mid-1920s. Although Arthur and Charlie sometimes hunted together in later years, it's not clear whether or not Ranger Woody was involved in Charlie's very first turkey hunt, but it is entirely possible that he was. What is clear is that both men loved to hunt turkeys and were very good at it. Charlie went on to become a nationally prominent turkey hunting writer and expert long after the Ranger's death.

Because of the various jobs he held with the state of Georgia and the U.S. Forest Service in the late 1920s and throughout the '30s, Charlie Elliott was an eye-witness to, and participant in, many of the historic events taking place during the time known as the "Ranger Woody Regime" in the North Georgia mountains. Charlie later documented many of those events through his prolific writing. Interestingly, the famous pipe-smoking comic-strip character Mark Trail, a forest ranger developed in 1946 (the same year Ranger Woody died), by iconic cartoonist Ed Dodd of Atlanta, was based on the pensive, pipe-smoking Charlie Elliott. Charlie and Ed Dodd were good friends. The comic strip survives to this day and now centers more on environmental and ecological themes. Photo courtesy of the Charlie Elliott Wildlife Center.

As Commissioner of Natural Resources and editor of *Outdoor Georgia* magazine, a popular monthly publication put out by the state wildlife agency, he was present during the first historic archery and firearms deer hunts held at Blue Ridge WMA in 1940, fondly known then as Rock Creek Refuge or simply the Game Reserve. (See Chapter 13 for the full story of that historic hunt.)

A decade later in 1950, Charlie became southeastern field editor for *Outdoor Life* magazine, a position he held for the next 40 years. During that time, he became a celebrated turkey hunter, writing two books on the subject. He also wrote hundreds of magazine and newspaper articles, along with some 20 books about hunting and fishing across North America during his long and productive career. Interestingly, the famous pipe smoking comic strip character Mark Trail, a forest ranger developed in 1946 (the same year Ranger Woody died) by iconic cartoonist Ed Dodd of Atlanta, was based on the pensive, pipe-smoking Charlie Elliott. Charlie and Ed Dodd were good friends. The comic strip still survives today and now centers more on environmental and ecological themes.

Since Charlie Elliott wrote numerous newspaper and magazine stories about his friend Ranger Woody during the late 1930s and early 1940s, I owe him a huge debt of gratitude for the many contributions he made to this book.

As a highly respected outdoor writer, Charlie Elliott has to be taken seriously when it comes to talking about his long-time friend Arthur Woody. One of the most popular stories regarding the subject of no shoes has been told over and over again during the last few decades. Charlie told it often and related it to me in a taped interview in 1995. It's impossible to say whether or not the story has real merit or if it is simply one of those embellished folk tales (Woody Myth) mentioned earlier. The story goes something like this:

Apparently the habit of going around in his bare feet didn't sit too well with some of Ranger Woody's Forest Service supervisors. Once, the visiting Forest Service Chief from Washington D.C. got wind of the problem and claimed he would make Ranger Woody tow the line. Among other more colorful and perhaps unprintable names, Ranger Woody often called officials from outside his native Union County "Yankees," often with a "damn" in front of it. A Yankee was the worst kind of outsider. Ranger Woody's precise definition of a Yankee was a man who had to travel away from home in order to get a job. Somehow he could never quite grasp the idea of having to travel hundreds of miles from one's home in order to make a living. After all, he spent his entire adult life working almost within sight of the tiny cabin where he'd been born. To his way of thinking, everyone else should find a way to do the same thing. The concept of leaving home to seek a career never sat well with him. Ranger Woody was perfectly content to stay right where he was, and he never had any desire to leave his beloved mountains. He felt that any man worth his salt should have a similar philosophy.

Wearing shoes might be one thing but there was more. It could be said that Ranger Woody had a stubborn streak as vast as some of the high mountain wilderness areas that surrounded the little valley where he lived in Suches, fondly known as the "valley in the clouds." To say that he had a mind of his own would be an understatement. In addition to the questionable subject of not wearing shoes, Ranger Woody was also well known for his refusal to wear a standard Forest Service uniform (except on very special occasions) throughout his three-plus-decade career. Usually he would appear in ragged old work clothes with his sleeves rolled up. After all, how could a man do any kind of outside work in a stuffy old, tight-fitting, wool uniform? And, much to the consternation of his superiors, he often refused to follow orders if those orders did not make good sense to him.

In some ways, Ranger Woody was a simple man. In other ways, he was a very complex individual. He was well-known for being a common-sense thinker who carefully liked to weigh all sides of an issue before making any type of important decision. But once that decision was made, there was no stopping him. Come hell or high water, he would forge ahead full-speed according to his most logical plan. If a certain mandate or rule happened to be clouded with the usual bureaucratic "gobbledy gook" that made little or no sense to him, as typically so many of the "official" Forest Service rules often seemed to be (even in those days), he frequently ignored it altogether.

One can only imagine how some of Ranger Woody's superiors must have constantly wanted to pull out their hair trying to make him conform. But this was one thing they could never do, and most of them eventually learned to live with it. Because the Forest Service desperately needed the valuable skills and services he brought to the table, officials simply put up with his "antics" year after year. To him, of course, his common-sense approach to problem solving was anything but an antic.

Ranger Woody lived by an ancient creed of self-sufficiency and independence, which had been bred into him through generations of tough mountain grit; and he was forever fighting the bureaucratic machine. This "courtship" between him and the federal government was one of the biggest ironies of his life. He detested big government, taxes and government regulations. However, his life's work – namely the conservation and protection of his beloved mountains – was so all-consuming and so important to him that he somehow managed to tolerate government regulations and red tape for over 30 years. But it never could have happened without plenty of fireworks along the way!

A lesser man might have given up early in the game, and there is no doubt that the Ranger's blood pressure boiled to dangerously high levels on many occasions. He was even known to have nosebleeds at certain times when his emotions got the best of him. Furthermore, he often had some choice words to say about matters where he and his bosses were in disagreement, words that are best left to the imagination, but somehow he persevered. Too much was at stake to do otherwise.

His life's work in husbanding conservation was much too important to him. It was not a job; it was a way of life, a calling, the thing he had been born to do. He lived it and breathed it every day of his life. Somehow he understood that he was serving a higher cause. In today's world, of course, a federal employee like Ranger Woody would have been hard-pressed to keep his job if he refused to obey a direct order by some authoritative superior. But those were different times, and time and again, he bucked the system and got away with doing things by the seat of his pants – his way.

One of his favorite sayings was, "Do what needs to be done and get permission later." He lived by that creed all his life. Once his mind was made up, he wasn't easily dissuaded. Time and again, his course of action proved to be the right course, so his superiors could not overly criticize his decisions. Since he demonstrated to his superiors more often than not that, as an insider, he could always get things done in a very difficult environment to most outsiders (as long as he did things *his* way) no one wanted to rock the boat. And they didn't. At least for most of the years he served in the Forest Service. During his final few years of service as District Ranger, he did butt heads with one particularly difficult supervisor who refused to let him "rule the roost," but even then, he emerged from many a skirmish unscathed.

You might say that the Forest Service was forced to put up with Arthur Woody and he was forced to put up with the Forest Service. Although this may sound quite strong, it is true nonetheless. So was it a "cosmic coincidence" that placed this gifted and driven man at Ground Zero in the mountains of North Georgia at a time in history when unfettered exploitation had all but destroyed the woods, the wildlife and the streams that once were so vibrant and full of life? Was it serendipity?

Whatever it was, it turned out to be a Godsend for the mountain region and for the people who lived in that region. No other living man could have accomplished what Arthur Woody did with the limited resources at hand, and in the relatively short amount of time he was allotted during his earthly journey. There was an old mountain saying that he loved to repeat: "You can't make a silver purse out of sow's ears." Yet he did it time and again through common sense, ingenuity and determination. His incredible list of accomplishments was nothing short of extraordinary.

Towing the Line

Although Ranger Woody learned to put up with the steady stream of Forest Service bureaucrats and curious Washington big-wigs from the National Park Service frequently stopping by to see him by way of the Forest Service offices in Gainesville or Atlanta, he had little use for some of them. While it is true that he made scores of life-long friends in the Forest Service during his 30-year career – especially with assistant rangers like Bill Bergoffen mentioned in Chapter 1 who were sent to learn from him (most of whom grew to idolize him) – he regarded most outsiders with distrust and disdain, especially those wielding authority. Again, that was his mountain upbringing.

Supposedly, when the visiting Forest Service chief mentioned earlier was told that Ranger Woody refused to wear shoes, he proclaimed to his men, "We've got to do something about this. I'll make him wear shoes, by God!"

So this by-the-book bureaucrat reportedly drove up to Suches to confront the man who was a non-conformist in every respect. The rest of his entourage reportedly went over to the Ranger Station just across the road from the Woody homestead (a several-acre complex of storage buildings and offices built on land donated to the Forest Service by the Ranger himself). The Chief's aids couldn't wait to find out what had happened. They returned later that day anxiously awaiting word of what had transpired. The story goes that they found their boss and Ranger Woody sitting on the front porch of the Ranger's house with their feet propped up on the railing. Both men were sipping on a glass of homemade apple-jack brandy, compliments of the Ranger, and both men were shoeless!

"It's good for the digestion," Ranger Woody reportedly told people with his ever-twinkling blue eyes and mischievous smile.

That's how the legend goes and the story has been printed many times over the years. Charlie Elliott loved to tell it. However, old photos of the Woody home place depict a long front porch with no railing; only a few well-used rocking chairs in which the Ranger, his family and some of his guests no doubt spent many a happy hour contemplating the problems The part about the apple-jack brandy… well, the Ranger wa always having an emergency supply on hand – for special gues occasions, mind you!

There are many such stories about Arthur "Kingfish" Woody. Some, like this one, have become very believable folk legends over the past seven decades. Is this story true? Or are many of these stories simply tall tales spun to fit the legend? Was Ranger Woody known as the "Barefoot Ranger" during his 30-odd-year career as custodian of one of the largest blocks of federally owned forestland in the nation? Certainly it is reasonable to assume that many of the stories told about him today, including those referring to his famous nickname, have become distorted and exaggerated over the years.

Separating Fact from Fantasy

In early 2013, while researching this book, I had the pleasure of interviewing Ranger Woody's two surviving granddaughters, Jean White McNey, daughter of Mae Woody, the Ranger's only daughter, and Lou Nichols, daughter of Ranger Woody's second son Clyne. Jean, along with her mother and brother Ned, lived with her grandparents from about 1934 to 1944, when she was between the ages of 5 and 15. Few people knew the Ranger in life as she did. This book would have been impossible to write without her help and input. Both Jean and Lou told me in unison, "If you're going to write a book about our grandfather, please don't call him the 'Barefoot Ranger.' We never once heard that nickname while we were growing up and we have no idea where it came from."

I was stunned.

"We never heard anyone call him that until long after his death," they both added.

As a teenager in the mid-1960s, I had done a lot of deer hunting and trout fishing in and around Ranger Woody's old bailiwick in Union County, and I had heard many intriguing stories about the "Barefoot Ranger." Ranger Woody became one of my early folk heroes in a big way back in those days. Years later, I even included a chapter about him in my first book, *Georgia's Greatest Whitetail,* published in 1986. In that chapter, I referred to him by that legendary and often used nickname. Now suddenly two close relatives who had known him well were telling me they had never heard anyone refer to their grandfather as the Barefoot Ranger during his lifetime. If he hadn't been known as the Barefoot Ranger while he was alive, how in the world did such a widespread folk legend get started? I was obligated and determined to try to find out.

So I started digging. The first written account I could find with that designation was published in 1965, almost 20 years after his death. After that, nearly every article about him I could find up to the present usually included that famous nickname. And you have to admit – the "Barefoot Ranger" is a catchy name. It sounds good. There's a certain mystique and romance to it. But when you take the magic out of the equation, how could a hard working and common-sense mountain man like Arthur Woody possibly go around without wearing shoes? It didn't add up.

A great many articles were published about Arthur Woody in the late 1930s and early 1940s. By the late 1930s, the eyes of an entire country were set upon the backwoods philosopher from Suches, Georgia. The public couldn't get enough of him. Never did I find a single reference in any of those articles using the much celebrated nickname. So the legendary name obviously came along 15 to 20 years after the Ranger's death. After that, it was repeated so often that the legend became fact. But how and where did it originate?

Arthur Woody spent most of his life outdoors. As a boy, he reportedly spent every available moment roaming and exploring his beloved mountains. Later on, during his 30-plus-year career of being in the woods almost every day fighting forest fires, working in sub-freezing temperatures in winter, restocking deer and trout to the woods and streams of the North Georgia mountains, managing forests, chasing poachers and arsonists up and down steep mountainsides, planting trees, overseeing the cutting of timber, building lakes, trails and roads in some of the most rugged country in the entire southeast, it seems highly unlikely that he could have done any of these demanding tasks without dependable shoes or work boots.

What's more, he did much of his work on horseback during many of those years. Being an excellent horseman and having grown up with horses, he spent his early years with the Forest Service often riding his favorite mounts Blackie and Queenie. In those days, before many of the rough cattle and wagon trails in the area were improved into viable roads for automobiles, it was much easier getting around the mountains on horseback. Over the years, the Ranger owned several beloved horses that carried him many a mile over many a rugged mountain gap. He continued working on horseback even into the early 1940s after many of the roads in the area had been greatly improved for modern vehicles.

"When he got home from work after a hard day in the woods, he often took his boots off and relaxed, but anybody would do that," Jean McNey continued. "Most people, including his wife June, called him 'Ranger.' After he started gaining a bit of notoriety in the mid 1920s, local people also called him 'Kingfish,' but never the 'Barefoot Ranger.'"

According to Jean, her grandfather, despite his great bulk, loved to swim in the then 80-acre lake he had built behind his house (Woody Lake, built in the early 1930s). "Papa was a swimmer," Jean said (she and her cousin Lou, as well as all of the other grandchildren, always called their grandfather 'Papa'). "During mild weather, he would often come home and go for swim in the afternoons. He loved to relax in the water. He would swim from the dock in his back yard to the dam and back (he must have been a powerful swimmer because the distance was considerable; over a quarter of a mile each way!). It was his way of winding down and getting some exercise after a long day at the ranger station or being out in the woods.

"Obviously he took his shoes off to go swimming. Otherwise he wore work boots most of the time. I remember one time when Papa was coming up from the lake after swimming one afternoon he stepped on some broken glass or some other sharp object in the lake and cut his foot very badly. Lanky Spaulding happened to be there that day (C.K. "Lanky" Spaulding served as the Forest Service Supervisor in Gainesville for several years during the mid 1940s.)

"Lanky was on the front porch down on his knees cleaning out that cut and Papa was just giving him down the country about something he had done and telling him how foolish he was and how wrong it was and that anybody ought to know better. I'll never forget that! It was embarrassing, but that was the Ranger for you."

Ranger Woody and Supervisor Spaulding apparently butted heads on a regular basis, right up until the Ranger's death in 1946. Spaulding was also the man responsible for having the hand-carved totem pole taken down at Woody Gap shortly after Arthur Woody died. The pole was a beautifully hand-carved telephone pole that stood over 20 feet tall, featuring a likeness of the Ranger standing at the top. It had been commissioned by the Civilian Conservation Corps boys at Camp Robertstown, and presented to him in the late 1930s or early 1940s just before World War II as a token of their fondness for him. (For more about the totem pole, see Chapter 8.)

When the U.S. entered the war in 1941, the CCC was disbanded out of necessity as most of the young men were needed for the war effort. The military-like training they had received as Corps members made them excellent soldiers. But just like so many of the young Forest Service recruits who had

served under Ranger Woody at one time or another, many of the "CC" boys had worked with the Ranger in various capacities – fighting forest fires, planting trees, stocking fish, building fish ponds in streams and doing numerous other tasks – and these young men had come to idolize him every bit as much as the Forest Service boys.

The totem pole had been placed on property belonging to Ranger Woody high atop Woody Gap near the spot where the Appalachian Trail crosses the gap. Supervisor Spaulding claimed

The hand-carved and hand-painted totem pole, standing over 20 feet tall, was a gift to Ranger Woody from his devoted army of CCC boys at Camp Robertstown (near present-day Unicoi State Park) as a gesture of their great respect and devotion to him. It was placed atop Woody Gap in the Ranger's honor on property belonging to the Woody family. Although the exact date the pole was erected is not known, it was likely put up in late 1940 or early 1941. At the time the pole was carved, no one could have predicted that the stark reality of World War II would mark the end of the CCC and the historic work that so many dedicated young men had performed for almost a decade across the mountain region. Note the two photos spliced together. A likeness of the Ranger stands on top of the pole wearing his ever-present hat. George Eastman, the carver, poses with Ranger Woody. Known locally as the "wood carver of Sautee," Eastman was a gifted artist who carved at least one other totem pole during this same time period. Made of poplar, that pole was presented to the people of Nacoochee Valley in White County. Photo circa 1940, courtesy of Jean McNey.

that the pole was a hazard to hikers and others passing through the gap, but he might have had the pole taken down for other reasons. By the early 1940s, Ranger Woody was the most famous Forest Ranger in the country. Certainly there might have been some animosity among some of his superiors. However, in fairness to Supervisor Spaulding, if George Eastman's pole had been made of poplar wood like the one erected in Nacoochee Valley, it might have begun to deteriorate after five or six years of being exposed to the elements.

According to Clyde Harkins, a former Camp Woody CCC member and local resident who knew the Ranger well when he was a boy, "Lanky Spaulding was the only Forest Service supervisor who ever gave the Ranger a run for his money!

"The Ranger pretty much ran rough-shod over all of the other supervisors over the years," Clyde said. "But he found his match with old Spaulding. Ol' Lanky didn't let the Ranger push him around. He was one of those people who always tried to put the Ranger in his place." (For more on Clyde Harkins and the CCC, see Chapter 10.)

Since the Ranger Station complex was located directly across the road from Ranger Woody's house, numerous Forest Service workers no doubt saw the Ranger in his swimming attire or sitting barefooted on the front porch after a long day in the woods. Perhaps some of the Ranger's fellow workers saw him walking around in his yard barefooted. Perhaps he even occasionally wandered over to his office at the Ranger Station after he had taken off his boots. Perhaps that is where the legend found its beginning.

Furthermore, during those hectic years throughout the 1930s and into the 1940s when so many projects were underway, the Woody household was often a hub of Forest Service activity. Forest Service workers were always stopping by the house at all hours of the day or night. Officials and spur-of-the-moment guests often spent the night with the Woody family, and the meals that June Woody and her daughter Mae "Maebird" White fixed for friends, strangers and other unexpected visitors became legendary. The Woody household was open to anyone and everyone. In many ways, it was much like a country inn where meals were often being served and where guests often spent the night. A great many of those visitors could have observed Ranger Woody in his bare feet. Perhaps that image somehow persisted and word of mouth formed the basis for the legend in later years.

When Ranger Woody was hospitalized in Atlanta in early 1945 for high blood pressure and a serious heart condition, an article in the Atlanta Constitution jokingly talked about him wearing pajamas for the first time in his life. The article stated that he was forced to take off his boots, but he refused to part with his beloved old hat – even in his hospital bed. An obviously staged publicity photo showed him in bed wearing both pajamas and hat. (See Chapter 15.) The article said nothing about the "Barefoot Ranger."

In regard to photographs, the evidence is irrefutable. Literally hundreds of photos were taken of the "Barefoot Ranger" after he became a local and later a state-wide celebrity in the late 1930s and early 1940s. In almost every one of those photos, Ranger Woody is wearing shoes or work boots. Only rarely do you see the occasional photo where he is shoeless. Despite this visual proof, a very catchy nickname somehow became a folk legend, and in the minds of many people, the legend became part of the man.

Ranger Woody's declining health in the mid-1940s might also have caused him to go shoeless more than normal. During the last year of his life, he suffered from severe heart and kidney disease. Each of these conditions no doubt resulted in poor blood circulation in his lower limbs. He might well have taken off his shoes or boots just to ease the pain and discomfort in his aching feet.

There is one more possible explanation. Up until very recent times, the image that many people in the outside world conjured up of a typical adult male growing up in Appalachia was that of an uneducated, gun toting, barefooted recluse in overalls, always missing a few teeth, and always wearing a crumpled hat. The look on his face would usually tell you that he would just as soon shoot first and ask questions later. One of the most famous Forest Service photos of all time, taken in the Cherokee National Forest in Tennessee in 1922 just a few miles north of Ranger Woody's Blue Ridge District, portrays four rough-looking mountain men who are all scowling at the camera. All four men are barefooted, and two are holding shotguns. The mountaineers in this classic photo easily could have been characters right out of James Dickey's famous novel *Deliverance.* And an appropriate caption for this photo might read something like: "Don't even think about messing with us."

For years, this photo was the all-time favorite "pin-up" photo in Forest Service offices everywhere; not because it represented four backwoods ruffians, but more because it represented just how far the Forest Service had come in reaching out to and working with these once misunderstood and remote mountain people. But to many outsiders and city folk, this was the only concept they had of Appalachia. In their view, the typical image of a mountain man was that of an uncouth, uneducated and often inbred hooligan who married his sister and lived like a hermit in some isolated mountain cove.

It made good press in the outside world to paint Ranger Woody in the same light. Here was an uneducated, backwoods, mountain hillbilly who had

Despite his legendary nickname, Ranger Woody really did dress up upon occasion! Posed here with an unidentified Forest Service official in front of a building (probably in Gainesville or Atlanta), this was one of those rare occasions when he saw fit to wear his fancy "city duds." He likely was attending an important Forest Service meeting. Photo circa late 1930s, courtesy of Jean McNey.

risen to great heights and become a legend in his own lifetime by instigating many innovative conservation policies that normally only a Harvard-educated man born with a silver spoon in his mouth might be capable of achieving. Why wouldn't he be portrayed as a barefooted, tobacco spitting dimwit. But Ranger Woody quickly showed the outside world that he was so much more. And by doing so, he quickly gained the respect of all those educated men who typically looked down on most uneducated mountain folk.

The earliest reference I could find that described Arthur Woody as the "Barefoot Ranger" appeared in *Whose Woods These Are, the Story of the National Forests.* In the first paragraph of Chapter 8, titled "Woody, the Barefoot Ranger," author Michael Frome commented:

> Ranger Arthur Woody was quite content to stay put in north Georgia, where he could watch trees, wildlife and people grow, and walk about unshod so his feet could breathe and feel the ground, and let the rest of the world revolve around him.
>
> Several paragraphs later the author added: ...Although he owned a pair of shoes, he would put them on only when the mountain trail was rocky or when he went to town. Dignitaries and Forest Service officials might or might not find him in his bare feet. They were welcome to take their shoes off, too, and learned that eating unshod helped in digesting ham, chicken, biscuits, cone pone, squash, beans and such dishes which they were served at Woody's table.

In the excellent book, *Touching Home*, published in 1976 and written by high school students in Fannin County with content much like that of the popular Foxfire book series, a chapter titled "Arthur Woody, the Barefoot Ranger of Suches," describes the Ranger in the following manner:

> He seldom wore a uniform and sometimes went barefoot.

Another reference to the Ranger's dislike for shoes by Charlie Elliott appeared in Charlie's 1992 autobiography *An Outdoor Life.* In that book Charlie made the following observation:

> One of my impressive stories about Woody concerns the reputation he held for years as the forest ranger with the best forest-fire record – with the least number of forest acres burned by wild fires – in the United States.
>
> His superiors conceived the idea that he should appear before the national organization of forest supervisors and rangers at their annual meeting in Washington and tell what steps he had taken to compile and maintain such a record.
>
> So his superiors arranged for him to appear before the national organization (the American Forestry Association) and tell how he had maintained such an excellent (fire) record.

> So they dressed him up, put shoes on him – he seldom wore shoes, winter or summer on the job, much to the discomfort of his superiors – and put him on the train to Washington….

During that infamous meeting in Washington, in typical Woody fashion, Ranger Woody made a frog-choker of a speech to those in attendance. I'll have more on that memorable speech in Chapter 7.

My good friend Emory Jones, a well-known author, historian and storyteller from White County who wrote the excellent book, *Distant Voices*, has a favorite saying: "It's a shame to ruin a good story with facts." Referring to Ranger Arthur Woody as the Barefoot Ranger makes for a good folk legend and good storytelling! In truth, he probably never went barefooted more than any other average person while he enjoyed good health. In the final analysis, a number of things could have contributed to the famous nickname, but the exact origin will likely remain a mystery.

One thing is certain: Whether you like it or not, today that famous handle is as much a part of the Ranger's persona as "Babe" was to Yankees slugger George Herman Ruth! In the minds and hearts of many, Ranger Arthur Woody will always be the "Barefoot Ranger."

Definitely the right man for the right job, Arthur Woody was an action man who made things happen. Because he dared to dream big, he overcame challenge after challenge during his long career and often achieved tasks that others deemed impossible. He liked to tackle problems head on, and he seldom shied away from difficult situations. Photo circa early 1940s, courtesy of Jean McNey.

CHAPTER 3
The Right Man for the Right Job

"I make a thousand dollars a day; most of it in scenery!"

Arthur Woody

At his core, Ranger Arthur Woody was a man of nature. The mountains were his heart and soul. He marveled at God's handiwork in the great outdoors, and the rolling hills of North Georgia became his everyday, lifelong, timeless cathedral. He cared deeply about his little corner of the earth and the environmental damage that had been inflicted to his beloved mountains during the latter half of the 19th century and early part of the 20th century. He spent his life trying to remedy some of that grievous damage.

His domain included nearly 200,000 acres of forestland north of Dahlonega, Georgia, in the Blue Ridge Mountains (known as the Blue Ridge Ranger District, this huge block of forestland eventually became one of the largest Ranger Districts in the nation). Although he never had much book learning, he must have been fairly intelligent because he commonly used words that were quite sophisticated. Some came directly from the works of William Shakespeare. He often used phrases like "get shed of," "nary," "purt," "purt nigh," "sit a spell," "don't go flying off the handle," "plumb tuckered out," "fetch," "nip and tuck," "tussel," "commence," "miser," and "tote." And what about the terms "dinner" and "supper?" To mountain folk, and most country folk as well, the noon meal will always be "dinner," and the evening meal will always be "supper."

If you think these phrases are colloquial "countryisms" from some redneck mountain hillbilly, think again. Many of those words and phrases originated in 16th century England during Shakespeare's time and even long before. You see, the rugged pioneers who settled the mountains in and around Union and Lumpkin counties were fairly isolated from the rest of the world. Many of the old Irish and Scottish words and expressions used hundreds of years earlier in the old country were still used quite frequently during the first half of the 20th century by Arthur Woody and his people.

In fact, it is believed that the classic term "y'all," one of the South's proudest and most widely used phrases in existence today, and one for which Southerners are constantly ridiculed by people in other parts of the country, also came from the old country as a derivative from "ye all" or possibly "ye aw." "Thou all" was a common term in the old country referring to the singular (one person), while "ye all" referred to the plural (more than one person). At some point, probably in the 1700s, "ye all" was shortened to "y'all" and it has remained that way ever since! Today that phrase practically defines the South and the congenial personality of its people. "Y'all come now, ya' hear!" was a phrase Ranger Woody no doubt used frequently during his lifetime.

Interestingly, there is also direct correlation between the Anglo-Saxon-Celtic roots of the "Swampers," who settled the Okefenokee Swamp country in South Georgia, and the mountaineers of North Georgia. Both groups of pioneers can be traced back to the same origins and their regional dialect, even 100 years later, was very similar in many ways. The difference is – one group went south to the remote Okefenokee Swamp region while the other migrated to a very remote section of the Appalachian Mountains.

In his excellent book, *Purt Nigh Gone, The Old Mountain Ways,* published in 2009, author, former U.S. Senator and Georgia Governor Zell Miller, who was born and raised in Towns County near Blairsville, devoted an entire chapter to the unique language that once dominated the mountains. Sadly, like many other mountain customs, the colorful dialect of the 20th century is "purt nigh gone" as Governor Miller alludes to in his very informative book. But if you listen carefully, you'll still hear some of these priceless expressions today, although many have disappeared. What a shame!

Kingfish the Man

Arthur Woody was a larger-than-life character whose fame grew to legendary proportions during the last few years of his life. He was an ardent conservationist. He believed wholeheartedly in the wise use of our precious resources instead of no use at all. He would have been appalled at today's generation of left-wing radical "preservationists" who think no trees should ever be cut or that wildlife should never be controlled or managed as a resource. He believed that God made the forests and the wildlife in those forests for people to use and enjoy and he spent his life trying to ensure that would happen.

In truth, he was also an early environmentalist. Two contemporary words we hear quite often these days are "biodiversity" and "ecology." Although it's doubtful Arthur Woody ever heard those expressions during his life, he knew their meaning, and he definitely emphasized both in his uncanny ability to manage the vast acres of mountain timberland under his authority. Amazingly, he was able to do this pretty much through pure instinct, since he had no formal training or education in forestry. Most of his training had come from studying the trees and plants and animals found in his native mountains during his constant wanderings as a boy. All his life he was infinitely curious about nature. His hands on, self-taught learning methods proved to be invaluable later in life when he mentored others coming up through the ranks in the Forest Service.

Arthur Woody possessed a wit like Will Rogers and he loved to play pranks on others. When it came to many of his timeless words of wisdom, he was often as wonderfully quotable as Mark Twain. Some who knew him claimed he was quiet and reserved with strangers until he got to know them. He had a heart as big as the mountains he protected, and he often helped people in need, sometimes even total strangers whom he did not know.

His tireless work in conservation was the catalyst that catapulted him to fame in the early 1940s. More specifically, his work in reintroducing deer to the North Georgia Mountains made him a legend in his own lifetime. His other accomplishments were extraordinary as well even though many of his groundbreaking deeds went unnoticed. In truth, some of his other achievements probably were equal if not more important than his work with deer, but he will always be remembered for that one remarkable feat. In his day, he became an immensely popular figure. Had there been 24-hour news coverage and television as we know it today, he no doubt would have appeared regularly on some of the TV news or reality shows.

By some accounts, he was not much to look at; but he had that rare blend of charisma and charm that made him always standout in a crowd. Whenever he walked into a room, people took notice. He had a commanding and dominating presence. His life has been characterized in many ways: untraditional, visionary, extraordinary, a cross between John Wayne, Daniel

Since his typical outfit for a day in the woods usually consisted of wrinkled work clothes, Ranger Woody was often mistaken for one of his workers. Once, while visiting Suches, the Forest Service chief from Washington D.C. saw a man in rumpled work clothes standing alongside the road. He pulled over and said, "Can you tell me where I might find Ranger Arthur Woody?" "I be him," the man answered. "No, I'm looking for Woody! Ranger Woody!" the chief insisted. "Yer lookin' at 'im," the Ranger said with a broad smile. Since he is wearing moccasins in this photo, Ranger Woody probably had just taken off his work boots to give his tired feet some relief after a long day in the woods. Photo circa early 1940s, courtesy of Jean McNey.

Boone and Davy Crockett; a backwoods philosopher, a self-made financier; stubborn to some, beloved to others.

Standing 6 feet tall and carrying a 250-pound frame in his later years, he was quite trim and fit in his younger days. But in later life he put on considerable weight because he loved to eat. Roscoe Reams, a Georgia native who became a legendary outdoorsman and nationally prominent trick-shooting archer in his own right in the 1950s, first met Ranger Woody in 1938 at age 14. The Ranger was then in his mid-50s. Roscoe described his first impression of Ranger Woody as "a federal man who was tubby fat."

That was an interesting observation indeed coming from a 14-year-old Atlanta boy. Just as Ranger Woody had a certain, inherent mistrust of most outsiders until he got to know them, Roscoe and his hunting companions were suspicious of anyone working for the government. However, the Ranger had a way of quickly endearing himself to most people, and it didn't take long for Roscoe to fall under his spell. (See Chapter 13 for more about Roscoe Reams.)

Arthur Woody loved life. He had a gregarious appetite for everything around him and a gregarious personality to match his size. Even if he did put on quite a few extra pounds in his later years, during the early 1900s he was known to be able to ascend steep mountain trails like a goat. According to Charlie Elliott, despite his bulk he could still get around in steep terrain in 1940 and he had a remarkable ability to read sign left by deer and other animals in the woods. He was blessed with that spark and spirit that made him appear to be almost 10 feet tall to some. And whether people liked him or not, he commanded a healthy respect in his community.

His deep blue eyes could cut through you like a knife, and his intense stare could penetrate your soul. Usually, though, he wore a friendly smile on his face that often revealed more than a little hint of mischief. He loved to look for the humor in most situations. In addition to his natural charisma, he could charm the pants off of Old Satan himself and he had a down-home style of humility that endeared him to most people. He was a people person. He genuinely loved people and most people loved him in return. This is not to say that he had no enemies. Because of his position in the community and his strong, sometimes overbearing personality, he definitely had his share of detractors over the years.

He could hold his own with the foulest rough-and-tumble mountain moonshiner who would just as soon shoot you as look at you, and he could be equally at home with a congressman or the governor of Georgia. He fit in well with everyone in between. He made no class distinctions among men. Everyone was equal in his eyes until proven otherwise. He was a self-made man and he had the confidence of a man who was not beholding to anyone. He was often known to use some very colorful if not downright crude language, which puzzled some people; but he was a man of his times. He was self reliant and determined.

Numerous photos were taken of Arthur Woody in the late 1930s and early '40s. Nearly every one of those surviving photos seems to depict a thoughtful, intelligent man who carried himself with confidence and resolve. Photos can tell volumes about a person's demeanor. Photos can tell you if a man is happy or sad, well adjusted or desperate, good-natured or mean-spirited. Photos can tell you if a man has a good heart. Arthur Woody's heart was in the right place. He was a man on a mission, and he seemed to know where he was going at all times. The sum-total of his many accomplishments bear this out.

Arthur Woody was also a dreamer. He looked well beyond following in his father's footsteps and giving in to the usual and accepted destiny of becoming a farmer like most other boys in his community. Although several stories about Ranger Woody written during the past few decades claim that he made part of his living buying and selling cattle just as his father had done, in truth, after growing up, he never wanted to see another bovine as long as he lived.

Likewise, during his adult life, he wanted nothing to do with farming or growing food in the family garden. He had no qualms about going out and shooting a mess of squirrels or an occasional turkey, or catching a big bass or some trout in Woody Lake for supper, but tending the family garden was always left to someone else. He wanted no part of it.

A Dreamer Who Made Things Happen

Arthur Woody dared to dream big, and through hard work he turned many of his dreams into realties. He was a dynamic individual who was driven to do the things that he did in life. He was a problem solver. If he recognized a problem that needed to be addressed, he tackled it head on, never shying away from any difficult challenge.

For all practical purposes, Arthur Woody should have been content to stay on the farm and eke out a meager living just like most other young men in his community had been doing for generations. But he was cut from a different cloth. Why some men choose to rise above the status quo in their lives while others – many, in fact – seem perfectly content to live a dull and mediocre existence is one of life's great mysteries. Why are some men so much more dynamic than others? Is it their upbringing? Is it their station in life? Is it their level of education?

Dynamic individuals are born with a special spirit and a spark. It is in their blood and in their genes. They possess that rare flame that refuses to be extinguished. They make things happen. They seldom think in negative terms. They refuse to give up. They overcome trials and hardships – even occasional failures –and never look back. They are so passionate about what they do that they are almost obsessed. Arthur Woody was just such a man.

When young Arthur came screaming into this world on the first day of April in 1884, automobiles were several decades away from replacing the horse and buggy. Electricity in rural mountain communities like Suches was a half-century removed from lighting up people's homes. Chester A. Arthur was serving the last few months of his presidency, and only 38 states made up the ever-expanding Union. Grover Cleveland, the only president to ever serve two non-consecutive terms, would be elected to his first term later that year.

Alaska became a U.S. territory. The passenger pigeon, once numbering in untold millions and once seen by the thousands in North Georgia's Lumpkin County as a winter resident, was now becoming extremely rare in the South. Within a few short decades, the species would be gone forever. The Washington Monument was finally completed after decades of remaining half built because of a nasty little "civil" war that claimed 600,000 American lives. The war had reared its ugly head during the 1860s and budget constraints had delayed the monument's completion. Construction began on America's first skyscraper – wonder of all wonders – a 10-story building in downtown Chicago, finished in time to be shown off at the 1885 Chicago World's Fair. Ringling Brothers premiered their first circus and the nation's first roller coaster screeched down a set of twisting, grinding take-your-breath-away tracks at Coney Island, New York.

It had only been a mere 8 years since George Armstrong Custer had perished with his troops at the Little Big Horn in Montana. And only 19 years had passed since Abraham Lincoln had succumbed to an assassin's bullet in April 1865. It was a time of great change to the country overall, but change had always come slowly to Union County, Georgia, one of the most isolated areas in the southern Appalachians. When it finally did come, it came swiftly during the early years of the 20th century, with the sweeping enormity of a great flood. Arthur Woody adapted well to change. In fact, he thrived on it.

A Friend to Many

Arthur Woody had a long history of helping those in need with no questions asked. He did this to such an unusual degree that one has to wonder how he kept anything for himself. But he was blessed. Although he reportedly had been a wild buck just like his father in his younger days, he obviously had been raised with a kindred spirit and a strong desire to help those less fortunate. He could often come across to "educated" people as being an old country bumpkin who murdered the King's English. He made an above average living during his lifetime and he shared his wealth freely and selflessly. However, you never wanted to get on his bad side. He might have been ridiculed by some because of his lack of formal education and his backwoods upbringing, but anyone who met him quickly realized this man was indeed visionary.

Despite his many good deeds he was not loved by everyone. Some people no doubt were jealous of him because of his fame and the things he accomplished during his lifetime. Although he always tried to put the needs of the people in his community first, certain job-related decisions he made in his conservation efforts or in community affairs did not always sit well with everyone involved. Like most families up and down the Appalachian chain, including the infamous Hatfields and McCoys, bad blood existed for one reason or another between the Woody family and certain other mountain families. Some of it dated back to the Civil War where families were torn apart. But much of it came about as a result of Arthur Woody's extensive land dealings. More on that later. Jealousy and envy seem to go with the territory when you are involved in as many controversial projects as Ranger Woody gladly shouldered and took responsibility for during his relatively short life. He understood that and he embraced it. He was nobody's fool.

Ranger Woody's extensive dealings in real estate no doubt contributed to his being disliked by some factions as well. Some of those ill feelings have been passed down through the generations and survive to this day. For years he bought parcels of land on behalf of the Forest Service; anywhere from a few acres to a few dozen acres, continually adding to his Rock Creek Refuge or adding to the National Forest system around the refuge.

Customarily he carried large sums of cash money in his pocket for the express purpose of buying land for the Forest Service. It is a wonder he was never robbed at gunpoint or murdered on some lonely mountain trail because everyone knew he always carried greenbacks in his pocket and he often traveled alone to very remote areas. He sometimes carried a gun, as was his legal right since he was a federal forest ranger. He was also entitled to wear a badge. Sometimes he had to arrest poachers and arsonists. It's a tribute to the great respect that he commanded in the community that he never was robbed.

Once a thief sneaked into his home late at night (the front door was never locked) and made off with his pants, or britches as he fondly called them, which he frequently took off and left downstairs near the door after a long day's work in the woods. That night his britches happened to contain his chain watch and a sum of money, and the thief made a clean getaway. (Read more about this humorous story in Chapter 5.)

During the course of his daily travels, if he ran across someone who wanted to sell a few acres, he would buy the land for cash on the spot. Later on, he would be reimbursed by the Forest Service. In situations where the Forest Service might not be interested in buying a certain parcel for one reason or another, he sometimes bought the land himself. These transactions often involved distress sales where the owner was only too glad to convert what he believed to be worthless land holdings into a few badly needed dollars. Ranger Woody no doubt later sold some of this land for a profit, as he had every right to do. Sometimes it took months to clear up clouded titles, and other times the titles could never be cleared. Any money he made was probably hard earned. Times were tough and you had to be tough to survive.

In truth, times were tough in the mountains long before the Depression plagued the country in 1929. By the early 1900s, many a mountain family was ready to throw in the towel and go somewhere else to make a new start. Many did. Some abandoned their played-out farms, never to return. The government often bought parcels of abandoned land for back taxes. In other cases, selling land to the government was the only salvation for some of those who stayed. The Depression years brought continued misery and hardship, and many farmers were only too happy to sell their unproductive acres for a few badly needed cash dollars that could put food on the table.

It is not clear when Ranger Woody started buying and selling land on his own account or when he started loaning money to others on a regular basis. It likely happened shortly after he went to work for the government in 1912. He probably started out on a very small scale. Apparently it didn't take him long to realize that he could make a decent living trading in land and loaning money. As time went by, his "business" (if you can call it that) grew considerably. By and by, if you lived in the Suches area and you wanted to sell a few acres or borrow a few dollars, Arthur Woody was the man to see.

On more than one occasion, Ranger Woody negotiated a land sale to the Forest Service with the stipulation that the owners could continue living on the property until they were able to make other arrangements. Sometimes he allowed elderly couples to remain on their property for the duration of their lives (essentially giving them a life estate). In more than one case, he even made sure destitute farmers or widows with children had food for their families, often delivering the food himself on horseback.

The Money Man

Ranger Woody made part of his living by charging interest on loans. If he loaned a large sum of money to an individual, he would often take a mortgage on that person's farm as collateral. In the case of a small loan, he would simply ask the borrower to sign a note. Sometimes he was forced to foreclose on a delinquent mortgage. It was the nature of the beast, and he no doubt made enemies doing this. But most of the money he loaned went to desperate people who needed it in the worst way.

Among several old promissory notes found in Ranger Woody's safe were notes made out to his father Abe Woody, indicating that Abe may have been in the money-loaning business before his son. The first was dated March 21, 1914 in the amount of $30 and made out to Abe L. Woody. The term was for six months at 8 percent. The second and third notes were in the amounts of $22 and $55. One was dated Dec. 26, 1916; the other was drawn up four days later on Dec. 30, 1916. The interest rate again was 8 percent. The first had a term of 9 months; the second 12 months.

$ 110.00 Oct, 21. 1929

Two months, after date I promise to pay to the order of

W.A.Woody,

~~Two hundred & ten~~ ---------- One Hundred and Ten DOLLARS

For value received, with interest, from date, at eight per cent. per annum until paid.

If collected by attorney at law after maturity, all costs of collection, including ten per cent attorney's fees, shall be added to principal and interest and be a part of the debt.

And each party hereto, whether maker, surety, or endorser, hereby waives all homestead and exemption rights under the laws of Georgia, or any other State, or of the United States, and further waives demand, protest and notice of demand, non-payment and protest; and the principal may be granted further time, after due, from period to period, on payment of interest, without releasing sureties.

(L. S.)

Due January 1, 1930. (L. S.)

Witness (L. S.)

SWORD PRINTING CO., HEMP, GA.

Typical of the dozens of notes Ranger Woody asked individuals to sign whenever he loaned them money, this $110 note, found in Ranger Woody's safe in 2014, was dated Oct. 21, 1929. Eight days later, on Oct. 29, the stock market crashed, marking the beginning of the Great Depression. Although the term of the note was for 60 days at 8 percent interest, only $60 had been repaid by Oct. 1932, three years after the money had been loaned. It's likely the balance was never paid. Although he did take appropriate legal action upon occasion, Ranger Woody always showed great empathy for people during hard times. Original note courtesy of Dr. Ed Woody.

The $30 note was signed by T.J. and Elizabeth Self. The $22 note remained unsigned. The $55 note bore the names "A.J. Ingram" and "Dusty Ingram" with "Xs" beside both names and the words "his mark" and "her mark" beside the names. (The $30 loan was probably made to the Ingrams as well. Apparently these were relatives of Abe's wife Eliza Ingram Woody who could not read or write.)

Based on the three notes made a few years before his father's death, it is entirely possible that Ranger Woody started loaning money to local people after his father's death in 1919 as a continuation of something Abe had started. Abe Woody reportedly made a good living through farming and other interests. One of those other interests might have been money loaning.

A number of other notes made out to "W.A. Woody" in the 1920s were found in Ranger Woody's safe as well. One in the amount of $110 was dated Oct. 21, 1929. Ironically, this note was signed 8 days before the historic stock market crash on Oct. 29, 1929, marking the beginning of the Great Depression. The term was for 60 days at 8 percent interest. (Eight percent seemed to be the standard rate that Ranger Woody and his father always charged.) Interestingly, despite the 60-day term, the back of the note showed that a $50 partial payment was received by Ranger Woody on Oct. 30, 1932. Another $10 was received on Oct. 5, 1934; a full five years after the original note had been signed.

Another note in the amount of $18 was signed to "W. A. Woody" on Nov. 9, 1923 for a period of 12 months. On Nov. 15, 1925, over two years after the loan was made, a partial payment of $5 was noted on the back of the note.

On Sept. 1, 1923, Ranger Woody loaned $100 to another individual for a term of 12 months. On Oct. 14, 1924, he received a partial payment of $50. On Jan. 22, 1926, he received another partial payment of $10. Then, on Nov. 20, 1937, 13 years after the loan was made, he received another $10 in partial payment.

Ranger Woody took a similar note for $50 on Oct. 1, 1928 for a 6-month period. On Oct. 4, 1933, he received a partial payment of $10.50. On Oct. 9 of the same year he received the additional sum of $12. And on Sept. 9, 1936, he received another $13.

These surviving notes clearly suggest that Ranger Woody could in no way have been the heartless "loan shark" that some people later accused him of being. Instead, the evidence strongly indicates his willingness to work with people who owed him money during very difficult times. Apparently he had great empathy for those who could not repay on time. Common sense dictates that most of the notes paid in full were probably torn up and destroyed on the spot. By virtue of the fact that these surviving notes remained in the Ranger's safe many years after his death, it is likely they probably were never paid. According to family sources, many notes owed to the Ranger secured by property were never paid.

Numerous stories exist about Ranger Woody tearing up unpaid mortgages and loaning money unsecured, but there were no doubt times when foreclosure or legal action was appropriate. It was said that he only foreclosed on people who deserved it, that is, the less desirable elements in the county that most law abiding citizens might just as soon see leave the area permanently. There is probably a certain amount of truth in this. It was also said that he had no qualms about foreclosing on someone who poached deer or trout inside his beloved game refuge. If a family was destitute and needed food, or if a certain deer happened to be destroying a man's crops, the killing of that deer was easily overlooked. But there was hell to pay for the man who deliberately poached one of the Ranger's deer out of meanness or spite.

And there were plenty of mean elements in the mountains. The mountains were full of tough and lawless people. The Civil Wars years proved that. Part of Ranger Woody's job was trying to keep peace with those elements as well. And the record shows that he did a remarkable job in that respect. But in situations where things got pushed to the limit, he was sometimes forced to take action that did not always sit well with certain people.

Charlie Elliott made this observation about the Ranger's loaning of money and his dealings in real estate:

> "The truth was that the ranger, through his ability to buy and sell land, had amassed a sizable bank account and was one of the wealthiest men in his position of anyone in the country ('country' meaning that portion of southern Union County where Ranger Woody lived and operated).
>
> "A large percentage of farmers and landowners in his region owed money to him that he had loaned at a good rate of interest. They were sometimes unable to pay back the money, but he never foreclosed on a mortgage unless the mountaineer failed to pay interest or became an undesirable character in such matters as helping him keep the forest land free for wildlife. In such a matter he would foreclose and send a truck to load their belongings and move them out of the country."

It was a hard business, and no doubt some hard feelings developed over the years. But based on numerous stories about how he went out of his way to help desperate Depression-era farmers and others who were about to lose everything, it is difficult to imagine an Arthur Woody who could have deliberately cheated people out of their land or money.

"He could never cheat anyone," Lou Nichols said. "He had a big heart, and he wasn't that type of person."

The evidence tends to support Lou Nichols' statement.

Furthermore, it's doubtful that Ranger Woody ever set out to get into the land business in the first place. Certainly he was not trained in any type of finance or in buying and selling real estate. It more or less happened because of unique set of circumstances. After the federal government had passed laws and provided funds to purchase cutover and eroded land that could be reclaimed and revitalized during the early part of the 20th century, Ranger Woody became a key link to the success of that process. By chance, he happened to live in the exact epicenter of where the first land transaction took place in North Georgia. The job of negotiating future land sales had to go to someone like Ranger Woody who knew the people and the area, and he happened to be the right man, for the right job at the right time.

So it was almost by default that Ranger Woody found himself negotiating sales for the government, and in time, for himself as well. After all, he had a family to support like everyone else. And history shows that he did a vast amount of good with the money he earned over the years.

Because he was financially independent at a relatively young age, Arthur Woody was able to devote nearly all of his time and energy into his real passion in life – conservation. Had he been forced to depend solely on his meager Forest Service paycheck as his only source of income, the outcome of his life's work no doubt would have been drastically different. In many ways, being financially independent was a huge blessing to his community and to his true passion.

Charlie Elliott said it best in a tribute to Ranger Woody after his death in 1946.

> "Woody's influence and kindliness reached beyond the boundaries of the forest. Legend are the stories of a helping hand he gave to his neighbors in need. His generosity was always so matter of fact, so casual, that many times it didn't dawn on one until later what a fine deed the Ranger had done.
>
> "His thinking was basic. He knew the need of community worship and education, and he helped build a church and a school. He took part in the Easter sunrise services held annually at Woody Gap. He worked to bring the mountains away from Indian trails to paved and gravel roads."

With his popularity, Ranger Woody might easily have been elected to public office. In some ways, you could argue that he was a politician of sorts because he wielded an immense amount of power in his community. The nickname "Kingfish" suited him well. Yet in truth, he did not have the temperament to be a politician. He detested laziness, people who lied, big shots and phonies. He respected and related to the common man, the man who toiled and worked hard every day to support his family and put food on the table. Of course, like most veteran politicians, his idea of good politics was doing things *his* way.

By 1927, most people called him Ranger Woody or just "Ranger," including his wife June. Some people in the community were beginning to call him "Kingfish," a nickname that seemed to fit the pillar of the community that he had become. Ranger Woody never flaunted his wealth. Most, if not all, of his money stayed in the community and he lived frugally most of his life, the way he had been brought up.

Mark Twain once said, "Everyone in Hannibal (Missouri) was poor but we just didn't know it." Such was the case with the Arthur Woody family of Suches. When Arthur Woody died, he left behind quite a bit of real estate that he had accumulated over the years, but very little cash money. For him, money had always been a tool like so many nails needed to build a house. It was to be used and shared, not hoarded, and he certainly never hoarded any of the money he earned.

"We were never in want," Jean McNey said, "But we never thought of ourselves as being wealthy or well-off either. We simply got by like everyone else."

A One-of-a-Kind Character

It is widely known that Ranger Woody ignored many Forest Service rules and regulations and seldom wore a Forest Service uniform. Most of the old photographs in which he appears (and there are many) show him wearing rumpled dark green work pants, or britches as he called them, with suspenders, and a wrinkled dark green shirt. That was his everyday "work" uniform. The suspenders became more commonplace as he put on more weight toward the end of his life. Sometimes the britches he wore would be opened at the top to accommodate an ever expanding mid section. He had a life-long love affair with June's homemade cornbread and it showed!

Although he knew every nook and cranny of the vast mountain region he grew up in around Suches, and often spent days at a time camping out with his children and roaming the mountains, he never had any desire to travel outside of the area or leave his native mountains. To make him leave, you practically had to pry him away from Suches, and that was the way he wanted it to be.

As with his definition of a Yankee, he also frequently described most government bureaucrats as "average men who had to leave their homes to make a living." Once a visiting forestry official asked him where the nearest bathroom was. "What do you need one of them for?" he responded with a puzzled look. "We only got about 180,000 acres of woods around here."

Ranger Woody might have been the original homebody, but his employer was in the habit of moving people around on a regular basis. Once, in the early 1940s, after he had established a reputation for doing such an outstanding job in his district, he was asked by the Forest Service if he would consider moving to another state to take over a forest district that needed a good overseer. "No, I think I'll just stay here," he said. "You can give my job to someone else, but you can never make me move."

By the late 1930s, after his reputation for restoring the mountain forests had spread far and wide, the University of Georgia offered him an honorary degree in forestry. The University had (and still has) an excellent school of forestry. Many of the outstanding foresters who had worked in the mountains with Ranger Woody over the years like Bonnell H. Stone and Charlie Elliott were graduates or attendees of Georgia. (Bonnell H. Stone managed land for the Pfister & Vogel Leather Company of Milwaukee, Wisconsin, and is recognized as the father of forestry in Georgia. Charlie Elliott studied forestry for three years at the University.)

"What do I have to do to get this-here honorary degree?" he asked.

"Just come down to Athens and we'll present it to you in a special ceremony," he was told.

"After I get it, will I know any more than I know now?" he asked.

"Well, no...."

"Then I think I'll just stay right here in Suches," Ranger Woody responded.

One possible reason Ranger Woody turned down the offer was because he hated getting up in front of crowds and "speechifying." He had done it once or twice before with disastrous results. He was a great supervisor, he worked well with small groups and he was great one-on-one with people, but he never felt comfortable getting up in front of crowds and talking about himself. That wasn't who he was.

Bill Bergoffen, who co-authored the letter reprinted in Chapter 1, recalled in a later letter to the Ranger: "...Reminds me of the time you got up at some dinner or other and remarked, 'I feel like a duck that's been fattened up for killing. I'm so full I can't quack!' Then you sat down."

That was typical for the Ranger – short and sweet. He was never one to make long-winded speeches.

Ranger Woody loved people; he loved the forest where he worked and loved his job. He had a very clear vision of what that job entailed and he was driven to achieve the many goals he had set. His co-workers would do anything for him. His natural magnetism made those around him always want to go that extra mile to please their boss.

"He was always doing something, working on some big project, sometimes several projects at a time," Jean McNey remembered. "Usually it had something to do with conservation."

He also loved food, and this inclination to eat probably cost him dearly toward the end of his life when he put on too many excess pounds and had serious problems with high blood pressure and a bad heart. Despite his bulk, he possessed an inordinate amount of energy and he worked hard every day. He was an excellent judge of character and he could usually size up a man within a few minutes of meeting him. He had no formal education, yet his common-sense wildlife and forest management techniques were eventually recognized as being brilliant. He set standards in a number of areas. Some of his methods are still in use today.

Ranger Woody seemed to know instinctively what would work and what would not work. For instance, in the 1930s, the Forest Service decided to collect grazing fees in the North Georgia Mountains from farmers who grazed their cattle on Forest Service land (based on the way things were done on the vast rangelands in the West). Ranger Woody was fit to be tied.

"It'll never work in our mountains," he protested. "Why these farmers have been grazin' their cattle in these hills for purt nigh 100 years. I know these people. If you make 'em start payin' for it now, they'll just set fires and burn the woods up. And the Forest Service will lose more money than any grazing fees would ever produce." He steadfastly refused to collect any grazing fees in his district.

Reportedly grazing fees were collected in another district to the west. Just as Ranger Woody had predicted, intentional fires were set because the local farmers were outraged; so much so that the ranger in the other district was forced to relocate. The Forest Service soon abandoned its idea to collect grazing fees in North Georgia.

White Whiskey

Among other things, the rugged people who settled the North Georgia mountains brought three important traditions with them from their native lands in Ireland and Scotland; a deep faith in God, a love of music and a penchant for consuming homemade spirits. Manufacturing and partaking in the consumption of mountain spirits was as natural to them as breathing pure mountain air. It was a way of life, part of who they were as a people.

Perhaps one reason Ranger Woody habitually refused to wear a uniform was because most mountaineers were highly suspicious of anyone working for the government, especially those who did wear uniforms. This probably originated from the fact that most mountain families up and down the Appalachians had at least one member who made some type of illicit spirits. The tradition of making moonshine had been passed down from father to son for generations. Oftentimes, those who made their own whiskey also sold a little on the side for extra income – especially when times were tough, and it seemed that times were always tough in the mountains.

(Georgia actually enacted a statewide prohibition law in 1908, well before the Volstead Act went into effect in 1920. Prohibition in Georgia lasted from 1908 to 1935. The National Prohibition Act was repealed in 1933. Even after prohibition ended, moonshiners were hunted down by the much-hated revenuers in a running war for several decades.)

Mountain folks did not take kindly to outsiders telling them they couldn't make or sell their much loved whiskey. But with the new laws in effect, it was a federal offense in America to distill alcohol without a federal permit. In effect, the making of "likker" in the woods made mountaineers tax violators, and the revenuers came after them unrelentingly to shut them down and destroy their stills.

Ranger Woody's Rock Creek Refuge included some acreage located in Dawson County, the most notorious county for the making of and running of illegal whiskey or "white lightning" in the nation during the 1930s and '40s. Highway 9, leading south from Dahlonega and Dawsonville to Atlanta, became known locally as "Thunder Road." A classic movie by that title was made in 1958 starring Robert Mitchum. The popular sport of stock car auto racing got its rough-and tumble beginnings in Dawson County. More than one former "tripper" (the man who drove the car and tried to outrun revenuers at very high rates of speed) won dirt-track races in Atlanta and other towns across the South during the sport's infancy in the 1940s and '50s. (Organized stock car racing later turned into what we know today as NASCAR, or the National Association of Stock Car Automobile Racing.)

Although he was never what you would call a heavy drinker, the gregarious Ranger Woody loved nothing better than to indulge in a shot or two of home-made apple-jack brandy or corn whiskey with good friends, and he often did so. Usually the apple-jack or white lightning was made by one of his neighbors. In fact, the Ranger always kept a good supply in his safe at the ranger station for any emergency that might arise such as the unexpected arrival of a special guest. And special guests seemed to be arriving on a regular basis.

While some mountain families made and sold whiskey for a livelihood, Ranger Woody always maintained that it wasn't his job to report moonshiners or illegal stills. Once he was ordered to appear in court over a case involving an illegal still. When the judge asked him point blank why he hadn't reported a still that he obviously knew about, he answered, "That wasn't my job, Your Honor."

To a large degree he was right. Since his "job" consisted of preventing forest fires and protecting the deer and other precious wildlife resources within his district, he knew it behooved him to remain on good terms with everyone, including those making whiskey. Moonshiners were often among the hardest and toughest elements in the mountains. To their way of thinking, it was a God-given right to make a little mountain whiskey on the side and Ranger Woody was not about to declare war on these people for obvious reasons. Had he taken a different position, it might have been just that – all-out war.

Once, when asked to enumerate some of the reasons why he had been able to maintain such an amazing fire prevention record in his ranger district over the years, he jokingly answered, "Wal, for one thing, I never was too awful good at smellin' a fresh still." In truth, he could smell a fresh still two miles away. He probably knew where every still in Union and Lumpkin counties was located, how much "white lightning" it was producing and the names of everyone involved.

According to former CCC member Clyde Harkins, (who served at Camp Woody in 1940 and who is somewhat of an authority on the subject of moonshine), the Ranger did have one steadfast rule that applied to anyone operating a still in his district. "Don't let your fires get out." It was that simple. As long as the local boys who operated stills watched their fires and didn't burn down the woods, the Ranger was content to continue having problems with his olfactory senses.

"On the other hand, if he didn't like you, watch out!" Clyde added.

The Winds of Change

Much has been written about Ranger Woody's various exploits over the years. Some is true; some has been greatly exaggerated as discussed earlier. It is understandable that tall tales about a man like Ranger Woody would eventually find their way into the printed material because he was such a remarkable character. However, many interesting aspects of the Ranger's life have never been brought to light.

Sadly, much of Arthur Woody's early life history has been lost to the ages because of little to no documentation. We know he went to work for the Forest Service in 1912 when he was 28 years old, but what did he do before that? He was married by the time he was 18 years old in 1901. But very little is known about his early life or what he did before going to work for the Forest Service. Fortunately, numerous stories were written about him in his later years after he attained some degree of fame. These stories paint a good and accurate picture of who this man was and they give considerable insight into what he thought, how he did things and his philosophies about life.

It is interesting to keep in mind that Ranger Woody's 33-year reign as a custodian of nearly 200,000 acres of mountain forests coincided with an extraordinary time in U.S. history. It was a time of monumental change. By 1918 when Arthur Woody became a Forest Ranger, automobiles had replaced the horse and wagon in most places. The U.S. had become a world power and

A rare photo of Ranger Arthur Woody in full uniform: when he first became a forest ranger in 1918, the idea of building a thriving national forest from cut-over, fire-scarred, eroded land was a relatively-new notion that had never been attempted before. Skeptics argued that it could not be done. Ranger Woody's idea for reclaiming the cutover landscape and returning it to the mountain paradise he had witnessed as a boy became his driving passion in life. He knew the mountain landscape should contain more than trees alone. He envisioned an outdoor paradise where hunters, fishermen, hikers and campers could relish in nature's bounty the way he had done in his youth. Photo circa mid-1930s, courtesy of Jean McNey.

was engaged in a nasty world war where American boys were dying on distant battlefields in France.

The country had finally filled out its boundaries and now boasted 48 shining stars on the American flag, a flag that, incidentally, Ranger Woody religiously flew proudly at the small ranger station in his front yard. And by this time, instead of exploiting our country's vast natural resources as Americans had been doing for two centuries, people in powerful positions were now thinking in terms of trying to conserve and protect what was left. Respected and forceful leaders like Theodore Roosevelt had led the conservation charge. It was now up to people like Arthur Woody who worked in the trenches to implement those much-needed changes.

The chain of events leading up to the establishment of what would eventually become the Chattahoochee National Forest during the early 1900s was nothing short of amazing. The national forest system truly is one of the federal government's greatest gifts to the American people. And as mentioned, Suches was the epicenter of the conservation movement in North Georgia. Few living men at that time in history could have taken the bull by the horns and done the type of job that needed to be done as well as William Arthur Woody. To him, of course, it was not a job at all. It was an all-consuming passion and his life's work.

Like many men who are passionate about what they do, Ranger Woody never punched a time clock and never worked a 9 to 5 shift. His was a job that required him to be wherever the action took him at all hours of the day and night. You might say his was the original "multi-task" job that involved three specific areas: managing and protecting the forests, restoring and protecting the fish and wildlife within those forests, and helping the federal government acquire land for the national forest system. When he wasn't busy tending to one of those important duties, he was doing community work in and around Suches, always working on some important project.

Much of his conservation and community work was done with his own money and resources. At the time, many of those projects never would have gotten started any other way. In regard to his duties as a forest ranger, any one of the three conservation-related undertakings mentioned above could easily have been full-time jobs administered by three highly qualified individuals. But Arthur Woody led the charge on all three of those fronts for over 25 years.

Of course, he always had the full help and support of his wife and children, and he had a lot of help and support from hundreds of hard working Forest Service employees and "CC" workers along the way. He certainly couldn't have done it alone. But there is no doubt that his vision and leadership spearheaded each and every successful project. Had he lived to witness some of Ranger Woody's most outstanding achievements, Theodore Roosevelt no doubt would have been extremely proud. Both men shared much in common.

In short, Arthur Woody was born to be a forest ranger. It wasn't practical to fight forest fires in a stuffy, tight-fitting wool uniform. Ranger Woody was a roll-your-sleeves-up-type of mountain man who got out there and got his hands dirty every day.

Was it divine providence that put the right man in the right place for a job that few others (if any) could have done as well as he did it? Any "outsider" brought in to do his job would have been run out of those mountains. But even an insider like Ranger Woody had to possess the skills, intellect, vision and dedication to accomplish the mammoth task of restoring, restocking, protecting and managing thousands of acres of forestland. And nothing like this had ever been done before. The idea of building a national forest from cut-over, fire-scarred, eroded land was a brand-new notion in those days. No precedents had been set to go by. Much of Ranger Woody's work was accomplished through instinct, determination and sheer stubbornness.

What Arthur Woody lacked in book learning he more than made up for with his God-given talent. His "unscientific" do-what-needs-to-be-done type of management – for both fire prevention and timber and resource management stemmed from one thing – common sense! He had a good feel for what needed to be done and how to do it and he accomplished his objectives through clear thinking and hard work. One of the most important truths he learned early on about conservation was that 80 percent of the job involved good people management. In that respect, he was far ahead of his time.

"He was amazing," Jean McNey remembered. "But he could also be quite blustery at times." Blustery may be putting it mildly. Although he had a heart as big as the mountains he came from, he had little patience for fools and by-the-book bureaucrats and he would often give them a piece of his mind if the task at hand was not to his liking. That is, if common-sense solutions were not used in the decision-making process, he would let people know what he thought. At times, he was known to use very convincing and sometimes "strong arm" methods to obtain his objectives.

By being such a "homebody" for 33 years, Ranger Woody established deep roots with every facet of his job. Those roots helped to create, anchor down and perpetuate one of the most amazing blocks of forestland in the United States. Judging by the Ranger's many accomplishments, this obviously turned out to be a tremendous benefit to the Forest Service, to the North Georgia mountains, and to the entire country.

Ma Woody looks lovingly up at her only child. Although she could be just as cantankerous as her famous son, she had a big heart, and young Arthur apparently inherited the desire to help others at an early age. Sadly, Ma Woody lost her husband Abe, 55, in 1919 after he was shot. Ranger Woody died in 1946 several years after this photo was made. Ma Woody lived to the age of 90. She passed away in 1957. Photo circa 1940, courtesy of Jean McNey.

CHAPTER 4
A Folk Legend is Born

"I'm now wearin' my seventh set of toenails. The other six were worn out on them miserable cattle drives."

Arthur Woody

He never made a lot of fanfare about who he was. He didn't have to. His actions spoke volumes and he never had to toot his own horn. Most people simply called him "Ranger." At home in Suches where he definitely ruled the roost, he was often known as "Kingfish" or the "Bull of the Woods." In later years, of course, long after his death, the outside world knew him fondly as "The Barefoot Ranger."

If anything important was going on in the community of Suches he was always right in the thick of every activity. If someone wanted to sell an acre or two, he was the man to talk to. If someone needed to borrow a few dollars, he was the man to see. To the outside world, he might have come across as being as country as cornbread (which he dearly loved all his life), but he had a quiet confidence about him that let you know in a hurry who was in charge.

William Arthur Woody was born in a log cabin just off Cooper Gap Road south of Suches, Georgia, on April 1, 1884. Perhaps it was serendipity that a man with such joy and goodness in his soul would be born on April Fool's Day because all his life he loved to laugh, he loved to have a good time, and he loved to play practical jokes on those closest to him.

Like his father before him, young Arthur Woody was of rugged pioneer stock, descended from a tough race of settlers who had moved into the headwaters of the Toccoa River while the area was still occupied by the Cherokee Indians. It seemed only natural that he would take to the high mountain ridges and deep valleys of his native homeland, and he soon became an avid outdoorsman and student of nature. He had an abiding respect for the Cherokee Indians who had lived in the mountains before his people and he always admired their many outdoor skills. He loved everything about his mountain paradise. He loved the scenic splendor, he loved the animals, and he loved to hunt and fish. He loved to study nature. Long before he went to work for the U.S. Forest Service, he knew every tree and plant in the mountains and the best uses for each type of wood. He knew the natural history of all the animals. Somewhere along the way, he developed a particular fondness for the beautiful and graceful white-tailed deer, which had been absent from his homeland for as long as he could remember.

He came from good stock – Abraham Lincoln Woody and Eliza Ingram Woody, known fondly in later years as Granddaddy Abe and Ma Woody (or "Granny" Woody). Ma Woody outlived her philandering husband by 40 years. Sadly, Abe died from wounds sustained in a tragic shooting at age 55. Despite his faults, Abe was a good man and a good father. Arthur's grandparents were Jonathan Wesley Woody Jr. (for whom Woody Gap was named) and Axey Seabolt Woody. Both were well-known personalities in their community. John Wesley was a highly controversial figure during the Civil War. He made a name for himself by being true to his convictions and remaining loyal to the Union. In so doing, he nearly lost his life. As a reward for his allegiance to the Union, he later became postmaster at Dahlonega after the war in the early 1870s.

While Arthur was still a boy, Abe and Ma Woody built a "modern" white frame house out of rough-hewn boards instead of logs in Suches only a few miles from where Arthur had been born near what today has become Highway 60. It was here in the valley of the clouds where young Arthur grew up and where his mother later spent the remainder of her life. Ma Woody lived in this house until she died in 1959 at age 90. Up until a few years ago, the ruins of that house could still be seen near the back side of Woody Lake.

Little is known about young Arthur's early childhood. "He didn't talk much about his boyhood," Jean McNey remembered, "at least not to me."

Like most mountain boys, he no doubt assisted his father doing farm chores and tending to the family cattle that roamed freely in the mountain meadows around Suches. The free-ranging cattle belonging to the Woody family were rounded up once a year and driven to the stockyards in Gainesville, a grueling 35- or 40-mile trip over extremely rough terrain. It took several hard days to make the trip. As soon as he was old enough to be of use, young Arthur went along. They camped out along the way, something the boy probably relished dearly.

In later life, Ranger Woody was quoted as saying, "I'm now wearing my seventh set of toenails. The other six were worn out on them miserable cattle drives." (Several written accounts claim that Arthur Woody and his father periodically drove their cattle to Atlanta. Although this is entirely possible, it's more likely that those cattle drives went to Gainesville instead. Gainesville had stockyards and rail facilities in the early 1900s and would have been much more accessible than Atlanta.)

Until much later in his life, the longest distances Arthur Woody ever traveled away from home were to Gainesville and possibly Atlanta a few times. Like most mountain boys, young Arthur developed a good work ethic at an early age. Although farm work was not to his liking, he was a hard worker and he knew how important it was to persevere and see a job through to the end, no matter how difficult. If he set his mind to something, he usually did it and did it well. But even in those early days he was fiercely independent. He didn't like to take orders from anyone, and good or bad, that trait stayed with him throughout his life.

Typical of mountain life in the late 1800s, Arthur attended grade school from the first through the fifth grade in a small one-room schoolhouse near Suches.

"I doubt if he made it all the way through the fifth grade," Jean said. "And he certainly never graduated from high school. But he educated himself in other ways. He was interested in everything. He was infinitely curious about the world around him, and he was always interested in learning new things, especially if it had to do with nature. He was a fast learner and he had a very good memory. And contrary to some of the tall tales about him that claim he was illiterate, he could read and write extremely well. As part of his job in later years, he read Forest Service reports on a daily basis."

As mentioned in Chapter 1, by the time most mountain boys were 11 or 12 years old, their rudimentary schooling usually came to an abrupt end because they were needed at home to work on the farm. High schools were nonexistent in the hinterlands of Union County when Arthur was coming along. The one or two teachers who taught the 20- or 30-odd children of all ages from 6 to 16 in the scattered and remote one-room schoolhouses (or church buildings), tried to teach the oldest students on a more advanced level, but there were seldom many older students present to teach.

A number of published accounts written during the past few decades state that Arthur entered North Georgia College in Dahlonega at the age of 16,

Edgar Guest once wrote, "It takes a heap of living, to make a house a home." Abe and Ma Woody's "modern" white frame house, where Arthur Woody grew up, experienced plenty of living during the late 1800s and early 1900s. Although Arthur was an only child, he was never alone. His mother took in numerous orphans during his childhood. Up until a few years ago, the ruins of the house could be seen near Woody Lake. Photo courtesy of Jean McNey.

an institution his grandfather John Wesley Woody had helped establish (also mentioned in Chapter 1, although no evidence could be found linking his grandfather to the college). Reportedly he left after only a few days or weeks, quickly returning to the mountains and the outdoor life he so loved.

"It seems clear that he was never cut out for academics, and I would be very surprised to learn that he ever went to North Georgia College," Jean McNey said. "He never said anything about it to me. And like so many of the stories about him, I think that one is more than likely pure fantasy. My Uncle Clyne and my mother Mae attended North Georgia College, as did several of Papa's grandchildren including me, but he never did."

Whether or not Arthur Woody received any type of formal education beyond grade school is really a mute point. His real education was attained through hard work and self determination. He was a lifelong student of human nature and his instincts about people were usually quite accurate. In many ways, he educated himself through hands-on experience, constant experimentation and living his life to the fullest every day. As his career progressed, others came to his district with forestry degrees from notable colleges around the country, but Arthur Woody didn't need a college degree to carry out his job and excel in what he was doing. Despite his lack of education, he constantly amazed his superiors year in and year out with his common-sense approach to forest and wildlife management. You might say that he earned his master's degree in the knobs and hollows of the southern Blue Ridge Mountains.

He achieved the "American Dream" through hard work and determination. He believed in the old motto "finish what you start," and he tackled any challenge head-on, using skill and ingenuity to get things done. He defined that uniquely American brand of American spirit that his forefathers and the founding fathers of this country had possessed. Although he hated to obey the rules, he frequently took chances and he thought far beyond his own life for the greater good of others.

He often came across to more educated people as being an illiterate country bumpkin who murdered the King's English. Sometimes, no doubt, that's what the man behind that knowing grin wanted people to believe. If he wanted something badly enough, he would find a way to make it happen. That's the way he had been taught by his father and that was the way of mountain people in general – innovative, creative, determined – making things happen with very little to work with, very little material wealth and very little outside help.

That same man also had a heart of gold. He was always looking out for the needs of his fellow mountaineers. Outside of his demanding job as a forest ranger, the compassion he had for other human beings was extraordinary. Throughout his lifetime he exhibited that compassion by demonstrating that he clearly cared about other people, and he wilfully helped those in need in a variety of ways. He seldom sought any type of recognition or repayment for his kindness. It was in his soul. He was born with a servant's heart. But even though he was a good man in countless ways, you never wanted to get on his bad side.

This is the oldest photo of Arthur Woody and his mother known to exist. It was probably taken in the late 1880s when young Arthur was about four years old. Elizabeth Ann "Eliza" Ingram, better known in later years as Ma or Granny Woody, was born Sept. 1, 1868 in Wildhog (near Suches). She married Abraham Lincoln Woody in 1883. After Arthur was born, she never had any more children. Photo courtesy of Lou Nichols.

He could get mad. He could lose his temper. He could go into a cursing rage. After all, he was human. But he seldom carried grudges and he seemed to have the ability to put things behind him very quickly and look to the future.

The Ravages of Civil War

The Civil War years were a living nightmare for Arthur Woody's grandfather and his large family. John Wesley Woody Sr., Arthur's paternal great-grandfather born in North Carolina in 1781, had moved his family from North Carolina to Lumpkin County, Georgia, shortly after the Cherokee removal of 1838 during the height of the gold rush frenzy. In the early 1840s, the Woody family homesteaded on land in the Yahoola Valley just north of Dahlonega that only a few years earlier had been traditional hunting lands of the Cherokees. John Wesley Sr. married Priscilla Treadway (also of North Carolina). Priscilla, who often spelled and pronounced her name as "Percilla," made a name for herself over the years as a highly skilled midwife who delivered scores of mountain babies. She was best remembered for having shared her name with many of the young girls she helped bring into the world. Both John and Priscilla were prominent and distinguished citizens in their community.

When war came in 1861, a number of Union County residents reportedly got together and attempted to deed their land to the Canadian government because they did not want to take sides and they certainly did not want to leave the Union. (The same thing happened in Dade County in extreme northwest Georgia as well.) Apparently nothing came of the effort, but a portion of the area near Canada Creek in Suches where a small community was located at the time became known as the "Canada District." The name stuck, and today the Canada District is listed as one of 14 districts in Union County, Georgia.

Many mountain citizens felt it was not their war. But the war came to them with a vengeance and impacted their families and their communities; not in the usual form of battles being fought on native soil but in other ways equally or even more harmful. Innocent boys 15 and older were eventually forced to join the Confederate Army by conscription, often against their will. Many never returned home, having died of disease or on some far-away battlefield. Lawlessness, generated by deserters, renegades and one faction against another ran rampant, causing considerable strife within mountain communities. Charles Frazier's best selling 1997 historical novel, *Cold Mountain,* set in North Carolina, describes in brutal detail much of the lawlessness that took place in the southern highlands during those trying times.

Found in Arthur Woody's safe, this portrait is believed to be a photo of his grandparents, Axey Seabolt Woody and John Wesley Woody Jr. Both were prominent figures in their community. Because of his devotion to the Union, John Wesley was appointed Postmaster of Dahlonega from 1874 to 1876. Woody Gap was later named in his honor. Photo courtesy of Dr. Ed Woody.

The Woody family suffered more than most. The old adage, "father against son and brother against brother" became a scourge to Arthur Woody's people. Conscription created a class of deserters across the state that often sought refuge from Confederate officials in remote mountain communities and turned them into hotbeds of guerrilla activity where innocent civilians, forced to choose sides, were caught in the middle.

At the outset of the war in 1861, then 80-year-old John Wesley Sr. ardently supported the United States. Slavery had never been a serious issue in his remote part of Union County. Unlike the southern two-thirds of Georgia where plantation life had flourished for generations prior to the Civil War, few men owned slaves in the mountains. During the gold rush days, a few wealthy mine owners used slave labor in Lumpkin County to work their claims, but only a handful of the isolated mountain families in Union, Fannin, White and Lumpkin counties who farmed for a living ever owned or wanted to own a slave. For the most part, mountain people did not support slavery, and many did not understand or support secession from the Union or the Southern cause in general. Typical of their isolationist attitudes, they simply wanted to be left alone.

John Wesley Sr. saw no reason why Georgia should leave the Union. His oldest son, John Wesley Jr., 41 when the war began, and John Jr.'s oldest son, Aaron Washington Woody (the only son old enough to go to war), also supported the Union. Records indicate that Aaron was born on June 3, 1845 in Dahlonega (making him almost 16 when the war started in April 1861).

Apparently, John Wesley Jr. was drafted into the Confederate Army through conscription during the early months of the war against his will. Like so many Georgians who were forced into the army, he promptly deserted and went home to his mountains. Reportedly, Aaron was conscripted into the army at the same time.

John Wesley Sr.'s other eight sons sided with the Confederacy (or at least, they all ended up in the Confederate Army, either by choice or conscription. Several of them later deserted, stating that they "did not like the way Confederate soldiers treated the Negroes." There were no doubt other grievances as well). This division understandably caused incredible heartbreak and fragmentation within the Woody family. This divisiveness was so great that after the war most of the Woody boys went their separate ways without ever reconciling their differences. Several left Georgia and moved to the Midwest, never to return. Others moved to other parts of the state.

Josiah Askew Woody, John Wesley Jr.'s younger brother by three years (born April 10, 1823 in Franklin, Georgia), became a devoted Baptist minister who started preaching before he was 20 years old. Records indicate that Josiah enlisted in the Confederate Army in the spring or early summer of 1861 for a period of three years. By July 1861 he'd been promoted to 3rd sergeant in Company B of the First Regiment of Georgia Regulars. The Georgia Regulars were sent first to Fort Sumter, and later up to northern Virginia where the regiment took part in the First Battle of Bull Run in July 1861. Josiah was given an honorable discharge some time after the Battle of Bull Run under the pretext that he was a minister of the gospel and therefore could not in good conscience serve as a soldier in battle. Reportedly he was given a traveling allowance from Manassas, Virginia, back to his home in Dahlonega and three months back pay. Witnessing the carnage during the Civil War's first great battle may well have been the reason he was so eager to be discharged from the Confederate Army.

Josiah Askew Woody, a Baptist minister and boyhood friend of Joseph E. Brown, who served as governor of Georgia during the Civil War, poses in his Confederate uniform (Note the sergeant stripes). Josiah Woody was so dedicated to the Southern cause that he turned against his father and older brother, John Wesley Woody Sr. and John Wesley Woody Jr., and tried to have them hanged for treason. He almost succeeded. Photo courtesy of Georgia Archives, Vanishing Georgia Collection, image No. lum191.)

Having been a personal friend of Georgia's wartime Governor Joe Brown since boyhood (Brown had been raised in Suches during the 1820s and '30s), with the governor's help Josiah was able to obtain an early discharge from the army. Josiah remained passionately loyal to the Confederacy. Within a year of returning to Dahlonega, and with the consent of Governor Brown, he was instrumental in forming a group known as the Home Guard, a volunteer group of older men not fighting in the war whose stated purpose was to catch deserters, Northern sympathizers (known as Tories) and outlaws and to try to stop some of the atrocities that were taking place against families whose men were off at war. Josiah originally intended for the Home Guard to be made up of local ministers and law-abiding citizens, but that intent was short lived. The Home Guard quickly turned into a renegade organization credited with committing numerous crimes against its enemies in the region.

Josiah was so dedicated to the Southern cause that he had his elderly father and older brother John Jr. arrested and put on trial for treason. Both father and son might easily have been hanged had it not been for an odd twist of events during the high-profile trial in Dahlonega in November 1863. Josiah reportedly testified against his brother. Later, when John Jr., who reportedly fired his corrupt lawyer and defended himself, was called upon to testify on his own behalf, he was said to have stated, "I did not begin the war and would not fight in it if I could help it." To everyone's amazement, both John Sr. and John Jr. were acquitted of all charges.

But John Jr.'s problems were far from being over. After their acquittal, he and Aaron were forced to hide out in the mountains for several months because the Home Guard led by Josiah Woody was still bent on hunting them down and hanging John Jr. Totally exasperated by the events of the past few years, John Jr., son Aaron and a close family friend known only as the "Caldwell boy," eventually made their way to Nashville, Tennessee in early 1864, where they enlisted in Company G of the 10th Tennessee Cavalry of the United States Army. The three Georgians saw considerable action in southern Tennessee and northern Alabama throughout the remainder of 1864, and during the early months of 1865.

At one point during a heated skirmish, John Jr. saved a tattered Union battle flag that he later brought home with him after the war. The flag was passed down through the family and eventually ended up in Ranger Woody's possession. Today it resides with one of the Woody family relatives in Wyoming. The Ranger told a number of people that his grandfather had carried the flag during the Gettysburg campaign. However, since the Battle of Gettysburg was fought in July 1863, seven months before John Wesley Jr. joined the Union

Bearing 36 stars, this tattered Union battle flag was picked up on a battlefield somewhere south of Nashville, Tennessee, by Arthur Woody's grandfather, John Wesley Woody Jr., during one of his many skirmishes with Confederate troops. For years, Arthur Woody mistakenly told people the flag had been rescued by his grandfather during the Battle of Gettysburg. However, John Wesley did not enlist in the Union Army until February 1864; seven months after the Gettysburg campaign had been fought. The flag now resides with Woody family descendents in Wyoming. Photo courtesy of Dr. Ed Woody.

Army in February 1864, that claim could not have been possible. As often happens, the Gettysburg story probably stemmed from a family story that had been passed down and exaggerated over the years. However, there is no doubt that John Jr. and Aaron saw plenty of action with the 10th Tennessee Cavalry in Tennessee and Alabama.

John Jr. attained the rank of sergeant, while young Aaron, who served as a bugler, held the rank of corporal for a short time. Aaron's rank was later reduced to that of private in April 1864 for some type of infraction. Later, he was court-martialed in New Orleans in early 1865 for an unknown offense (probably for refusing to obey orders, a distinct Woody trait). Both father and son were mustered out of the Army in August 1865.

John Wesley Sr. died in 1866 shortly after the war ended. Even though he had lived 85 long and productive years, the war no doubt took a heavy toll on him and his will to live because of what it did to his family. Since John Jr. and Aaron had supported the Union cause and later served in the Union Army, they were rewarded for their service after the war. John Wesley Jr. was appointed postmaster of the Dahlonega post office from 1874 to 1876. He became a leading citizen in Lumpkin County during the 1870s. Woody Gap was later named in his honor.

Aaron Woody became sheriff of Dahlonega in 1867 during Reconstruction. At the time, the town was still occupied by Union forces, and an infantry soldier reportedly was shot on the town square by a local young man. The existing sheriff, reportedly named Kelly, refused to arrest the man, and the Union commander relieved him of his duties and made Aaron Woody the new sheriff. A few years later, Aaron left Georgia and migrated west like several of his brothers had done, reportedly to get away from the horrors of the Ku Klux Klan, which had been terrorizing people in the mountain region. Aaron died in Hood River, Oregon, in 1923.

After John Wesley Sr.'s death in 1866, Priscilla moved to Dahlonega where she ran a boarding house and sold milk to gold miners. The small pen where she kept her milk cows reportedly was located where the old courthouse now stands. She later purchased a quarter acre lot in the Porter Springs resort spa area nearby, where she and son John Jr. operated a prosperous hotel.

After the war, Josiah Woody moved to Taliaferro County, Georgia, near Crawfordville where he served several years as a Baptist minister. In 1869 he moved to Platte County, Missouri. He never reconciled his differences with his brother. He died on Nov. 25, 1899, in Lincoln, Kansas.

Today, various factions of the Woody family whose roots can be traced back to North Georgia are scattered across the country from California to Chicago, from Missouri to Wyoming. Those interested in finding out about their heritage are still trying to make sense out of what happened 150 years ago during a very difficult time when families were torn apart by a vicious and costly war that changed America forever.

Ranger Woody's Roughneck Father

With their own blend of justice, mountain folk evolved from a tough, hard element. They didn't come any tougher than Abraham Lincoln Woody. Born in the Yahoola Valley in strife-ridden Lumpkin County on July 23, 1864, during the misery and confusion of the Civil War, John Wesley Woody Jr. named his seventh surviving son (as of that time) in direct defiance of the Confederacy after a beloved president who was trying so desperately to restore the Union. Another son, born four years after the war ended in

To all whom it may Concern.

PAID Aug 2 1[illegible]

Know ye, That John Woody a Sergeant of Captain James M. McGill's Company, ("G") 10th Regiment of Tennessee Cavalry VOLUNTEERS, who was enrolled on the Fifteenth day of February one thousand eight hundred and Sixty four to serve Three years or during the war, is hereby **Discharged** from the service of the United States this Thirty first day of August, 1865, at Nashville Tennessee by reason of Special Orders No 13 from [illegible]

(No objection to his being re-enlisted is known to exist.*)

Said John Woody was born in Lumpkin Co in the State of Georgia, is Forty four years of age, Five feet eleven inches high, Fair complexion, Dark eyes, Dark hair, and by occupation, when enrolled, a Farmer.

Given at Nashville Tenn this Thirty first day of August 1865

*This sentence will be erased should there be anything in the conduct or physical condition of the soldier rendering him unfit for the Army.

[A. G. O., No. 99.]

Commanding the Reg't.

James M McGill
Capt Co G 10 Tenn Cav

On Aug 1, 1865, John Wesley Woody Jr. received an honorable discharge from the United States Cavalry. He had attained the rank of sergeant in the 10th Regiment of Tennessee Cavalry Volunteers where he and his son, Aaron Washington Woody, saw considerable action against Confederate forces across southern Tennessee. Discharge papers courtesy of Dr. Ed Woody.

1869, was named Ulysses S. Grant Woody for the same reason, in honor of the restored Union that had finally been saved at such a heavy cost.

It seems that Abe Woody was always having close calls. Even as an infant, he had a close "skirmish" with Rebel forces. At the time he was born, John Wesley Jr. was a fugitive because he refused to fight in the Confederate Army. He reportedly was hiding out in the mountains when a contingent of Rebel soldiers and members of the Home Guard raided the Woody home shortly after Abe was born, under the guise of looking for the baby's father. Knowing full-well he would not be there, they were probably more intent on terrorizing the family. Fearing that the soldiers would kill him because he was John's son, baby Abraham was hidden in a corn meal barrel by the women of the house.

Two different stories have been passed down about what happened next. One story tells about how little Abe was discovered by a member of the Home Guard, yanked out of the barrel and was only seconds away from being bashed to death against the rock fireplace; however, the screams and appeals of the horror-stricken women in the house, who begged for his life, won the day and prevented the baby from being murdered. A second story says that while the outlaw Rebels ransacked the house, the baby was never found in its hiding place. Therefore the boy's life was spared and young Abe Woody grew up to fight another day. If he had been found, the story says, he probably would have been taken outside and bludgeoned to death for sheer spite.

Perhaps it was prophetic that young Abe Woody had made his grand entrance into the world under such dire circumstances. With that kind of beginning, it is little wonder that he grew up to be rough, tough and self-sufficient. Like many mountain men of his era, Abe Woody was a hard-drinking, hard-living man who loved to have a good time. Not much is known about his life. Records show that he married Elizabeth Ann Eliza Ingram, in Suches on Nov. 23, 1883. Their only child, William Arthur Woody, was born the following year on April 1, 1884. At a time when it was a common practice for mountain families to raise large families of 10 or more children, why Arthur was an only child remains a mystery. Ma Woody survived both her husband and her only son.

Although young Arthur was an only child, he apparently had plenty of company while growing up. According to Jean McNey, Abe and Ma Woody took in and raised a number of orphan and homeless children over the years. Most of that "raising" probably was carried out by Ma Woody. "They were always taking in someone," Jean said, remembering stories that had been told to her as a little girl. There is much conjecture that several of those orphan children might have been fathered by Abe.

One of the orphan children reportedly was a full- or half-blooded Cherokee Indian girl. The U.S. Census of 1900 shows a number of people living in the Woody home when young Arthur was 16 years old at the turn of the century. According to that census, living under the roof of 32-year-old Eliza Woody and 36-year-old Abe Woody was a 4-year-old girl named Carrie who is listed as having been adopted (Note: Carrie was listed in the census as white but she might well have been part Cherokee Indian), a white male named Camer Butler (no age shown) who was listed as a servant, a white female named Elisabeth Lunsford (no age shown) who was also listed as a servant, and 76-year-old Anne Woody (listed in the census report as "Anne," but probably Abe's mother Axey Elizabeth Seabolt, born in 1824).

In those days, it was not unusual to have farm help or domestic help living with a family. Like most mountaineers in Union County, Abe Woody made his living through farming and trading and raising a few cattle that ran freely in the mountains. He apparently provided well for his family, and his ability to earn a decent living in a variety of ways certainly rubbed off on his son.

Over the years, Abe Woody was involved in more than his share of scrapes and close calls. During the early 1900s, he was severely cut across the abdomen in an ugly knife fight. According to Clyde Harkins, who served in the CCC in 1940 at age 15 and knew Ranger Woody well, "Knowing he would be dead if he didn't get to a doctor, Abe hoisted himself up onto the back of a mule and managed to ride from Suches to Dahlonega to seek medical attention. He was split open like a watermelon, and during that 15-mile ride over some of the roughest terrain in North Georgia, he held one hand over the long open slice in his abdomen to keep his entrails from spilling out."

A lesser man would have died from pure shock, loss of blood or the mule ride alone. Not Abe Woody. Nor did he die from any later infections.

"When he got to Dahlonega," Clyde continued, "they laid him out on a table in the doctor's office. The doctor sewed him up like an old hound dog that had been split open by a hog. A few weeks later he was as good as new."

The next time around, Abe was not so lucky. The following article appeared in the *Dahlonega Nugget* on Sept. 5, 1919:

> Dr. Head received a message from across the mountain in Union County stating that Abe Woody had been shot by Will Palmer, one of his relatives. Upon arrival to the home, the Doctor found Mr. Woody suffering with a dangerous wound in the side made by a gun. Miss

> Daisy Ingram, his sister-in-law, with one arm half shot off below the elbow, and Mr. Perkins, one of the men who was looking after the government timber over there, with a long gash in one of his arms made by a pocket knife. The Doctor asked no questions. Dr. Head went to the foot of the mountain with a truck and carried Woody and Miss Ingram to Dr. Downey's Hospital in Gainesville.

> A follow-up article appeared one week later:
> *'Dahlonega Nugget*, Sept. 12, 1919:

> Mr. Abe Woody, who was shot over in Union County on the 30th of August by Will Palmer, died at Dr. Downey's Hospital in Gainesville on Friday night at about 12 o'clock. The remains of the deceased was carried back home for internment (Sp).

Abe Woody was shot on August 30 and died 12 days later on Sept. 12. He was 55 years old. Arthur Woody was 35 at the time. He had just become a full-fledged Forest Ranger one year earlier and was just starting to come into his own as a community leader in Suches as well as a powerful force within the Forest Service. It is not known how Arthur Woody responded to his father's death or whether or not Abe Woody's killer was ever prosecuted for the shootings. In an interview years later, he told the writer, "My father got killed by a boy he raised." Will Palmer might have been tied to the Woody family by marriage. He was believed to have been married to an Abercrombie, but he was probably not a blood relative.

"I heard stories that Papa went out looking for the fellow who shot his father with his own gun but I don't know if anything ever came of it," Jean McNey said.

Apparently nothing did come of it because Will Palmer reportedly owned a garage or tire store in Dahlonega a number of years later. Since Abe Woody had long been the family patriarch as of that time, the responsibility now fell to his son. Ranger Woody shouldered that responsibility with his usual energy and common-sense determination. He saw to the needs of his mother and plowed ahead into history. After all, destiny waits for no man and he had a great deal to accomplish!

Marrying Young

At the age of 17, Arthur Woody married Nancy Emma Abercrombie on Sept. 1, 1901. He affectionately called his wife "June." She was 7 years older than her husband. He often said that he married June because she was so much smarter than he was. In later life, she always referred to him as "Ranger." He sometimes jokingly referred to June as "Old Woman."

"If I keep calling her that long enough, it'll fit one of these days," he jokingly liked to say.

June was from a third generation family in Suches. He loved to kid her about "Abercrombie" idiosyncrasies. Arthur and June had three children: Walter W. Woody born July 13, 1902; Clyne Edward Woody born April 30, 1905; and Mae Woody born July 15, 1907. Both boys followed in their father's footsteps and had long, distinguished careers with the Forest Service. Both boys also helped their father with many of his timely and innovative projects. Like many of her close relatives, Mae was destined to become a respected school teacher.

Hard Times and Exploitation – Curse of the Iron Horse

Prior to the time Author Woody was born in 1884, tens of millions of board feet of white pine, hemlock, chestnut, white oak, poplar and hickory covered the mountain slopes where he grew up. Trees standing 100-feet tall and so thick that a man could not reach around them were too numerous to count. It was said in those days that one out of every four trees in the forest was a mighty chestnut. A few years after young Arthur was born, the great, unstoppable fire-spitting iron beasts slowly pushed into the virgin mountain country that he grew up in, making vast stands of timber accessible for the first time in history.

The leather industry was at its peak in the late 19th century. Tannic acid, extracted from the bark of chestnut trees, chestnut oaks and hemlock trees, used in the tanning process, was in heavy demand. The railroads were financed and built by wealthy out-of-state businessmen who accumulated large tracts of acreage in the southern Appalachians for as little as $1 per acre. The common practice for these companies was to come in, cut every available tree, and then sell the land and move on to another promising location with little regard for any damage left behind. Heavy erosion on the hillsides and pollution of the streams and rivers was commonplace.

Within a few short decades, much of the once splendid forestland resembled the surface of the moon. Because of its remote location and difficult access, the area around Suches did not suffer as badly as other areas that were more accessible to the east. Still, much of the picturesque forestland that Arthur Woody had known as a boy was destroyed. By 1910, the once breathtaking views of vibrant green forests filled with tall pines and hardwoods, so common to the southern Blue Ridge Mountains, were replaced with scenes of vast cut over wasteland areas and badly eroding mountainsides for as far as the eye could see. The devastated and bomb-ridden battlefields of France during World War I a few years later couldn't have looked much worse than many a mountain ridge and valley in North Georgia. They resembled bomb zones in their own right.

By 1900, the natural resources of an entire nation had been exploited to the point of being a national embarrassment. A few visionary conservationists of the day like Theodore Roosevelt began taking a keen interest in the sad state of affairs. People began to realize for the first time that America's precious natural resources were not so boundless after all. In an effort to reclaim some of this badly depleted forestland in the east, the federal government began purchasing cutover, eroded land throughout the southern Appalachians. During the first few decades of 20th century, tracts of all sizes and shapes were purchased in eastern Tennessee, western North Carolina and northeast Georgia for what was originally known as the Cherokee National Forest.

During those early years, no man alive did more to help the Forest Service procure land than Ranger Woody. His work in that area alone is extraordinary. He negotiated sales and often paid cash for land himself on behalf of the Forest Service. His cohort Ranger Nick Nicholson likewise helped negotiate a number of land sales for the Forest Service in Rabun County and surrounding areas in northeast Georgia, but Ranger Nick never purchased any land with his own money like Ranger Woody did on a regular basis.

As mentioned, a few disgruntled mountain families disapproved of the Ranger's methods and in later years some even accused him of "stealing" land belonging to their descendents; that is, buying it for a song and reselling it to the Forest Service for a big profit. It's doubtful that could have happened for a number of reasons. First, the Forest Service always had a maximum price it would pay per acre and everyone knew it. Secondly, most of the landowners selling land during the Depression were desperate and they were glad to get anything they could for it. Thousands of acres were foreclosed upon. Thousands more were abandoned and eventually sold for back taxes.

"Several times during the Depression and afterward Papa bought land from people who were destitute because they desperately needed the money," Jean McNey recalled. "I remember one family in the Rock Creek area named Bellisle that owned 680 acres. After he bought their land, he let them live on it for the

Ranger Woody poses with a young chestnut sapling. At a time when the devastating chestnut blight was killing tens of thousands of mature trees in the southern Appalachians, the Ranger apparently tried his hand at planting some seedlings in an effort to save the species, all to no avail. Photo courtesy of Jean McNey.

The hollowed out skeleton of an enormous chestnut tree killed by the blight and millions like it were all that remained of a species that once served as an important food item to numerous woodland creatures including deer, bears and turkeys. The forest giants numbered in the millions; some 21 percent of all trees in the southern Appalachians were said to be chestnuts. Photo probably taken by Charlie Elliott, circa 1930, courtesy of the Charlie Elliott Wildlife Center.

rest of their lives because they didn't have anywhere to go. He also made sure they got by all right with food and other necessities."

Since Ranger Woody was fairly well-off by the time he was 40, one might pose the question: Why did he pour his heart and his life's blood and in some cases, much of his personal fortune, into a gruelling job that demanded long hours, much time spent away from home (usually seven days a week rain or shine), and certain inherent dangers like forest fires, ornery poachers and potentially dangerous arsonists, freezing temperatures and other daily hazards that living out in the elements almost guaranteed? And as a man who never liked to take orders and often refused to obey the rules, why did he spend over 30 years of his life tolerating government red tape and stubborn bureaucrats when he easily could have taken a much less demanding pathway in life?

The answer is simple. Improving his mountain community was his life's work. He was driven to do the things he did. The mountains were his heart and soul. The woods and wildlife he protected were his passion. He woke up every morning of his life raring to go. He likely would have done the job for no pay at all!

What's more, he loved to share his passion with anyone of a similar mind. Anyone who agreed with his plans for improving his beloved mountain country became an easy candidate for his inner circle. This included many professionals that he worked with over the years, fellow co-workers with the Forest Service and the state as well as people like Charlie Elliott who shared his love for the wilderness. (Through his own job with the state of Georgia, Charlie had a hand in laying out hiking trails in Vogel State Park as well as that part of the Appalachian Trail that crossed Blood and Black Mountains in Union County.) Many of these professionals became lifelong friends and they expressed their love and respect for the Ranger in a number of heartfelt ways after he was forced to retire due to failing health in 1945.

In addition to his professional friends, throngs of sportsmen from all walks of life revered Ranger Woody because of what he had done to bring deer hunting and trout fishing back to the mountain region. No wonder he soon became the most famous Forest Ranger the country had ever known!

Ranger Woody had little use for smooth talkers or phonies. He was a mountain man, a product of a sometimes unforgiving landscape. He worked hard every day of his life and he expected others to do the same thing. Perceived social class meant nothing to him. A man's ranking or level of education didn't impress him in the least. Although many high ranking politicians and government officials ultimately sought his friendship, he showed the same respect for the lowest ranking laborer as he did for the governor of the state; it was what a man held in his heart that mattered most to him. And even though he may never have read a complete book during his entire lifetime, he could read most men like an encyclopedia.

A Real Job – Working for the Man

In 1912, when 28-year-old Arthur Woody told his father that he'd been offered a job working with a survey crew with the U.S. Forest Service, his father reportedly hit the roof. "You'll starve to death working for the government!" he informed his son.

But the job was right up his alley. Arthur was hired to help cut out and mark boundary lines on the newly acquired tract of land known as Cherokee Refuge No. 2, just west of Suches, encompassing some 31,000 acres in the Rock Creek/ Noontootly Creek area of Fannin, Gilmer, Lumpkin and Union counties. (Today Noontootly Creek is known as Noontootla Creek.) Shortly after the Weeks Act was passed in 1911, the land had been purchased from the Gennett family for $7 per acre. It was the first tract of land to be acquired in Georgia by the federal government with federal funds.

While the government later purchased many more thousands of acres of cutover land in the area for $1 to $2 per acre, much of the Gennett tract still contained virgin timber, thus justifying the higher price. Arthur Woody knew this land like the back of his hand and the Forest Service was no doubt very pleased to have someone with his knowledge working on the crew. (As mentioned, this initial land purchase was the beginning of what would eventually become part of the Cherokee National Forest. Later on, it would be called the Georgia National Forest and finally, as each state consolidated its individual forest within state boundaries, the Chattahoochee National Forest.)

Abe Woody was adamantly against his son working for the Forest Service. If the truth be known, he was probably more than a little embarrassed because working for the government in any capacity was not a popular vocation in the mountain region. Nonetheless, a stubborn Arthur Woody took the job.

At the time Arthur Woody was hired by the Forest Service, all government people were lumped together with "revenooers," and were not to be trusted. Fifty years earlier President Abraham Lincoln and Congress had established the Internal Revenue Service during the Civil War to collect taxes on luxury items to help pay for some of the extensive costs of the war. Alcohol was one of the "luxuries" included in that tax. Since almost every Georgia mountain clan had someone in the family who made and sold mountain spirits, the new law made it illegal to produce any untaxed whiskey.

Local mountaineers deeply resented this tax and many refused to pay it. Being the incredibly resourceful people they were, local mountaineers resorted to hiding their home-made stills deep in the woods. Since they often worked under the cover of darkness by moonlight, these operators soon became known as "moonshiners." The ongoing war between moonshiners and revenuers would last for the next half century.

By default, Arthur Woody was now one of those "gover'munt" men that most mountaineers despised and avoided. Most people in his situation would have been considered traitors and become outcasts in the community. Not Arthur Woody. With his down-home charm and charisma, his immense popularity in the community, and his ability to win people over, he would see to it that the Forest Service and its many programs were eventually accepted by the local mountain folk with open arms. Thanks in part to the efforts of Arthur Woody, the Forest Service was soon seen as a friend to the people. It became an icon in North Georgia. Many a down-on-his-luck mountaineer drew a pay-

Taken in front of the Dahlonega Post Office with a group of postal workers in 1910, this photo is probably the oldest adult photo of Arthur Woody known to exist (dressed in black, standing second from right in back). He would have been 26 at the time. The significance of the photo is not known, although Arthur Woody's grandfather, John Wesley Woody Jr., had served as postmaster nearly 40 years earlier in the 1870s. Photo courtesy of Georgia Archives, Vanishing Georgia Collection, image No. lum144.

check from the Forest Service for work rendered during the hard years of the 1920s, '30s and '40s, and that pay-check went a long way during hard times.

Prior to 1912, Arthur Woody probably had never given a second thought to working for the federal government. But to him the U.S. Forest Service was a good fit. Looking at the big picture, this seemingly inconsequential decision would change his life forever. On Oct. 1, 1912, he became an axe man with a survey crew, cutting trails and marking boundary lines through the wilderness on lands he had hunted and fished all his life. Officially, this newly acquired government land was known as Cherokee Refuge No. 2 as mentioned, being part of what was then known as the Cherokee National Forest, which at the time included all federal lands purchased in Georgia, Tennessee, North Carolina and South Carolina. (Cherokee Refuge No. 1 was located in North Carolina, having been part of the vast Vanderbilt land holdings.) Over the ensuing years, most local people, including the Ranger, referred to this newly acquired Forest Service tract as "Rock Creek Refuge."

No doubt Arthur Woody was well-suited for the job. He was in his element. He was tall, strong and in top physical condition. Ever since his boyhood days, he had spent countless hours in these very knobs and mountain hollows chasing after his favorite quarry – wild turkeys and squirrels. Or, he might be found fishing the streams for the few remaining brook trout hidden away in mountain alcoves that he loved so much and fondly referred to as "specks."

In addition to the usual mistrust of any government worker, like most mountaineers, Arthur Woody and his father Abe detested big government. President William Howard Taft, who had been hand-picked to succeed Theodore Roosevelt, was leaving office. One month after Arthur Woody was hired by the Forest Service, Taft would be replaced by democrat Woodrow Wilson, and the Woody's detested democrats and their wasteful spending habits with a passion. But Arthur Woody took the job anyway, not knowing what the future might have in store for him. Little could he know that this job would set the stage for an extraordinary career in conservation that would span the next 33 years!

Abe Woody's maverick son quickly advanced to the position of surveyor, a job he no doubt relished, plotting out various new lands acquired by the Forest Service. Since fire control and fire fighting on National Forest lands became an immediate priority with both federal and state authorities, he also began to gain valuable experience regarding forest fire control and fire prevention methods. With his easy going and fun loving ways, Arthur Woody knew virtually all of the landowners in the area. Since he was so well liked and trusted by these local people, it was only natural that he soon found himself helping the Forest Service acquire additional lands for the National Forest system.

Little could he imagine what a blessing in disguise this would turn out to be for his future, his family and the community at large. No one could have predicted that the very tract of land Arthur Woody was surveying would play such a large role in his later life as a Forest Ranger. Eventually his beloved Rock Creek Refuge would be expanded to nearly 40,000 acres and go by a number of different names in the years ahead: the Noontootly National Game Refuge, the Rock Creek-Noontootly Refuge, the Blue Ridge Refuge, the Blue Ridge Game District, the Blue Ridge Ranger District and finally, the Blue Ridge Wildlife Management Area (WMA), the name by which it is still known today. To clear any confusion, the Blue Ridge Ranger District originally included the initial 31,000-acre land purchase. As the district was expanded to include nearly 200,000 acres of national forestland, the Rock Creek/Blue Ridge Refuge grew to 40,000 acres and became a self-contained wildlife management area within that much larger ranger district.

(Note: Formal development of game management on national forest lands nationwide had its beginnings in Georgia when President Calvin Coolidge proclaimed the establishment of the "Noontootla Game Area" on August 5, 1924. But 12 more years would pass during which time a significant amount of prodding of his superiors took place by Ranger Woody before the area was officially declared the "Blue Ridge Wildlife Management Area" in 1936. Not only was Ranger Woody's Rock Creek Refuge the first tract of land in Georgia purchased by the federal government, but thanks to his vision for what it could become – a refuge where fish and wildlife species were every bit as important as the forests and should therefore equally managed and protected – it ultimately became the first official wildlife management area in Georgia and the first of its kind in the nation. Today, hundreds of management areas are found across the U.S.)

Under the watchful eye of soon-to-be "Ranger" Arthur Woody, the Rock Creek Refuge would make history in many ways over the next few decades. In 1928, it would be the release site of and home to the fledgling deer herd that soon would become the basis for a much larger herd that eventually would expand across the entire mountain region. And in 1940, nearly three decades after Arthur had spent long days in the woods cutting and marking its boundary lines as an axe man, it would make national headlines by being the site of Georgia's first modern deer hunt of the 20th century.

Forest Service Advancement Record for William Arthur Woody

Oct. 1, 1912 – Hired as an axeman on a survey line crew working in the Rock Creek area.

May 1, 1915 – Forest Guard hired to protect the game refuge (Salary $50 per month).

July 1, 1918 – Promoted to Forest Ranger (Annual base salary $900).

July 1, 1928 – Promoted to Senior Forest Ranger (Annual base salary $2,000).

Sept. 16, 1930 – PR. Forest Ranger (Annual base salary $2,300); note: It is not known what the letters "PR" stood for. The initials could have designated "Park Ranger."

April 16, 1935 – Promoted to District Forest Ranger (Annual base salary $2,600); presiding over nearly 200,000 acres.

Sept. 1945 – Forced to retire from Forest Service due to failing health.

THE ORIGINAL BOY SCOUT
Doing What He Was Born to Do

Forest Service officials must have seen something special in the hard-working and enthusiastic man from Suches. On May 1, 1915, Arthur Woody was promoted to Forest Guard at a salary of $50 per month. A Forest Guard's duties were described as "protecting all forest lands from fire, trespassers and poachers." Most of this work was done in the Rock Creek Refuge from horseback, and it must have been a life that Arthur Woody relished. After all, he was actually getting paid to work in his mountain heaven.

Initially, very little work was done regarding wildlife management inside the refuge. Because forest fires were the scourge of the southern Appalachians, a heavy emphasis was directed at fire prevention and putting out fires once they started. The 31,000-acre refuge contained millions of board feet of valuable timber, and the Forest Service didn't want to see it go up in smoke. All roads leading into the refuge were gated off and locked. Unauthorized trespassers were cited if caught on the property. Despite the emphasis on protecting trees and preventing fires, Arthur Woody was already thinking ahead of the curve.

He had big plans for his refuge. Fire protection was important, but why not reintroduce and protect certain fish and wildlife species as well – namely brook trout and white-tailed deer – that once had been so plentiful in the area. Soon he would be doing that very thing.

After serving as a Forest Guard for three years, Arthur Woody was promoted to the position of Forest Ranger on July 1, 1918. This was a historic event, one that paved the way for all of his future endeavors. Ranger Nick Nicholson had been named Georgia's first official Forest Ranger in 1912, and now Arthur Woody was the state's second. In order to become a Ranger, an applicant had to pass a written examination.

As with his contemporary, "Ranger Nick" as he was fondly known, the skills required for the Ranger's test were second nature to Arthur Woody. They involved things he had been doing all his life. Of note in the 1908 Forest Ranger Examination issued by the U.S. Civil Service Commission under the heading "Skills a Forest Ranger must have," all applicants were required to have "various horsemanship skills such as saddling and bridling a horse and riding at a trot and canter."

Of course, having been around horses all his life, Arthur Woody could do those things blindfolded. Other required skills included camping and packing abilities (the use of pack animals by Forest Service personnel was quite common out West, but much less common in the southern Blue Ridge) being able to use a compass and being able to measure distances in rods, yards and feet. The test also included a variety of questions about fire prevention, fighting forest fires, forestry practices, being able to identify trees and knowing the specific uses of the wood from those trees. Once again, Arthur Woody's expertise in all of these areas was considerable. A certain amount of knowledge was also required in regard to scaling and grading logs and knowing which trees made the best logs for lumber, railroad ties, fence posts, furniture, ax handles, etc. There were questions about grazing practices (again, this applied mostly to the western states) and questions about knowing land areas (how many square feet in an acre?).

Needless to say, Arthur Woody reportedly did very well on the exam. Being a fast learner, what he didn't know he quickly picked up. The Forest Service was happy to welcome a promising new ranger into its ranks. At the time, no one could predict that this soft-spoken man from Suches would become one of the most beloved forest rangers in the history of the organization.

Forestry Practices

"At the time he became a Forest Ranger, the science of forestry and forest management was still in its infancy but Papa was a woodsman and he used common sense management practices," Jean McNey said. "From the time he was a small boy, he observed what was happening in the woods. He studied everything in the forest. He knew every kind of tree and leaf and what the wood could be used for. He knew which trees produced which kinds of mast for wildlife and people. He had seen firsthand the devastating effects of widespread clear cutting of vast tracts in the mountains during the early 1900s, and after he became a ranger he was very much against clear-cutting any timber on Forest Service land.

"He often used this analogy whenever the question of clear cutting came up: 'You can take the most beautiful woman in the world and put some big, ugly scars on her face and she's not so beautiful any more. That's what clear-cutting does to the mountains.'

"When it was time to harvest a certain stand of timber, he preferred to go in and selectively mark certain trees to be cut so that the timber around them would mature and continue to grow. He was always making way for future crops. This insured a healthy forest for future generations. He refused to follow the old standard practices of going in and clear-cutting everything in sight with no regard for what would be left for the future. Papa's methods of marking trees and selectively cutting are still used as a means of harvesting trees with minimal damage to the surrounding trees and habitat."

Today, while clear-cutting is still a valuable tool in forest management, its use is typically restricted to much smaller tracts that are earmarked for replanting after the harvest instead of the much larger tracts of the old days that might include entire mountains where little regard for the future of the forest or the land was shown after the harvest. For instance, in the pine tree country of South Georgia, where the terrain is much flatter, clear-cutting today is often appropriate on tracts with little timber value or growth potential so that they can be replanted and managed for maximum productivity.

As with the plants and trees of the forest, Ranger Woody also knew much about the habits and behaviour of the various creatures that lived in the mountains because he had studied them all his life. He had a lifelong fascination for wildlife and he loved to watch all wild creatures. As his young protégé Roscoe Reams once commented, "Nothing got by Arthur Woody. Nothing missed his eye. That included both the four-legged variety of critters as well as the two-legged kind!"

Managing the vast timber resources and trying to attain Forest Service goals was an important job. Ranger Woody dedicated his life to the proposition of protecting and perpetuating the renewable timber and wildlife resources in his vast Blue Ridge Ranger District. He understood how important it was to restore the natural balance in the mountain region. At the same time, he never forgot about the people who lived in the mountains or their needs. According to Clyde Harkins, if a farmer needed boards for a new barn or house, Ranger Woody was only too glad to grant permission to go out and cut several good "board trees" so that a family's needs could be met. Sometimes he issued written permits; other times he simply gave verbal permission or granted his approval with a handshake.

As if the Ranger didn't already have enough on his plate in preventing and fighting forest fires, and in managing the forests for optimum health and growth, he apparently took it upon himself to experiment with trying to propagate young chestnut saplings after the great chestnut blight started killing tens of thousands of trees in the 1920s and '30s in the mountain region. Although very little is known about the specifics of what he did, several surviving photographs indicate that he tried to plant a number of young chestnut trees in hopes they would somehow avoid the blight and become re-established. Did he spray them with some chemical? Did he try to isolate the trees from other trees in the forest? We'll never know the answer, but his efforts were in vain. It must have been difficult for the Ranger to stand by helplessly and watch countless thousands of beautiful chestnut trees – one of the most common trees in the mountains and the very trees that fed his beloved turkeys – succumb to a cursed blight.

A Life of Irony

Arthur Woody's professional life contained many ironies. Like most mountain men, he detested many aspects of the federal government and didn't want the government intruding into his personal life in any way. Although he never quite fit the mold and never fell into that all-too-easy trap of becoming a complacent government bureaucrat, he managed to keep his job with the Forest Service for over 30 years, knowing in his heart that the government was responsible for protecting the forests and the creatures that dwelled within them. More importantly, perhaps, he knew that the government also did much to improve the plight of his mountain people.

Even though he disdained big government, Ranger Woody knew that the Forest Service proved to be worth its weight in gold for all of the innovations in conservation it championed nationwide, as well as the economic impact it had on the mountain region. He knew there would always be a certain amount of waste in big government, but he also realized that the nation's forestry program was one shining example of tax dollars being well spent. He probably never would have admitted it, but deep in his heart he also had to agree that the Forest Service turned out to be that one-in-a-million government agency that actually performed a worthwhile service. In so doing, thousands of jobs were created in the North Georgia mountains that were desperately needed by hard-working Americans who had suffered greatly during dire economic times.

Despite his refusal to wear a Forest Service uniform on a regular basis and his steadfast refusal to conform with many Forest Service rules and regulations, Ranger Arthur Woody went on to become one of the most beloved and highly respected forest rangers ever to join the ranks of that service. During his tenure, he also attained fame and legendary status that few people in life ever receive – due mainly to his amazing accomplishments. And even though his star has somewhat faded in recent decades because many of those who knew and loved him in the mountain region are now gone, he was definitely one of the most productive and beloved Georgians of the 20th century. He no doubt enjoyed the attention he received in later life, but doing his job and helping others was always his first priority. After his death in 1946, the legendary status he had gained had been well-earned.

Wearing his perpetual smile, Ranger Woody poses on the front-porch steps with his beloved granddaughter, Jean White (McNey) who was around 15 at the time. As valedictorian of a senior class that contained a whopping seven students, she would soon be graduating from Woody Gap High School. A very bright student, Jean enrolled in North Georgia College in Dahlonega after graduating from high school. Ranger Woody was extremely proud of Jean, who in many ways was a "chip off the old block." Photo circa 1944, courtesy of Jean McNey.

CHAPTER 5
Life with Papa
A Granddaughter's Reflection on Living with Arthur Woody

"A woman can throw away more with a tablespoon than a man can bring in with a shovel."

Arthur Woody

My grandfather was an amazing man," Jean McNey remembers. "A number of greatly exaggerated legends have been told about him, but still he was amazing. He could be a mean and difficult old so-and-so when he wanted to, but he was always very kind and helpful to needy people. If someone needed money to go to the hospital, he would pull it out and give it to them on the spot.

"Once, during the time we were living with my grandparents, there was a knock on the door. It was a local farmer. He and my grandfather talked for a few minutes in private out on the porch. After the man left, my grandmother June, said, 'Well I suppose he was wanting money. Did you let him have any?'

"'Yes,' came the quiet answer.

"'Did you get anything in writing from him?' June asked.

"'No.'

"'What if he never pays you back?' she asked knowingly, as if this same thing had happened many times before (and it had). 'You have nothing in writing from him to say that he owes you one dime.'

"'What was I supposed to do?' my grandfather responded. 'Did you want me let his kids starve?'

"I think the amount was $20," Jean remembered. "In those days, that was a lot of money to someone who really needed it."

"Papa would always carry a few hundred dollars in his pocket," Jean remembered well. "He would often bump into someone who had an acre or two of land for sale while he was out and about during the day, so he got in the habit of carrying cash with him. He would often buy the land on the spot for the Forest Service. He bought some land on his own as well. If the Forest Service wasn't interested in buying a certain parcel for whatever reason, he might buy it himself. Sometimes he did it just to help people out.

"I was attending North Georgia College when he died in 1946. I came home to be with my family. Three or four days after the service, a man named Bob Meaders from Dahlonega whose family we knew stopped by our house. 'Mrs. Woody, I know this is a bad time for me to be coming by,' Mr. Meaders said apologetically to my grandmother, 'but I wanted you to have this in case you might need it for some of the funeral bills and other expenses.' He handed my grandmother (June) a check for $3,000. 'The Ranger loaned it to me a while back and I wanted to make sure it got repaid.'

"That was a staggering amount in those days. My grandfather had left no record of ever having made the loan. If Mr. Meaders hadn't come by on his own volition, no one would have ever known about it."

This unexpected check must have been a windfall to June Woody and the family. It no doubt went to good use. In today's dollars, that amount would have equalled nearly $30,000. Although Ranger Woody was considered to be a wealthy man by most mountain standards (mostly through his considerable real estate holdings) the family did not have a great deal of cash on hand at the time of his death. In fact, the Ranger never hoarded money or kept large quantities of ready cash. He always kept some cash on hand, but he put most of his money to work by loaning it out (usually taking a note or mortgage in return) or he bought land. Prior to his death, his health had been rapidly deteriorating for many months, and the family was left with very little ready cash.

"Another time," Jean remembered, "Papa returned home in a somewhat somber mood after attending the funeral of a mountain farmer he had known for many years. He went downstairs and opened his safe. He went through his papers and located a mortgage that he proceeded to tear up and throw into the fire. When my grandmother (June) asked him what he was doing, he answered, "If that widow woman ever comes by and inquires about the loan on her farm, tell her it was cleared up before her husband's death."

These and other stories about the generosity of Arthur Woody are legion.

"During the Depression, my grandfather lent money to the Union County school board so that the teachers could be paid," Jean remembered. "For a time, the school board had no money for salaries. Papa knew that those teachers' paychecks were probably the only money coming in to some of those families since many of the men were out of work. The school board eventually paid him back when things got better, but he never charged any interest on the money."

Mrs. Miriam J. McNey, or Jean as she prefers to be called, has a wealth of rich childhood memories regarding her larger-than-life grandfather. Jean's mother, Vella Mae Woody, born July 15, 1907, was Arthur's third child and only daughter. Mae had two children of her own: Jean, the oldest, born in 1929, and Ned, born in 1933. In 1934, when Jean was 5, Mae and her children moved in with Arthur and June Woody.

"I lived with my grandparents from the winter I was 5 years old to the summer I was 15 when I entered college," Jean said. "My relationship with 'Papa' was very close. He was really a surrogate dad to me. My dad left and my parents divorced when my brother Ned and I were very young. Ned was also very close to Papa. I lived with my grandparents for 10 years. I called my grandfather Papa and my grandmother June, as did almost everyone else who knew her, although her real name was Nancy Emma.

"Papa took me places all the time around the mountains and once he even bought me a piano. I often fished with him for trout in one of the fish-rearing ponds in the game reserve and we always had the best time together. Whenever we went on one of our little fishing excursions, he would call it 'scientific' fishing to determine how fast the fish were growing because technically, we were breaking the law since trout season was usually closed. However, one of the game wardens sometimes baited my hook."

Ranger Woody was an avid fisherman all of his life. He loved to catch (and eat) the over-sized largemouth bass he had stocked in the lake he had built behind his house in the early 1930s (Woody Lake). Over time, the lake gained quite a reputation for producing exceptionally large bass. The Ranger loved to fish for trout, bream and other species from the many freshwater lakes in and around Suches as well. But no other fish compared to the Ranger's beloved mountain trout that he had so painstakingly restocked into the streams and lakes of Union County. He had a deep reverence and special affinity for his trout, especially the native mountain brook trout that he fondly called "specks." He loved nothing better than to steal away to some secluded spot, sit on a creek bank and spend an afternoon trying to outsmart one of his favorite "pet specks."

"I know most of the big trout by name," he once said. "But you have to be smart to get 'em on a hook!"

Ranger Woody held these fish in awe almost to the same degree he did his beloved white-tailed deer, which had over time become like children to him. Sometimes he would talk to his trout and name individual fish. He had started stocking non-native rainbow and brown trout in the streams in around his Rock Creek Refuge back in 1918, and perhaps his deep reverence for all trout was due in part to all the work he had put in trying to replenish the empty streams of North Georgia with these beautiful and noble fish. He had also spent considerable time, money and energy restocking native brook trout whose numbers had been depleted to dangerously low levels by the early 1900s. To him, the mountain streams and rivers that he grew up exploring as a boy were not the same unless they were teeming with trout.

An Appalachian Redneck at Heart

"My grandparents had a very congenial relationship," Jean said. "They both stayed incredibly busy. June kept pretty busy feeding Forest Service personnel, feeding guests who were apt to stop by at any time, and helping Papa see to the needs of his junior rangers. We had a phone in the house before the Ranger Station was built, and if a fire broke out somewhere, she would usually take the call and get word to Papa or set things in motion for a crew to get out immediately and begin fighting the fire. Later, the Blue Ridge Ranger Station was built across the road from our house (within yelling distance) and there was always something going on there. Oftentimes the men sleeping over at the Ranger Station would eat breakfast and other meals with us because there were no eating facilities there and the nearest restaurant was probably 15 to 20 miles away. Occasionally one of the junior rangers would rent a room from us and stay with us a while.

"My grandmother was both a hard worker and a constant worrier. I could measure her love for me by the way she worried about me. She was the family gardener, and I helped her do the gardening, even to the extent of 'bugging' the beans in those pre-pesticide days. I was expected to go outside and pick all the bugs off the beans and put them in a jar. That was a formidable job because the numbers of bugs seemed infinite. June was the original 'organic' gardener long before the word was invented. Whenever I'd tell her I just couldn't pick every bug off every single leaf, in an exasperated voice she'd say, 'You can, but you just don't have the will to do it!'

"At harvest time in late summer or early fall, she and I would collect the vegetables. My mother would cook them, and all three of us had a hand in

The Woody home place as it appeared around 1920. Built on a hillside that eventually overlooked Woody Lake, June and Arthur Woody raised their three children here. Granddaughter Jean McNey also grew up here. The tiny building in the front yard, erected after Arthur Woody became Georgia's second forest ranger in 1918, served as Ranger Woody's first official ranger station for several years during the early 1920s. (Note the American flag hanging in the front). A much larger Forest Service complex, including a two-story house that served as offices, along with several large outbuildings to store equipment, was built directly across the road in the late 1920s on six acres Ranger Woody deeded to the Forest Service for $1. The large Woody garden can be seen just behind the small Ranger Station. Woody Lake, not seen in the photo, was built directly behind the house. A few years after Ranger Woody's death in 1946, June and daughter Mae renovated the dilapidated old house by replacing the weathered wooden siding with a new brick exterior and remodeling inside. Photo courtesy of Jean McNey.

canning them for the winter. Beans were a staple in our diet. We ate beans so often that almost every day June would ask, 'Is it time to put the beans on yet?"

Although Jean jokingly likes to refer to herself as "an original, sixth generation North Georgia mountain redneck," nothing could be further from the truth. Unlike her grandfather, who might well be described as having been more than a little rough around the edges, Jean is a very well educated and refined lady, thanks in part to her beloved Papa who encouraged her along the way and made sure she received a good education. One thing she definitely inherited from her grandfather was a keen wit and an enduring "Woody" sense of humor. Today Jean lives in a modern brick structure on the site where the historic old clapboard house she grew up in with her grandparents once stood. The house was remodeled and "modernized" with brick siding several years after the Ranger's death in the later 1940s.

In many ways Jean is a chip off the old block. Much like her grandfather, she is extremely intelligent. She grew up with a strong work ethic and she was determined to make something of herself from an early age. Unlike her grandfather, she came along at a time when getting a good education was possible through hard work and a strong desire to go to college. After graduating from high school, she immediately started attending college during the summer session without taking any time off. After earning her degree, she then received a Master's Degree at Emory University. She began teaching almost at once, never taking any time off after graduation. Woody women had been inclined to be teachers for several generations, and Jean was no exception. Teaching was in her blood.

"The rewards of teaching have never been in the salary you earn," Jean said philosophically. "They come with making a difference in people's lives. I think every teacher likes to think he or she has done that at some point in their career.

"My mother was a teacher and my aunt was a teacher. In fact, after my mother attended North Georgia College for two years, she taught for two years in the little one-room school at Mt. Zion Church. In those days, the roads around Suches were so poor that she rode a horse to school every day. (Mt. Zion Church is located north of Suches on Highway 180 just south of Lake Winfield Scott. The original one-room wooden building has long since been replaced with a modern brick structure.)

"She attended high school in Blairsville for a while in the early 1920s," Jean continued. "After school let out in the afternoons, she would often get a ride in an automobile down to a spot just west of where Vogel State Park is now located, and she would walk up through Sosebee Cove and meet Papa on his horse near Wolf Pen Gap. Then they'd ride double together all the way home. Things were quite a bit different in those days but life was good!

"Back then, a female usually had only two choices as far as a vocation went: being a teacher or being a secretary in a town like Dahlonega or Gainesville. In Suches, there weren't too many jobs for secretaries. I always enjoyed literature and grammar so I became a teacher. I was valedictorian at Woody Gap School. That means I was sixth from the bottom since there were just six people in my high school graduating class! I attended North Georgia College right after graduating when I was 15 and finished there in three years at age 18. I was valedictorian there, too, but many of the students were much smarter than I was.

"I went on to get my Masters in English from Emory University and graduated when I was 19. After that, I took some summer courses at Peabody College in Nashville. (Peabody College merged with Vanderbilt University in 1979.) After graduation from Emory, I came back to Suches to teach. My friends at Emory couldn't understand why in the world I would want to come back to the mountains.

A beaming Ranger Woody holds grandson Ned, 7, as the family poses in front of the hearth. From left to right, granddaughter Jean, 11, wife June, and daughter Mae, or "Maybird," pose for the camera. Both children had a very close relationship with their grandfather during the years they lived with him until his death in 1946. Note the family cat in the foreground and the electric stove in the corner, indicating the house recently had been electrified. Photo circa 1940, courtesy of Jean McNey.

"'That's where my roots are,' I told them. 'After all, I'm a sixth generation Appalachian redneck at heart!'"

"Papa gave me a bible when I graduated from college. I took it with me everywhere I went and I still have it today."

Jean likes to tell the story about how Ma Woody, her great-grandmother, approached her one day shortly after she graduated from Emory University and asked her about her future plans. Ma Woody, who lived just around the lake from Ranger Woody's house, could be just as cantankerous and blustery at times as her famous son. "Well, what do you plan to do this summer now that you're all through with your schoolin'?" Ma asked, knowing that Jean had been attending college nonstop for nearly four years without a break ever since graduating from high school.

"I'm going to take some summer classes up in Tennessee so I can start teaching in the fall," Jean answered.

Ma seemed to take offense at Jean's answer. She bristled and said, "Is school the only thing you ever think about? Why Abe Woody could make more money in one week walking across this porch than you can make in a whole year teaching school!" (Her husband, Abe, had died in 1919 at age 55. Ma Woody never remarried.)

"She was right," Jean said with a smile. "I could have made a lot more money doing something else, but being a teacher was what I had always wanted to do."

Knowing how Ma Woody could be, Jean never took any of her negative comments too personally.

"Ma Woody was a character in her own right," Jean said. "She lived to be 90 years old. She died in 1959, outliving her husband by 40 years and her son by 13 years. It must have been very hard losing her only child, especially since they had been so close. She always called everyone, 'Honey.'

"In 1949 and 1950 when my mother and I taught at Woody Gap School, we would often walk from our house down to the school (about a mile). Ma Woody would always get mad if we didn't stop on our way home to see her. On days when we failed to stop by, she would sometimes say horrible things about my mother to the neighbors.

"One time, when we did stop by to see her, she said, 'Mae, I reckon I've nearly been out of my head. They say I've been talkin' about you and saying terrible things about you. Have I?'

"She knew exactly what she had been saying. It was just her way of making excuses. But we understood."

After finishing her summer classes at Peabody at age 20, Jean began teaching that fall at Woody Gap School, the school her grandfather and uncle (Walter Woody) had built eight years earlier (and the high school from which she had graduated). After four years of teaching at Woody Gap School, Jean was offered a position at Truett McConnell College in Cleveland, Georgia.

"I lived right on the square in Cleveland right next to Nix's old Department Store," she fondly remembered.

After spending three years at Truett McConnell, Jean moved back to her old alma mater of North Georgia College and taught there for four years.

"Then I met someone special – Tom McNey – and we got married," Jean said. "Since Tom was an Air Force man, we left home and traveled about for the next 13 years. I didn't think I would ever teach again. But after Tom retired from the Air Force, we came back to Suches and Tom started teaching science at Lumpkin County High School in Dahlonega.

"As soon as we moved back to Suches, I was offered a job at Woody Gap where I taught for a year. The principal there called and said, 'We just got word that under the Isolated School Bill we can hire another teacher if we can get one right away. Will you come teach for us this year?' So I did. After all, Woody Gap was special to our family. My grandfather had been the driving force behind building the school and I had a vested interest in it myself. I had washed every window in the building, mopped the floors and helped put together the playground equipment just after it opened in 1941.

"As time went by, our daughter Lisa started attending Lumpkin County High because Lisa couldn't get some of the courses she needed for college preparation at Woody Gap. She rode to school with Tom each day and it worked out well since the drive to and from Dahlonega was no short trip. As soon as our son John finished middle school, he attended Lumpkin County High as well.

"Then, in late 1977, Tom had a serious heart attack and couldn't work for a while. I had been away from teaching for several years while the kids were growing up and I knew nothing at all about teaching science. But we both knew how important it was for our children to continue getting the classes they needed at Lumpkin County High, and so I told Tom, 'If you'll make the lesson plans and tell me what to do and grade all the papers, I'll be your substitute.' And that's what we did.

"I had been doing that only a short time when the principal came to me one day and said, 'Jean, I have a job for you. I'd like for you to start working with the kids and help them prepare for the SAT. I can always find another substitute for Tom.' (Then known as Scholastic Aptitude Test, the SAT was given to evaluate a student's readiness for college.)

"I told him that SATs hadn't even existed when I was in school back in the '40s and that I knew nothing at all about them. But he insisted and that's what I ended up doing for the rest of that school year. The next August, I ran into that same principal one day in the bank in Dahlonega, and he said, 'Oh, Jean, I'm so glad to see you. School starts in two weeks and one of my English teachers has resigned. You've got to come teach English for me.'

"I said, 'But I don't have a teaching certificate.'

"He said, 'We can work that out and get you a temporary certificate.' So I continued teaching at Lumpkin County High until John graduated in 1983. Then I returned to Woody Gap School and taught there for 8 more years. That was really convenient since the school is within walking distance of my house. I retired permanently in 1991. Looking back, I know it's been a good journey for me."

A Die-Hard Republican

Coincidentally, Jean happened to live with her grandparents during a very historical era – from 1934 to 1944. This 10-year period closely paralleled the years Franklin Delano Roosevelt served his four terms as president (Roosevelt was in office from March 4, 1933 to April 12, 1945). A lot happened in the mountain region during that decade. The adverse effects of the Great Depression were felt well into the late 1930s, and World War II started in 1941. Jean was an eye-witness to a number of historical events involving her grandfather.

"Papa was a dyed-in-the-wool Republican like his father before him," Jean said. "He didn't like Roosevelt (FDR) or any of his programs. He often complained bitterly about many of the government's 'big spending' programs. Like many mountaineers, Papa thought people should be self-sufficient and not dependent on government for anything. He hated the New Deal when it first came out. But even before the New Deal, he hated the fact that the government wasted so much tax money on what he considered to be 'foolish' projects."

Despite his political leanings, Ranger Woody quickly learned to take advantage of several of Roosevelt's Depression-era "New Deal" programs. One in particular, the Civilian Conservations Corps (CCC), turned out to be a gift-horse in disguise for many of his local projects requiring manpower. After Camp Woody (F-1) was established in Suches in 1933, and Camp Enotah was established near Blairsville around the same time, the "CC" boys, also known as "Roosevelt's Tree Army," worked on dozens of projects in Union County under Ranger Woody's careful direction. Had it not been for these hard-working boys who grew to idolize Ranger Woody, many of the projects they took on that benefited the community and the forest and wildlife in the area might never have been completed.

"Papa was very sad when Roosevelt died in Warm Springs, Georgia, on April 12, 1945," Jean remembered. "He said, 'I never liked his politics, and I didn't agree with much of anything he did, but I certainly didn't want the damned old devil to die.'"

At the time of Roosevelt's death, Ranger Woody was struggling with his own health problems. Certainly he must have felt a strong sense of empathy for the physically worn-out and war-weary president.

Home Cooked Cornbread Always a Favorite

"In addition to raising all of our meat and vegetables, the Woody women did a lot of baking around the house," Jean remembers. "We cooked a lot of homemade cornbread. Papa never liked loaf bread. He called loaf bread 'moonshine bread.' But he absolutely loved homemade cornbread and that's what he ate most of the time. Mae, June and Ma Woody made the best cornbread in the world in an old Dutch oven. Every morning for breakfast we had cornbread, biscuits, ham and gravy. Every morning!

"After he got sick in 1944, he was told by his doctors to watch his diet and not eat certain things in order to lose weight and get his blood pressure under control. Cornbread was one of the items he was not supposed to eat. June tried to help him watch his diet by decreasing his portions, but he'd just go off to some neighbor's house and eat all he wanted. She later said she wished she hadn't been so strict on him during that time because it didn't do any good anyway. His health never did improve.

"Papa hated sweet potatoes," Jean remembers fondly. "But June loved them. So did most other people in the family. Whenever she fixed them for everyone else he would say, 'You can give an Abercrombie a sweet potato and a biscuit and they can make it all the way around the world without having to stop.' (June's maiden name was Abercrombie, and the Ranger loved to poke fun at her family.)

"June always wanted things done yesterday. We had an electric stove in the house long before the power line brought in the electricity needed to operate it. That's the way she and Papa always did things. After it had sat there a while someone asked Papa why he had a stove that he couldn't yet use and he said, 'Because I don't want to cut one more stick of stove wood than I absolutely have to!' (Before electricity, everything was cooked on a wood-burning stove or in the Dutch oven at the fireplace.) In truth, the Ranger enjoyed cutting wood. Even though he disdained working in the garden, he never seemed to get tired of cutting wood for the stove or the fireplace.

"Our first electric power was generated from the spillway in the lake. It served our house, the Forest Service office across the street, and several nearby houses. I'll never forget the first time we turned on the power. It was probably in the mid-1930s and it was quite an event. Everything had to be perfectly coordinated and everyone had to make sure all of the light switches were turned on when the electricity was first hooked up because the initial surge of energy would have blown everything out if only one or two of the light bulbs had been turned on."

A MOUNTAIN MAN THROUGH AND THROUGH
Being Self-Sufficient the Mountain Way

"Papa possessed a deep sense of home and place all his life. He never had any desire to leave Suches, especially in later life. He loved rambling all over the mountains. He was in his element when he was in the wilderness, and his idea of traveling probably consisted of putting in 15 or 20 miles on his horse in his beloved mountains and camping out for the night.

"I never remember my grandfather ever putting a foot in the garden or milking the cow," Jean said. "We always had a large garden where we grew enough vegetables to put up for the entire year. And he never set foot in that garden. He was always doing something else. He was a lot of things, but he was not a farmer. My mother (Mae), my grandmother (June) and great grandmother (Ma Woody) always did all of the gardening and milking. Of course, as soon as Ned and I were old enough, we were expected to do a lot of the gardening and all the milking chores.

"Papa much preferred to be out in the woods. When he was growing up, Suches was virtually all woods, and he loved his home and his surroundings. The mountains were sacred to him. He did do a lot of hunting for squirrels and turkeys, but never deer because there weren't any. We frequently ate squirrels and rabbits and other small game. As soon as his grandson Dick (born in 1925) was old enough to handle a gun and hunt, he and Papa would keep count to see who could kill the most squirrels. They had the best time hunting together and they brought home a lot of squirrels! We ate a lot of squirrel gravy!

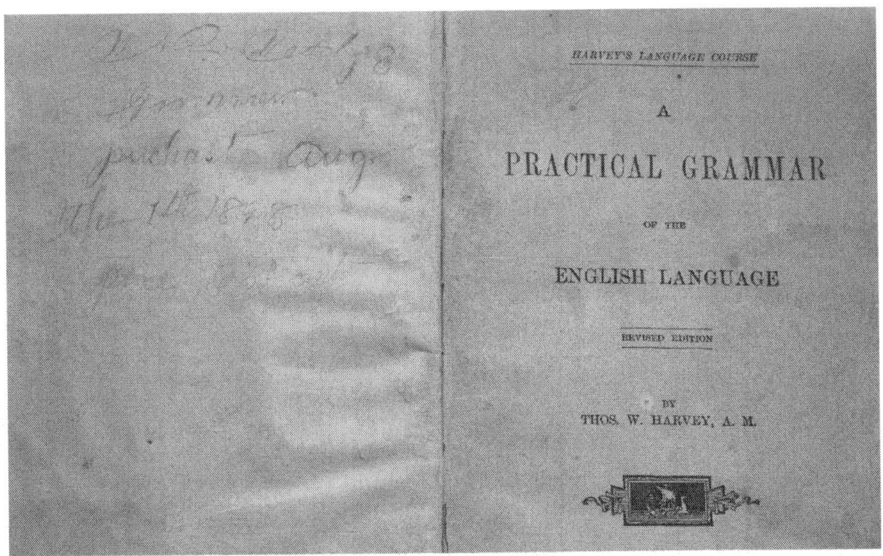

HARVEY'S LANGUAGE COURSE

A

PRACTICAL GRAMMAR

OF THE

ENGLISH LANGUAGE

REVISED EDITION

BY

THOS. W. HARVEY, A. M.

Young Arthur Woody's well-worn grammar book contains the following hand-written inscription: "W.A. Woody, grammar. purchast Aug. the 1st, 1898. price .65 cents." The previous page contains a short inscription in his rough hand writing that reads: "Arthur Woody's book, Price 65 cts, Aug.1st, 1898." The Ranger would have been about 14 when he acquired this book. He likely was still in the fifth grade at that age. Photo by Duncan Dobie.

"Papa loved being outside and never got tired of being in the woods. I remember Ma Woody saying that when he was a tiny baby, she would put him in a box by the edge of the cornfield while she was hoeing and weeding and he would sit there all day long and watch her, as content as he could be. He never got fussy when he was outside.

"Although he was a mountain man through and through, Papa never had any cattle of his own and to my knowledge he never wanted to own any (other than the milk cows we kept for milk and butter). Our milk cows occasionally had calves and Papa would let Ned and me raise them and then sell them. Sometimes we raised two at a time and we sold them for around $30 each when they were old enough. Before refrigeration, we had a covered springhouse in the back yard behind the house. That's where we kept fresh milk and butter in cold water running through a trough, so that it would stay cool during the day.

"Like most mountain families, in those days we raised just about everything we needed to run a household. Over the years, June and my mother fed dozens of outside guests as well, mainly Forest Service personnel who worked at the ranger station across the road. But Papa frequently had special dinner guests as well. A congressman might drop by for a visit, and Governor E.D. "Ed" Rivers was a regular visitor. Forest Service dignitaries from Washington were also frequent guests. Someone was always stopping by to have dinner with the family. Once, Marjorie Kinnan Rawlings came all the way from Florida to visit Papa."

In his incomparable style, Charlie Elliott eloquently described one such dinner at the Woody home in an article that appeared in the May 1939 issue of *American Forests* magazine. He and Ranger Woody had been out working together all day in the mountains and they came home tired and hungry. Charlie was a frequent guest at the Woody home and often spent the night when he and the Ranger were working together on a particular project.

> "Supper hour was one of the most delightful of the day. The Ranger warned me that I would have to take 'pot luck,' which turned out to be golden brown ham and gravy, several fried chickens, biscuits the size and color of an October moon, a variety of vegetables and coffee. Around a huge log fire that evening I learned much about this mountain land with its vanished race (the Cherokees) and it present people, much about its rich legendary lore and richer history."

It may have been a 'pot luck' supper to Ranger Woody but to most people in today's world that meal would have been a feast. Mind you, this was a typical evening meal in the Woody household, guest or no guest. The Woody's always ate well, and Ranger Woody's waistline reflected his great love for the unequaled home-style cooking provided by June and Mae!

"At any given time, we probably had at least two dozen chickens, some for laying eggs and some for eating," Jean continues. "We also had at least one pig in the pen if not two or three and at least one or two milk cows. I can remember having to milk two cows in the morning before coming in and getting ready for school.

"We bought staples like sugar, coffee and salt at an old country store down Cooper Gap Road. I remember that Papa used to settle up with the store owner and pay his bill once a year because the amount was too small to pay off every month. It was usually around $300 per year.

"At hog killing time in the fall, after the first frost in late October or early November, Papa's son Clyne would always come over and butcher the hog. Papa never liked doing that job.

"Even the lake behind our house served a useful purpose," Jean said. "In addition to its recreational value and the fact that it provided fish for us to eat, Papa set up a grist mill at the spillway so that we could grind our own corn. Later, he used the spillway to generate electricity to our house. When the county-wide electric power line finally reached us in the late 1930s, my mother talked Papa into enclosing the back porch and making it into a kitchen. She also talked him into adding a third bedroom upstairs in a space that had never been finished.

"I remember that one of the glass panes in the kitchen door always had a crack in one corner of it because as the new kitchen was being finished, Papa had to transport a lot of the building materials including that door up Horseshoe Ridge in a wagon pulled by horses. Somehow one of the panes got cracked during that very rough trip and it stayed that way for many years.

"We usually had one or two yard dogs that always stayed outside, and for several years Papa kept a bloodhound that he used for tracking arsonists and poachers."

Free from Want – the Independent Spirit of Mountain People

"In the early 1900s mountain people were very clever and displayed a lot of ingenuity," Jean said. "They could do marvellous things with what they had, and often that was very little. They were fiercely independent and seldom depended on outside help.

"In the early years of settlement, the people in this part of the country were much like 17th century English people: reserved, self-sufficient, determined and very ingenious. They found ways to get things done. A lot of the rich language they used was Shakespearean, Celtic, Scottish and Irish that dated back to the 16th and 17th centuries. Growing up, I heard Papa use words that I had never heard or read anywhere else before. I wondered where they had come from. Later on, after I got to college, I read Chaucer and Shakespeare and I understood.

"I remember Papa talking about going to visit a man named Postell who lived way up in the Nantahala Gorge. This fellow lived with his wife and children in a one-room cabin with a dirt floor that had been built virtually on the side of a steep mountain slope. Although the family was almost destitute, you would have never known it through Mr. Postell's actions and speech. Probably being of Scottish descent, the proud old mountaineer carried himself as though he were related to English royalty. Once, when Papa rode up to the man's cabin on his horse, he greeted the man in his typical robust manner: 'How ya' been gettin' along, Josephus?'

"'Well, so-so, Ranger,' the old mountaineer answered matter-of-factly. 'I'm not vastly rich, but I'm alivin' free from want.'

A Penchant for Nicknames

"Papa nicknamed everyone. At various times he called me 'Hootie doll,' 'Tootie doll or 'Bootie Doll.' He called my cousin Lou Nichols 'Tweedy doll.' He fondly called June 'Old Woman,' and he frequently called my mother 'Maybird.'

"Mr. Howard Tritt, who had lived across the road from us since I was a small girl and who was well-known for running a grocery at that location for many years was always known as 'Fid.' I never knew his real name until after I had grown up because Papa always called him Fid, and that's all I ever heard. I don't know whether he ever played a fiddle or not, but I doubt it.

"Papa also had names for all his deer as well."

Ranger Woody's Safe

"Papa had a large, 2-ton safe in the basement where he kept all of his important papers," Jean said, "things like mortgages, deeds on property he

Dr. Edward Woody poses by the legendary safe once owned by his great grandfather, Ranger Arthur Woody. After the Ranger's death in 1946, the vintage safe was placed in one of the small buildings at the old Ranger Station used by Dr. Woody's grandfather, Walter Woody, as an office for his cattle operations. During Ranger Woody's life, the much-storied safe always held several important items; a sum of cash money, a stack of promissory notes and deeds to secure debt, and a respectable supply of applejack brandy. The neglected office has not been used in many years, thus its cluttered appearance. Photo by Duncan Dobie.

For many years, Ranger Woody's safe has been housed in this now weather-worn building at the old Ranger Station that served as Walter Woody's office during the 1950s and '60s. Photo by Duncan Dobie.

owned, notes on loans, and IOUs from different people. Later he moved it over to his office at the ranger station. After he died, we found a stack of IOUs inside. Some had been paid, many were still outstanding. Although some of the people later repaid the money they had borrowed to my grandmother, many of those notes were never collected. And similar to the story mentioned at the beginning of this chapter, several people eventually repaid loans to June about which nothing in writing had ever been recorded.

"Papa never kept a lot of cash on hand, but you could always count on him to have a supply of homemade apple jack brandy or corn whiskey in the safe to share with someone on a 'special occasion.'"

Mae Outwits Her Father for a New Radio

"Radios were non-existent in Suches during the early 1930s," Jean remembers. "Television was still over 20 years away, and there were no movie theatres in the mountains. I remember that even after the power line came through in the late-1930s, no one in our area owned an electric radio. One day, out of the clear blue, my mom said: 'Papa, why don't you buy us a radio?'

"'Nos 'em, nos 'em, nos 'em!' answered Papa (his way of saying no ma'am). 'We don't need a dern radio!'

"Well, he and my mom talked about it for a while and finally Papa said, 'Tell ya' what, Mae… If you can open my safe you might just find enough cash money inside to buy that radio you've been a'wantin'."

At the time, Ranger Woody's safe was still downstairs in the basement.

"Unbeknownst to Papa," Jean continued, "my mother had watched him open that safe many times and she had memorized the combination. But he didn't know that and she never let on. As he stood there and watched her turn the dial to all of the correct numbers and finally swing open the big door, he shook his head and exclaimed: 'This ain't fair! You've cheated, you've cheated, you've cheated! You knew the combination all along!'

"Despite having allowed my mother to get the best of him, he bought the radio after all, a big radio at that; and he got addicted to it right away just like millions of other Americans. Soon, at Papa's insistence, we were all sitting around listening to Gabriel Heatter's newscast every night because that's what *he* wanted to listen to."

(Gabriel Heatter (1890–1972) was a popular radio personality during the 1930s, '40s and into the '50, at which time television began to replace radio in many American households. Heatter was often quoted for his words of wisdom. He was immensely popular during the war years in the 1940s, and he frequently gave up-to-date news reports about what was happening in Europe and in the Pacific.)

Today, a little more rusted and a little worse for the wear, the Ranger's infamous safe still resides in one of the dilapidated storage buildings at the old ranger station.

Caught by June Cheating at Cards

"Papa and June loved to play a game called "Set Back," a card game that was popular back in the 1930s. They played often in the evenings and one night June caught him cheating. Papa always got a great kick out of agitating her. At the time, we had an Ashley wood-burning stove/heater (before we had electricity). June, acting as if she were furious, grabbed the deck of cards, opened the door of the heater and tossed them into the fire. Papa got a great laugh out of that. He thought it was hilarious. It was all in good fun and getting caught by his wife just tickled him to death."

Behind every great man is a great woman, and June Woody stood behind her man every step of the way as Arthur Woody's amazing career launched him into legendary status. The Ranger, as he was fondly known, "ruled the roost" in Suches from about 1915 to 1945. Arthur and June Woody dedicated their lives to helping others and doing things to improve their community. Over the years, June, daughter Mae, and the rest of the Woody family worked tirelessly to support Ranger Woody's endless projects. Photo circa 1940, courtesy of Jean McNey.

Greeting the Day

"Papa was an early riser all his life. He loved to greet the new day. He'd always be up early in the morning before anyone else because he always had a lot to do. Getting up early was a lifelong habit. During the winter months, he would start the day off by building a fire in the fireplace (since that was the only source of heat we had in the house before we had electricity). We later put in an Ashley wood-burning stove as noted above.

"The bedrooms where Ned and I slept were upstairs. At that time the house had clapboard siding with little to no insulation. I can remember when it snowed sometimes the snow would work itself between the cracks in the boards and come fluttering into my bedroom. At night in winter, before going to bed, I always heated a big round rock by the fireplace. I then wrapped the rock in a towel and put it at the foot of my bed to stay warm. Back in those days it got so cold during several winters that the lake froze over. The ice was so thick that I was able to go ice skating. I remember once when a neighbor drove a truck out on the ice.

"In the mornings, when Ned and I would wake up, we'd yell down, 'Papa, is the fire hot yet?' He usually had a few choice words to say. Sometimes he would say, 'You two are up there a lyin' in yer' warm beds while yer' poor ol' grandpap is down here all alone needed yer' help.'

"But he'd always end up building us a cozy fire and have things nice and warm for us when we came downstairs.

"Christmas Day was always special. We would wake up earlier than usual around 4 a.m. and Papa would already be downstairs stirring around. We would yell down to him about the fire and he'd yell back, 'Ya' better come a runnin.' Old Santa's done walked the log!' (Meaning that Santa Claus indeed had found his way down the chimney and magically walked across the logs in the fireplace and left presents for everyone under the tree.) We couldn't wait to go downstairs and open our presents."

Mountain Nectar

"My grandfather didn't drink a lot and I never saw him drunk, but he liked to take a little drink now and then, especially with friends," Jean remembers. "He was never what you would call a heavy drinker, but like most mountain men of his time, he grew up during an age when making home-made liquor was a way of life.

"Papa sometimes had a toddy in the morning and he often had one at night," Jean said. "Occasionally he'd have one in the middle of the day, especially if an important friend or dignitary came by for a visit or if there was some other special occasion to celebrate.

"Dr. John W. Turner, a prominent physician in Atlanta, built a cabin near Lake Winfield Scott. He started coming up to Suches on a regular basis, and he and Papa became good friends. Whenever Dr. and Mrs. Turner came to Suches for the weekend, Doc and Papa would get together and go romping out in the woods somewhere. After Papa had his first stroke and became ill, he naturally wanted Dr. Turner to treat him. It was Dr. Turner who put him in Georgia Baptist Hospital in Atlanta to try to get his heart and kidney conditions under control. Later on, during the final stages of my grandfather's illness, Dr. Turner came by the house to see him frequently.

"Since they enjoyed each other's company so much, Papa and Dr. Turner eventually hid a bottle in a stump out in the woods on some property Papa owned on Little Rock Creek near the game reserve. They loved to sneak off to their secret spot and have a little 'nip' together. After Papa's health had deteriorated to the point that it didn't look as if he would recover, he told Dr. Turner one day, 'Now Doc, our bottle is still over there. When I'm gone, I want you to go over to our stump and have a drink to remember me by!'"

The good doctor no doubt honored that bittersweet request.

More Mountain Spirits – The Joshua Ingram Story

Speaking of mountain spirits, Jean recalled a humorous story that she remembered hearing several times as a child.

"An old man named Joshua Ingram who lived locally was arrested and charged with making moonshine," Jean said. "When his trial date came up in Blairsville, he appeared in court in his usual outfit – well-worn bib overalls. He was a small, swarthy man who frequently tugged on his long white beard out of nervous habit. When his case was called up, he stepped up in front of the judge pulling on his beard. Seeing the man's name, the judge, who apparently had a wry sense of humor, decided to have some fun. He looked down from his bench and said, 'Are you the Joshua who commanded the sun to stand still so the troops could organize to fight the famous battle at Jericho?'

"'No, sir,' Joshua answered meekly. 'I'm just the Joshua who made the moonshine.'

The judge was so taken by his honesty that the case was promptly dropped and Joshua went home a free man.

Do Mountain Folks Ever Do Anything Besides Make Moonshine?

"In the late 1940s, my first cousin Dick Woody (Walter's son) married a girl named Eileen from Wyoming who had attended Brenau University in Gainesville," Jean said. "They met while she and her best friend were in school there. Since the wedding was held in her hometown in Wyoming, many of the Woody family members traveled out West to attend. (Ranger Woody had died several years earlier.)

"During the ceremony, I happened to be sitting next to the father of the bride's best friend who had also attended Brenau. At one point he looked at me with an odd expression and asked, 'What do you mountain people do to earn a living besides making moonshine?'"

Being the dedicated teacher she was, and in classic Woody fashion typical of her grandfather, Jean responded with the perfect comeback. "Well, when we're not making moonshine, we educate Westerners' daughters!" she said.

Memorable Easter Sunrise Services with Governor Ed Rivers

"Governor E.D. "Ed" Rivers came up here and stayed at our house many times," Jean said. "Papa always called him 'Little Eddie.' I loved it when he came to visit because I got to ride in his limousine and I thought I was really something. In those days, the governor's limousine wasn't nearly as spacious as the ones you see today (stretch limos), but it was larger than a regular automobile. Inside it had little jump seats that would pull down and they were just the right size for a child like me. I loved riding in that vehicle.

"For several years in a row during the late 1930s and early 1940s, Papa arranged to have Easter sunrise services conducted from Woody Gap. Governor Rivers always came up and officiated. WSB Radio in Atlanta would come and do a live broadcast of the service and the entire community would turn out and participate.

"One evening, before an Easter Sunrise service, I remember we were sitting around the fire after dinner. Papa suddenly reached down and unlaced his shoes and said, 'Little Eddie, you can sit here and talk to the womenfolk as

Ranger Woody poses on the front porch with his two beloved grandchildren, Jean, 8, and Ned, 4, who lived with their grandparents from 1934 until the Ranger's death in 1946. Jean was attending college in Dahlonega when Ranger Woody died. The Ranger was a surrogate father to both children in numerous ways. Photo circa 1937, courtesy of Jean McNey.

long as you like, but I'm going to bed. It's past my bedtime.' With that, he took his shoes off, put them near the hearth, got up and went to bed."

(Governor E.D. "Ed" Rivers – Eurith Dickinson Rivers, 1895-1967 – served two consecutive terms as governor of Georgia from 1937-1941. He was quite fond of Ranger Woody and enjoyed staying with the Woody family.)

A Little Bit of "Woody Wisdom"

"While attending North Georgia College, my mother was sitting out on the front lawn with a cadet one afternoon who apparently thought she was very attractive," Jean remembered. "One of her professors happened to see them sitting and talking together. Later on, in an attempt to tease her about being seen with a boy, he jokingly commented, 'I bet you don't even know what love is.'

"'Oh yes I do,' Mae quickly replied. 'I know plenty about love.'

"'Oh, yeah…Tell me what you know then,' the professor said. "What is your definition of love?'

"'That's easy,' Mae told the startled professor. 'Love is a little bit of heaven come down to earth to raise hell!'"

It's entirely possible and likely that those thought-provoking words of wisdom were borrowed from Mae's unabashed father. It would have been just like the Ranger to say something like that.

Please Cash Those Paychecks

"Papa was well-known for giving the Forest Service accountants down in Gainesville fits because of the way he did things," Jean said. "For one thing, he was not good about cashing his Forest Service paychecks in a timely manner. On more than one occasion, Mr. Crawford Dupree, the bookkeeper in the Gainesville office, (who was sort of a sissy; Papa always called him 'Sister DuPree') would come up to Suches and say, "Ranger, please do cash your checks. I can't balance my books until you do."

"A day or two later, Papa would get around to opening his big 2-ton safe in the basement and sure enough he'd have a stack of Forest Service paychecks stowed away that had not been cashed. On his next trip to Dahlonega, he'd cash them at the bank."

Marjorie Kinnan Rawlings Comes to See the Ranger

"In September 1942, while World War II was raging, we received word that Marjorie Kinnan Rawlings, author of *The Yearling,* wanted to come to Suches to meet Papa and write a story about him. I was 13 at the time and that created quite a bit of excitement because she was a very famous author. I'm not sure how it all came about, but I feel certain she must have read something in the newspapers or magazines about Papa's involvement with bringing deer back to the mountains. By that time, his deer program had gotten quite a bit of national publicity. Since she had written a best-selling book about a boy and his fawn, it was my understanding that she was interested in writing a factual story about Papa and the many deer he had raised. I don't know whether she ever completed a story or not. We never heard any more about it."

Published in 1938, *The Yearling* won the Pulitzer Prize in 1939. Over the years it has become a literary classic for people of all ages, but especially for

After winning the Pulitzer Prize for her 1940 blockbuster novel, The Yearling, Marjorie Kinnan Rawlings traveled to North Georgia to meet Ranger Woody and write a story about his work with deer. During her one-night visit to the Woody home in September 1942, she signed a copy of her best-selling book, Cross Creek, to young Jean White (McNey), then about 13 years old. The book was apparently purchased by Ranger Woody's good friend, Clint Davis, Forest Service photographer, before Mrs. Rawlings arrived. It is not known whether or not Mrs. Rawlings ever wrote or published a story about Ranger Woody and his deer. Photos courtesy of Jean McNey.

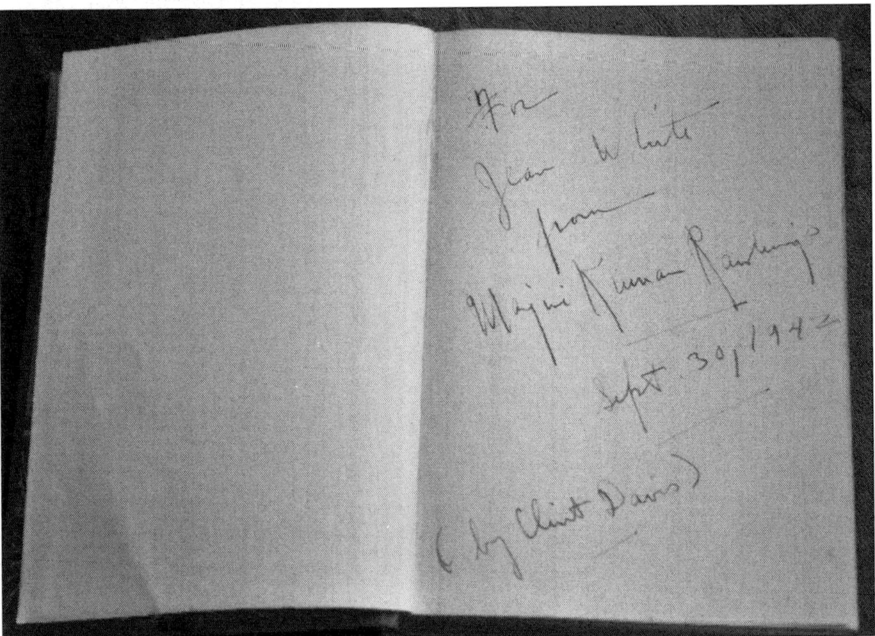

young-adult readers. In 1946, the book was made into a classic film starring Gregory Peck. In 1942, Mrs. Rawlings published *Cross Creek* and it too became a best seller.

Unlike *The Yearling,* which was a fictional story, *Cross Creek* was an autobiographical account about how Mrs. Rawlings had moved to the wilds of central Florida during the Depression years, and come to know the local people who were often referred to as "Florida crackers." In certain ways, the Florida crackers in her book were much like Ranger Woody and his Georgia mountaineers in Suches.

Marjorie Kinnan Rawlings drove up to the North Georgia Mountains from her home in Florida with Julia Scribner Bigham, daughter of Charles Scribner, whose company, Charles Scribner's Sons (Scribner Publishing), published all of Rawlings' works. At the time, Scribner's was also publishing the works of Ernest Hemingway, F. Scott Fitzgerald and Thomas Wolfe.

"As I remember, she first drove to the Forest Service headquarters in Gainesville, Georgia, where she met with Clint Davis, a Forest Service photographer and public relations man, and also a very good friend of Papa's," Jean said. "Clint brought the two ladies up to Suches one afternoon to have dinner and spend the night with us. I don't think they could have found Suches on their own."

Although there was an age difference, Marjorie Rawlings and Julia Bigham were very close friends. Bigham later served as the literary executor of Rawlings' estate and edited *The Marjorie Rawlings Reader* published in 1956. In a Sept. 30, 1942 letter written to her husband Norton Baskin from Atlanta, Mrs. Rawlings wrote "preparing for trip to mountains. Story beginning to shape up." So she certainly must have been planning to do a story about Ranger Woody. In a postcard sent to her husband from North Carolina on October 30, she wrote "gathering material in Blue Ridge mountains."

"I had read some of her stories in school and was enthralled with her," Jean said. "After dinner, we were all sitting around in the living room that night when Papa embarrassed us all by looking at Mrs. Rawlings and saying, "Well, young lady, I'll be honest with you. I've never read any of your books. Only read one book in my life and that was about how to be a good supervisor. But my granddaughter here has told me all about *The Yearling.*

"Actually I don't think Papa ever read a book on supervising or any other book in his whole life. But our good friend Clint Davis, who was always thinking ahead, had brought with him a copy of the recently published bestseller *Cross Creek.* I'm not sure whether he just happened to have it or whether he went out and bought it the day before because he knew Mrs. Rawlings was coming for a visit. I suspect that he went out and bought it. At any rate, after dinner, we all sat around talking and Ms. Rawlings agreed to read a passage from the book; a somewhat humorous story titled 'the pig is paid for.'

"To my horror," Jean remembered, "I was asked to leave the room because the story touched on the delicate subject of pigs 'breeding' and a sow 'taking.' My mother didn't think I was old enough to hear that sort of stuff. That made me so mad because I had been around farm animals all my life, and I had known for a long time all about how animals bred and how little piglets were made. So I listened in, anyway, from the other room.

"Later on, Clint asked Ms. Rawlings to autograph the book to me and she did. I still have the autographed book today, a little worse for the wear because it somehow ended up in the library at Woody Gap School for a while and it was apparently read many times before I was able to get it back. That was really a nice thing for Clint Davis to do! I'll never forget his generosity. He was always a good friend to Papa and our family; he loved Papa dearly like so many of the other Forest Service men did."

During the late 1930s and up until his death in 1946, Ranger Woody had no better or more loyal friend in the Forest Service than Clint Davis. Davis served in public relations and was a gifted photographer. He took many historic photos for the Forest Service in Georgia and North Carolina during those ground-breaking years that appeared in various publications. After the U.S. entered World War II, Davis served with distinction as a U.S. Army photographer in the Pacific Theatre. Photo courtesy of Jean McNey.

Shortly after the visit from Marjorie Kinnan Rawlings, Clint Davis went off to serve his country in the Pacific where he was involved in taking top-secret photos for the military. After the war, he resumed his old job with the Forest Service, spending much of the latter part of a very successful career in Washington D.C.

Chip Off the Old Block

Jean's brother, Ned White, was a chip off the old block, with many of the mannerisms and expressions of his grandfather. One day when he was about seven years old, he was watching Forester Bryce Ledford Jr. drive in from a scaling job. The truck Ledford was driving had seen its better day, and when it stopped with a rattle and roar Ned observed, "Bryce, your truck is just like my pants."

"How's that?" Ledford asked.

Ned responded, "Two or three wear 'em out before we git 'em!"

The Case of the Ranger's Stolen Britches

"Papa was very patriotic," Jean said. "During the early days of the war, he proudly put up a flag pole and hung an American flag out in the front yard. One year, on his birthday, April 1, April Fool's Day, he got up and couldn't find his pants. He always called his pants 'britches.' He looked all over the house, and finally he looked outside. Lo and behold, his britches were hanging from the top of the flagpole! The Woody family never locked any doors, and someone, probably one of his assistant rangers, apparently had sneaked inside during the early morning hours and taken his britches outside as a birthday and April Fool's prank. He got a big laugh out of that.

"Some time later," Jean continued, "Ranger Woody's britches disappeared again. This time it was no prank. They'd been stolen by a thief. He always kept some cash in his pocket as mentioned earlier, sometimes as much as three or four hundred dollars in case he ran across some land to buy for the Forest Service. No doubt this is what the thief was after.

"Most people knew that Papa always left his britches downstairs near the front door, so it was very easy for someone to sneak up on the porch, open the front door and grab them. His pocket watch and his Forest Service key to the locks on some of the gates in the game reserve were also in his stolen britches."

Apparently this incident happened during the winter on a particularly cold night in the late 1930s. At the time, assistant ranger Bill Bergoffen was renting an upstairs bedroom in the Woody house. Bill had a dog named Jinx that sometimes stayed in his bedroom at night. In a letter written to Ranger Woody in November 1945, shortly after the Ranger's forced retirement due to failing health, Bill mentioned the incident:

> "How very often I've thought about the time your pants were stolen! I knew you must have cussed me for having Jinx in bed that night and not on guard like any respectable dog ought to be. But, dammit man, it gets cold in those North Georgia hills… and I never did mind the fleas for the heat Jinx afforded. By God, those were the days!"

"The key was later found over on the other side of Wolf Pen Gap in Sosebee Cove," Jean remembered. "Of course, Papa had a good idea who did it. He had ways of finding out things like that – nothing ever got past him – although it probably would have been difficult to prove. Later, the watch turned up after it had been sold to a third party and Papa bought it back because it meant a lot to him.

"After hearing about his stolen britches, the ladies in the Forest Service office in Gainesville got one of those large, old-fashioned corsets with staves in it and they sewed a little pocket on one side and put a penny and a key in the pocket. They sent him the girdle with a note saying, 'Ranger, we know this belongs to you because it has your money and your key. This is so you don't lose your key again, and so you'll always have a little money in your pocket!'

"He sent word back thanking them for their thoughtfulness along with a note that said, 'I'd like to reward each one of you by buying you a pair of panties and I'll be glad to come and help you put them on if you'd like!'

"That was my Papa!"

HARRY L. ROSSOLL

Ranger Woody poses with a female bloodhound used to track down poachers and arsonists. During the late 1930s, he owned a very popular male bloodhound named Pete that became a mascot and favorite among the CCC boys at Camp Woody. Photo circa 1925, courtesy of Jean McNey.

CHAPTER 6
Of Forest Fires and Flaming Speeches

"Once, when my grandfather was asked how he handled 'crown fires,' that is, fires so hot and furious that they jumped from one crown of a tall tree to another and often from one ridge top to another, he answered, 'Run like hell and pray for rain!'"

Jean McNey

Long before the first white settlers ever crossed a high mountain pass, the Cherokees (along with many other eastern Indians) commonly practiced large-scale burning of ground litter and understory up and down the Appalachian chain. This practice was noted by William Bartram who visited the southern mountains in 1776. This frequent burning of ground litter created large open glades or pastures as they were later called by the whites. Constant burning by controlled fires kept much of the terrain relatively open at the ground level. In the spring, new green growth (grasses and forbs) attracted wildlife like deer and turkeys, made hunting somewhat easier and kept predators at bay. Wolves, bobcats and mountain lions didn't have anywhere to hide. The Cherokees also gathered a variety of nuts for food – chestnuts, beechnuts, hickory nuts and white oak acorns – and regular burning made nut gathering much easier.

The whites quickly adopted many Indian customs. Early settlers and homesteaders habitually burned off large areas each spring and fall, creating green forage for their free roaming cattle in the spring and fall with little regard for any sustained damage to the land. Of course, the fires often got out of control and burned many hundreds of acres of forestland. Even if the fires were kept under control, this widespread burning not only damaged older trees but killed any young seedlings that were trying to make their way out of the ground. One of the toughest jobs the Forest Service faced after acquiring land for the National Forest system in the North Georgia mountains during the early part of the 20th century was trying to convince local landowners not to set intentional fires because of the great damage those fires inflicted.

Shortly after acquiring its vast acreage in the early 1900s, and well before the federal government began buying land in the mountains, large landowners like the Gennett family (from whom the first large tract of land in Georgia was purchased) had made attempts to control fires on their holdings by hiring forest guards and trying to educate local individuals about the great harm that random burning could cause. As soon as land ownership began transferring from individuals and companies to the federal government, fire fighting and fire prevention became a top priority within the Forest Service.

Fire prevention throughout the entire national forest system is still an important priority today. Great strides have been made in averting and controlling fires during the last 100 years. In the late 1800s, large-scale fires in the West had burned millions of acres of priceless timberland, destroyed houses and other personal property and taken dozens of human lives. The problem was no less devastating in the southern Appalachians.

From the start, the most perplexing problem the Forest Service faced was in trying to gain the cooperation of the local mountaineers. At times, it seemed like an impossible job. In addition to providing a negligible amount of forage for their hogs and cattle, farmers burned off their land to help get rid of insects and snakes. The first recorded fire prevention efforts in North Georgia took place about 1913 by Ranger Roscoe "Nick" Nicholson through personal contact with the local people in Northeast Georgia's Rabun County. (Ranger Nicholson's Tallulah District covered much of Rabun County.) Since Ranger Nicholson, who became an official Forest Ranger in 1912 (six years ahead of Ranger Woody), knew most of the people in his district personally (as did Ranger Woody), he knew which farmers regularly burned off their grazing land each year and he went to great lengths to try to educate and encourage these people to stop the indiscriminate burning. But the habit of burning annually seemed to be ingrained in the mountain culture, and in some cases no amount of talking or education seemed to help. When caught after setting intentional fires, violators were seldom punished to any real degree.

At the time Ranger Woody was hired to work on a survey crew in 1912, fire prevention and fire fighting steps were being taken in Union County as well. When he was sworn in as a forest guard in 1915, a large part of his job description included "the protection of forestry lands from fire, trespassers and poachers."

It goes without saying that Ranger Woody and Ranger Nicholson were two of the driving forces in the forest and conservation movement in the North Georgia mountains during the early 1900s. Although very little is known about their personal relationship, the two men worked together at times and their careers followed many similar paths. Each made groundbreaking strides in their respective forest districts. Clyne Woody, Ranger Woody's son, worked for a time with the Forest Service in Tiger, Georgia, in Rabun County. According to Lou Nichols, Clyne's daughter, her father worked with Ranger Nicholson on a number of projects and the two men got along extremely well.

In *A Historical-Socio-Political Study of the Chattahoochee-Oconee National Forests* written by Norman Bruce Alter in 1971, a former Ranger himself, the author commented:

> "In other cases, funerals were the most effective prevention since some people had to pass on before the fires died down."

Because of the frustration level created over this matter, there were no doubt times when both Ranger Nicholson and Ranger Woody probably would have liked to expedite a few of those funerals in order to remedy what seemed like a never-ending problem. (Norman Bruce Alter served as District Ranger in the Tallulah District from 1952 to 1961, taking Ranger Nick Nicholson's place after his retirement in 1952. Ranger "Nick" had served 40 years with the Forest Service, seven years longer than Ranger Woody).

Alter goes on to mention that Ranger Nicholson and one of his Forest Guards invested personal funds in a female bloodhound to use for tracking arsonists around 1926:

> "There are several accounts of successful employment of the dog and two of her pups. It was considered a successful fire prevention measure until cars became more common, and the dogs could not track them."

Ranger Woody also acquired a bloodhound he named Pete about this same time. It is not clear which of the two rangers purchased a tracking dog first. The two men were certainly in contact with each other, and in all likelihood after one acquired a bloodhound the other followed suit because the idea made good sense. Both Ranger Woody and Ranger Nicholson reportedly used their bloodhounds to successfully catch a number of poachers and arsonists. Pete was reportedly very popular with the CC boys at Camp Woody in Suches, and even stayed with them from time to time during the mid-1930s when their manpower was used regularly to fight fires.

In regard to Ranger Nicholson's bloodhound, former Regional Forester J. Herbert Stone was quoted as saying:

> "Ranger Nicholson, of Rabun County, Ga., also employed a bloodhound. One of the firebugs whom Nick had had his eye on up in that area, had been setting fires each year in the spring to get the country in shape for his stock. The year after the bloodhound's reputation had gotten around, a friend of his asked if he was going to burn the woods that year and he answered, 'No sir, not me. I don't want any bloodhound tearing the seat out of my britches.' The result was that the fire record for that particular drainage improved tremendously."

In addition to trying to put a stop to the widespread burning, the Forest Service, through its early rangers and foresters, also hoped to encourage the local people and small timber companies to practice "enlightened silviculture and forest conservation," especially on lands that had been cut over. But it took many decades before this idea took root among private landowners.

The Scourge of North Georgia

Widespread burning by farmers had become almost a ritual since the gold rush days, but there were other causes of forest fires as well. Sometimes fires were started by lightning strikes during electrical storms. As soon as trains pushed into the North Georgia region, sparks from wood-burning engines and skidders set off blazes that burned thousands of acres. Most fires were man-caused, and many of those were intentionally set for one reason or another by disgruntled individuals.

"One time a man got lost in the mountains," Jean McNey remembered. "He purposely set a fire, knowing that a crew would be dispatched to the area and that he'd be found. Another time a fire started by accident at a moonshine still. (This no doubt happened quite a few times over the years.) After the fire had been extinguished, my grandfather grabbed some containers and filled them with what was left of the moonshine at the still. He then hid the containers in a deep ditch beside the Cooper Gap Road, and covered them up with leaves and branches. A few days later, he went to check on the hidden moonshine and it was nowhere to be found. The moonshiners who operated the still apparently found it first and reclaimed it. Within a day or two, they were back in business!"

Speaking of moonshine, stills were quite common in the mountains during the years that Ranger Woody served with the Forest Service. Over that nearly 30-year span of time, he received many accolades for his phenomenal fire prevention record (see Ranger Woody's "speech" at the end of this chapter). One of the reasons often cited for his amazing record was his uncanny ability to get along with the local people. This included people from all walks of life, both good and bad.

Practically every mountain family could claim at least one relative who made some variety of illegal "likker." Many of these people were the salt of the earth; their families had been making mountain spirits for their own consumption for generations and the custom had become a way of life. Even

Ranger Woody poses in front of a split rail fence at Hightower Gap within his beloved Rock Creek Refuge, circa 1930. The small structure behind him contains a variety of fire-fighting equipment which, in the event of a fire, would be distributed to local volunteers. The fence appears to contain chestnut rails, probably obtained from salvaged trees killed by the great chestnut blight. Most of the mature chestnut trees in North Georgia were dead or dying by the mid-1930s. Photo courtesy of Jean McNey.

though they might sell a little moonshine on the side in order to make an extra dollar or two during difficult economic times, these people certainly did not regard themselves as criminals. But no government agency was going to tell them they couldn't continue to do what they had been doing for decades. It is also true that some of the roughest elements in the mountains were also involved in the making and selling of moonshine.

So Ranger Woody was forced to walk a fine line. Should he report these people to the authorities and have them arrested and risk having his beloved mountains set afire and destroyed, or should he go about his business and leave them to their own devices? It was not an easy call. Even though he was never a heavy drinker, like his father before him he had grown up with a decided preference for homemade corn whiskey and apple jack brandy. Suffice to say he had one hard and fast rule when it came to dealing with local moonshiners: "Don't let your fires get out!" It was that simple. If any of those fires did get out and burn up any of his forests, there would be hell to pay.

It is likely that Ranger Nicholson faced the same situation in Rabun County and probably handled it in a similar manner.

"When Papa first became a Ranger (1918), a telephone switchboard was installed in the living room of our house," Jean said. "At first, wire was primitively strung by hand with work crews from tree to tree across the mountains. Later paths were cut out and proper poles were erected to carry the wire. Two or three men working for the Forest Service also had telephones as well as several local individuals who were appointed forest guards or fire marshals. These men were paid by the Forest Service. They were given a supply of shovels, axes, rakes, saws and other light equipment with which to outfit a crew."

It is entirely possible that a telephone could have been installed in the Ranger's house before 1918, while he was still serving as a forest guard, because fire fighting at that time was such an important priority with the Forest Service. Later on, beginning in 1933, The CC boys were invaluable in fighting fires, building roads that could get to remote areas in case of fires and in stringing miles of telephone wire across the mountains in the mid-1930s.

In a June 13, 1937, story appearing in the Atlanta Constitution titled "Forests Coming Back, Georgia Ranger Says," penned by Harold Martin, Ranger Woody shared these gems of wisdom about fighting forest fires in the early days:

> Hard work in the old days. No roads back into the hills, no trucks to travel in. No telephones, right at first.

UNITED STATES DEPARTMENT OF AGRICULTURE

FOREST SERVICE

FIRE LAW ENFORCEMENT SUGGESTIONS FOR FOREST GUARDS AND FIREMEN

1. Upon discovery of a fire your duty as a guard or fireman is to put it out, if possible, by your personal work. If you are unable to put it out promptly, you should make the strongest effort possible to place it under control so as to prevent its spread. Should your efforts to put the fire under control fail, you should obtain help in the manner provided by the general fire instructions issued to you by the ranger in charge of your district.

2. Immediately after the fire is under control, or if it is out, or the direction of the work of the fire-fighting crew is taken over by some other employee, or you have so arranged the work on the fire line that you can do other things, you should investigate fully the cause of the fire. If you suspect that the fire was started *unlawfully* by a rancher, smoker, cam... logger, or by any person, or by any corporat... ground lying close to the point where the fi... carefully examined for horse, wagon, auto, ... other clues, such as paper scraps, empty foo... fruit peelings, pieces of cloth, or other things... the discovery of the person who started the ... what you have seen or collected near, or at ... fire started should be made. Any tracks foun... in your diary, and if you find any article w... serve as a clue, or as evidence in the case, ... in your diary and then deliver it to the ra...

3. Even though you have personal kn... received trustworthy information, as to th... *fully* started the fire, you should make full ... what you have seen, and of what you have ... the point where the fire started. Do not t... much. As soon after as possible, you sho... with the ranger in charge so that together ... value, or the importance, of what you ha... value or importance of articles you have c... or importance of what you have heard reg... fire and the person responsible for it.

4. If the land on which the fire is sp... United States and it supports a stand of ... or a growth of young trees, a prompt e... over which the fire is likely to spread sh... that you may be able to obtain reliable inf... notes, as to the percentage of the trees a...

5. Of the greatest importance in ev... caused fire was started, is to locate by ...

Revised, Jan., 1923. Form D. 1—F. 18 A

FIREMAN'S REPORT

(To be filled out in duplicate.)

.... National Forest

Ranger Dist. .... Fire No. ....

Name of Fire ....

Map. 1″=1 mile. Location: Sec. ...., T. ...., R. ....

NAME OF CREEK OR RIDGE

....

Fire started in ....
(Specify character of ground cover. Example: Grass, slash, needles, etc.)

Slope .... Exposure ....
(Gentle, moderate, steep, etc.) (NE., SW., N., S., etc.)

Altitude, approximate ....

CAUSE OF FIRE (Check one.)

Lightning ....
R. R. Engines ....
R. R. Right of way ....
Camp fire ....
Smokers ....
Brush burning ....
Incendiary ....
Lumbering: Donkeys ....
Lumbering: R. Roads, loaders ....
Lumbering: Slash burning ....
Lumbering: Sawmills ....
Miscellaneous .... (Specify cause.)

CLASS OF PEOPLE RESPONSIBLE (Check one.)

Tourist .... Fisherman ....
Stockman .... Rancher ....
Timberman .... Miner ....
Hunter .... Others .... (Specify class.)

HOW DID REPORT REACH YOU?

CHECK ONE

TELEPHONE MESSENGER SIGNAL

From .... (Name of person.)

When did you receive report? .... (Hour a. m. or p. m.) (Date.)

When did you start to fire? ....

What means of travel in going? .... Distance ...... mi.

When did you reach fire? ....

When was fire controlled? .... When left? ....

Was it out when you left it? ....

When do you think fire started? ....

How big was it when you reached it? ....

How big was it when you left it? ....

How long did they work? .... (man-hours).

8—4437 U. S. DEPARTMENT OF AGRICULTURE FOREST SERVICE

Within a few short years of becoming a Forest Guard in 1914, Arthur Woody began to amass an extraordinary fire prevention record. These U.S. Forest Service directives, titled "Fire Law Enforcement Suggestions for Forest Guards," and "Fireman's Report," dated January 1923, once belonged to the Ranger's good friend, Charlie Elliott. They were found in one of Charlie's old scrapbooks from the early 1930s. Courtesy of the Charlie Elliott Wildlife Center.

> Man walked 8 or 10 miles (to the fire) in the morning to where he was going to work and worked eight hours and lay down in the woods wrapped in his blanket. Got up and cooked a little snack and worked again all day.
>
> Tromped miles to fires and fought 'em best they could with nothing much to fight 'em with but axes and hoes and rakes.
>
> Easier to put out fires now. Lose a lot less acreage, though it costs a lot more.
>
> Used to take a ridge or a stream and backfire from there and stop it after it had burned through the valley from the other ridge. Stopped it that way, but lost a lot of timber in between. Used to take a day to get a crew into a fire, walking and on horses. Now, with the roads the CCC built, and the CCC crews to fight 'em, and the trucks and the chemical tanks and the equipment, we can stop one right quick.
>
> With no fires to ruin 'em, the forests will come back quick. Maybe....

"Whenever a fire broke out somewhere, June, and later my mother Mae, when she was old enough, would usually take the call at our house," Jean continued. "They would immediately notify the closest person to the fire by telephone and that man would quickly round up a crew to fight the fire. The crews, made up of local individuals, were also paid by the Forest Service. Although it was hard and dangerous work, in many cases this was a much needed source of income for men who were struggling to feed their families, and some were quite happy to see fires break out. Many men actually looked forward to this work because they knew they would be paid. But it also created problems at times; some fires were deliberately set by desperate men who saw a way to earn a few dollars getting hired to put them out."

Roscoe Reams, who fished in Rock Creek Refuge as a teenager and developed a close friendship with Ranger Woody in the late 1930s, remembered stories he had heard about the much coveted shower facility located at the Ranger Station:

"There was a shower located in the U.S. Forestry facility near Suches, and it was public knowledge that anyone in the community could use the shower if they wanted to. But there was a catch. In those days, very few people had running water in their houses, and the Forest Service shower was a popular commodity. But if you used that shower, you had to promise Ranger Woody to join in and help fight any local fires when called upon. A lot of men used that shower, and they gladly helped out whenever a fire started somewhere in the area."

Norman Bruce Alter made an important point in his 1971 paper about the dedication of the Rangers' wives whenever a fire broke out:

> "Here is a good place to pay homage to the wives of the men in the Forest Service and especially the Rangers' wives. In the days when help was very limited, these women often served as part-time telephone operators or messengers. Sometimes it fell to them to get a fire crew rounded up and on its way or to send out rations to crews on the fire line – all without pay until recent years when some were put under contract to perform certain services such as reading weather instruments."

Since Ranger Woody and Ranger Nicholson were often away from their homes when a fire did break out, their wives did do an extraordinary job in getting the word out and making sure that crews were organized and dispatched to the scene of the fire as soon as possible.

In fact, throughout Ranger Woody's long career, June helped her husband in countless other ways as well, day in and day out. Not only was his job a seven-day-a-week endeavor, but June, Mae and other family members were always ready to help out in any way – fixing countless meals over the years and seeing to the needs of Forest Service workers.

In a section called "Home-Grown Rangers Do Best" from the U.S. Forest Service Publication, *Mountaineers and Rangers: A History of Federal Forest Management in the Southern Appalachians,* Ranger Woody is praised for his amazing ability:

> How were the mountaineers persuaded not to burn? According to an early ranger, "It took a great deal of educational work with lectures in schools, moving pictures, and literature to overcome the practice." The effort was a gradual one which evolved as a system of trust developed between the Forest Service and the mountain people. This system was often founded upon the selection and placement of rangers and forest technicians who had grown up in the mountains and knew them well…
>
> A classic example of a local resident who became an outstanding ranger was W. Arthur Woody, native of northern Georgia, who started as a laborer in 1912 and became a District Ranger there July 1, 1918. He retired in 1945. Known for his accomplishments in restocking the forest with deer and protecting wildlife, Woody was also renowned for his ability to get along with the mountaineers of his home. Woody enlisted local boys to help watch for and fight fires and resorted to his own methods of punishing

Ranger Woody stands on the porch of Mount Lebanon School in 1926 and points to a sign that reads: "Help Prevent Fires." Since fire prevention was such a key issue with the U.S. Forest Service in the teens and 1920s, great efforts were made to educate the local people about the importance of preventing forest fires. During the 1920s, the Forest Service initiated a program of going into schools, churches and community meetings and teaching fire prevention techniques by showing movies and using other visual-aid teaching tools. In some cases, these were the first moving pictures that school children and other mountain residents had ever seen. Mount Lebanon School was one of five independent, one-room school houses in the Suches area of the Cherokee National Forest in the late 1920s. It was similar to the one-room school Ranger Woody attended as a boy some 30 years earlier. The five schools were consolidated 14 years later in 1940 with the opening of Woody Gap School in Suches. Photo courtesy of Jean McNey.

> incendiarists. His sons, Clyne and Walter, who also became foresters, as did his nephew and grandson, tell the tale of Woody tracking a fire-setting turkey hunter with a bloodhound, jailing him, and then returning him to the scene of the fire, whereupon the hunter finally confessed."

And just what were Ranger Woody's "own methods of punishing incendiarists" and other lawbreakers like deer and turkey poachers? Since the historic record does not tell us for certain, we'll have to leave that up to our imagination. However, as noted, numerous stories have been passed down claiming that he had no qualms about foreclosing on the farms of people who he deemed "undesirable characters" and moving them out of the area. Although this probably was true to some extent, the fact that he *did not* foreclose on many other loans that were in default tells us that he was not a ruthless money monger only out to take advantage of the poor and disadvantaged. If and when he did foreclose, he must have had ample reason to do so.

Since he was a federal forest ranger, Ranger Woody had the authority to carry a badge and sidearm, which he sometimes did, and he had the authority to arrest lawbreakers, which he also did upon occasion. But he seldom forced his authority upon others in the community; probably because he knew this would separate him from the people in his district. This is also why he seldom wore an official uniform. He knew how important it was to get along with his people and he always went to great pains to simply be one of the boys.

But there was no mistaking who he was or what he could do if necessary. After all, he was the Kingfish! From that standpoint, he was looked upon by most with great respect; partially out of fear, partially out of adoration. No one wanted to be on his bad side. He loved guns, and when he did carry a sidearm during his almost daily jaunts in the mountains, it was probably more for

Clyne Woody (right), worked with Ranger Nick Nicholson (left), for several years in Rabun County (unidentified man in center). In addition to helping the Forest Service acquire much land, Ranger Nicholson faced many of the same challenges in his Tallulah Ranger District as Ranger Woody did in his Blue Ridge District. Both men were driving forces in the forest and conservation movement in the North Georgia mountains during the early 1900s. As Georgia's first forest ranger, Nick Nicholson served for 40 years, from 1912 to 1952. Because of the excessive logging that took place in Northeast Georgia during the early 1900s, Rabun County today boasts the highest percentage of national forest land of any county in the mountain region. Photo circa 1944, courtesy of Jean McNey.

shooting an occasional snake or a much hated wildcat (because they preyed on his deer) than trying to impress people with his authority. But there were times when he also carried a sidearm for protection. There were some tough elements back in those hills.

Jean McNey tells another story about a local fire that she remembered hearing from her grandfather when she was a young girl:

"After a fire had been intentionally set and put out by a local crew, an assistant ranger who was working under Papa at the time, tracked a mule belonging to an old-timer from the scene of the fire right into the old gentleman's barn using Papa's bloodhound. When the assistant ranger reached the barn, the mule was hot and sweaty. The strong circumstantial evidence certainly made it appear as if the old farmer had set the fire. The assistant ranger questioned the mule's owner. Although the old man couldn't explain where the mule had been, he vehemently denied setting the fire.

"The assistant ranger reported back to Papa that the farmer denied setting the fire. However, he was positive the old man was lying because he hadn't been able to explain why his mule was so sweaty or why the tracks led from the fire to his barn. The old man kept saying over and over again, 'I didn't do it. I didn't do it.'

"Then the somewhat arrogant assistant ranger said, 'Ranger, I don't know how you deal with these dumb mountain folks. They're so dumb, you can't reason with 'em.'

"Papa decided to go see the mule's owner to determine what had happened for himself. When he returned, he told the assistant ranger, 'The farmer didn't set the fire. He was telling the truth all along.'

"'What do you mean?' the assistant ranger asked incredulously. 'That can't be right. That old man is guilty as sin.'

"Turned out the man's son-in-law was mad about some property division," Jean continued. "So in an act of revenge, he had taken the old man's mule without his knowledge and set the fire, knowing it would look like the old man had done it. Papa had a nose for figuring out things like that. I'm sure he gave that assistant ranger a piece of his mind for condemning mountain people. 'Maybe mountain people aren't so dumb after all,' he no doubt told that haughty assistant."

The vast majority of forest technicians and assistant rangers who worked under Ranger Woody for any amount of time quickly came to regard him as a mentor and hero. And there were dozens of such young men. Many were in awe of Ranger Woody's knowledge and abilities. A few, however, who might have been long on education and short on experience, came to the Georgia Mountains with a definite "attitude." Ranger Woody had no use for these "damned technicians" or "damned Yankees" as he often called them, especially those who viewed most mountain people as stupid and illiterate. He no doubt made life more than a little difficult for this particular brand of government bureaucrat.

The First Fire Towers

Records indicate that Ranger Woody was involved in building at least two fire towers in the Suches area as well as a replacement lookout tower on Brasstown Bald. One of the first fire towers in the Suches area, if not the first, was Rocky Mountain fire tower. The short wooden structure and cabin (located on Rocky Mountain just north of Suches), was probably built around 1920 or 1921. At the time it was built, the area was accessible by horseback only. All building materials had to be sledded in by horse team. A cabin was built beside the tower due to its remote location. For a while, Arthur Woody's son Walter and his wife lived in the cabin and manned the tower. Walter's wife also taught school in Union County.

Ranger Woody sits on the front steps of the cabin next to Rocky Mountain fire tower built in 1920 or 1921 (just north of Suches). Being one of the first fire towers in the area (if not the first), building materials for the cabin had to be sledded up the mountain trail by horse team. The tower was made from trees cut on the site. George Burns, who lived with the Woody family for a time and did odd jobs for Ranger Woody, stands in the doorway. For a while, Ranger Woody's son, Walter, and Walter's wife, Mina, lived in the cabin and manned the fire tower. Mina taught school in Union County. Photo courtesy of Bud Braddock, U.S. Forest Service retired.

Local CCC camps provided a much-needed source of labor for other fire towers that Ranger Woody wanted to build. In fact, he had long thought about building a fire tower and some type of visitor's center on the top of Bald Peak (Brasstown Bald, also known as Enotah Mountain, sometimes spelled "Enota"), Georgia's highest point. The fruition of that dream was made possible by the willing boys of "Roosevelt's Tree Army."

About the same time the Rocky Mountain lookout tower was built in the early 1920s, the Pfister & Vogel Leather Company of Milwaukee, owner of thousands of acres in the area, had built a rough wooden lookout tower made from chestnut and locust wood on the top of Bald Peak (Brasstown Bald). From that high point, company fire guards could see smoke from any direction, especially in areas where logging operations were being conducted.

By the early 1930s, the original wooden fire tower was in bad repair, and Ranger Woody began to talk about building a new tower on Bald Peak as well as some type of observation deck for visitors. The CC boys provided the work force that made this dream a reality. Reportedly the Ranger sat at his kitchen table (the same table from which he later drew plans for the Dockery Lake dam) and drew out a rough sketch of the stone viewing station and lookout tower in less than a week's time. His plan called for the CC boys to improve an old logging road that led up to the bald and make it accessible by automobile. While under construction, the CC boys camped nearby. The rock station and lookout tower were built using local stone and timber.

The project was completed during the summer of 1935. The Woody granite tower was replaced by a modern steel tower in 1947, one year after the Ranger's death. Today, the present stone structure, visitor's center, and educational facilities, completed in 1965, includes a very informative "Man and the Mountain" program hosted by a talking manikin of Arthur Woody wearing crisp khaki shirt and pants, an outfit the Ranger seldom if ever wore. Practically every photo taken of Ranger Woody in the late 1930s and early '40s shows him wearing his well-worn and wrinkled dark green work clothes, not khakis. Several states including North Carolina and Tennessee can be seen from the observation deck, which offers a breathtaking 360-degree panoramic view of the North Georgia mountains in every direction.

The Black Mountain fire tower is located a few miles east of the old Blue Ridge Ranger Station in Suches. It can be reached by hiking up Forest Service Road No. 81, about 500 yards from Woody Gap. It's about a one-mile hike to the tower from the road. The original tower on Black Mountain is believed to have been built by contract using steel under Ranger Woody's supervision in 1927. It was replaced by a 33-foot tall steel structure in 1949. Today the tower

Ranger Woody (on right) poses with a group of CCC officials and civilians in front of the Black Mountain fire tower near Woody Gap. Reverend Claud Boynton, who served as a civilian supervisor and chaplain for the CCC boys at Camp Woody, stands sixth from left. The original steel tower on Black Mountain is believed to have been built by contract under Ranger Woody's supervision in 1927. It was replaced by a stronger, 33-foot-tall steel structure in 1949. Photo circa 1935, courtesy of Jean McNey.

is used mostly as a mounting structure for communications antennae. It is listed on the National Historic Lookout register as U.S. 703, GA 6.

As recently as the 1960s and '70s, many of the much taller fire towers found across the southern two-thirds of Georgia were still in active use. Unlike most of the fairly short towers in the North Georgia Mountains that were built on the highest points in the area, fire towers built in central and South Georgia in the mid-1900s where the terrain is rolling or flat often stood at least 100-feet tall. Sadly, only a few dozen of these historic and once important landmarks remain in the state today. They stand as silent sentinels to a bygone era.

Ranger Woody's Immortal Speech
(Undoubtedly the Most Famous Speech Ever Given by a Forest Ranger)

When it came to making speeches, Arthur Woody was not what you would call a polished orator. In fact, there is good evidence to suggest he never liked having to get up in front of groups to talk. Throughout his life he tended to shy away from "speechifying." Despite his possible public speaking weaknesses, with his down-home personality and charisma, he might well have been a successful politician had he ever decided to run for office, but that was not necessary. "Kingfish" literally ran the community of Suches without holding any type of elected position. Local politicians sought him out all the time, and he no doubt loaned some of them money. But only a few times in his life did he ever agree to stand up and give a speech.

One of those rare times was referenced in a letter written to Ranger Woody by his special friend Bill Bergoffen from the U.S. Forest Service office in Washington D.C. (No date appears on the letter, but it was probably written in mid-September 1945. This was a week or two before Ranger Woody's official retirement ceremony in late September because a later paragraph in the letter refers to Bill Bergoffen's "post-war" project of visiting the Ranger soon. Japan had surrendered on Sept. 2.)

Bergoffen wrote:

> Reminds me of the time you got at up at some dinner or other and remarked: "I feel like a duck that's been fattened up for killing. I'm so full I can't quack!" Then you sat down. Remember?

In truth, the Ranger loathed most politicians for good reason, and he certainly wanted as little to do with the government establishment as possible. But he did attain one milestone in his life that many politicians never achieve. His most famous public address – actually it might be stretching it a bit to call it a true speech because it was only a few sentences in length – is something that people still talk about to this day. Like many other things the Ranger did in life, this unforgettable "utterance" caused quite a sensation.

Most politicians fail miserably at saying anything with real substance, but on rare occasions certain elected officials do offer inspired words of wisdom that go down in history as being true gems of oratory genius. David Crockett, a Tennessee pioneer born 100 years before Arthur Woody under very similar circumstances, was known for delivering homey yet powerful speeches in Congress. After being elected to his first term, he gave an unforgettable introductory speech to Congress by saying, "I'm David Crockett, fresh from the backwoods. I'm half horse, half alligator and a little touched with snappin' turtle." He and Ranger Woody would have gotten along famously. They were both fresh from the backwoods.

Another successful speech maker was Abraham Lincoln, for whom Arthur Woody's father was named. In November 1863, several months after one of our nation's most horrendous battles occurred during the Civil War – the Battle of Gettysburg, fought in July 1863 – an under-the-weather President

Lincoln followed Edward Everett's tedious, two-hour dissertation by making a few "appropriate remarks" of his own. Lincoln's short and to the point address was less than 250 words in length and contained only 10 sentences. It was considered pitiful by several "learned" people who listened to it that day. Today, of course, Lincoln's extraordinary Gettysburg Address is considered to be one of the greatest speeches of all time.

Ranger Woody was no Abraham Lincoln, and his frog-choker of a speech turned out to be less than 50 words and contained only three or four sentences. But it turned more than a few heads and certainly grabbed the attention of more than a few bored attendees at the special dinner where it was given. With his wit, wisdom and down-home ability to say what was on his mind, he usually had little trouble getting his point across.

After having been given an award by the American Forestry Association for maintaining one of the best forest fire prevention records in the nation in his Blue Ridge Ranger District, he was asked to attend an Association meeting in Washington D.C. to receive the award and give a short talk about how he'd been so successful with his fire record. The precise date of the meeting is not known, but it probably took place in the late 1930s.

The exact wording of Ranger Woody's speech is lost to the ages, but several variations have been printed in various publications over the past few decades and each version gives a good idea of what was said. Typical of Ranger Woody's oratory history, the speech was short, sweet, to the point. It was also absolutely stunning to those who heard it.

Before the advent of the iconic "Smokey the Bear" character in 1944, the Forest Service campaigned for fire prevention by placing signs along roads and on the backs of government vehicles. Photo circa 1940, courtesy of Jean McNey.

The earliest reference I could find to Ranger Woody's immortal speech appeared in a well-written article in the October 1941 issue of *Outdoor Life* titled: "Dixie's Game is Coming Back," by Arthur Grahame. The article talked about how conservation efforts in the North Georgia Mountains helped restore the many fish and game species that had all but disappeared by the early part of the 20th century. Toward the end of the article, the author mentioned Ranger Woody:

> One of the chief attractions of this area is Ranger Woody himself. Born and raised almost within sight of his ranger station, he knows the mountain people better than any outlander can ever know them. Unlike most of the rangers of today, he didn't learn his forestry in college, but he's one of the most competent men in the Service. A few years ago the American Forestry Association awarded him a medal for his remarkably successful work in fire prevention. The presentation was made at a big dinner in Washington. Entirely unabashed, Woody made a speech that had the gentlemen in white shirt fronts standing on their chairs.

Indeed Arthur Grahame was right. And then some! Here are several variations of what Ranger Woody said:

In his classic and well-researched book, *Whose Woods These Are, the Story of the National Forests*, published in 1962, author Michael Frome writes:

> Once he (Arthur Woody) was honored at a formal dinner for a nationally outstanding fire record (of only four acres burned in a year). "Tell us, Ranger," the toastmaster asked, "how did you achieve this fine record?"
>
> "Well, you have just got to know the people," Woody confided to his audience. "I fish with the men, buy candy for the kids, and tell each and every woman if I wasn't married I'd sure like to make love to her."

A similar account appears in the book *Touching Home*, produced by the students of West Fannin High School photo journalism class, edited by Kathy Thompson, and published in 1976:

> When he received an award for fire prevention at a banquet in Washington D.C., he was asked to tell his methods. He stood up and said, "You have to know your people; I kiss all the babies, fish with the men,

> buy candy for the kids, and tell the women that if I wasn't married I'd sure like to make love to them." Then he sat down.

It's entirely possible that the account in *Touching Home* was borrowed from Michael Frome's highly acclaimed book.

In *An Outdoor Life, the Autobiography of Charlie Elliott*, published in 1994, Charlie Elliott gives a slightly different version of the speech:

> One of my impressive stories about Woody concerns the reputation he held for years as the forest ranger with the best forest-fire record – with the least number of forest acres burned by wild fires – in the United States.
>
> His superiors conceived the idea that he should appear before the national organization of forest supervisors and rangers at their annual meeting in Washington, and tell what steps he had taken to compile and maintain such a record.
>
> So his superiors arranged for him to appear before the national organization (the American Forestry Association) and tell how he had maintained such an excellent (fire) record.
>
> So they dressed him up, put shoes on him – he seldom wore shoes, winter or summer on the job, much to the discomfort of his superiors – and put him on the train to Washington....
>
> The program chairman who introduced him to the convention gave a long, flowery introduction, going into great detail about what an unusual and colourful character the ranger was and giving the comparative facts of his forest-fire record. After about 30 minutes of this, the chairman concluded by saying, "And now we have brought Ranger Woody all the way up here from Georgia to tell you how he has accomplished such a magnificent record."
>
> The assembly settled back for a long, dry discourse on procedures. Arthur Woody lumbered to his feet, gave a nervous cough and said, "I speak to the dogs, pat the chillun on the heads, shake hands with the men and sleep with the women." Then he sat down.
>
> There was a moment of half-stunned silence that burst into a pandemonium of laughter, cheers and a standing ovation – all of which broke up the meeting for the remainder of that session.

A slightly different version appeared in the Summer 2005 issue of *Georgia Backroads:*

"Wal, I take notice of the whole family. I speak to the hounds, pat the chillun' on the head, drink likker with the men, and sleep with the women."

A much more refined version comes from *The Best of 'I Remember Dahlonega'* by Anne Dismukes Amerson:

> "Well, I tell you. I take a drink with all the men, kiss all the babies on the head and tell all of the women they are looking younger every day."

Another more refine version that appeared in the Summer, 1990, issue of *North Georgia Journal* said:

> "Wal, you just have to know your people. I kiss all the babies and buy them candy, tell all the women if I wasn't married I'd be in love with them, and I go fishing with all the men." After pausing a moment, Woody reportedly added with a chuckle, "And I keep a trained bloodhound chained to my back door."

Yet another account about the secret to his success in keeping down fires was given to me over the phone by Mr. William Gooch, whose family had homesteaded in the Suches area. Mr. Gooch told me that as a boy, he used to ride around with Ranger Woody in his truck. Here is his version of how the story was told to him:

> "I ain't never criticized a man's dog and I ain't never criticized a man's wife. Instead I'd always tell her that her cookin' is real good. Last of all, I ain't never smelled a workin' still in my whole life!"

Ranger Woody no doubt told people that he was never able to smell the unmistakable aroma of mash being heated by a fire in some remote section of woods because he had bigger fish to fry. He had to keep the peace with everyone, including renegade moonshiners. Preventing forest fires was not an easy task, and he used every means at his disposal to get the job done. Apparently his methods worked!

In addition to the accounts cited above numerous magazine articles published over the past few decades have included similar renditions of the speech. Most of the magazine accounts were probably taken from one of the books mentioned.

While the exact wording of Ranger Woody's epic speech is lost to the ages, his unabashed words certainly woke up some of the sleepy dinner guests and raised more than a few eyebrows. Obviously for the sake of good taste, his actual words probably have been watered down over the years. Perhaps it is best to leave the exact wording to our imagination. We do know that our beloved Ranger could be somewhat crude at times, but he was always candid and truthful. He said what he thought. Whatever he said on that unforgettable night definitely turned a few heads and caused the entire audience to gasp. Fighting forest fires is a tough business. No wonder he had the best fire prevention record in the nation!

Ranger Woody smiles broadly as he poses with Elsie Freeman, a garden club member from Atlanta who had traveled to Suches with a group of women to meet Georgia's most acclaimed forest ranger. The Ranger dearly loved receiving attention from, and hugging, the ladies. Photo circa early 1940s, courtesy of Jean McNey.

CHAPTER 7
Stories that Made Arthur Woody a Folk Legend

"My weakness – women, wine and song. But I've never been able to sing and I don't drink a whole lot!"

Arthur Woody

Ask any old-timer in the mountains of Union County if they've ever heard of Ranger Arthur Woody, and chances are they'll smile shrewdly and say: "Oh, yes. I've heard some real whoppers about the Kingfish!" The hills are full of tall tales, half-truths and folk legends about Arthur Woody. Although some of the stories are highly exaggerated or altogether untrue, many of the amazing stories about this remarkable man have been documented. These credible accounts help paint a solid picture of who he really was.

On Loaning Money
From an Interview with Charlie Elliott (1994)

The stories about Ranger Woody loaning money to those in need are legion. When it came to collecting on those loans, much depended on the individual and how Ranger Woody saw that individual in his eyes. Was the man trustworthy? Was he a friend? Was he someone the Ranger truly wanted to help? With certain people, it was strictly a business proposition. If the interest was not paid on time or if the loan went into default, the individual in question might suffer the consequences. With other individuals, the Ranger probably knew in advance that he would never collect a penny of the debt.

Charlie Elliott remembered a conversation he once overheard between Ranger Woody and a local farmer. Charlie said the conversation took place during the Depression in the mid-1930s when the man was obviously short of cash and facing dire circumstances. The man had come to the Woody home and the conversation went something like this:

"Hello Lewis," Ranger Woody said, standing on the front porch. "How ya' a'doin'?"

"Doin' fine, Arthur. And yerself?"

"Couldn't be better," Arthur answered with a smile.

"Nice weather we been havin'," Lewis said.

"Yeah, right nice," Arthur agreed.

"Arthur, I need to borrie $75. Do you think you could let me have it?"

"Seventy-five is a heap of money, Lewis," Arthur said. "And money's pretty hard now. Maybe the bank'll let ya' have it."

"I don't know about that, Arthur."

"I ain't got that kind of money just layin' around, Lewis, but I'll tell ya' what. I'm goin' down to the bank (in Dahlonega) tomorrow and I'll ask 'em about it."

"I sure would appreciate anything you could do, Arthur. I need it real bad."

The next day, Ranger Woody again met with Lewis.

"Lewis, I talked to the folks at the bank when I was down there."

"Yeah, what'd they say?"

"They said they might consider loanin' you the money, but you'd have to sign a note. Let's see, your farm's about 300 acres, ain't it?"

"Yes, Arthur, that's right, 300 acres."

"Well, if you'd sign a note and put up the farm, I think they'd loan you the $75."

According to Charlie, "Ranger Woody then made the loan himself, never having had any intention of involving the bank. If the man didn't pay it back, as was often the case, he'd have the option of foreclosing. He collected interest on the note every year, and if the man was caught setting fires or poaching, he'd be moved out of the county."

A "Sobering" Commencement Address at Woody Gap School

From an Interview with Charlie Elliott (1994)

Frank Gross of Union County was a popular and highly-respected public servant and politician elected to the state senate of Georgia in the late 1930s. He did much for Georgia, and being from Union County, he especially did a lot for Union and Fannin counties. Frank loved to hunt and fish, and he and Ranger Woody became great friends.

Frank was also a close friend and long-time hunting and fishing partner of Charlie Elliott. Long after Ranger Woody's death in 1946, Frank and Charlie hunted elk in Wyoming and fished for trout across the North Georgia mountains. Charlie wrote several magazine articles in *Outdoor Life* about various hunts he and Frank shared in the 1950s and '60s. Frank is best remembered for his work on behalf of the local schools in Union County as well as for his support of the Forest Service. He helped set up a wildlife conservation area along Rock Creek in the Blue Ridge WMA that eventually was named in his honor. Today it is known as the Frank Gross Recreational Area in Fannin County.

Woody Gap School, which offered grades 1-12, opened its doors in Suches in midterm in January 1941. At the end of the school term in late May or early June, Ranger Woody asked Frank to give the commencement address to the graduating high school class and the student body. (This may have been the very first graduating class in 1940, or it could have been a year or two later. Even though the graduating class would have been very small with no more than 8 to 10 students, this was an important community event and a large turnout was expected.)

On the appointed day, Frank arrived early and stopped by the Ranger's house. After a brief chat, they walked across the road to Ranger Woody's office at the Ranger Station. Since the two men had a little time to kill before Frank's address, Ranger Woody opened his safe and produced a quart bottle of applejack brandy made by one of his neighbors. No doubt this was a treasured cache, brought out only on special occasions and shared only with special friends. The two men enjoyed a tasty little "swaller."

"That applejack was so dern good," Frank later told Charlie, "that we decided to take a second swallow. The third was much better than the first two, and then we had two more before we drove over to the school which was just a mile down the road.

"The school auditorium was overflowing with more people than I knew lived in the county," Frank told Charlie. "When I stood up to speak, I was refreshed, relaxed, and never felt better."

Frank was also quite inebriated. Ranger Woody, who could usually hold his mountain spirits with the best of them, did not seem to have a problem.

A few days after Frank had given his speech, he told Charlie, "You know, I stood there and made what I thought was one of the funniest speeches I'd ever given and nobody laughed but me."

Always quick witted like Ranger Woody himself, Charlie looked at Frank and said, "You and Ranger Woody should have passed out the applejack to all the adults before the commencement address began. That way, everyone would have laughed along with you for sure!"

Ranger Woody's reaction to Frank's address apparently went unrecorded, but with his fun-loving sense of humor, he no doubt got a big kick out of his friend's impeded performance.

An Unforgettable Act of Kindness

From an Interview with Lou Nichols (2013)

Lou Nichols, daughter of Clyne Woody, did not spend as much time with her grandparents as her cousin Jean McNey because her family moved away from Suches when she was a small girl. Both of Arthur Woody's sons, Walter and Clyne, had long careers with the Forest Service. During the war years, Clyne was transferred from a post in northeast Georgia to east Texas to supervise a prisoner-of-war camp containing German prisoners. Each summer, he brought his family home to Suches to visit for summer vacation, and Lou often spent part of her summer with her grandparents and her cousin Jean.

"One summer afternoon in the early 1940s, we were all sitting out on the front porch like we commonly did," Lou remembers, "Jean, Papa and me. I was probably 10 or 11 years old.

"A young man around 16, who lived in our community, came walking down the road out in front of the house. He was carrying his meager belongings in an old flour sack attached to a pole over his shoulder like hobos used to do. Since Papa always had a nickname for everyone, he yelled out something like, 'Hey, Stogey, where ya' goin'?'

"'I'm going down to Mt. Berry to school,' the young man answered proudly.

Mt. Berry School, or Berry College as it soon became known, in Rome, Georgia, was a considerable distance from Suches. In all likelihood, the young man probably planned to walk to Dahlonega – a distance of some 15 miles – and then try to hitch a ride by automobile over to Rome, Georgia, at least another 120 miles. In those days, mountain folks without transportation thought nothing of walking from Suches to Dahlonega and back. It was done on a frequent basis.

"'Ya' got any money in yer' pocket?' Papa asked the boy.

"'Fifty cents,' the boy answered.

"'Yer' gonna need more than that,' Papa said. He called the boy over and pulled out a wad of bills – maybe 10 or 15 dollars – and put them in the young man's hand.

"'Now you let me know how yer' gettin' along down there in school and if you need any more you jus' holler!' Papa told him.

"That young man graduated from Berry College and later came back to Suches and taught at Woody Gap School for several years," Lou said. "He became a prominent citizen in the community. I'm sure he never forgot Papa's generosity. That's the way Papa was. If he thought somebody needed something, he would always make sure they had it."

A Georgia Road Paved in Gold

From an Interview with Charlie Elliott (1995)

Charlie Elliott loved to tell the following story and it appeared several times in print. All Georgians should be proud of the fact that the capitol building in downtown Atlanta has a beautiful gold dome made from gold mined in and around the Dahlonega area. According to Ranger Woody, at least one road in the mountains might lay claim to the fact that it was paved with Georgia gold as well!

"Ranger Woody was an avid Republican," Charlie said. "He hated all Democrats, and he especially hated most of Roosevelt's policies. 'Them Democrat spendthrifts throw our money away,' he would often say. When the Civilian Conservation Corps first came to North Georgia, he tolerated them, believing they were grossly wasting taxpayers' money building roads and doing other jobs in the community, but it didn't take long for Ranger Woody to change his tune. Within six months, the Ranger's loyal "CC" boys were implementing all types of conservation projects under his careful supervision.

"We spent a lot time in the truck driving around together," Charlie said. "Once we were driving around looking at the new road across Woody Gap that was being covered over with crushed gravel rock. (Due to the endless mud, early mountain roads were notoriously known for being almost impassable during wet weather, and paving them with gravel made a significant difference in getting around by automobile.) For seemingly no reason, he stopped the

Charlie Elliott jots down a few details in his notebook. He began the habit of taking notes for future reference at an early age. Because of the numerous conservation projects in which he and Ranger Woody were jointly involved beginning in the late 1920s and ending with the Ranger's death in 1946, Charlie developed a keen insight into the man that he would later pen numerous stories about. Of all Ranger Woody's many friends and admirers, Charlie was one of the closest. Photo circa 1929, courtesy of the Charlie Elliott Wildlife Center.

truck, got out and picked up several pieces of crushed gravel that recently had been spread down on the roadway. He examined the rocks and put them in his pocket. There was a rock quarry nearby on land he owned where the stone being crushed to spread on the forest roads had come from.

"The next time we were together, I asked him what he had done with the small chunks of rock he had picked up on the road.

"'Why I had them assayed,' he answered.

"'For what?' I asked.

"'For gold,' the Ranger said. 'I thought I recognized some little flecks of gold in some of them rocks.'

"And what were the results?" I persisted.

"'Oh that gravel being crushed in the quarry is running about $30 per ton in gold content," he answered slyly. "Some of the best around these-here parts."

Charlie was speechless for a moment or two before he was able to ask, "Good gosh, why didn't you stop them? Did you tell anyone about it?"

"Nope," the Ranger grumbled. "For once I wanted one dern road in Georgia the Democrats paved in this forest to be worth what it cost!"

Although Ranger Woody initially did a lot of grumbling about Roosevelt's "wasteful" spending programs and the formation of several Civilian Conservation Corps in the area including Camp Woody in Suches, little could he have known at the time how indispensable "Roosevelt's tree boys" would be to him with many of his important conservation projects during the mid to late 1930s. In return, his "CC" boys learned to love him like a father.

But this didn't keep the Ranger from complaining about Democrats. It's very likely this incident occurred in late 1933 or 1934 just as the newly formed ranks of the CCC were being put to work improving local roads with crushed gravel. The road in question is the very steep stretch from Suches to Woody Gap that eventually became Highway 60, the very road Ranger Woody and his son Walter contracted to build with their own work crew before the CC entered the picture.

A Legendary Bear Track

From an Interview with Jean McNey (2013)

Sometime in the mid-1930s, Ranger Woody obtained two black bear cubs that reportedly had been captured in South Georgia. He named the lovable little cubs Mike and Ike, and built a cage for them behind his house. As soon as they were old enough to fend for themselves, he planned to release them in the refuge.

Jean did not like the cubs at all.

"They were stinky, nasty and dirty," she said. "I was about 7 or 8 and I had good reason to be mad at them because one day one of them stole my lollypop that I was sucking on. I tried to share it with him and he ate the whole thing, stick and all. I was furious.

"They escaped from their cage one afternoon and went swimming in the lake behind our house (Woody Lake). Papa dispatched his assistant ranger to go out and collect them in a canoe and put them back in their cage. When the assistant ranger returned, his pants legs had been shredded from the feisty cubs. Everyone got a good laugh out of that except for the assistant ranger!"

For the most part, bears had been absent from the North Georgia mountains since the late 1800s. A reasonable population existed in the mountains of North Carolina because they had long been protected in that region. Ranger Woody had a keen interest in restoring bears to his Blue Ridge Refuge. Whenever the opportunity availed itself, he would acquire a cub or two and eventually release them in the refuge. He protected his bears as vehemently as he did his turkeys and deer.

Ranger Woody poses with Mike and Ike, two lovable but mischievous bear cubs, circa 1935. As soon as they were old enough, the cubs were released inside Rock Creek Refuge. Jean McNey, who was about seven or eight when the cubs shared a cage behind the Woody house, remembered them as "stinky, nasty and dirty." Photo courtesy of Jean McNey.

One day Ranger Woody discovered a huge bear track inside the refuge. In an article in the October 1940 issue of *Outdoor Georgia* magazine, titled "Big Tracks in Georgia's Wilds," the author stated:

> Few persons realize that the black bear is a common animal in Georgia. Bears occur generally throughout the southern part of the state and are found in several of the large river swamps which stretch like giant fingers away from the coast.
>
> Black bears recently were introduced again into one of the management areas of the Chattahoochee National Forest (Blue Ridge WMA). There the huge black animals are increasing, both in numbers and in size. Not long ago United States Forest Service Ranger Arthur Woody, of Suches, discovered an enormous black bear track near his home. Actual measurements of the track were 10 1/2 by 7 1/2 inches. The ranger estimated this animal weighed more than a quarter of a ton! To prove to incredulous persons that such bears did exist in the Blue Ridge Mountains, Arthur Woody poured concrete into the tracks and allowed it to harden. Now if his story of the tracks is doubted, he will make more tracks to prove it.

> Most persons have a horror of meeting a black bear in the woods. The truth is that even where black bears are numerous, the average hunter or fisherman seldom sees one.
>
> Black bears are hunted as big game in the south. Those who trail the black furry creatures like to think of themselves as hunters on a dangerous mission, or that bear hunting in Georgia is comparable to hunting lions in Africa or tigers in India. That is not true, since a black bear will usually run from a man in the woods, and many times when he is wounded will keep on running.

Ranger Woody had a lot of fun with his concrete bear track. After making the casting, he attached to it a long stick that could he used as a handle. Later on, he used the casting of the track to lay down a fake trail in areas where he suspected poachers to be frequenting. The ruse worked perfectly. When the would-be poachers saw the tracks, they reportedly left the area immediately.

"That ol' bear track did more to turn away poachers in the refuge than three game wardens put together!" Ranger Woody was quoted as saying on more than one occasion.

"GOVERNMENT PROPERTY BELONGS TO EVERYONE"

From an Interview with Jean McNey (2013)

Known as the Blue Ridge Ranger Station (sometimes referred to as the Suches Ranger Station or Blairsville Ranger Station), a large Forest Service complex was constructed just across the road from Ranger Woody's house in the late 1920s on approximately six acres of land he deeded to the Forest Service for $1. After the Ranger Station was abandoned in the late 1940s for a more modern facility closer to Dahlonega, the land was deeded back to Walter Woody, Ranger Woody's son. (Later still a new Forest Service facility was built near Blairsville on Highway 515 West, where it remains today.)

A two-story house in the front of the complex near the road served as an office with makeshift barracks upstairs where Forest Service personnel could spend the night whenever duty called. Each room on the ground floor of the structure, including the Ranger's office, was paneled in beautifully grained chestnut wood from floor to ceiling, salvaged from dying trees killed by the blight. The building also contained a much heralded shower facility, a luxury the hard-working men of the Forest Service learned to love, especially during the blistering days of summer.

Described by Charlie Elliott as a tiny "shanty," the first official Ranger Station in Suches was indeed a doll-house-size structure built in Ranger Woody's front yard around 1920. Ranger Woody and his ever-expanding staff of Forest Service personnel quickly outgrew the small space. By the late 1920s, a much larger facility was constructed just across the road on land donated to the Forest Service by Ranger Woody. Photo courtesy of Jean McNey.

By the mid-1930s, the Blue Ridge Ranger Station was a bustling, hub of Forest Service activity in southern Union County. Photo circa 1932, courtesy of Bud Braddock, U.S. Forest Service retired.

A view of the Blue Ridge Ranger Station office building from which Ranger Woody operated during his most productive years. The structure was originally built by Ranger Woody as a house for a noted Forest Service game warden from North Carolina who Ranger wanted to hire, but the transfer never went through. Photo circa mid-1930s, courtesy of Jean McNey.

The original Ranger Station office structure, as it looks today, has been well-maintained over the years. Photos by Duncan Dobie.

Most of the rooms inside the Ranger Station, including Ranger Woody's private office, were paneled in beautifully-grained chestnut boards salvaged after the devastating blight began to kill thousands of chestnut trees in the southern Appalachians in the late 1920s. Photo by Duncan Dobie.

Dr. Ed Woody, grandson of Walter Woody, and great-grandson of Arthur Woody, stands by one of the original warehouse buildings at the Blue Ridge Ranger Station. Photo by Duncan Dobie.

Behind the two-story office building stood four or five large outbuildings. Over the years, the Ranger Station accumulated quite a bit of machinery and equipment for road building and fire fighting. Other various types of construction materials were stored in large wooden buildings on the property. A little worse for the wear, the original Ranger Station office building and most of the out-buildings are still standing today.

Charlie Elliott described Ranger Woody's office in detail in a story he wrote in the May 1939 issue of *American Forests* magazine:

> The Ranger Station, itself, had spread from a small, one-room shanty (in Ranger Woody's front yard) to several large buildings (just across the road) with office space, desks, clerks and garages. Arthur Woody's office was draped with skins and pictures and game heads. Each trophy was a mute but sufficient basis for a delightful story from the lips of the Ranger. One antlered head which interested me particularly was a large buck, which had been hamstrung and brought down by two wildcats.
>
> "I wouldn't have believed it," Arthur said, "but we found the deer soon after he had been killed. He fought with the cats for half a mile and the tracks in the snow were so easy to read that you didn't have to be a Boy Scout to tell what happened."

If a certain piece of big equipment at the Ranger Station wasn't being used at the time, Ranger Woody had no qualms about loaning it out to local farmers who might need it for some special purpose. This discreet practice obviously stretched Forest Service regulations. "Why not," he often said to those closest to him. "After all, it was bought with taxpayers' money wasn't it? So it belongs to all the people, doesn't it?"The bureaucrats might have argued that point.

"Periodically one of the bookkeepers would come up to the Ranger Station from Gainesville to do a complete inventory of all Forest Service property," Jean remembered. "He and Papa would spend several hours walking around the complex checking off various items on his list. One time (probably in the early 1940s), just as the bookkeeper was finishing up, he looked down at his list and said, 'Ranger, there's just one item that seems to be unaccounted for – a Caterpillar Tractor Company bulldozer, serial number such and such...'"

Because of its sheer size, a bulldozer would be hard to miss. As luck would have it, Ranger Woody had recently loaned it to a local farmer who needed to do some clearing on his property. Allowing local farmers to use government property was something the Ranger strongly believed in. In his opinion, it not only encouraged good public relations, but during times when he needed extra manpower to fight forest fires, he could usually call on these same people to lend a helping hand. In most cases, they were only too happy to help out!

But this time the Ranger was in a real pickle.

"Knowing that the bulldozer had to be accounted for on the 'government' inventory list, Papa did some quick thinking," Jean said with a grin. "He walked over to a big pile of twisted metal scraps and other rubble on the ground and said, 'Thar she is…'

"The Forest Service bookkeeper looked down at the pile of rubble, and then he looked quizzically at Papa. Then he shook his head and put a check beside the space next to the missing bulldozer. He probably knew something was amiss but he knew better than to ask what it was. So he took the Ranger's word for it. Apparently everything was in good order with the inventory list and nothing more was said about the subject. The next time the accountant showed up, the yellow bulldozer was parked in a prominent spot – no worse for the wear – so that he could not miss it!"

Mentioned in Chapter 6 by Roscoe Reams, Jean McNey also noted the importance of the shower facilities at the Ranger Station.

"The showers also served an important function for Papa," Jean continued. "Local farmers who were willing to help Papa fight fires and help with other projects when necessary were allowed to use the shower facilities on a regular basis. Many of these people had no running water in their primitive cabins or houses. Being able to take a shower after a hard day's work in the scorching summer heat was a luxury that few local people ever enjoyed, and Papa was repaid many times over when he needed their help!"

He Couldn't Stay Mad for Long

From an Interview with Lou Nichols (2013)

"It was not Papa's nature to stay mad for very long but he was human, and he did get upset from time to time," granddaughter Lou Nichols remembered. "One time, when I was about 8 years old, June and Mae asked him to do something that he didn't want to do. It made him so mad that he lost his temper and walked through the house muttering, 'Them damn women! Them damn women!' He was furious.

"He marched through the house from the front door to the back door and out into the back yard. In those days, there were a few fields and the garden

No matter how angry or upset he might be, Ranger Woody couldn't stay mad for long. Granddaughter Lou Nichols reminisced that sooner or later, that "million dollar" smile would always reappear on his face, and the anger would evaporate. Photo courtesy of Jean McNey.

to one side of the house but everything around the house was heavily wooded (today everything is open) and he quickly disappeared into the nearby woods. He was gone for 20 or 30 minutes, and then he came back inside the house whistling as if nothing had happened. That's how he got rid of his anger.

"Walking in the woods always had a calming effect on him. When he returned, he came in through the back door and walked all the way through the house to the front door, just the opposite of what he had done earlier. He never stopped. He went out the front door and sat down in a chair on the porch."

Charlie Elliott often told a similar story about anger control. "When he (Ranger Woody) was mad or angry, he would usually leave the scene, returning minutes later to say, 'I'm not mad now. I've just been out in God's amazing creation and I can't stay mad for long.' Of course, he was referring to the breathtaking mountain scenery all around.

"Ranger Woody wasn't much at toting a bible," Charlie added. "And he was even worse about quoting it, but he and his maker seemed to have a mutual understanding that served him well throughout his lifetime."

June Woody's Pet Mallards

Ranger Woody was always gracious about allowing friends, neighbors, and even perfect strangers, to fish in Woody Lake behind his house (see Chapter 9). During the winter, ducks often landed on the lake, and he occasionally allowed friends to do some duck hunting as well.

The following story, titled "A Duck Hunt," appeared in the Atlanta Constitution. It was written by well-known sports writer Jack Troy. No date appeared with the story, but it probably was written in 1942 or 1943 because it mentions the war.

A Duck Hunt

By Jack Troy

And there was another time that Woody gave Clint Davis and I permission to shoot ducks on his lake.

Davis and I walked around the edges and slipped up on a flock of ducks in a cove. We had noticed along the way that several wild-appearing mallards swam unconcernedly about, ignoring us completely.

"He was how big?" Iconic Atlanta Constitution sports writer Jack Troy discusses the finer points of fishing with his good friend Ranger Arthur Woody. Jack wrote numerous stories about his friend Ranger Woody during the early 1940s and often fished in Woody Lake. Note what appears to be a fox tail attached to the front of Ranger Woody's Dodge truck. Photo circa 1941, courtesy of Jean McNey.

Well, to make a long story short, we fired away and got a couple of ducks in the cove. We felt pretty happy about it and took them over to Woody's house.

"My Gawd, men," Woody exclaimed. "You've gone and shot two of the old lady's pet mallards. I don't know what she's going to say when she gets back."

(For many weeks Ranger Woody had both men believing they had killed several of June Woody's tame mallards. They avoided going by the house whenever she was at home. Months later Ranger Woody finally confessed that he'd been joking all along.)

Davis and I didn't wait to hear (what June Woody would say). And it wasn't until the next year that we timidly approached the Woody domicile that the sly old ranger admitted he was kidding.

It was good to see official Army photographer, Sgt. Clint Davis, back with us for a spell. He has been away a year, photographing secret stuff in the islands (Pacific). What islands, I am not at liberty to say. Anyway, Clint will be going back soon. He's doing a great job.

Ranger Woody poses in front of the Blue Ridge Ranger Station office in Suches with Clint Davis, a close friend and a highly respected Forest Service photographer who was based in Gainesville before World War II. Judging by Ranger Woody's "spruced up" appearance, the two men were probably filming some type of documentary for the Forest Service. Photo dated May 19, 1940, courtesy of Jean McNey.

(Forest Service photographer Clint Davis was a very special friend to Ranger Woody and his family. During World War II, he served his country well as mentioned above. After the war, he resumed a long and distinguished career with the Forest Service.)

The following undated article probably appeared in a Forest Service publication in the late 1930s while the author was still working in Georgia. As mentioned in Chapter 1, Bill Bergoffen was one of the Ranger's most ardent admirers.

The Ranger's Corner

By W.W. Bill Bergoffen, Forest Ranger
Toccoa District, Chattahoochee National Forest

Praise for a Fellow Ranger

"It is requested that you transfer to the Blue Ridge District to assume duties as assistant to the Ranger." So stated the supervisor's letter to me just two years ago. Little did I realize that there lay ahead of me the most interesting 14 months that I was ever to experience. I am more concerned in this article with the story of that Ranger than with my own activities on his district.

The Blue Ridge Ranger District – some 200,000 acres of National Forest land, representing in part the earliest purchase in Georgia by the government over 20 years ago. There grew up with this National Forest unit the man who is now called affectionately and variously, "Ranger," "Kingfish" and "the Bull of the Woods."

For nearly 20 years the Ranger has administered his district, seen it grow from small scattered parcels of land to a large compact district. His intimate knowledge of his country and his people has helped him to achieve an enviable reputation for fire prevention. Under his supervision there has come into being a large network of forest roads, a well-stocked game area, and many fine forest improvements.

Not always has the Ranger gone about his duties in a modern automobile. It is only recently that he has had the large force of workmen and the CCC to accomplish the many jobs on his district. In earlier days Ranger and his black horse, "Queenie" were inseparable companions as they made their rounds about the district looking out for fire and other trespass. Sometimes he would be gone from the station for a week or two at a time, camping out in lovely, though lonely, forest camps or on some high mountain top far above the land he so carefully supervised. His days stretched out in rapid fashion, month at a time building telephone lines; backbreaking work on forest trails and roads. Through it all Ranger worked among his forest people. Known to have a large warm heart, he was depended upon to help in all manner of crisis. The most interesting of all was the time he was reputed to have aided in bringing a squalling husky baby into the world. All forest neighbors – his people, fish and game even the forest trees and flowers know him as a friend.

As cordial to the humblest farmer, as to many congressmen, this ranger is a democratic individual and a fine forester and a gentleman.

All this I learned during my stay in his district. No wonder, therefore, that I should have enjoyed my fourteen months association with this man. I pay this tribute to a large man of some two hundred forty pounds, and twinkling blue eyes, rosy fat cheeks, and ready whit and humor – my friend Ranger W.A. Woody.

Praises, too for his fine wife, "June," who has helped in no small measure in giving the Ranger his widely known reputation which is his today.

Roscoe Reams and the Ranger's Breadbox

From an Interview with Roscoe Reams (2000)

Roscoe Reams, who is prominently mentioned several times in later chapters, first met Ranger Woody in 1938 when Roscoe was 14 years old. He had come up to Rock Creek Refuge from his home in Atlanta to hunt wild hogs with some older men who loved to hunt and fish in the mountains. Over the next few years, Roscoe and the Ranger became very good friends and the Ranger became a beloved mentor to Roscoe (see Chapter 10). Roscoe became an avid trout fisherman and often stopped by to see the Ranger whenever he was in the area hunting or fishing. As soon as he was old enough to do his patriotic duty (18), Roscoe joined the Navy and was shipped off to the Pacific. Sadly, by the time he returned home after the war ended, Ranger Woody had passed away. Roscoe deeply regretted having been away during the Ranger's memorial service. He and Charlie Elliott were also life-long friends. They hunted and fished together for over 50 years. Roscoe died tragically in an auto accident in 2008 at the age of 84. He had never slowed down from pursuing his passion for hunting and fishing.

"Arthur Woody was widely known for loaning money to neighbors," Roscoe said. "In those days, he sometimes kept cash money in a perforated bread box in his kitchen. I'm sure a lot of people knew about it, but no one in the local community would ever attempt to steal money from Arthur. Most people didn't even have locks on their doors in those days, but if someone had tried to sneak in and steal Ranger Woody's money they probably wouldn't have gotten very far. He would have caught them for sure, and there would be hell to pay. People knew better than to ever try and cross Arthur Woody."

(As mentioned in Chapter 5, Ranger Woody kept a large safe in the basement of his home where he no doubt kept small sums of greenback dollars with which to make loans. He later moved the safe to his office across the road at the Ranger Station. This incident probably took place in the early 1940s after the safe had been moved so it's entirely plausible that some cash was kept in a bread box at home. Also as mentioned in Chapter 5, unbeknownst to Roscoe, a thief did sneak into the Ranger's house one time and stole the Ranger's "britches" containing a sizable amount of cash and his pocket watch. See Chapter 5 for the full story.)

"Anyway, one day while I was visiting the Ranger at his house and we were sitting on the back porch shooting at stumps way out across the lake with an old military rifle he owned. While I was there, a man stopped by to borrow some money. The Ranger went inside the house, opened the bread box, counted out the money and loaned it to the man right then and there. He didn't even have a lock on that bread box.

"He loaned money to people all the time like that," Roscoe continued. "If it was a large amount, he would take out a lien on the person's farm. If they didn't pay him back, he could always foreclose, but he didn't always do that. It depended on the person. With him it was pure business. This was also how he protected his free-roaming deer once the numbers started increasing in the area. He'd tell people, 'You'd better leave those deer alone or else I'll foreclose on you.' Seldom did anyone ever try to shoot one of Arthur's special deer!"

ck deer
the area
set for
will be
number
after a

d by a
by the
October
e public
eceipt of
lications
ve so as
r. Prior
will be
packets
rvice or
eligible
nters is

the still
allowed.
shooting

compart-

Guides—No guides are necessary. The full responsibility for making the hunter's trip a pleasant one lies with the officers on detail,

It is against the law to shoot does.

who will instruct, advise, and cooperate with

dium h
sights,
trigger
shooting
The
pounds,
close p
long w
the fine
ter. Th
Americ
inch se
bored
double

A ne
a clean
tial for
scores.
rugated
bolt, ar
firing i
type sa
rifle.
It ha
one an

Two does in the snow, Blue Ridge WMA, 1940. Courtesy of Outdoor Georgia magazine and the University of Georgia Library.

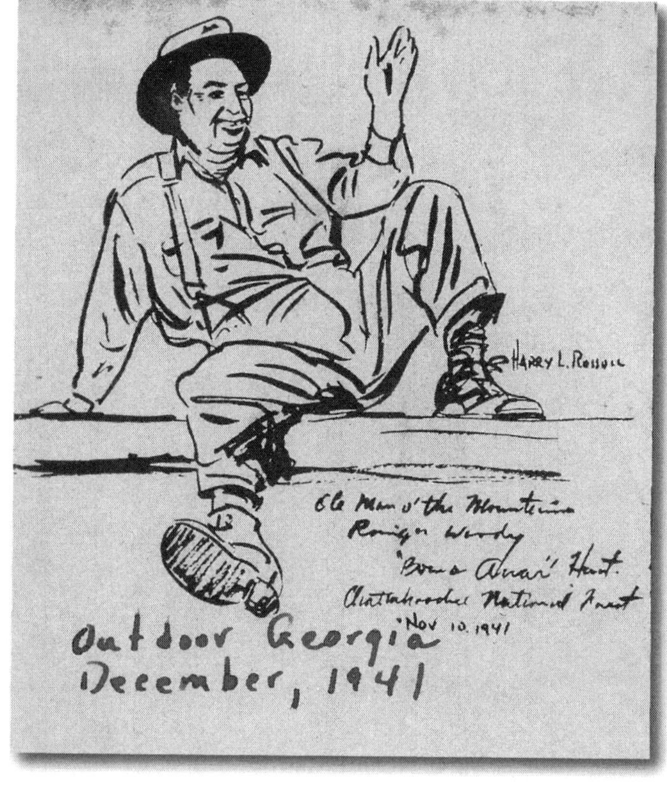

Drawing of Arthur Woody by Harry L. Russell, with handwritten caption: "Ole Man o'the Mountains, Ranger Woody, November 1941. 'Bow & Arrar' Hunt. Chattahoochee National Forest, Nov. 10, 1941," as it appeared in Outdoor Georgia magazine, December 1941. Courtesy of Jean McNey.

SECTION TWO –

A New Era in Forest and Game Management

On Feb. 16, 1925, Ranger Woody negotiated the sale of a unique, 178-acre forest preserve to the U.S. Forest Service. Today known as Sosebee Cove, and originally owned by F. Alonzo Sosebee, the property has long been a true mountain treasure. This remarkable photo of the Ranger and an unidentified man standing at the base of two giant poplars or buckeyes is believed to have been taken in Sosebee Cove in the mid to late 1920s. Photo courtesy of Jean McNey.

CHAPTER 8
30 Years of Visionary Accomplishments and Innovations

"A man's wealth is in his friends, not his money."

Arthur Woody

The "Ranger Woody Regime"

Arthur Woody was a virtual powerhouse of energy and ideas. He never slowed down until failing health forced him to submit to the inevitable at the relatively young age of 61. And even then, he certainly didn't do it willingly. Much was accomplished during the fast-paced decades of the 1920s, '30s and '40s when "Kingfish" ruled the roost in Suches. Because it was a time like none other in the history of conservation, it is little wonder that Ranger Woody's 30-plus-year career with the Forest Service, along with his many years of service to his community, became known as the "Ranger Woody Regime."

Many of his visionary achievements took him into new and uncharted territory. He was a true pioneer who often flew by the seat of his pants. His instincts usually carried him through most situations with flying colors. He never rested on his laurels after some major project was completed. Instead, he immediately forged ahead into the next big project, often working on two or three important enterprises at the same time.

During the years between 1918 and 1945, the pulse of Suches was very much regulated by Ranger Woody and various family members who were always there to support him. Nothing went on in the southern portion of Union County without the Ranger's influence and input. More often than not he had the final word. From road building to church issues, to helping people in need, he literally had his finger in every pie. And like Charlie Elliott often stated, "Almost everyone in the county owed him money at one time or another."

After the Blue Ridge Ranger Station was established across the road from the Woody home place during the late 1920s, a long tradition of feeding Forest Service personnel and visiting dignitaries began in the Woody household. The ever-growing numbers of hard-working Forest Service personnel had to eat, and since there were no eating establishments within many miles of Suches, June and Mae Woody were relegated to perform this vital service. They did it gladly year after year. No doubt it started out on a small scale, but it quickly grew to epic proportions.

The meals fixed by the Woody women weren't simply light snacks designed to tide someone over. They were always full blown country breakfasts or lavish "suppers" made from the finest homegrown ingredients and always made from scratch. Breakfast usually consisted of ham and gravy, bacon and eggs and biscuits and cornbread. Suppers always boasted several kinds of meats – ham, beef, chicken and wild meats like turkey when available – along with multiple platters of homegrown vegetables.

It's likely the Forest Service eventually began to reimburse June Woody for the dozens of meals she and Mae prepared and served during any given month. At times it must have been like feeding a small army. A writer interviewing Ranger Woody once asked, "You can't possibly grow all of the food that you serve in your little garden can you?" "Oh, no," he answered. "We get vegetables like corn, beans and tomatoes by the bushel basket from neighbors all around as well as chickens and eggs and beef and other types of meats."

In many ways the Woody household must have resembled a country inn of yesteryear. Decades later, when prominent restaurants like the nationally famous Smith House in Dahlonega opened its doors, the country-style cooking and mouth-watering platters of food might easily have resembled the delicious spreads that June and Mae routinely prepared.

Ranger Woody served on numerous committees and local boards during those fast-paced years, many of which are lost to time. For instance, in 1939, he served a two-year term on the State Parks Advisory Committee. He no doubt had considerable influence on issues involving at least two local parks built in the area – Vogel State Park and Lake Winfield Scott. During the war years, he apparently served on the local draft board. In the early 1940s, when then

17-year-old Clyde Harkins petitioned him for permission to join the war effort by enlisting in the service, Ranger Woody flatly refused his request by saying, "You already got four brothers who have gone off to war, and I ain't lettin' another Harkins boy put hisself in danger." Clyde had to wait until he was 18 before he could enlist on his own and serve his country.

On Wealth

Ranger Woody has often been described as having been one of the wealthiest men in his community. It certainly didn't start out that way. He came from very meager beginnings and his story is one of the great rags-to-riches stories of the Depression era. In many ways it is astonishing that he was able to prosper during that difficult time period. How did he do it? For one thing, he was a natural trader. "He loved to trade anything," Jean McNey said, "mules, land, guns, and he always liked to think he was getting the better end of the deal."

Ranger Woody was cut from a different cloth. Something in his psyche was different. He had no intention of being a poor farmer all his life. There were much bigger fish to fry. Attaining a reasonable degree of financial security was only part of the equation.

After he started working for the Forest Service in 1912, his primary focus in life quickly turned to the numerous conservation projects that would occupy his time for the remainder of his life; fire prevention, re-establishing and protecting the forests, restocking trout and establishing a deer herd. These important objectives were all-consuming as well as time-consuming passions. He was driven by his passion to see them through to completion.

The evidence suggests that making money was a secondary objective. But make no mistake about it: He was a shrewd and calculating businessman.

Conservation Initiatives and Achievements
A Mountain Paradise, A Vision of What Could Be

What was Ranger Woody's greatest contribution to the conservation effort in the North Georgia mountains during a long and productive career filled with many striking accomplishments? Obviously his work with stocking trout, deer, turkeys and bears into the streams and forests has to be at the top of the list. But the novel idea of making his beloved Rock Creek Refuge into a true wildlife reserve as well as a forest preserve – a place where deer and other wildlife could be restocked, protected and grown in numbers while the forest was being regenerated at the same time – was a concept that he pushed relentlessly with the Forest Service until it finally became a reality. His idea of having a refuge inside the forest preserve eventually evolved into the modern wildlife management area system in Georgia as we know it today. Because of its success, it quickly spread to other states. This may well have been his single greatest contribution to the conservation movement.

When Arthur Woody first went to work for the Forest Service as a lineman on a survey crew, later graduated to the positions of forest guard in 1914, and finally became a full-fledged forest ranger in 1918, the stated mission of the U.S. Forest Service was to re-establish the badly depleted forests in the mountain region. Fire prevention and restoring the forests by growing and protecting trees were the top two single-minded priorities. At the time, there was room for little else. Ranger Woody was fully on board with those important objectives, and he did an exemplary job in both areas, but his vision went far beyond simply growing trees in a protected forest.

Perhaps his almost utopian vision of what the mountains could once again become had been etched in his mind from his personal boyhood experiences and some of the stories he had heard during his younger days. In an article written by Harold Martin which appeared in the Sunday American section of the Atlanta Constitution on June 13, 1937, titled "Forests Coming Back, Georgia Ranger Says," the author quoted Ranger Woody as saying:

> "My granddaddy came here to these mountains from Virginia (by way of North Carolina) nearly a hundred years ago. Built him a cabin and took up farmin', right over yonder in the valley, not more'n hollerin' distance from where old Joe Brown, the wartime Governor (Civil War), growed up farmin' with a bull hitched to his plow.
>
> Granddaddy growed up here and raised his family. When he come here the woods was full of game. The virgin growth was on the hills. Land was rich and timber was plentiful. Bear and deer by the thousands in the woods, turkey and pheasant (ruffed grouse) – all you could shoot.
>
> Then the country got thick settled. Somebody livin' in every cove. Smoke from a cabin in every holler. They killed off the game till there wasn't a deer left, killed off the turkey, killed off the bear.
>
> The loggers come, the big lumber companies bought most of the hill land and the folks moved out of the coves and the hollers. The loggers cut over the woods, cleaned out the woods, took the big timber, butchered the

> woods. Folks with stock burned the timber, thought it 'greened' the woods for better grazin', ruined the timber year after year."

Of course, this article was written nearly two decades after Arthur Woody became a forest ranger, and much had happened to restore the forests during that time. But from his earliest association with the Forest Service, his vision included not only restoring the forests, but also restoring the fish and wildlife that had once been such a prominent part of those forests. Equal in importance, his vision also included allowing people to enjoy those forests filled with fish and game as a form of outdoor recreation the way he had enjoyed them as a boy. In other words, his vision included utilizing the land by its citizens through hunting and fishing, camping, hiking, canoeing, and studying nature the way he had always done.

The idea was simple: The government had acquired all this land and made it into a national forest in which to grow and protect trees for the future. Why not set some of that land aside within the national forest specifically for wildlife as well so that the fish and game species that had been wiped out years earlier could be reintroduced and enjoyed by the hard-working Americans whose tax dollars had paid for the land in the first place? Of course, the land he wanted to set aside for this specific purpose was his beloved Rock Creek Refuge!

In the *History of the Chattahoochee-Oconee National Forest* report written by Rachel G. Schneider, the author makes the following observation:

> The goal to manage timber, wildlife soil and water, and recreation resources in the proper balance was hard to do. Scientific forestry practices were not widely accepted. It was in this setting that rangers Roscoe Nicholson and Arthur Woody came to work for the Forest Service. These men did much to gain the support of forestry practices that nurtured the agency through its infancy.

Through Ranger Woody's stubborn tenacity and constant prodding, and thanks to the heavy involvement of state wildlife officials who shared his vision for a wildlife reserve on federal land, he became the driving force behind the "refuge" or "wildlife management area" system that later developed in Georgia and across the nation. And it all began at the 31,000- acre Rock Creek Refuge (eventually to become 40,000 acres). Rock Creek Refuge (Blue Ridge WMA) was the first of its kind in Georgia and the nation. Due to its success, many more WMAs were established in the mountains and throughout Georgia in the years ahead.

In a November 1972 article written in *Outdoor Life*, titled "The Blue Ridge Hunt," author Charlie Elliott made the following observations:

> That first WMA (Wildlife Management Area) was rugged, primitive wilderness. About the only management that the deer and turkeys received was protection, though a few small feed patches were planted in the forest in later years (by Ranger Woody!).

Both Charlie Elliott and Ranger Woody firmly believed that the "refuge" or wildlife-management-area system was the future of hunting in the South. Fish and animals could be protected and the surplus could be taken by hunters and fishermen. Both men strongly supported opening more WMAs on federal lands in North Georgia during the mid-1930s. In his *1972 Outdoor Life* article Charlie also noted:

> The WMA is one of the big factors in the future of hunting – and possibly much of the fishing. More acreage is being turned over to the state each year for management. A good percentage of this is national forest land and a healthy chunk belongs to the pulp-and-paper and big timber interests, which have found that such an arrangement is one of the best public interest tools they can employ.

Charlie's words, written decades ago, have proven to be very prophetic.

So in addition to working toward protecting and enhancing the forests, Ranger Woody lobbied tirelessly to his Forest Service supervisors to make his vision a reality. He knew in his heart that the mountain region could once again become a sportsman's paradise and he dedicated his life to making that premise a reality.

In the early 1900s, however, few Forest Service officials shared his vision for a forest that could provide multiple uses. During the teens of the 20th century, Forest Service leaders in Washington believed that all national forest lands in Georgia and the southeast should be self-sustaining and managed for maximum timber production and monetary return. While protection from forest fires was also major priority, little thought was given to anything else outside the goal of growing trees for a profit. The idea that the forests could be used for multiple uses in the future – namely enjoying the fish and wildlife resources that lived within those forests, or enjoying the recreational benefits those protected forests could afford the taxpaying Americans who financed them in the first place – was not readily embraced by government officials.

From a political standpoint in Washington D.C., large expenditures of money for land could be justified if the forests eventually became self-sustaining and paid for themselves through timber sales, but there were little, if any, additional monies available to finance any extracurricular activities like the restoration of fish and wildlife resources.

After it had become apparent to Ranger Woody that the Forest Service was either too busy, too preoccupied or too financially strapped with its stated goals to put into motion any of his ideas about fish and wildlife, he did what he always did. He took matters into his own hands. He plowed ahead by stocking trout and deer into the refuge on his own volition with his own money. Later on, of course, after realizing the potential benefits of what he was doing, the Forest Service quickly got on board and began to put resources into the Ranger's various fish and wildlife programs.

In fairness to the Forest Service, it faced a formidable task in preventing fires and protecting the few trees that still remained after the devastation of the early 1900s. Manpower was limited and the Forest Service had to answer to the federal government for every move it made. No one thought beyond the immediate goals of preventing fires and growing trees. No one except Arthur Woody that is! He saw the amazing potential in his mountain forests. Despite the apparent tunnel-vision maintained by his superiors, he plotted and schemed and kept the pressure on. Slowly, he began to see that potential being realized.

Ranger Woody adamantly believed that the forests belonged to all the people, especially those mountain people who lived closest to them. He also believed that the various recreational uses mentioned above should be as much a part of the overall management plan as growing trees. All of these things were close to his heart and he fought hard to get his point across. Through his relentless "prodding," attitudes began to change. His oft spoken quote, "We should look to the forests as a source of good as well as wood," bears proof he knew and understood that in addition to growing trees, his beloved mountain forests could provide numerous benefits to people everywhere.

Much like forest management, wildlife management was in its infancy during the early 1900s. It was pretty much learn as you go, and consisted primarily of putting animals (deer, turkeys and bears as well as trout and other fish in the streams) in the refuge and protecting them so that their numbers would increase. Very little thought went into any type of habitat management specifically aimed at deer and other wildlife. The idea of carrying capacity, that is, the number of deer the area could support without over-browsing and

Today known as the father of forestry in Georgia, Bonnell H. Stone (second from right standing next to Ranger Woody), did much to improve roads in Union County and was instrumental in having the land for Vogel State Park donated to the state by the Pfister & Vogel Land Company of Milwaukee, Wisconsin. Stone served as chief forester for the company's vast land holdings in Georgia. The photo, which includes two unidentified forest workers on the left, was taken during the planning and mapping-out of the Appalachian Trail across Georgia, a project in which Ranger Woody was heavily involved. From its inception, Ranger Woody was a dedicated proponent of the trail and did everything he could to see that it was built across his ranger district. Charlie Elliott (not pictured), also did much of the on-site legwork. Photo circa 1929, courtesy of Jean McNey.

damaging the range, was still years away. But wildlife experts learned quickly and many improvements and innovations were made along the way. Even Ranger Woody knew and understood that a certain number of deer would ultimately have to be taken out of the refuge through controlled hunting each year in order to keep the herd at a healthy level. Interestingly, the first signs of over-browsing were not seen in the Blue Ridge WMA until 1949, three years after Ranger Woody's death. That year, an effort was made to reduce the deer herd by allowing some does to be taken for the first time.

Conservation Initiatives and Achievements:

Arthur Woody's most important achievements in conservation are listed in chronological order below.

1912-1940 –
Purchasing Land on Behalf of the Forest Service

Ranger Woody assisted the Forest Service in acquiring many thousands of acres of abandoned and cutover mountain land to be placed into the national forest system and reclaimed. In many cases, he paid for the land himself in cash and was later reimbursed by the Forest Service. By doing this, he was able to acquire key pieces of land for the government that might never have been acquired otherwise.

1912-1945 –
Exemplary Record in Fire Prevention

Ranger Woody accrued an exemplary record in fire prevention and restoration and management of mountain forests. He helped design and built at least three local fire towers 1) Rocky Mountain, built in early 1920s just north of Suches with materials sledded in by horse teams; 2) Black Mountain (just east of Suches), believed to have been constructed in the mid 1920s, and 3) designed the Bald Mountain fire tower (at Brasstown Bald) and had it built by his ever-dependable "CC" boys. He planted tens of thousands of trees through the willing CCC labor force drawn from several CCC camps in the area. He worked tirelessly on disease control, and executed numerous forest improvement plans by taking out undesirable or burned over trees and opening up the forest for new growth, ultimately benefiting thousands of acres of mountain forestland.

1918 –
Ranger Woody's Trout Program

By his own initiative, the Ranger ordered a shipment of rainbow trout from a fish hatchery in Denver, Colorado, and picked them up at the train station in Gainesville, Georgia. He and his son Clyne delivered them by wagon to the mountains and introduced them to Rock Creek and other streams in his forest reserve. Later on he ordered many more shipments of rainbow trout from Colorado as well as brown trout from Washington State. Both species were introduced in dozens of mountain streams. He improved the native brook trout habitat and restocked brook trout in numerous areas where they had been fished out.

Realizing the need to raise hundreds, if not thousands of fingerling trout, Ranger Woody experimented with building several small trout-rearing pools at Woody Lake behind his house. Later he built larger rearing pools at Rock Creek Lake inside the Rock Creek Refuge. Those original trout-rearing pools were eventually taken over and managed by the Forest Service. A much larger trout-raising facility was constructed on Rock Creek by the U.S. Forest Service in 1937. The hatchery remained under Forest Service authority for 23 years. On April 13, 1960, a cooperative agreement was signed that transferred ownership and management to the U.S. Fish and Wildlife Service, which still runs the facility today. The hatchery became known as the Chattahoochee Forest National Fish Hatchery on Rock Creek. The primary responsibility of the Chattahoochee Forest National Fish Hatchery today is to raise rainbow trout, but it also raises some brook and brown trout which are stocked throughout the region. (See Chapter 9, A Monumental Fish Story.)

Early 1920s, 1930s –

Ranger Woody lobbied and worked tirelessly to have Rock Creek Refuge made into a fish and wildlife sanctuary that ultimately would become the first wildlife management area in the state of Georgia, as well as the model for similar WMAs in many other states across the nation.

1925 –
Sosebee Cove, Preserving a Natural Treasure

Although it was only about 178 acres, Ranger Woody knew the small tract of land known as Sosebee Cove just off of Wolf Pen Gap Road was a one-of-a kind treasure. He often rode one of his favorite horses through the tall poplars, buckeyes and other large second-growth trees on the property belonging to old Mr. Sosebee, and he was quick to take note of its natural splendor. At the time, the road was not much more than a wagon trail, but eventually it was improved into a passable road for automobiles. Later still, it became Highway 180, running north-easterly from Highway 60 in Suches to the Gainesville Highway (Highway 129) at Vogel State Park.

The Sosebee property dropped off the main road into a beautiful bottom or cove. In the spring and fall it was alive with nearly every variety of wildflower found in North Georgia. With its wealth of timber and other natural wonders, the Ranger knew this property was unique to the mountains. He urged the Forest Service to buy the tract; not to be cut, but to be kept it in its pristine state as a natural preserve. Parts of the tract had been cut around the turn of the century, but its timber value was still substantial.

On Feb. 16, 1925, 41-year-old Ranger Woody successfully negotiated a sale between the property's owner F. Alonzo Sosebee and the Forest Service for the unheard of price of $10 per acre. At the time, that was one of the highest prices ever paid for mountain land in Georgia. (Today, of course, we know that was a bargain!) Sosebee Cove was said to contain one of the best stands of yellow poplar in the state. Only a few years later the timber value was estimated to be worth many times the price paid for the land. In the mid-1960s the timber value was estimated to be around $2,000 per acre, or just over $350,000, quite an increase over the mere $1,780 purchase price.

Because of the part he played in purchasing the property and his deep reverence for this land, Sosebee Cove was made into a memorial after the Ranger's death (Sosebee Cove Scenic Area) and the hiking trail that loops through the forest was named in the Ranger's honor. As mentioned in several guide books, the numerous trees and plants found within the confines of the preserve make this spot a botanist's dream. According to Don Pfitzer, author of *Hiking Georgia,* one massive buckeye tree at the beginning of the trail is 17 feet in diameter (and one of the largest recorded buckeyes in the state).

1927 – to Present
Ranger Woody's Deer Program

Ranger Woody began his legendary program to reintroduce deer to the North Georgia mountains by initially purchasing five fawns from the Pisgah Game reserve in North Carolina for the sum of $100. He also worked tirelessly to manage and improve wild turkey population through hatching eggs, protecting young poults and placing dozens of young turkeys inside the refuge. Although these methods often failed for the most part, he also protected the few wild flocks that remained in the area, and this vigorous protection proved to be the best way of increasing turkey numbers. Likewise, he vehemently protected the small black bear population and released bear cubs in Rock Creek Refuge on a number of occasions. He stocked bob white quail in Rock Creek Refuge as well. (See Chapter 10 for more on this work.)

1929 – History in the Making
Ranger Woody's Appalachian Trail Initiative in Georgia

During the early 1920s, the idea for a trail following much of the Appalachian chain was proposed by Benton MacKaye, a Pennsylvania forester. The idea was later expanded to build a trail from Maine to Georgia. In 1925, the Appalachian Trail Conservancy (ATC) was formed to advance the idea in all states that would be affected. Four years later in 1929, the ATC contacted Ranger Arthur Woody to seek his advice on building the Georgia portion of the trail. From the outset, the Ranger was highly supportive of the idea. At the time, however, the proposed map-drawn route included only a 20-mile section of the trail in Georgia which ended in the Cohutta Mountains just south of Chattanooga.

Ranger Woody and others believed the trail should have a much larger presence in Georgia and that it should traverse several of the more scenic portions of his ranger district. With his vision of a mountain paradise that could be utilized by people from all walks of life for hunting, fishing, camping and hiking, he threw himself into the project full bore. When the question came up about the best possible route through Georgia, Ranger Woody recommended his friend Roy Ozmer, a well-known outdoorsman and somewhat eccentric woodsman who, in later years, became the infamous "Hermit of Pelican Key" in the Everglades of southern Florida. Ozmer was hired by the ATC on Ranger Woody's recommendation to scout out the best potential route for the trail. In 1929, he walked from Georgia to Virginia seeking the most beneficial route.

Everett "Eddie" Stone, who served as Assistant State Forester in Georgia, was also a friend to Ranger Woody. When he heard about the proposed trail, he joined forces with Ozmer and mapped out an alternate route that would begin at Mt. Oglethorpe (in Pickens County near Jasper) and run in a northeasterly direction across Ranger Woody's Rock Creek Refuge into the Nantahala Mountains in North Carolina. This alternate route would span some 79 miles of rugged terrain in Georgia and cross over imposing and historic areas like Springer, Blood, and Tray mountains into North Carolina. All three men heartily supported this alternate route.

With considerable opposition to his plan, due mainly to the proposed location of where his route would enter North Carolina, Stone solicited the help of the ever-reliable and good-natured Charlie Elliott, then serving as Assistant District Forester for the state of Georgia, to aid in clearing and marking his proposed route.

History in the Making
The Building of the Appalachian Trail

Note: It is very likely that Charlie Elliott took most of these photos.

Arthur Woody poses with his friend Roy Ozmer, a well-known outdoorsman and jack-of-all-trades, after a day of notching trees for the proposed Appalachian Trail across Blood Mountain in 1929. Upon Ranger Woody's recommendation, Ozmer was hired by the Appalachian Trail Conservancy to scout out the best route for the trail across the North Georgia mountains. In 1929, Ozmer walked from Georgia to Virginia looking for the best route. He received the help of E.B. "Eddie" Stone, assistant state forester in Georgia. Stone in turn solicited the help of Charlie Elliott, another assistant state forester, who ended up doing much of the legwork in laying out and marking that portion of the trail across Blood Mountain from Neels Gap to Woody Gap. Photo courtesy of Jean McNey.

Serving as assistant district forester with the Georgia Forestry Department, Charlie Elliott (left), then about 23, poses with assistant state forester Everett "Eddie" Stone (right) on Blood Mountain. Stone recruited the personable young forester to solicit a small army of volunteers to help mark and maintain the proposed footpath through Georgia. According to Charlie, at the beginning of the project, Stone dragged him out of bed and carried him through the black skies and howling winds "to places where not even the gods would be caught on a day like that." As expected, Charlie did an outstanding job promoting the trail and soliciting a small army of dedicated volunteers. Photo circa 1930, courtesy of the Charlie Elliott Wildlife Center.

With his ever-present pipe in his mouth, Charlie Elliott poses with a group of hearty volunteers who helped mark the trail in 1931. "(Eddie) Stone said to me, 'I want you to organize the Georgia Appalachian Trail Club.' Just like that. Just like I could go out into the street and round up 50 people who would walk with me up the summit of a mountain. Most of the folks I knew had never even seen a mountain."

A hard-working group of Forest Service workers put some serious sweat equity into the historic wilderness trail across Blood Mountain. Photo circa early 1930s, courtesy of the Charlie Elliott Wildlife Center.

Carving a foot path across the rugged and steep terrain of Blood Mountain was a formidable job. Photo circa early 1930s, courtesy of the Charlie Elliott Wildlife Center.

Two unidentified workers prepare to place a "Blood Mountain" directional sign along the Appalachian Trail near a creek crossing. Photo circa early 1930s, courtesy of the Charlie Elliott Wildlife Center.

Ranger Arthur Woody (center), Roy Ozmer (right), and an unidentified man (left), take a break from exploring the best route across Blood Mountain for the historic, soon-to-be Appalachian Trail foot path. Ten years after Ranger Woody's death in 1946, Ozmer made a name for himself as the well-known "Hermit of Pelican Key" in the Everglades. Photo circa 1929, courtesy of the Charlie Elliott Wildlife Center.

A stretch of the completed foot path across Blood Mountain. Photo circa 1930, courtesy of the Charlie Elliott Wildlife Center.

In an effort to stem some of the opposition, Charlie organized a group of Boy Scouts to hike the proposed trail across North Georgia and end up at Mt. Oglethorpe on the very day in which a monument was being dedicated to General Oglethorpe, Georgia's founder. The publicity stunt worked and Stone eventually persuaded his detractors to approve his route for the trail. The trail across Georgia was completed by the end of 1931.

Charlie Elliott was given the task of setting up a network of volunteers from local hiking clubs in Gainesville and other nearby areas to help with much of the work that took place on that portion of the trail traversing Blood and Black mountains. At first it was a daunting job, but he eventually recruited several volunteer groups, including numerous dedicated women, who worked tirelessly with the Forest Service to maintain the trail, help build shelters and put out markers and signs.

With the arrival of the CCC boys at Camp Woody in Suches in 1933, as well as several other camps in the area camps near present-day Vogel State Park and Unicoi State Park, this formidable new labor force also did much to improve and maintain the trail in Georgia under the direction of Ranger Woody and the Forest Service. Thanks to the skills of those dedicated "CC" boys, the famous two-room rock shelter on Blood Mountain, built in 1937, proudly stands today as a monument to those hard-working individuals. Being the oldest shelter on the trail, it is also the only walk-through structure on the entire trail.

1930s –
Trying to Save the Chestnut Trees

During the late 1920s and early '30s, when countless thousands of chestnut trees were dying in North Georgia from the great chestnut blight, Ranger Woody experimented with planting chestnut saplings. Little is known about how many trees he planted or how he went about this enterprise because the trees obviously did not survive. The great chestnut blight wiped out tens of millions of chestnut trees up and down the Appalachian chain. After many of the trees had died, Ranger Woody embarked on a program to salvage the wood for a variety of uses.

1933 -1941 –
Roosevelt's Tree Army Invades Suches

Ranger Woody quickly realized the value of the Civilian Conservation Corps when Camp Woody and several other camps in the area were established in 1933. He promptly arranged for son Walter to become the civilian supervisor at Camp Woody. Two years later in 1935, Ranger Woody was also instrumental in having Reverend Claud Boynton appointed to the duel position of camp chaplain and one of the work supervisors. This was during the height of the Depression, and both men sorely needed the extra income they received to support their families.

With the arrival of the "CC" boys in Suches and other mountain camps, a new day was dawning in the North Georgia mountains. Reverend Boynton led his eager young men in all facets of their work; building and improving roads and trails, crushing rock, and spreading tons of gravel over some of the newly improved roads that were previously impassable whenever it rained; working on erosion control, planting tens of thousands of trees on burned-over acres, fighting forest fires and in some cases helping to catch arsonists, stringing miles of telephone wire across the mountains and working diligently to try to control disease and insect infestation in forest trees. Ranger Woody exerted great influence over which projects would become priorities, and he was always heavily involved in all of the CC's many forest-related enterprises.

With the help of such a willing and strong army of young men who apparently worked well under the direction of son Walter, Rev. Boynton and various other leaders, the CC boys also built three lakes in the area, improved the Ranger Station in Suches, built amenities in Vogel State Park and Lake Winfield Scott (campgrounds, beaches, and rock grills still in use today), and helped improve that portion of the Appalachian Trail that spans Union County as mentioned. Oftentimes, boys from several local camps including Camp Enotah near Blairsville and Camp Robertstown near Helen would work together on important projects. As discussed in Chapter 6, the CC boys built at least three fire towers in the area, including a new rock structure at Brasstown Bald. They also stocked thousands of trout in dozens of local mountain streams, and improved the habitat in many of those streams by building fish pools and small rock dams.

Two views of the sprawling CCC Camp Woody, F-1, home of CCC Co. 1404, May 1936, Suches, Georgia. Photo courtesy of Bud Braddock, U.S. Forest Service retired.

Community Initiatives and Achievements:

According to the Ranger's granddaughter Lou Nichols, "Papa was always very community oriented. He wanted the local people to be able to enjoy some of the modern conveniences and inventions that improved mountain life; things like electricity, indoor plumbing and telephones. He shared everything he had and got great pleasure in doing things for other people like letting them fish in his lake. He believed that local mountain residents should always have first dibs at hunting, fishing or enjoying federal land."

Ranger Woody's most important community achievements are listed in chronological order below.

Late 1920s –

Ranger Woody was committed to seeing that a new road was built from Stonepile Gap to Suches. He and son Walter were heavily involved in the project. Later, when the CC boys appeared on the scene, he was deeply involved in building and improving a number of other roads in the area.

1930s –
Ranger Woody the Lake Builder

Ranger Woody was involved in building four historic lakes in the Suches area.
Woody Lake – originally 80 acres, constructed near his home around 1933.
Dockery Lake – 5 acres, constructed in the mid-1930s.
Lake Winfield Scott – 22 acres, constructed in the late 1930s.
Lake Trahlyta – 20 acres, constructed inside Vogel State Park in 1937.

Woody Lake

"Woody Lake was built in early 1930s with the help of the C.C. boys," Jean McNey remembered. "Papa decided to build the lake since he knew a ready work force was available. At the time, a creek ran through the property but much of the land was a bog. There were lots of swampy areas that couldn't be used for anything else, so building a lake made a lot of sense. Papa figured out where the dam should go over a natural spillway of granite where a beautiful waterfall had once cascaded over the rocks."

Heavy veins of granite criss-crossed the area. During the 1930s, Ranger Woody operated a quarry near his home from which CC workers crushed the granite rock and spread it over many of the local roads in the area. (Since most of the early roads were muddy wagon trails, graveling these roads with a solid rock base greatly improved automobile access and mobility in the area.)

"Papa built up both sides of the waterfall with heavy rock and made a beautiful 80-acre lake. He stocked it with bass, bream and trout. The lake was unusually fertile and within a few years it was producing some enormous bass in the 10- to 14-pound range."

Sadly, Woody Lake has been greatly reduced in size in recent years because of heavy siltation. "We've been told that there's not much we can do about it," Jean said in 2013. "Because the lake has a natural rock dam, it can't really be drained. And it would be very expensive to try to dredge it out. And even if we tried to do that, I've been told that might become a 'wetlands issue" with the state and the EPA.

"Papa always wanted the local residents to have access to all of the fishing lakes in the area, and people from near and far were always welcome to fish in Woody Lake. All they had to do was ask. Of course, he loved to fish and

State of Georgia

DEPARTMENT OF NATURAL RESOURCES

Division of State Parks Historic Sites and Monuments

Know all by these presents that Arthur Woody

has been duly appointed a member of the Vogel

State Park Advisory Committee

Committee, to serve for a period of two years from the date of this appointment.

This 2 day of August, 1939

Approved by: Ed Rivers
Governor.

E. L. Bothwell
Director, Division of State Parks, Historic Sites and Monuments.

Ranger Arthur Woody was heavily involved in the planning and building of Vogel State Park and Lake Winfield Scott. This State Parks Advisory Board Certificate was issued to the Ranger in 1939 while his good friend E.D. "Ed" Rivers served as governor. Certificate courtesy of Jean McNey.

swim in the lake himself. He felt the same way about hunting in the woods. If someone needed a deer for food, he thought they ought to be able to shoot one; or catch a fish in any lake for food. Knowing that local people would eventually have to pay fees to hunt and fish in the mountains (as they do today) would have greatly upset him."

Today, Woody Lake is a well-known landmark in Suches. People still occasionally knock on Jean's door and ask for permission to fish, although the fishing is not as good as it once was during its "golden" days. Jean can remember ice skating on the lake as a young girl during several particularly frigid winters. (For more on fishing in Woody Lake, see Chapter 9, A Monumental Fish Story.)

Dockery Lake

In all likelihood Ranger Woody initiated the construction of Dockery Lake as a flood control measure. The lake was named for Andrew John Dockery, a homesteader who had come to the area in the 1850s. Situated on small tributary to Waters Creek, the 5- to 6-acre lake was built by a CC crew in the mid-1930s according to specifications that Ranger Woody reportedly drew up on his kitchen table. Reportedly, when Forest Service engineers found out he had authorized the construction of the lake without their approval or technical advice, they were said to have been furious. Upon examining the finished product, they insisted the dam would never hold up.

"The first time we have some heavy rains and a little flooding that dam will wash away," the officials reportedly maintained.

Following federal guidelines, those same engineers later built two more flood-control lakes farther downstream from Dockery Lake on Waters Creek. A year or so later, heavy rains washed away both government dams. Ranger Woody's dam held like the Rock of Gibraltar, never faltering. It still stands proud and strong, although it has been strengthened over the years!

Today the lake is a popular destination and Dockery Lake Recreational Area offers camping, hiking, picnicking and fishing for trout (the lake is stocked with trout). Hikers can enjoy the 3.4-mile Dockery Lake Trail, which provides access to the nearby Appalachian Trail.

Lake Winfield Scott, 1942 –

Lake Winfield Scott is an 18-acre lake located just north of Suches at the headwaters of Cooper Creek in the shadow of Blood Mountain, where a historic battle to the death between Creek and Cherokee Indians was said to have been fought. The pristine mountain lake was built by the CCC under the direction of Ranger Woody and the Forest Service in the late 1930s. It was completed in 1942. It was the last project in Georgia, and one of the last in the nation, before the CCC was disbanded due to the U.S. entering World War II. The high-mountain lake is stocked with trout and other species and surrounded by breathtaking mountain scenery.

A trail circles the lake giving anglers easy access to most good fishing spots. The Appalachian Trail runs nearby across Blood Mountain, and two trails that start at the lake eventually join up with the main trail. During the lake's construction, CC workers put sand on the beach and built rock grills and other rock structures that remain strong and sturdy to this day. Clyde Harkins worked on several of the rock projects in 1940. (See Chapter 10, A Voice From the Past.)

The lake was named after legendary General Winfield Scott. Known as "Old Fuss and Feathers," General Scott was responsible for removing the Cherokees from the area in 1838 and pushing them westward on the "Trail of Tears." He was the hero of the war with Mexico a few years later during the 1840s. As the ranking Union general in 1861, he was placed in charge of all Union forces for a short time at the outset of the Civil War.

Ranger Woody must have been deeply proud of the part he played in the construction of Lake Winfield Scott because of what it represented. By the late 1930s, thanks in part to the Ranger's relentless pressure, the Forest Service had revised and expanded its original goal of growing trees for profit to utilizing the national forest for "the greatest good for the greatest number of people." This new-found, "multiple-use" philosophy was something Ranger Woody had been promoting for nearly 20 years. It no doubt came about in part as a result of his farsighted vision and influence.

Lake Trahlyta

Lake Trahlyta, a beautiful 20-acre mountain lake located in Vogel State Park, was created in 1937 when the CC boys dammed up Wolf Creek. The lake was named for a Cherokee maiden who according to legend is buried a few miles from the park at Stonepile Gap. The 233-acre tract that makes up Vogel State Park was donated to the state by the Pfister &Vogel Leather Company of Milwaukee, Wisconsin, in 1927. Vogel State Park was Georgia's second state park and today is one of the oldest state parks in the nation. In addition to building the dam, CC workers also built cabins, picnic areas, and camping areas within the park. A museum inside the park is dedicated to the various Civilian Conservation Corps camps in the area and its enduring legacy.

As director of Georgia's newly organized Parks Department in 1937, Charlie Elliott, along with his good friend Ranger Arthur Woody, had considerable involvement and input in the building of the park and the lake. In addition to laying out some portion of the nearby Appalachian Trail on Blood Mountain, Charlie also helped lay out some of the trails within the park.

Rock monument with bronze plaque built by the CCC boys at Vogel State Forest Park. In part, the plaque reads: Dedicated to Fred Vogel Jr. and August H. Vogel, President and Vice-President of the Pfister & Vogel Leather Co., Milwaukee, Wisconsin. Much of the park was built by the CCC boys from several local camps during the early 1930s. Photo circa mid-1930s, courtesy of the Charlie Elliott Wildlife Center.

Ranger Woody the Road Builder

Nothing had more impact on improving the poor mountain roads in the mountain region than the arrival of the CCC work force in 1933. But Ranger Woody had been working on various road improvement programs long before the CC boys put their muscle into the effort, and a gargantuan effort it proved to be. The Ranger's primary motivation for building and improving roads in the area was to help his people jump into the 20th century. To give an idea of just how poor the roads were in the early 1920s, the following except from an old newspaper clipping describes in detail what mountaineers faced on a daily basis. The column had no date and no publication name, but it was believed to have run in the Atlanta Constitution in the late 1940s:

> Woody was born and reared in what was formerly known as "Canada" or the "Canada District," the valley in which he was reared on the north side of the mountain. When the Chattahoochee National Forest was organized, the ranger station was built near Arthur's home and it is still from that point that forest rangers work out. "Canada" valley was formerly reached from the south side of the mountains (from Dahlonega) through Grassy and Cooper's Gaps, over rough roads that would try men's souls. (Before Woody had his CCC boys build the new road across Woody Gap.) The old mountaineers, to whom time meant but little, "spelled" their way, meaning pull awhile and rest awhile to give their (horse or mule) teams a breathing or resting spell, up and down them. Later, the Model T Ford came along and it was something of a job to negotiate the mountain gaps with it. It also had to "spell" its way across in that it would run a while and get hot, then you would have to fill your radiator with an extra supply of water with which you started from the bottom and let your engine cool off. Sometimes, it would take half a dozen tries before you got to the top, and then after much pushing besides. But this is a thing of the past now for not only Woody's (Gap), but Neal's (Gap) and Unicoi (Gap), as well as all other major gaps, are negotiated in high gear over other hard-surfaced or semi-hard-surfaced roads. (Note: spelling and punctuation as originally appeared in article. "Woody" Gap has no 's'; Neel or Neels Gap has no 'a'.')

It was a well-known fact that roads leading out of Suches were steep and impassible if it rained. Horses and wagons could usually work their way through the mud after expending considerable effort, but when automobiles came along, they frequently got hopelessly stuck. Ironically, they often had to be pulled out by the very horses or mules they had replaced. Jean McNey remembered that, "Before the road from Suches to Woody Gap was built, that portion of the road in front of our house (later to become Highway 60) was not much more than a wagon trail."

Prior to the new road being built, the trip from Dahlonega to Suches was challenging at best. Flat tires were common and had to be patched on the spot with pieces of rubber and glue. Brakes frequently rusted out after numerous creek crossings. Many were the stories about cars having to go up steep hills backwards to get better traction and having to stop often to let the radiators cool down and to fill radiators with water. When trying to negotiate steep downhill grades, drivers often tied a section of tree trunk to the back bumper of their car in order to slow the vehicle down and help save the brakes.

The legendary story about the road that Arthur Woody built told many times over the years by Charlie Elliott and others goes something like this: Knowing what a difficult time people had trying to get from Suches to Dahlonega (Dahlonega was the closest town to Suches where people could buy the goods they needed), Ranger Woody asked the appropriate governmental authorities (not clear which agency; department of transportation possibly) to build a new road in a westerly direction from Stonepile Gap up the side of Black Mountain and across Woody Gap into Wolf Pen Gap Road in Suches so that the people living in the area could reach Dahlonega more easily. In all, the distance from Stonepile Gap to Suches was about 8 miles, but it covered some incredibly rugged and steep terrain.

At that time, a reasonably good road led from Dahlonega up past Stonepile Gap all the way to what eventually would become Charlie Turner's Corner at its intersection with Highway 19-129 leading northward to Blairsville. So it made sense to Ranger Woody to build an 8-mile stretch of road from Stonepile Gap up to Suches so that access to Dahlonega would be greatly improved. However, the response the Ranger got from public roads officials was that the state did not build roads; it only improved them. Undaunted and in his typical "do what needs to be done and ask for permission later" fashion, the Ranger said, "Okay, I'll build the dern road myself!"

Apparently the road from Stonepile Gap across Woody Gap and down into Suches was built in two segments by two different work crews. According to her excellent book, *I Remember Dahlonega,* author Anne Dismukes Amerson states that Henry Moore of Dahlonega was contracted to build the segment from Stonepile Gap to Woody Gap. It is not known what Arthur Woody's involvement was, if any, in that portion of the road. However, Ranger Woody was heavily involved in building the short, but very steep segment, from Woody

Gap to Suches because his son Walter was contracted to have the road built (almost certainly at the Ranger's direction). In her book, Anne Amerson quotes Herman Caldwell as saying he thought construction on the road got underway around 1926:

> I was 17 when work was started on the Woody Gap Road. Walter Woody had contracted to build the road from Suches to Woody Gap, and I asked for a job, but he wouldn't pay me but $1.50 a day because I was so young. Then I went to Henry Moore, who was contractor for the road from Stonepile Gap to Woody Gap, and asked him for work. He wanted to know how old I was. "Herman, you're pretty small," he said, "but I know the Caldwells, and they're good workers. Can you roll a wheelbarrow and handle a pick and shovel?" I told him I could. "Well, then, I'll pay you $2.00 a day like the rest of the men," he said.

Herman goes on to talk about how well he was treated by Henry Moore. Then he described some of the working conditions:

> We didn't have any power saws, so trees had to be cut down by a crosscut saw with a man on either end. The stumps had to be dynamited. We dug up little trees with picks and shovels. A man operating a panscraper pulled by two mules would scrape up the dirt and drop it below the road.
>
> We had to watch out for mountain rattlesnakes. They're not lazy like diamondbacks, but will throw their tails up and go to singing, ready to get you if you get close to them.
>
> After the road was finished, the state put in a crusher, and the road was graveled with rock that came from a quarry about halfway up the mountain. (In all likelihood, the gravel was put down by the CCC boys after their arrival in 1933.)
>
> ...Working on the road was hard work, but I hated to see it come to an end. ...We had fun joking and working together as we made a road out of wilderness.

And make a road out of wilderness they did! At the other end of the road higher up the mountain in Suches, the Woody father-and-son team did very much the same thing. They collected some primitive scraping equipment, several teams of mules from local farmers and a crew of able-bodied men with axes and shovels and forged their way up the mountain to Woody Gap. Ranger's Woody's primitive engineering of the road was nothing short of amazing as the much-improved Highway 60 that it ultimately became still follows the original road route today.

The project reportedly took just over a year to complete. The exact dates of construction are somewhat sketchy, but Herman Caldwell's recollection of 1926 as being the starting date is probably accurate. Prior to that time, the shortest way to get to Suches from Dahlonega was by way of Grassy Gap Road as mentioned, a very steep and difficult road to negotiate just south of Suches often described as "having a lot of steep hills that were straight up and down."

Both segments of the road were no doubt funded by the state of Georgia, but Ranger Woody probably paid some of the expenses out of his own pocket for which he might have been reimbursed later on. Legend tells us that as soon as the primitive road was completed after many months of hard work, the Ranger contacted the appropriate governmental authority down at the state capitol and said, "Now here's your road; come and improve it!"

Eventually the road was improved by the state. With help from the CC boys in the mid 1930s, a layer of crushed gravel was placed over the often muddy and rutted dirt surface. Jean McNey remembered that it was finally "blacktopped" over Woody Gap around the time she graduated from Emory University in 1949. Today known as Highway 60, the road built by the Woody father and son team crosses Woody Gap at its intersection with the Appalachian Trail. It continues down Black Mountain into Suches, where it meets Highway 180 that runs northeast to Lake Winfield Scott and Vogel State Park.

"While the road was being laid out in front of our house, Papa liked to tell the story about a local man who came looking for work one day," Jean said. "This man was known for two things: having a somewhat theatrical way of talking and having an aversion for any kind of real work (although he liked to tell people about how hard he worked). He approached Ranger Woody one day while the crew was clearing brush and scraping the roadway and asked for a job. The Ranger pointed over to a stack of tools and said, 'Grab you a shovel and start a'diggin.'

"The man looked at Ranger Woody and in his theatrical style said, 'Oh, no Ranger. What I had in mind was a boss's job like yours. I want to be able to tell the men, 'Men, turn them shovels to the sun just like you do, Ranger!'

"Papa apparently made it clear to the man that if he wanted to work he would have to get his hands dirty like all of the other men," Jean said. "I don't remember what the end result was, but I suspect the man wasn't really interested in working so he probably went on his way."

After the road was completed, a well-earned celebration took place in Suches for all the men who had worked on it. Jean remembered that her grandfather went out and shot several wild turkeys for the feast. Although turkey numbers in the area had gotten relatively low by that time, Ranger Woody protected the small population that remained and he always knew where to find a few of the resident flocks if he needed one or two birds for an occasion such as this. Once again, thanks to the culinary skills and hard work of June, daughter Mae and Ma Woody, the men feasted in style on wild turkey and other prepared foods. They no doubt enjoyed a few toasts with a little mountain nectar as well.

The crew building that portion of the road from Stonepile Gap to Woody Gap also had a celebration in Suches when that stretch of the road was completed, but it is not clear if two separate celebrations took place or if one combined celebration was held for both work crews.

Other Important Community Initiatives

Mid 1920s –
The Suches Blue Ridge Ranger Station

Upon becoming a Forest Ranger in 1918, Arthur Woody built a tiny 6x8-foot building about the size of a children's playhouse in the front yard of his home to serve as his official Ranger Station and office. Ever the loyal patriot, he made sure an American flag hung proudly on a flagpole next to the tiny building. He and his ever-expanding number of assistants and technicians quickly outgrew this tiny structure. Knowing that he wanted to have an office close by, Ranger Woody donated about 6 acres of land directly across the road from the Woody home place to the Forest Service for the site of the new Ranger Station. The Forest Service actually paid him one dollar for the deeded land. Years later, when the Ranger Station was shut down and relocated closer to Blairsville, the land was deeded back to Ranger Woody's son Walter.

Reportedly, the first structure built on that land was a house intended for an assistant ranger from North Carolina that Ranger Woody wanted to hire. William Huber had been an assistant ranger working in the Pisgah National Forest during the 1920s. Having apparently been very successful at catching arsonists, he was sent down to Suches to help Ranger Woody solve a particularly perplexing problem involving a local firebug. The arsonist was quickly apprehended and Ranger Woody was so impressed with the young man's ability that he offered him a job working in Suches as his personal assistant. The question came up about housing, and Ranger Woody committed to building the assistant ranger a splendid house on property he owned just across the old road from his own house.

A beautiful two-story house was built on the property using the finest woods found in the forest; cherry, poplar and oak. Most of the rooms were paneled in chestnut, probably salvaged from dead or dying trees during the great chestnut blight of the 1920s. Much to the Ranger's disappointment, however, the transfer never went through. A few years later, Ranger Woody donated the land, house and all, to the Forest Service. The house was made into an official office for Forest Service personnel and a number of large outbuildings and garages were erected on the property. (See Chapter 7 for detailed photos of the Ranger Station.)

Ranger Woody maintained his office at the Ranger Station right up to his retirement in 1945. Today, the original house and outbuildings are still standing. The house is in excellent shape, having been rented from time to time over the years, but the outbuildings are beginning to show signs of age and are in need of renovation.

Early 1930s
The Great Depression

Ranger Woody willingly loaned money to Union County School Board during the height of the Depression so that the teachers would continue to receive badly needed paychecks. The money was later paid back without interest.

Mid 1930s
Enticing a New Preacher to Stay in Suches

After hearing him deliver a guest sermon that was very much to his liking, Ranger Woody offered to build a house for Reverend Claud Boynton of Macon, Georgia, to entice him to stay in Union County and serve the people of the mountains. Rev. Boynton accepted the Ranger's offer, and ultimately became a much loved and highly respected community leader and ultimately a legend in his own time. As mentioned, Ranger Woody also arranged for Rev. Boynton to get a supervisor's position with the CCC in Suches during the Depression years so that he would be assured of receiving a regular paycheck. Rev. Boynton proved to be an excellent supervisor as well as a respected spiritual leader with the CC boys, positively impacting many of the young men. (For more on Rev. Boynton see Chapter 10.)

Late-1930s
Improving Mt. Lebanon Baptist Church

"When the church attended by the Woody family needed a new building, Papa arranged to have some white pine timber that he owned harvested for the interior walls," Jean remembered. "He also gave the church $300 for a new roof. The old wooden structure has since been replaced with a brick building."

Incidentally, as of 2015, Jean McNey still attended Mt. Lebanon Baptist Church where she played the organ nearly every Sunday.

(Whenever anyone in the community needed boards for any kind of construction project – a home or a barn – they would go out into the woods and search for a good "board tree." Ranger Woody was well-known for allowing local residents to cut such trees on government property, as long as they first asked permission. He staunchly believed that all of the National Forest property belonged to the people, and that they should always be able to benefit from the forest's resources when needed.)

Late 1930s, Early 1940s
Easter Sunrise Services, Woody Gap

Originally proposed by his good friend Reverend Claud Boynton, Ranger Woody initiated and supported a series of Easter Sunrise Services held on Woody Gap during the late 1930s and early 1940s. The services were broadcast live by Atlanta's WSB radio and usually attended by Governor E.D. "Ed" Rivers. This popular Easter event became a yearly tradition during the early years of World War II.

1940 -
Woody Gap School

"Prior to the early 1940s, five separate one- and two-teacher grammar schools operated in our portion of Union County and no high school existed in the Suches area," Jean said. "Two of those schools were one-room school houses, and the other three conducted classes in church buildings. In the early 1920s, my mother Mae had to go all the way to Blairsville to attend high school, and the logistics of getting her to school and back home each day on very poor roads presented a serious challenge. In the mid-1930s, Papa's oldest son Walter came up with the idea of consolidating all of those one-

Ranger Woody's special friend, Governor E.D. "Ed" Rivers, loved to attend the Easter Sunrise Services atop Woody Gap held during the late 1930s and early '40s. Standing behind the governor on the right side of the photo with Ranger Woody is Reverend Claud Boynton. Reverend Boynton was one of the driving forces behind the popular Easter services. Note the Woody Gap totem pole in the background. Photo circa 1940, courtesy of Jean McNey.

room schools into one central schoolhouse in Suches that would serve all of the children in the area. Papa and Walter also decided that high school classes should be offered in the new school. When Papa approached the county, either the school superintendent or county commissioner, I'm not sure which, about available funding, he was told that the county would be willing to invest $10,000 in the project under one condition: The school would have to be built on the former property of Governor Joe Brown, Georgia's infamous governor during the Civil War. (Governor Brown had grown up in Suches. For more on Governor Brown, see index.)

"Walter located the current owner of the property, arranged a sale and Papa bought the land – a 20-acre parcel. Papa then deeded the land to the county. Once the construction got underway, the granite rock that was used on the exterior of the school building was quarried from the dam area of Papa's lake (Woody Lake) just down the road. Papa also donated lumber and other building supplies to the project and everyone in our family volunteered time and energy into getting the school ready to open.

"Eventually a medical clinic, a volunteer fire department building, and a community center were also built on part of the original 20 acres. Today these structures are located just across Highway 60 from the school building. Papa and our entire family were always very supportive of the school. For the next few years, he auctioned off the boxes at special 'box suppers' held to raise money for the school (until his health prevented him from doing it in the mid-1940s).

"I remember helping with putting together some of the playground equipment when I was around 12 years old. We also scrubbed floors and washed windows inside the school building. I remember that each classroom contained an Ashley wood burning stove that got plenty of use during the winter months."

Plans got underway to build a single school structure in Suches in 1936. This modern school would consolidate the scattered one-room schools of Mt. Lebanon, Mt. Zion, Cooper's Creek, Sprigg's Chapel and Valley into one central location that would offer grades K through12. Ranger Woody and his son Walter made numerous trips to Blairsville (and reportedly Atlanta as well) to get approval and work out all of the details for getting the school built. Woody Gap School was dedicated in November 1940.

The school opened its door in January 1941 at mid-term. It was named to honor both father and son, Arthur and Walter Woody, who had worked so hard to get it located in Suches. The building included a large auditorium, a dining room and transportation facilities so that the children of Suches could receive the best education possible. The man who never made it beyond the fifth grade must have been proud when the doors opened and the children from many of his good friends in the community started attending Woody Gap School.

Today known as an "isolated school" with excellence in education as a primary goal, Woody Gap School is the smallest public school in Georgia. Average annual enrollment in the kindergarten, primary, middle and high school runs around 80 to 90 students.

Fittingly, when the doors of the school first opened in 1941, Ranger Woody's daughter Mae White proudly served as one of its teachers, a position she maintained for several years. The Ranger's beloved granddaughter Jean graduated from Woody Gap School in the spring of 1945 at age 15.

Dedication Exercises

WOODY GAP HIGH SCHOOL
Suches, Georgia

Saturday, November 30, 1940
11 a. m. Eastern Standard Time

PROGRAM

CLAUD C. BOYNTON, Master of Ceremonies

NATIONAL ANTHEM .... BAND
INVOCATION .... DR. J. M. NICHOLSON
ADDRESS .... FRANK SHULER
County School Superintendent
ADDRESS .... ARTHUR WOODY
U. S. Forest Ranger
PRESENTATION OF BOARD OF EDUCATION AND COUNTY OFFICIALS
MUSIC BY BAND
ADDRESS .... JUDGE TOM CANDLER
ADDRESS .... COL. PAT HARALSON
ADDRESS .... C. A. STRICKLAND
INTRODUCTION OF STATE SCHOOL SUPERVISOR H. G. JARRARD
DEDICATORY ADDRESS .... M. D. COLLINS
State School Superintendent
ADDRESS .... GOVERNOR-ELECT EUGENE TALMADGE
MUSIC BY BAND
BARBECUE DINNER AT 3:00 P. M.

Dedication program for the opening of Woody Gap School, dated Nov. 30, 1940. Note that Eugene Talmadge was the new governor-elect of Georgia. Program courtesy of Jean McNey.

Jean's graduating class contained a whopping seven students. After graduating from Emory University several years later in 1949, Jean, like her mother, also taught at Woody Gap School for one year before becoming a college teacher at Truett-McConnell College in Cleveland. Years later, she returned to Suches and taught at Woody Gap for another span of eight years.

Woody Gap School, past and present, was built on 20 acres donated by Ranger Woody. It was erected on the site of the old home place of Governor Joe Brown, who served as Georgia's governor during the Civil War. The granite used to build the school, also donated, came from the Woody quarry just across the highway from the school. While the school was being built, many members of the Woody family (children, grandchildren, nieces and nephews) volunteered their services by painting walls, cleaning windows and doing other various light construction jobs. Jean McNey helped assemble the playground equipment. The school opened its doors in January 1941, at mid-term. After graduating from Woody Gap School in 1944 and attending college, Jean came full circle by becoming a teacher at Woody Gap School in the late 1940s. Three generations of Woody women have taught at Woody Gap School since it opened its doors in 1940: Ranger Woody's daughter, Mae Woody White; Mae's daughter, Jean; and Jean's daughter, Lisa McNey Sweet, who began teaching English at the iconic school in 2015. Photo courtesy of Jean McNey.

The Woody Gap Totem Pole
A Special Gift to the Ranger from the "CC" Boys

CCC boys carved this totem pole to honor Woody, who, in the inset, tries a hand at an unfamiliar art

14

As much as Ranger Woody criticized many of the "wasteful" programs initiated by the Roosevelt administration during the height of the Great Depression, the arrival of the CCC work force to the mountain region in 1933 marked the beginning of an amazing relationship between the Ranger, the Forest Service, and the "Satan's of Suches," as well as boys from other camps in the area.

By the late 1930s, the various CCC camps in the area including Camp Woody had been in operation for almost seven years. Although new faces were constantly replacing those who mustered out after a 12-month enlistment, most of the CC boys had one thing in common: They idolized Arthur Woody, and they did anything he asked of them. Although the camp was supposed to be run like a military operation, to many it seemed much more like a permanent summer camp for young men. The boys worked hard and accomplished a great deal. They also played hard. Everything they built was built to last, and many of the rock structures they erected throughout Union County and the state are still standing strong today as a testament of their skill and workmanship.

In an article by Arthur Grahame that appeared in Outdoor Life magazine in October 1941, a bird's eye-view of Ranger Woody's carved likeness stands watch atop the one-of-a-kind Woody Gap totem pole. The pole was commissioned by the loyal CCC workers as a tribute to the man they had come to know and revere for nearly 10 years. Ironically, Pearl Harbor was attacked one month after this article was published, forever putting an end to the CCC and its enduring work across the U.S. Article excerpt courtesy of Outdoor Life magazine.

It is not known how the idea actually came about, but at some point during the late 1930s (possibly early 1941), the CC boys of Camp Robertstown (Co. 456, F-3) commissioned a well-known and gifted local wood carver named George Eastman, known as the "wood carver of Sautee," to carve a wooden totem pole as a tribute to the hard-working forest ranger they had come to know and love so much. Since the primary business of the Forest Service revolved around trees, what better shrine could the "tree" boys give Ranger Woody than a carved tree, or totem, showing some familiar visual images of their seven or eight year history in the area? (It is not known what part, if any, Camp Woody played in the carving of the pole.) Probably made of poplar, the 20- to 24-foot totem pole depicted numerous CCC and Forest Service objects. At its base, the tree measured about two feet in diameter.

The first scene at the bottom and obvious front of the pole depicted a painted relief of a pick, a shovel and a double-bladed ax, all tools of the trade of the CC boys. A painted relief of the Forest Service-Department of Agriculture logo was carved just above the three almost life-size tools. Surrounding the logo and wrapping around the pole were painted dogwood blossoms, branches and reeds. A relief of a bird (unknown species) sat on a limb just above the logo. Above the bird were the carved identification numbers of Camp Robertstown as shown below:

C.C.C.
Co
456
Camp
GA F3

A painted white cross was carved just under the ID numbers, indicating the strong faith shared by many of the boys. A cluster of oak leaves appeared just above the CCC identification numbers, with a black bear standing above the leaves. An emblem of an eagle and shield (obviously symbolizing America), with the face of a lady carved just above that (could this be Lady Liberty?). The crowning achievement of the totem stood at the top. A likeness of Ranger Arthur Woody in full uniform donning his always-present fedora stood watch at the very top of the pole. Obviously the Ranger appeared to be gazing out over his vast forest domain.

The painted totem pole was by every definition a beautiful work of art and a fine tribute to Ranger Woody. Every relief in the carving was symbolic of some important CCC or Forest Service symbol. Nothing is known about how the totem was presented to the Ranger, but it was placed in a prominent spot on the side of Woody Gap near the intersection of the road and the Appalachian Trail on land belonging to Ranger Woody. The pole was set in a concrete base and a rail fence was erected around it. Photographic evidence indicates that it was placed at Woody Gap in 1939 or 1940. The totem became an immediate and well-known landmark.

Shortly after the Ranger's death in 1946, C.K. "Lanky" Spaulding, the supervisor of the Chattahoochee National Forest in Gainesville, had the pole removed, claiming it was a hazard to pedestrians because it might fall on someone. If it had been made of poplar, the wood most commonly used by George Eastman in similar carvings, it might well have been starting to show

Ranger Woody and his good friend Governor E.D. "Ed" Rivers admire the beautifully-carved totem pole while attending an Easter Sunrise Service atop Woody Gap, circa 1940. Photo courtesy of Jean McNey.

signs of age by 1946. Being a very soft wood, poplar does not last long when exposed to the elements. On the other hand, however, it was a well-known fact that Supervisor Spaulding and Ranger Woody had butted heads on more than one occasion, and his reasons for removing the pole might well have been personal. No one knows what became of the pole. It seems to have disappeared without a trace. One rumor claimed that the top of totem depicting Ranger Woody eventually showed up at a popular barbecue restaurant in Athens, Georgia, in the late '50s or early '60s, but that rumor was never substantiated. Like so many other important relics of that amazing era, a beautiful work of art was lost.

Woody family members were understandably upset because the totem had been placed on private property, and they did not think the Forest Service had a right to take it down. Since the Ranger had been such a popular and powerful figure in the community, perhaps Supervisor Spaulding wanted people to forget Ranger Woody's legacy as quickly as possible. Whatever the reason for its removal, a work of art on Woody Gap was lost forever. Truly this marked the end of the "Ranger Woody Regime." A new day was dawning in Forest Service protocol in the North Georgia mountains.

Ranger Woody loved to "sneak off" to fish for his beloved "specks," or brook trout, native to North Georgia, whenever he could. By the time he became a full-fledged forest ranger in 1918, however, they had become increasingly rare. He restocked many of the local streams with native brook trout and introduced non-native rainbow and brown trout purchased with his own money. He eventually began to spawn brook trout from eggs bought in the Northeast and grown in fish-rearing ponds that he built himself. Later on, the Forest Service took over his trout stocking initiative and greatly expanded his original program. Ranger Woody knew where all the good fishing holes were located on every stream in his beloved Rock Creek Refuge. Photo courtesy of Jean McNey.

CHAPTER 9
A Monumental Fish Story
The Ones That Didn't Get Away

"I know most of the trout by name. If I'm lucky, I might get one of them on a hook."

Arthur Woody

Most fish stories fall into the category of being exaggerated tall tales. But when it comes to the work Arthur Woody did with restocking trout in the streams of North Georgia, the story is every bit as remarkable and important as his work with white-tailed deer. In fact, the Ranger's work in this area alone should rank right up there with other great achievements in conservation that took place in America during the early decades of the 20th century.

Unfortunately this is one of the least documented aspects of Ranger Woody's diverse career. Many of the details involving his tireless work in restocking the streams and lakes of his mountain domain from 1918 to the late 1930s with a variety of fish were never maintained or preserved to the degree that his high-profile work with deer was recorded, so many of the particulars are lost forever.

Based on bits and pieces of various written accounts, though, plus several firsthand accounts that have been passed down through the years, it's apparent that Ranger Woody spent considerable time and energy on his trout restocking efforts. Much of the early work was done on his own initiative with his own money and resources.

The Ranger seemed to have a clear vision for what he wanted to do. Having grown up watching his beloved "specks," or native brook trout, slowly disappear in many of their familiar haunts, he set out to restore these delicate fish in high mountain streams where they could once again thrive. But he didn't stop there. He brought in non-native rainbow and brown trout and established viable populations of these popular game fish as well. This was an amazing gift to the countless thousands of sportsmen who have enjoyed fishing for trout in the North Georgia mountains for nearly a century now. The truth is, if Ranger Woody hadn't taken it upon himself to stock rainbow and brown trout in his beloved Rock Creek Refuge in 1918, and if he hadn't expanded his stocking efforts to other nearby creeks and streams in the early 1920s, the North Georgia region might have a totally different complexion today.

Perhaps one reason this area of the Ranger's career received very little attention during his lifetime, and in the years following his death, is because fish may not capture the emotions in the same way a deer might do. Sportsmen are passionate about their trout, but fish don't touch your soul like deer are capable of doing. Another reason the trout program received such little attention is because it was a fairly low-profile activity. Ranger Woody and his helpers simply went about their business without much fanfare.

Although trout were unquestionably beautiful creatures to Ranger Woody, and to the countless thousands of sportsmen (both past and present) who loved the challenge of trying to outsmart them, they may not have had the hypnotizing effect on people that Ranger Woody's deer were able to generate in later years. With large brown eyes that can stare right through you, or an imposing set of antlers, deer can make a man do strange things. Trout can't stand in a field staring at you, or majestically bound away through the woods, although they certainly have their own brand of majesty and magic. For the most part, they often go unseen until they are on a hook. Nonetheless, the Ranger had a burning passion to see his beloved "specks" swimming in every stream where they could survive, and he was a true pioneer in placing all three species of trout in mountain streams.

A Love Affair with Trout

For a man of the mountains, Arthur Woody had an unusual affinity for water and the creatures that lived in that water. Although it's likely that he never saw a beach or an ocean during his lifetime, he loved to swim in the lake he built behind his house and he swam there often. That love of swimming almost cost him his life in 1944 when he suffered his first stroke at age 60 while swimming across Woody Lake one afternoon as he often did in mild weather.

During his long career, he had a hand in building and stocking four lakes in the Suches area and he did much to clean up and improve many of the mountain streams and rivers that flowed through his district. He had grown up stalking native brook trout in some of those very streams, some of which today have grown to become legendary trout waters. It was only natural that after many of the streams had been polluted with logging debris and depleted of fish, he would start a crusade to replenish the area's waterways with those beautiful fish in some of the familiar haunts he had known as a boy. He said many times that he believed God and nature had intended for every mountain stream to be teeming with trout. To his way of thinking, a mountain stream or river without a trout swirling to the surface after a tasty morsel was akin to a pristine country church with no congregation.

Shortly after being promoted to the official rank of Forest Ranger in 1918, one of the first things he did was to set about procuring and releasing a

Originally built on land he owned near Rock Creek Lake in the 1920s, Ranger Woody's primitive fish-rearing ponds proved so successful for raising trout that the Forest Service took over his operation in the early 1930s. With the help of the "CC" boys in 1933, the Forest Service greatly improved the Ranger's original ponds inside the Rock Creek Refuge (seen here). Note the rock structure, a trademark of the CCC's enduring work in the area. The Chattahoochee Forest National Fish Hatchery was established on Rock Creek in 1937 by the Forest Service. In 1960, the National Fish Hatchery was officially handed over to the U.S. Fish and Wildlife Service. Photo courtesy Charlie Elliott Wildlife Center.

shipment of non-native rainbow trout into some of the local streams in Rock Creek Refuge. Under his direction, trout were soon placed in Noontootly Creek (today known as Noontootla Creek), Smith Creek, Little Rock Creek, Cooper Creek, and the Toccoa River, now regarded as one of the best trout rivers in Georgia.

Fishing was a lifelong passion for Ranger Woody. He loved to fish for bass, bream and anything else that might be found in a mountain lake or stream. But his mountain trout were special. They were his children. In a December 1940 article written in *Outdoor Georgia* magazine titled "Deer Hunt" by Jim McGraw, which described the first deer hunt of modern times held in the Blue Ridge WMA a month earlier in November, the author made the following observation:

> Every trout fisherman in the Southeast knows the creeks Noontootly, Jones, Montgomery, Mill, Rock Creek, and Rock Creek Lake in the refuge. Many thousands of rainbow and native trout (brook trout) have been released in those streams and in the lake. Each year, trout fishermen eagerly await the announcement of open dates on those streams. They flock to Rock Creek Lake throughout the week-ends of summer. In countless deep pools on those creeks, the trout have grown wise and huge and hungry and only an expert fisherman can take them on flies or other artificial lures. Fifteen years of management have made this wildlife area one of the most popular trout havens in the state.

While Ranger Woody no doubt received a great amount of satisfaction knowing that sportsmen across Georgia enjoyed fishing for the trout he had had such a big hand in restocking and protecting, there was nothing in the world Ranger Woody enjoyed more than stealing away from a hectic work schedule for an hour or two and sitting along a peaceful trout stream in some secret spot trying to outsmart one of his "pet" trout.

"It was probably good therapy for him," Jean McNey recalled. "He found much consolation and solace in fishing for his beloved specks, his terminology for the native brook trout that had come close to being wiped out in the mountain region."

Fly fishing up and down the Appalachians from Maine to Georgia, and especially in legendary haunts like the Catskills and Adirondack mountains of New York State, has been a popular outdoor pastime since America was founded. Trout fishing is as American as apple pie. The task of making it possible for sportsmen to once again hunt deer in the North Georgia

Mountains was incredibly important in its own right, but restoring trout to the mountains has no doubt impacted substantially higher numbers of outdoorsmen over the past 75 to 80 years. And Ranger Arthur Woody was the man who started it all.

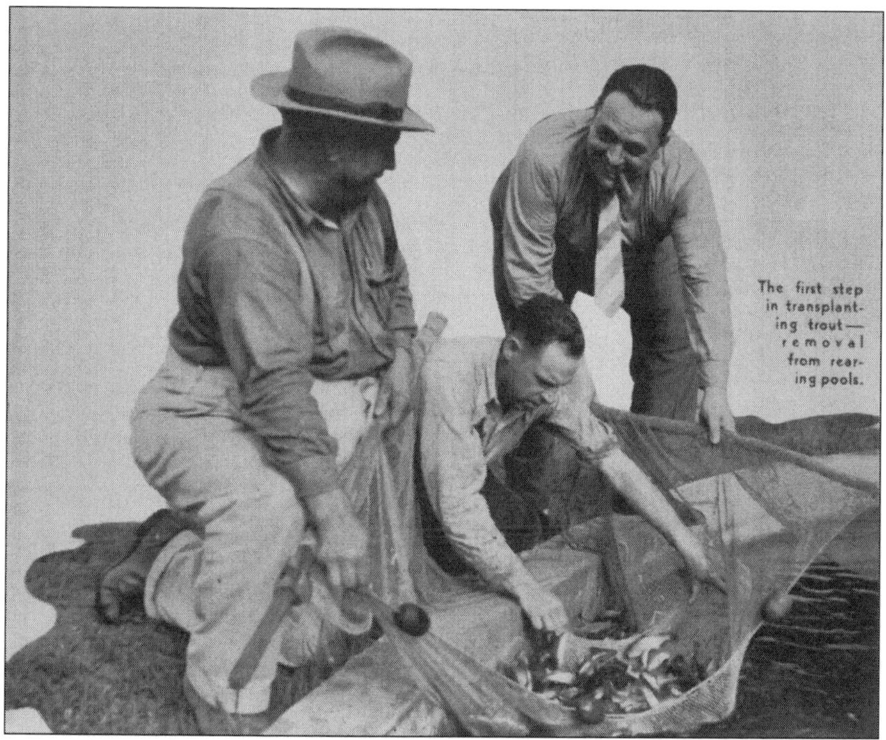

Ranger Woody lends a hand in netting a batch of trout fingerlings from a pool at the fish hatchery on Rock Creek. The fish will soon be placed in the local streams in and around Rock Creek Refuge. From an article in Outdoor Georgia magazine, early 1940s.

In his classic book, *Whose Woods These Are, the Story of the National Forests,* published in 1962, author Michael Frome reflects on the visionary man who understood human nature and knew how to use psychology on people better than most trained professionals:

> For almost 25 years he never went south of Gainesville, the outpost of the mountains. Once friends suggested he go to Florida for his health. "Me go down there and drink wiggle-tail water?" And then, with a sense of home and place a man like him would feel, "What's the use to live if it can't be right here?" He loved his home country and he knew every bit of it. Brook trout, which he called "specks," were his favorite fish. "I

know the big trout by name," he said, "and if I'm smart I can get them on a hook."

As a ranger, Woody considered game and fish equally important as timber. His homily on this subject to young foresters who trained under him was, 'We should look to the forests as a source of "good" as well as "wood." I wonder, what would Carl Alwin Schenck, the Prussian forest meister, have thought of this roughhewn mountaineer who refused to wear a uniform or to measure forestry in terms of lumber profit?

Yet his philosophy prevailed on one of the largest ranger districts in the Forest System. Operations were not always in strict accord with prescribed methodology. He ignored rules and regulations and requests for written reports. After all, Woody defined an expert as "an average boy away from home." But his district excelled in fire prevention, timber management and game protection."

The Makings of a Trout Paradise

It happened in 1918. For reasons we may never know, Ranger Woody took it upon himself to order an unknown quantity of non-native rainbow trout from a privately owned fish hatchery near Denver, Colorado. This was nearly 10 years before he would purchase five fawns in 1927, a later action marking the beginning of a modern mountain deer herd that would grow substantially during the decade of the 1930s. We do know that he had just been promoted to the respectable position of "forest ranger" by the U.S. Forest Service, but why he took this ground-breaking action at that particular time is lost to the ages.

The fingerling trout were shipped to Gainesville, Georgia, by railroad in large barrels. Ranger Woody and his son Clyne met the train and loaded the barrels onto a truck. Clyne later recalled that he and his father hauled the barrels by truck to the foot of Black Mountain, and then transferred them over to a horse-drawn wagon. From there the globe-trotting trout were painstakingly hauled up Grassy Gap Road, across Grassy Gap, and over to the game refuge, a strenuous trip to say the least. It's a wonder that any of the fish survived, but one thing is certain. With all of that jostling up and down steep grades in those barrels, they couldn't have suffered from a lack of oxygen inside those barrels!

(Note: Since numerous shipments of trout and other fish species were brought into the area in the years following that first shipment in 1918, some of the later shipments might well have been picked up at the rail depot in the town of Blue Ridge, in Fannin County, instead of Gainesville. However, interviews with Clyne Woody in his later life specifically mentioned Gainesville as the initial pickup point.)

This was before the road from Stonepile Gap to Suches was completed over Woody Gap, and very few improved roads existed in the area in those days making automobile travel very difficult. The best way to reach Suches from Dahlonega was by way of the steep and rugged Grassy Gap Road route, but it was a grueling journey and one that automobiles often failed to complete because of the steep grades that often burned up brakes and overheated strained radiators.

Those first trout were placed in Rock Creek and several other streams within the refuge. Thus began a very primitive trout stocking program that the Ranger continued to enhance and improve upon for the next 20 years. Additional shipments of rainbow trout were ordered from Colorado, and reportedly several shipments of non-native brown trout were ordered from a hatchery in Washington State. Ranger Woody and Clyne solicited the help of several local men to assist them in releasing the fingerling trout in a number of local cold-water mountain streams.

Forest Ranger George Schaeffer gives two young hikers some pointers about trout fishing as he looks down on an ideal trout pool and possibly at some fish below a waterfall somewhere inside Ranger Woody's beloved Rock Creek Refuge. U.S. Forest Service photo, 1943.

In her very informative book, *I Remember Dahlonega,* first published in 1990, author Anne Dismukes Amerson quoted Harman Caldwell of Dahlonega, whose father had assisted with hauling and putting out several shipments of fish:

> In those days (1918 through early 1920s) there were no fish in the streams, except minnows and horny heads. Then Ranger Arthur Woody told Daddy how he could order trout from the state of Washington. My brother Pool rode with Daddy in a two-horse wagon loaded with wooden barrels to Gainesville to pick up the fish when they came in. My other brother, Henley, and I helped put five or six little trout in every creek hole we could find. Five years later people were catching trout as long as your arm.

(As mentioned, the fish were in all likelihood picked up by motor truck in Gainesville, not by horse and wagon, and transported to the foot of Black Mountain where they were then placed in a two-horse wagon.)

Ranger Woody built his first primitive fish-rearing enclosures on Woody Lake behind his house in the early 1920s. Later on he constructed several fish-rearing ponds on land he owned next to the game refuge on Rock Creek. He also began ordering native brook trout eggs that could be hatched and reared from a hatchery somewhere up in the northeast, possibly upper New York State. Most fish hatcheries around the country in the late 1800s and early 1900s were privately owned and easy to do business with.

The invasion of the "CC" boys into Camp Woody in Suches and other similar camps in the area in 1933 proved to be of great benefit to all of Ranger Woody's various conservation projects, but it was especially important to the trout stocking efforts. Suddenly Ranger Woody and the Forest Service were provided with a small army of willing and able-bodied workers to carry out dozens of projects, including the labor intensive job of hauling heavy fish canisters and barrels to remote streams and hand distributing those fish safely into the water. The CC boys also improved streams by building special trout pools and small dams, and did much to improve trout habitat across the mountains in general. This stream habitat improvement continued after the war and after Ranger Woody's death in 1946. It was carried out by hired workers, some of whom had been former CC members 10 years earlier, and funded by money provided by the Pittman-Robertson Act.

It is not known to what extent the Forest Service was involved in Ranger Woody's initial stocking efforts in 1918. Did Ranger Woody initiate this action

A group of CCC boys place canisters of young trout in a local stream. The hard-working boys often carried the heavy canisters long distances to reach remote streams. From an article in Outdoor Georgia magazine, early 1940s.

on his own? It seems likely that he did, just as he did with his deer program 10 years later. The Forest Service was probably aware of his intentions, and he likely had its blessings to proceed full-speed ahead, but it would be several years before the government became actively involved in any trout-stocking or stream-management programs. Certainly, by the time the CC boys appeared on the scene in 1933, the Forest Service had begun to play a much larger role in both the trout-stocking and deer-stocking efforts.

Ranger Woody continued to purchase rainbow and brown trout throughout the 1920s. He also continued to expand his primitive trout-rearing pools. Eventually the Forest Service stepped in and built larger and more efficient concrete pools. As some of the local lakes and state parks were developed in the early 1930s, pike, musky and other lake species were also brought in and released. Long before the first deer hunt in 1940 was conducted at Rock Creek Refuge in 1940, trout fishing inside the refuge and in other nearby streams had become very popular with Georgia sportsmen.

In 1937, realizing the need for a larger and more modern trout raising facility, the Forest Service constructed the Chattahoochee Forest National Fish Hatchery on Rock Creek. In 1960, ownership and management of the hatchery was transferred to the U.S. Fish and Wildlife Service. Over the years the hatchery has raised and released millions of trout. Today its primary focus is aimed at raising rainbow trout, but smaller numbers of brown and brook trout are also grown and released into mountain streams.

"Scientific Fishing" with Ranger Woody
A Young Girl's Unforgettable Fish Fry

"Papa often took me with him on trips around the refuge and we frequently went fishing together," Jean McNey recalled. "He originally built a fish-rearing pond on the hill behind our house (on Woody Lake). There he raised trout and later put them out in nearby streams. By the time I came along, he had built a small pond we called Edmondson Pond near Rock Creek inside the game reserve and stocked it with trout. Then he built two more ponds on some land he owned on Little Rock Creek (below Rock Creek Lake). The Forest Service later took over all of the Ranger's fish-rearing ponds (probably in the mid-1930s), and eventually built a large fish hatchery on Rock Creek in 1937.

"As a young girl, I remember going to several of the ponds with him to do what he always termed 'some scientific fishing' to find out how much the fish had grown. Technically, we were breaking the law because trout season was not open. But Papa would wink at me and say, 'This is the only way I can find how much these fish have grown.' Then he would smile broadly.

"One time about 20 Forest Service workers and some of their family members had a big fishing party at Edmondson Pond. I got so excited about 'shagging' trout that I waded out into the pool with a pair of white shoes on! We later built a fire, cooked the fish and stuffed ourselves. Everyone had a great time in spite of the fact that one very self-righteous Pennsylvania Dutch wife of an assistant ranger declared that 'her George would never eat any of those disgusting fish!' I guess eating mountain trout was beneath her. As things

Under Ranger Woody's careful direction, a group of 4H-Club teenagers are being shown how to improve a trout pool inside the Rock Creek Refuge. The young adults were attending a Wildlife Conservation Camp at Camp Washsega, near the fish hatchery, as part of a summer conservation project. Photo 1941, courtesy of Jean McNey.

turned out, however, George couldn't get enough. He must have eaten at least eight of those delicious fish!"

"Papa never abused the law or took advantage of his position, but in situations like that there were more than enough fish to go around and everyone who participated had a great time. The game warden would often bait my hook for me. I remember getting so excited whenever we went trout fishing."

Catching the Ranger Red-Handed

From an Interview with Roscoe Reams (2000)

"During one of my hog hunting trips to the mountains as a teen, I decided to go down to a spot on the creek where I knew there were some big trout," Roscoe recalled. "There used to be a dam right below a homestead known as the old Lyle place. The CC had built a log dam across Rock Creek to keep the red-eyed bass from swimming upstream. In late winter, right below that dam, a lot of trout and bass typically congregated in a certain pool. We had finished hunting for the day, and I decided to slip down there to the creek to take a look around and see if I could see some big trout in that hole.

"It was a week or so before trout season opened and we couldn't hunt hogs in there any more after the season opened because people would see us and no one was supposed to be in there hunting." (Note: Roscoe and his older companions were given special permission to hunt wild hogs inside the refuge in late winter by Ranger Woody, and the local refuge game wardens, before trout season opened because the hogs were doing considerable damage to the habitat. Ranger Woody wanted to remove as many hogs as possible, so that they would not compete with the deer for food.)

"Not too many people knew about this particular hole. I went sneaking down there tip-toeing along, and wouldn't you know it, there was old Arthur Woody. He had broken off a long branch, and he was sitting on a rock, fishing for trout out of season. With the noise of the waterfall there, he didn't see me or hear me coming. I backed out and retraced my footsteps up the hill. He never knew I was there.

"Of course, I'm sure he just wanted to catch one or two fish for supper, but I got a big kick out of it nonetheless, because he was always so adamant about making everyone obey the game laws to the letter.

"The trout fishing was fabulous back then. The area had been stocked by the CC, beginning back in 1933, and 1938 was the first year I fished it.

Roscoe Reams shows off an outstanding rainbow trout taken in his beloved North Georgia mountains in the early 1960s. Roscoe began fishing for trout in the Rock Creek Refuge with some older friends at age 14 in 1938. He soon befriended Ranger Arthur Woody, and his life was never the same. The Ranger was his greatest trout-fishing mentor. After World War II ended, Roscoe was still in the Navy in June 1946 when his dear friend died. He deeply regretted missing the Ranger's funeral. Roscoe later became a renowned sportsman in his own right and enjoyed a close friendship with Charlie Elliott for over 50 years. (See Chapter 12 for more about Roscoe Reams.) Photo courtesy of Mrs. Elinor Reams.

(Actually Ranger Woody had begun stocking the streams in and around the refuge as early as 1918. When the CC boys came along, the increased workforce greatly enhanced the program Ranger Woody had started by stocking many other streams in the area, building dams, building fish pools, and making many improvements to the habitat.)

"In those days, trout fishing season on both Rock Creek and Noontootly Creek was only open for two weeks. Those creeks were closed the rest of the year. One year I went over there and camped out for a solid week, staying over near Rock Creek Lake. I was there from Saturday to Saturday, and I only saw two other people fishing during that whole time I was there. I caught a lot of fish. The only other people I saw during that week were two doctors from Athens, and I thought, 'Boy, this is getting crowded!'"

Brief History of the Three Species of Trout in the North Georgia Mountains

Brook trout, which are actually not trout at all but members of the char family, were native to the southern Appalachian Mountains in limited numbers. Heavy logging and farming began to take its toll on native brook trout in late 1800s. Since they were a popular food item, mountain people caught them in traps and seining nets, and in some cases even used explosives to kill them. By the early 1900s, after much of the mountain forests had been clear cut, their numbers dropped to dangerously low levels. Fire, erosion and siltation added to the problem. Before long, native "brookies" were only found in isolated pockets. Ranger Woody worked tirelessly over the years to reintroduce his beloved specks into remote streams where they had been fished out.

Clyde Harkins, who went to work with the CCC at Camp Woody in 1940 and knew Ranger Woody well, caught a few native brook trout growing up with his brothers in the headwaters of Cooper's Creek. By then, however (1930s), many of the remote streams contained only "rough" fish, species no one wanted for food. "Most of the trout were gone by the time I was old enough to catch them," Clyde said.

As one of his jobs with the CC in 1940, Clyde worked in some of the local streams and building trout ponds and pools, a job he dearly loved doing. After World War II, he worked off and on for the Forest Service continuing to work on various stream improvement projects.

Rainbow trout are native to the American west. Ranger Woody introduced both rainbow trout and brown trout to the North Georgia Mountains around

1918 as mentioned. Brown trout, native to the British Isles and most of Europe, were introduced to the western U.S. in the 1800s. Today, thanks to the far-sighted vision of Arthur Woody, rainbow and brown trout dominate most North Georgia streams while populations of native brook are still found in certain areas in much lower numbers.

Brown trout and brook trout spawn in October and November, whereas rainbow trout spawn in the spring. Approximately 2,800 of Georgia's 5,400 miles of trout streams support wild trout populations where the fish reproduce. About 142 miles of streams support native brook trout.

Ranger Woody and His Bass

"Papa loved to fish for bass almost as much as he loved fishing for trout," Jean McNey recalled. "Once he was fishing in Woody Lake behind our house and he hooked a nice, 'eating size' bass. After a short fight the bass broke off. A little while later, Papa spotted an extremely large water snake (non-poisonous), at least 5-feet long, swimming in the lake. He grabbed a rifle and shot the snake. When he went to retrieve it, he discovered that the snake had swallowed the bass he had previously hooked. He cut the snake open and recovered the lost bass and his lure from inside the mouth of the fish. He was tickled to death!"

Legend has it that Ranger Woody once found a 20-pound bass floating belly up in Woody Lake. Reportedly he took it over

Ranger Woody and an unidentified worker show off a fine largemouth bass at the Blue Ridge Ranger Station located just across the road from Woody Lake. The fish was likely caught by the Ranger and he no doubt planned to eat it. Over the years, many 10-pound-plus "bucketmouths" came out of the fertile mountain lake. Photo circa 1938, courtesy of Jean McNey.

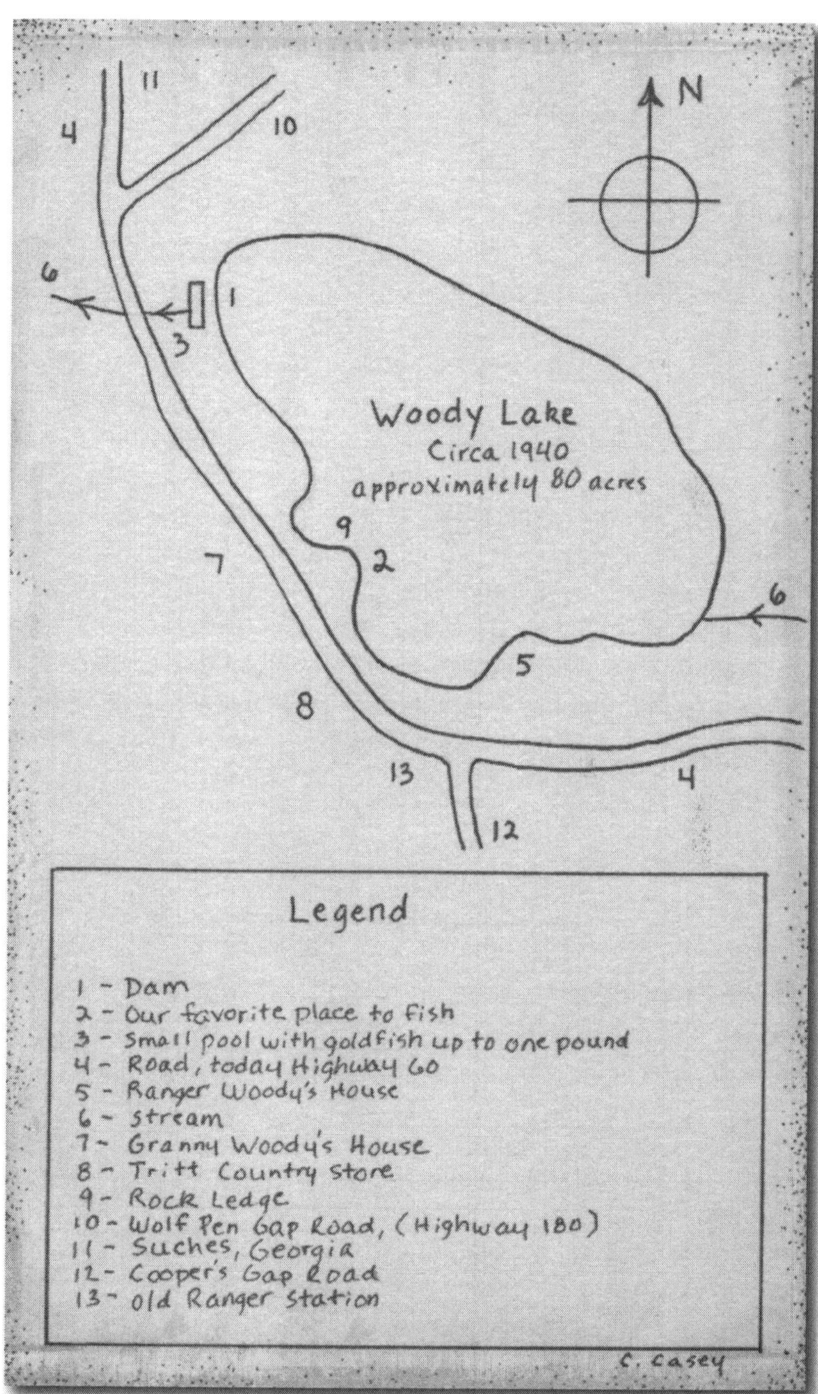

Woody Lake as it appeared in the 1940s. Map originally Drawn by Horace Shelton Jr. (2013).

to Tritt's Grocery Store across the road from his house and had it weighed to verify the size. For years he told stories about that mythical fish, and he often suggested to those fishing in the lake that there were other fish of that size in Woody Lake begging to be caught. Twenty pounds might have been an exaggeration, but over the years, some extremely large bass weighing in the 14- to 15-pound range were wrestled out of Woody Lake.

Ranger Woody was always happy to allow people to fish in his lake. All anyone had to do was ask permission. This included local residents as well as total strangers. Over the years, a number of avid fishermen came up from Atlanta to fish the lake on a regular basis. (Even today, Jean McNey still follows her grandfather's 70-year tradition of allowing people to fish in the lake.)

In addition to his beloved trout, the Ranger had a special affinity for his bass. After Woody Lake was built with the help of the CC boys in the mid 1930s, and after the Ranger had stocked it with bass, bream and trout, it wasn't long before people started catching some bragging-size bass in the 4- to 5-pound range. After a few more years, people started landing some 10-pound-plus "bucketmouths." Perhaps the lake was unusually fertile because of the fertile valley it had been built in. Whatever the reason, the lake produced some mega-bass, especially during the decade of the 1940s. As mentioned, the size of the lake has been considerably reduced due to the heavy siltation that has occurred over the years.

Fishing for Ranger Woody's Bass

From an interview with Horace E. Shelton Jr. (2013)

Growing up in the early 1940s, Horace E. Shelton Jr. of Atlanta fished in Woody Lake with his dad Horace Sr. on a number of occasions. Horace holds some fine memories of meeting Ranger Woody in person and staying in Ma Woody's house.

"My dad was a locomotive engineer for Southern Railway and he frequently made the run from Atlanta to Chattanooga. He loved to fish more than anything. He often went to Lake Chatuge in North Georgia with my uncle and several close friends. He started taking me with him when I was about 6 or 7 years old. I'm not sure how he met Ranger Woody. I think it's very possible that he and my uncle were just driving around in the mountains one day and saw the lake behind Ranger Woody's house and stopped by to ask permission to fish in it, and he said yes. At that time (early 1940s), the road across Woody Gap was a gravel road. I'm not sure when it was finally paved. In fact, almost all the roads in that part of the country were gravel back then.

"Not only did Ranger Woody give my dad permission to fish in the lake, but he made arrangements for Dad and his friends to stay in his mother's house (located on the other side of the lake). We hit it off right away with Granny Woody. She was a character just like her son. She was probably in her late 70s at the time and we used to love to listen to her tell stories. Can you imagine? Opening your house up to a couple of perfect strangers from Atlanta? Those were different times, all right! Granny Woody did not have a telephone, so whenever we went up there to fish for a couple of days we just showed up unannounced. But she always treated us like family. As I grew older, she always hugged me and told me how much I had grown.

"At the time, a very nice lady named Emma Townsend lived with Granny Woody and took care of her. She always cooked for us and we enjoyed her cooking very much. Mrs. Townsend was from Dahlonega and we heard that she sometimes walked all the way from Dahlonega to Granny Woody's house (a distance of at least 15 miles). That would have been quite a walk but in those days mountain folk were known to walk long distances without thinking much about it!

"Miss Emma usually fixed us ham or fried chicken with cream gravy and one or two delicious home-grown vegetables. She always made scratch biscuits that melted in your mouth. If the fishing was good, she might cook up some of our fish. On one or two occasions when we happened to catch a big snapping turtle in the lake, we'd take it back to the house and cut its head off with an ax. Then she would dress it and fry it up for us. We'd have fried turtle for dinner that was out of this world!

"Granny Woody always had a fire going in the fireplace, even in the summertime. After supper we always sat around the fire in the evenings, listening to her tell stories as she poked at the fire with a poker. Even though I was very young at the time, as I sat there looking at her wrinkled face in the glow of the fire as she talked about old times and mountain traditions, I knew in my heart that my dad and I were experiencing some true mountain magic. I'll never forget those special times!

"I remember seeing Ranger Woody for the first time when I was about 6 or 7. That would have been around 1944. To me he was a big, intimidating man, and I was kind of scared of him. One time when I was talking to my dad, I referred to the Ranger as being fat. Dad, a big man in his own right who weighed about 220 pounds, corrected me by saying, 'No, Son, he's not fat. He's heavy.'

Horace Shelton Jr., wearing his Sunday best just like his dad, proudly helps show off a fine stringer of bass (with one trout on the end) caught in Woody Lake circa 1943 or 1944. Horace was probably six or seven at the time. Pictured left to right are: young Horace; Lloyd Harris, a friend of his dad's; Horace E. Shelton Sr. and Jack Shelton, Horace's uncle). Photo courtesy of Horace E. Shelton Jr.

Horace E. Shelton Sr., Jack Shelton and Lloyd Harris with a 10-pound-plus bass caught in Woody Lake. Photo circa mid-1940s, courtesy of Horace E. Shelton Jr.

A view of Woody Lake, Suches, Georgia. Photo circa 1950, courtesy of Horace E. Shelton Jr.

Horace E. Shelton, Jr., at age 14, with his dad, Horace E. Shelton Sr., showing off a beautiful 7- to 8-pound-plus largemouth bass caught in Woody Lake. Photo circa late 1940s, courtesy of Horace E. Shelton Jr.

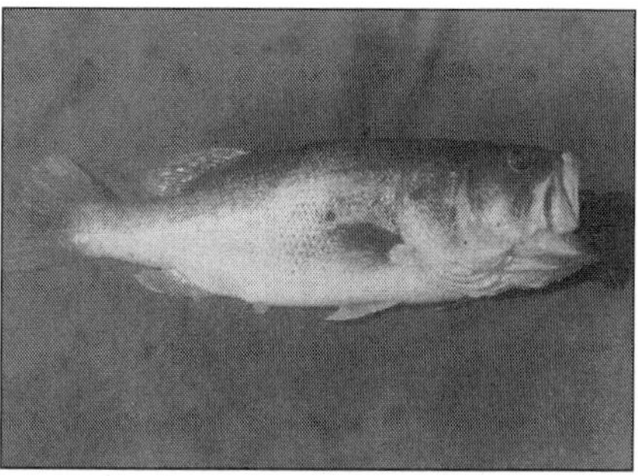

Caught by Horace Shelton's good friend Hoyt Ogle in 1946, this 14-pound largemouth bass is the largest fish ever caught in Woody Lake by the Shelton group. Before his death, Ranger Woody often bragged about record-size bass in his lake, and he was happy when fishermen caught them. Photo courtesy of Horace E. Shelton Jr.

Ma Woody, or Granny Woody as she was fondly known to the Sheltons, always welcomed young Horace and his father into her home, cooked for them and treated them as if they were family. Photo courtesy of Jean McNey.

Another fine stringer of bass caught in 1943 or 1944. Pictured are Horace E. Shelton Jr. and his dad's fishing pal, Lloyd Harris. Photo courtesy of Horace E. Shelton Jr.

"Ranger Woody was just a big, heavy old man to me, but always very nice to everyone in our group. Every time I saw him, he had on dark green work clothes. The manikin up at Brasstown Bald has him dressed in khakis, but I never saw him in khakis. He always wore that dark green.

"When Dad first met Ranger Woody, he told him there were some big bass in the lake. He told us the story about one day noticing a dead fish floating in lake. He went over and got it. It was a huge bass. He took it up to the store and had weighed it. He said it weighed 20 pounds on the store scales.

"He kiddingly told us he thought he might have a world record in his lake and he wanted someone to catch it. He told Dad he knew there were some other bass in the lake approaching that size and he wanted someone 'to catch one of the big'uns to prove it.' Although Dad and his friends caught some huge bass over the years – the largest being about 14 pounds – they never did catch one that big."

(Ranger Woody was well aware of George Perry's world-record largemouth bass caught on June 2, 1932 in Montgomery Lake, an oxbow off the Ocmulgee River in Telfair County, Georgia. The bass weighed 22 pounds, 4 ounces and has remained the world-record largemouth bass for many years. Perry landed his world record using a Creek Chub Broken-Back Wiggle Fish. Did the Ranger really think he might have a potential world record or was he pulling some legs? Probably a little of both! George Perry's record was tied in 2009 when Manabu Kurita of Japan caught a largemouth also weighing 22-pound, 4-ounces on July 2, 2009, on Lake Biwa, an ancient reservoir northeast of Kyoto, Japan.)

"Dad enjoyed a good drink from time to time. On several occasions when we were fishing at Woody Lake, he would get with a man named John Tritt who lived across the road from Granny Woody. They'd sneak off somewhere and buy a bottle of moonshine. One time John bought two bottles for himself. Since he was inclined to drink a little too much, he had some sort of arrangement with Granny Woody to let her keep his bottle at her house and dispense drinks to him whenever she thought he needed one. Well, according to their agreement, he went in and gave her one of the bottles, and she gave him a drink. Then he went outside in the apple orchard behind the house, sat down and leaned back against a tree, and drank the entire second bottle of moonshine that Granny Woody didn't know about. He got so drunk that he couldn't stand up. He started calling out for help.

"My dad asked Granny Woody if he should go and help him. 'No, let him sit there,' she answered. 'When he gets cold enough, he'll sober up and go home.' Sure enough, the next morning he was gone. I guess he had gotten up and gone home like she said.

"The back part of Granny Woody's house had two separate rooms. As you went in to the right you entered the kitchen where there was a large wood-burning cook stove and a dining table. On each side of the table were a couple of benches where people sat and on one end was a chair where Granny Woody always sat.

"We slept in the left front room of the house, which served as a guest room. The room contained two double beds, and since we usually had three or four people in our party it was pretty full. The room had a door to the outside porch, so that we could get up early and leave to go fishing without bothering anyone.

"The right front room was the sitting room. It contained a large rock fireplace, several clocks and chairs and two beds with quilts where Granny Woody and Miss Emma slept.

"We had some good experiences up there and we caught some beautiful bass. Ranger Woody and his mother were awfully good to us. They were good folks. As mentioned, the biggest bass we ever caught was one that weighed 14 pounds. It was caught by my dad's friend Hoyt Ogle in 1946, the year Ranger Woody died. I remember that the lower lip of that fish was so big that you could barely get a hook stringer around it.

"We usually fished with Baltimore minnows that we brought with us. They looked just like goldfish only they were brown. They didn't last long. We always fished off the bank. There were no boats for us to use. One of my jobs was to catch little bream to be used as bait for large bass. There was a little indention in the shoreline and I put rocks around it and made a little pool. Whenever I caught a bream, I'd put it in that pool.

"We fished with a couple of rods and reels and two or three Calcutta cane poles rigged with linen line. The place where we fished was kind of a point. There was a rock ledge about 20 feet out in the water, and we put a minnow on the cane pole and threw it out over the ledge. If a big bass struck, he'd go deep and pull the line against the ledge and usually break it off. So the object was to get him over the ledge before he broke the line. I probably know everything there is to know about that portion of Woody Lake. I still remember it like it was yesterday.

"After a day's fishing, we'd always show Ranger Woody our catch. No matter how big our fish were – and we caught several bass over 10 pounds – he would look at them, shake his head and say, "These here are right nice'uns, but next time I want you to catch one of the really big'uns!"

"Dad must have known that Ranger Woody was very sick in the summer of 1946 because we drove up to Suches to see him shortly before he died. My mother was with us. When we got to the Woody house, Dad went into the house alone while we sat in the car. When he came back out he was very somber as he drove off. 'How is he?' my mother asked.

"'Not good. He didn't even know who I was,' Dad told us. A short time later we heard that Ranger Woody had passed away. After having known him when he was healthy and vibrant, I know it was a quite shock for my father to see him in that condition. We continued going up there after the Ranger's death and Grandma Woody was always very cordial.

"I even took my grandson up there in 2012. He caught one bream. We got permission from Jean. I was hoping we'd have some luck and catch one of those fabled Woody bass, but all he caught was a bream. Still we had a great time and being there brought back some special memories."

A Different Kind of "Fish" Story – Big Bass with a Rifle

From an Interview with Roscoe Reams (2000)

As a budding 14-year-old outdoorsman growing up in Atlanta during the late 1930s, Roscoe Reams started going to the mountains to hunt wild hogs with some older friends as mentioned earlier.

"Ranger Woody and the local game warden, a Mr. Sprinkle, were more than happy to allow us to come into the refuge and help remedy what they considered to be a serious game management problem," Roscoe remembered.

Roscoe soon became an avid trout fisherman, and he frequently fished in the refuge during the very short two-week season in the spring. The Ranger apparently took a strong liking to young Roscoe, and the two became good friends. Ranger Woody always called Roscoe "Boy." During the five or six year period Roscoe spent in the mountains before the war took him away in 1943 when he was 18, he also became a lifelong friend of Charlie Elliott as noted. After Ranger Woody's death in 1946, Roscoe and Charlie hunted and fished together for the next five decades. During those years, Roscoe gained national fame as a renowned trick archery shooter and as a nationally acclaimed turkey hunter.

"One time in the spring when I was in the mountains I went up to visit the Ranger at his home in Suches," Roscoe recalled. "We were sitting on the back porch talking and looking out over the lake. He never called me by my name. He always referred to me as 'Boy.' In addition to his Savage Model 99 that I coveted because I had killed several deer with it (see Chapter 13), he had an old military rifle with iron sights that he was very proud of, a Springfield or Enfield, I forget which, and he brought it out and started bragging about it. There was a stump sticking out of the water across the lake about 300 yards away, and Ranger Woody looked at me and said, 'Boy, you reckon I can hit that ol' stump out there?'

"We talked about the yardage, and I said, 'Well, if your rifle is sighted in at 100 yards, you'll have to hold her a little high…'

"Ranger Woody took a rest on the wooden railing of the back porch, aimed and POW! He came pretty close, but his shot was a little short."

"'Boy, you think you can hit that stump?' he asked me.

"'Probably not,' I answered. 'But I'll give it a try.'

"Ranger Woody handed me the rifle. I laid it on the railing, intentionally held it a little high and pulled the trigger. My shot was long enough, but it went a little bit to the left. We were talking and laughing about our shots, when maybe three or four minutes later, we noticed something light colored floating in the water near the stump. It really grabbed our curiosity, so we walked all the way around the lake to see what it was. Darn if we hadn't killed a trophy-size largemouth bass with that high-powered rifle bullet. Apparently the bass had been swimming close to the stump and the concussion had killed it.

"'That's against the law,' the Ranger said jokingly with a big grin on his face. 'I reckon we'll just have to eat it to get rid of the evidence!'

"So we got a small boat and retrieved the fish, cleaned it and fried it up for lunch. It was delicious. It must have weighed 4 or 5 pounds."

Conclusion

After Ranger Woody's forced retirement in 1945 due to failing health, he confided to Charlie Elliott that he actually looked forward to retiring and to spending the remainder of his days in the woods and on the streams of his district. That's when he recited his now famous quote:

"I know the big trout by name," he told Charlie, "and I'll have to be smart to get 'em on a hook."

Sadly it was not to be. The man who had devoted his life's energies into stocking and restoring trout to the mountains would never be able to personally enjoy the fruits of his labor because his health deteriorated very rapidly. But he was very proud of what he had accomplished. And he must have known in his heart that as a result of his efforts, thousands of avid sportsmen would be able to enjoy some of the finest trout fishing in the nation for decades to come. Today the Chattahoochee Forest National Fish Hatchery, nestled deep within in the Blue Ridge WMA, is a permanent shrine to the extraordinary groundwork initiated by Arthur Woody almost 100 years ago!

A noticeably slim Arthur Woody displays a fine turkey gobbler, circa mid-1920s. Since there were no deer in the mountains to hunt when he was growing up during the early 1900s, he cut his teeth hunting small game – squirrels, rabbits and turkeys. To a lesser degree, he sometimes hunted quail and grouse and the occasional 'coon, 'possum or wild hog. Ranger Woody had a particular passion for turkeys and he dearly loved to hunt squirrels with his grandsons. Even after turkey numbers began to decline, the Ranger always seemed to be able to locate a flock and shoot one or two for special occasions like Christmas, Thanksgiving, or when important guests like the governor of Georgia might be coming for dinner. Pictured with his beloved Savage Model 99, believed to be a .250 or .250/3000 caliber, he developed quite a reputation for hunting turkeys with a rifle instead of a shotgun, a common practice in his day. Photo courtesy of Jean McNey.

CHAPTER 10
A Love Affair with Wild Turkeys

"A true woodsman and student of nature, Woody championed wildlife fundamentals. He preferred to increase and improve native species of game, leaving the exotics to the laboratory. Brook trout, which he called "specks," were his favorite fish, and the turkey was the bird for which he worked to restore in the mountains near his home at Woody Gap."

John Martin, Editor and Publisher
Southern Outdoors, July 1, 1946

"My grandfather had a special fondness for wild turkeys," Jean McNey recalled. "He loved to hunt them, and he could always go out and get one or two for the table, especially if we had a guest coming for supper or, if we happened to be celebrating some special holiday during the year."

Next to his beloved deer and trout, wild turkeys were the most important wild game animal in Ranger Woody's life. He had a lifelong passion for his mountain turkeys. He hunted them as a boy, and during the 1920s and '30s, at the height of his restoration work with deer, he protected the local turkeys and worked hard at trying to rebuild a viable turkey population inside Rock Creek Refuge. He protected his turkeys as vehemently as he protected his deer.

He frequently collected eggs from nests found by local farmers and mountaineers. After hatching, he placed the young poults in pens and much like his deer, released them into the refuge as soon as they were old enough to survive. Apparently those efforts often proved futile because most of the hand-raised birds succumbed to predators. Undaunted, Ranger Woody always had an alternate plan for every endeavor. Simply protecting the remnant populations of turkeys inside the refuge brought considerable success and their numbers slowly increased. It is interesting to note that the great chestnut blight of the 1920s and '30s, and the subsequent loss of a favored and highly important food item, greatly impacted not only turkeys, but deer and bears as well. It was especially devastating to the turkeys because chestnuts were always more abundant and much more dependable as a food source than acorns, and had long been a mainstay of the turkey's diet. However, all three species apparently adjusted to the loss of chestnuts amazingly well.

Most of the turkeys Ranger Woody killed in his later life were for special occasions as Jean mentioned – holidays like Thanksgiving or Christmas or at times when a special guest like Georgia Governor E.D. "Ed" Rivers was planning to stop by for dinner. As with his boyhood exploits, very little information was ever recorded about Ranger Woody's turkey hunting experiences or about his efforts to rebuild the local population. In this respect, his actions always spoke louder than his words. He was a doer, and he quietly went about the business of protecting *his* turkeys with little fanfare.

Several articles written about the Ranger in the 1940s mention his efforts to increase and protect the turkey population inside the refuge. Charlie Elliott and others were fully aware of the successful efforts Ranger Woody made to protect and increase the turkey population in the area.

A Seasoned Turkey Hunter

Modern turkey hunters would be interested to know that many of the turn-of-the-century old-timers hunted turkeys with a rifle, usually their deer rifle. Ranger Woody was no exception. His preference for hunting the big birds was a trusty Savage lever-action Model 99 shooting a very small center-fire bullet instead of a shotgun. (The caliber was believed to be .250 or .250/3000, a very fast bullet that produced a velocity of over 3,000 fps). Even in his later years when the turkey population in southern Union County was still relatively low, he always seemed to have an uncanny ability to go out and shoot a turkey (or two) just about any time he felt the urge to do so.

Because he was such an ardent conservationist, one has to speculate that Ranger Woody must have had a good idea about the numbers of turkeys in the area, and he must have felt comfortable shooting an occasional turkey for the pot. Those numbers must have been sufficient for the limited hunting he and others did in the area. It's doubtful he would have continued hunting turkeys if they had been in serious danger of becoming totally wiped out.

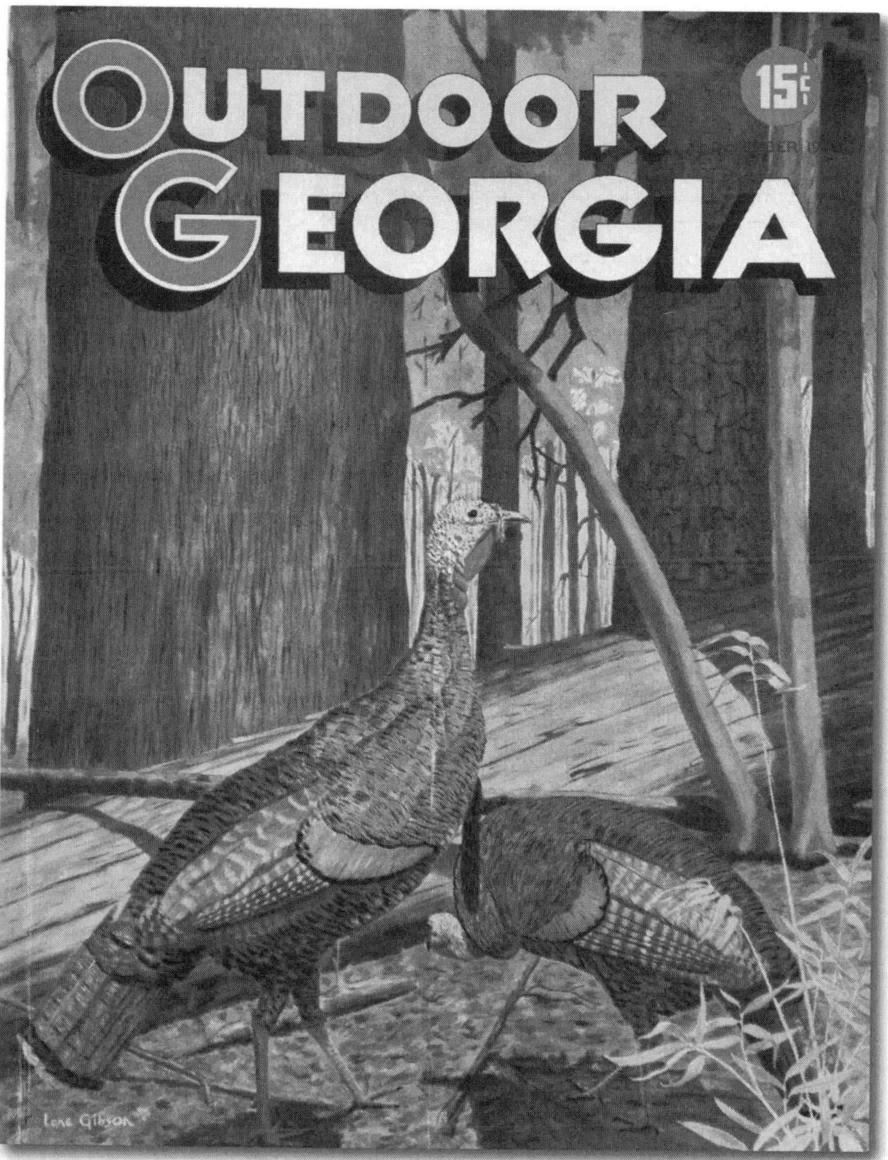

In 1940, Charlie Elliott served as editor of the state-sponsored and very popular Outdoor Georgia magazine. The December 1940 issue featured a story he wrote about the historic deer hunt at Blue Ridge WMA. Roscoe Reams attended the five-day archery hunt, while Charlie attended both the archery and firearms hunts. Photo courtesy of Outdoor Georgia magazine and the University of Georgia Library.

Mountain turkeys are fairly predictable in their habits because of the terrain and the limited amount of seasonal foods like acorns, which are often concentrated in specific areas. Ranger Woody probably kept very close tabs on several resident flocks. Mountain flocks tend to be quite large, and he probably had a good idea of where the local turkeys roosted, where they spent most of their time feeding in the woods, and where they gathered in mountain coves.

It's not unusual to see mountain flocks with 20 to 30 birds or more. If the Ranger wanted to shoot a single bird for table fare, he likely did it only when he knew the flock was healthy and strong and when plenty of younger birds were coming along to replace the older ones. This is all conjecture, but knowing how the Ranger felt about managing and utilizing the fish and other wildlife resources in his native mountains, it makes sense.

Jean McNey likes to tell the story about the celebration that took place in Suches after the road from Woody Gap to Suches was completed in the late 1920s.

"Papa and Uncle Walter had hired a crew of probably 25 to 30 men to carve out the road up to Woody Gap, and it was a long and challenging job," Jean said. "I remember hearing the story about how my grandfather went out and shot a couple of turkeys and June and Mae cooked up a special dinner for all of the men who had worked so hard on that very difficult project. There was a large celebration in Suches marking the completion of the road."

Upon completion of the new road from Suches to Woody Gap in the late 1920s, spearheaded by Ranger Woody and his son Walter, a celebration was held in Suches. The road connected to the recently completed road that ran from Woody Gap to Stonepile Gap (later to become Highway 60), making access to Dahlonega much easier by automobile. Ranger Woody reportedly went out and shot several wild turkeys for the milestone celebration. Two unidentified men appear to be feasting on turkey legs, likely provided by the Ranger's trusty Savage rifle. Photo courtesy of Jean McNey.

Henry Moore, a contractor from Dahlonega, had hired a similar crew to build that portion of the road from Stonepile Gap to Woody Gap, where the two roads merged into one (see Chapter 8). It is not clear whether or not the celebration in Suches included both crews of workers or just the Woody crew, but it is likely both crews took part in the noted celebration. The construction of the road from Stonepile Gap to Suches was a significant event to the mountain folk living on the northwest side of Black Mountain because it made access to Dahlonega much easier. In essence, it opened up a very remote part of the mountains. Eventually that important road became Highway 60.

No open or closed season existed on wild turkeys in the mountain region during the early 1900s, and the big birds were hunted by local mountaineers on a year-round basis because of the delicious meat they provided. Both hens and gobblers were fair game. Baiting by corn and shooting one or more turkeys off an evening or morning roost was not considered unethical or unsportsmanlike. After his 40,000-acre Rock Creek Refuge became off-limits to any kind of hunting (prior to 1940, only trout fishing was allowed inside the Refuge), the local turkey population was also protected by default and allowed to increase in numbers during the years between 1927 and 1940 when the deer herd was expanding.

By the early 1900s, native wild turkeys had been decimated in North America (like many other wildlife and game species) because of habitat destruction, commercial hunting, and lack of hunting regulations. As mentioned, in the North Georgia Mountains of Union County where Arthur Woody grew up, turkeys were never completely wiped out. As a result, turkeys were never "officially" stocked in the Blue Ridge Refuge by either the state of Georgia or the federal government during the nearly three decades Ranger Woody managed the Refuge. After his death, turkeys were live-trapped in other areas and stocked in various mountain locations during the late 1950s and early '60s through funds provided by the Pittman-Robertson Act. But none were ever stocked in Blue Ridge WMA because after Ranger Woody's death in 1946 the Refuge contained a respectable native population.

Interestingly, it was not until 1955 that the first legal turkey season of the modern era was opened to hunters in Blue Ridge WMA, nine years after the Ranger's death. However, during the first few archery hunts held in the refuge in 1940, 1941 and 1942, the rules stated that archers could shoot one wild turkey. None were ever taken by the budding archers, and the all-too-effective firearms hunters who came in right after the archers were never given that same opportunity.

Hunting with Dogs

Ranger Woody loved his dogs, and always had several around the house, but it is not known whether or not he ever used a hunting dog in conjunction with his turkey hunting. There is no evidence to suggest that he did. Many veteran turkey hunters who plied their trade during the early 20th century in the Southeast frequently used a dog to help locate a flock. Once a flock was located, the dog was then sent in to scatter the flock so that the birds could be called in by the hunter as they attempted to reassemble. This custom was quite common in the coastal plain areas of the South.

In the high country where Ranger Woody hunted, however, it would have been a little more difficult because a scattered flock near the top of a mountain might pitch off the side of that mountain and glide over to the next valley a full half a mile away, making it difficult to call them back in. In the coastal plain country of Georgia and the Carolinas where the terrain is much flatter, a single gobbler from a scattered flock would be much easier to call in because it probably flew only a short distance when the flock was disrupted.

A Never-ending Feud with Hawks and Wildcats

Ranger Woody was an excellent rifle shot. He loved to shoot and he got plenty of practice.

"He hated hawks and wildcats (bobcats) with a passion," Charlie Elliott remembered. "And he had good reason to feud with those highly proficient predators. Hawks preyed on his young turkeys and bobcats frequently preyed on his deer. He declared war against both species and went to great lengths to hunt them down whenever he could.

Charlie remembered one time when Ranger Woody had a clutch of young turkey poults in a pen inside the refuge that he intended to release as soon as they were old enough. Young turkeys can fly at a very young age (at least well enough to get from the ground to a low lying tree limb to avoid predators like bobcats), and the Range had clipped their wings so they couldn't escape the enclosure. One by one, the young birds began to disappear. Ranger Woody soon discovered that every day or so a hawk was swooping down into the pen and carrying off one of his precious poults.

"He was furious," Charlie said. "From that time on, he shot every hawk he could get a bead on."

"Once, when we were driving along, we saw a big red-tailed hawk circling over a mountain valley," Charlie continued. "As the hawk steadily drew closer, Ranger Woody slammed the truck to a stop and grabbed his old lever-action .30-30. He jumped out and took aim. Blam! The hawk crumpled!"

"That's one hawk that won't be killin' no more of my turkey chicks," the Ranger proudly told Charlie.

According to his autobiography, Charlie Elliott killed his first wild turkey in the North Georgia Mountains in 1923 on his first-ever turkey hunt at the age of 18. After attending the University of Georgia in the early 1920s for several years, he went to work in Union County as an assistant regional forester for the Georgia Department of Forestry. His job put him in close touch with Ranger Woody, who was 21 years his senior. The two men became good friends and worked together closely for the next two decades until the Ranger's death in 1946.

The following quote is from a story I wrote in the March 1989 issue of *Georgia Sportsman* magazine titled "The True Colors of Charlie Elliott." At the time I interviewed Charlie for this story in 1988, I had no reason to question him about the "old mountaineer" who directed him to the old home place where he killed his first wild turkey. It is entirely possible that the mountaineer he referred to could have been Ranger Arthur Woody. If not the Ranger

Charlie Elliott, known in later years as "the Old Professor" in turkey-hunting circles, shows off two fine mountain gobblers taken while hunting with his lifelong friend, Roscoe Reams, in the late 1980s. Charlie's passion for hunting turkeys began some 60 years earlier as a youngster when he became acquainted with Ranger Arthur Woody. Photo courtesy of Mrs. Elinor Reams.

himself, it was probably another mountaineer with whom the Ranger had put Charlie in touch.

> "There were few turkeys in the state back then and this old mountaineer had told me where I might find some," Charlie said. "I had an old Model 12 (Winchester), 12-gauge, and I went to this old home place that the mountain man had told me about. I no sooner got out of my car and started walking around when a gobbler flushed right in front of me. I shot him in the air. When I got back, the old man said, 'Boy, you sure got him fast.' I said, 'Yeah, there's nothing to this turkey hunting!"

Of course, Charlie later known fondly in turkey hunting circles as "the Old Professor," learned a lot more about the art of turkey hunting over the next six decades, and he went on to become a nationally acclaimed turkey expert. Among the 20-some-odd books he wrote during his lifetime, two were about turkey hunting, and several others contained some of his favorite turkey hunting stories. He also wrote numerous magazine articles in *Outdoor Life* about his turkey hunting adventures. His early interest in outsmarting cagey old mountain gobblers no doubt was heavily influenced by his close friend and mentor Arthur Woody. Since he and the Ranger each shared a lifelong passion for hunting wild turkeys, it is likely they hunted together from time to time (although I could find no written evidence to verify this).

Roscoe Reams began a life-changing friendship with Arthur Woody in 1938 when he was 14 years old. He went on to become a nationally-known trick archery shooter during the 1950s and '60s, as well as a nationally-known turkey hunting expert in the 1970s, '80s and '90s. He and Charlie Elliott became the best of friends in the early 1940s. The two men hunted and fished together for over 50 years. Ranger Woody had a profound influence on the lives of both men. Photo courtesy of Mrs. Elinor Reams.

Ranger Woody's Turkeys –
The Purest Strain in the Mountains Today

At age 15, Herb McClure of Cleveland, Georgia, started turkey hunting at Blue Ridge WMA when the first modern season was opened in 1955. Born in 1940, the year the first deer hunt took place in Blue Ridge, Herb went on to become a well-known expert on hunting mountain turkeys in his own right. In 2012, he published an outstanding book titled *Native Turkeys, and a Georgia Mountain Turkey Hunter.* In that book, Herb explains that the native mountain birds in Union County, and more specifically in Blue Ridge WMA, were never completely killed out (thanks to Ranger Woody's efforts to protect the population and his efforts to continually increase turkey numbers during the '20s, '30s and '40s). That's why little to no restocking was done in that specific area in later years while other sections of the mountains were being repopulated.

As a result, Herb believes the turkeys found in Blue Ridge WMA are the purest strain of native birds found anywhere in the North Georgia Mountains. Because of their "pure-blooded" status, Herb also believes these native turkeys are darker in color and traditionally have been much more difficult to hunt – that is, much harder to call in and kill over the years. He should know. Herb killed his first Blue Ridge gobbler in 1956, the second year that a spring turkey season was held (ten years after Ranger Woody's death).

Even today, although some of the native Blue Ridge birds have no doubt had their gene pool diluted to some extent by turkeys moving in from other areas, the mountain birds in the southern portion of Union County remain very tough and challenging to hunt. Thanks to Ranger Woody's efforts, some of Georgia's most notable turkey hunters who came along in the 1950s – men like the legendary Arthur Truelove (with whom Herb hunted on a number of occasions) cut their teeth hunting the elusive "black" birds of Blue Ridge WMA. Since 1955, other pioneer turkey hunters like Herb McClure and Roscoe Reams consistently outsmarted tough Blue Ridge gobblers for many decades. Their success is a real tribute to Ranger Woody's tireless efforts.

Taking pride in one's marksmanship has been a mountain tradition for generations. In the late 1800s and early 1900s, many an old-time turkey hunter preferred to draw down on a wary gobbler with his deer rifle in areas up and down the Eastern Seaboard where whitetails and turkeys had not been completely wiped out. It was not until the mid-20th century, when the first modern seasons were being established, that most shotgun-only laws were put into effect in Eastern states. But even today, a few states still allow rifle hunting for turkeys.

Herb McClure's excellent book contains detailed historic facts about turkey hunting in Ranger Woody's Blue Ridge WMA in the 1950s after the first spring hunting seasons were established. Courtesy of Herb McClure.

The debate between using rifles or shotguns for turkey hunting in the South goes back to the first modern legal turkey hunting seasons in the 1950s. Hunters who wanted to test their calling ability might opt for a shotgun in order to "get 'em in close." Hunters who wanted to test their marksmanship at longer distances might opt for a rifle. Some early 20th century hunters split the difference by using over-and-under rifle/shotgun combinations. The idea here was to kill him close with a shotgun pattern if possible, but if he hung up out of shotgun range, the hunter could always resort to shooting him with the rifle barrel.

In the classic book, *The American Wild Turkey* by Henry Davis, the author talked about his preference for a small, center-fire rifle over a shotgun for hunting turkeys in the early 1900s. He believed it took a real marksman over a shotgun hunter to place a shot precisely at the top of the wing so that the bullet put the turkey down for good (without destroying much meat) and prevented it from being able to fly away and possibly become lost.

> "I've found that the best place is where the wings join the body," the author stated. "It's a much larger target, albeit not a huge target, but much better than a head shot. A gobbler's head seems to be constantly moving and bobbing. Shot with a .22 Magnum and a 40 or 50 grain hollow point, not too much meat is destroyed either. A lot of states don't allow for using a rifle on wild turkey so check your game laws."

For decades, turkey hunters have traditionally collected the beards and spurs from their trophy gobblers just as deer hunters collect the antlers from the bucks they kill. When Herb McClure first began hunting turkeys in the Blue Ridge WMA in the mid-1950s, he often stopped by the hardware store in Dahlonega to pick up shells or other supplies. Herb remembers seeing a string of long turkey beards hanging on one wall in that old store, and he was told by a salesman working in the store that the gobblers once sporting those 10- and 12-inch-long beards were said to have been killed by none other than Ranger Arthur Woody.

One can only imagine the rich stories the Ranger must have shared around the campfire concerning his remarkable turkey hunting exploits.

At a spry 88, CCC veteran Clyde Harkins poses near his garden in 2014. "Back in my CC days, we worked hard but we also had a good time," Clyde said. "The WPA, which originally stood for Roosevelt's 'Works Progress Administration' (and was later changed to 'Works Projects Administration,') had a totally different meaning to us. To us the initials stood for, 'We Piddle Around.' And we did! We had fun whenever we could, but we also did an awful lot of hard work." Photo by Duncan Dobie.

CHAPTER 11
A Voice from the Past
Clyde Harkins and the CCC

"Ranger Woody was a pretty good fellow! I never would have gotten into the CC without his help. The Forest Service people all loved him. He did a lot of good things for the forest and the mountain people in general."

Clyde Harkins, Civilian Conservation Corps member,
Camp Woody F-1, 1940

The Civilian Conservation Corps was a Godsend to the people of the North Georgia Mountains. Its legacy to Union County was especially significant, where an initially pessimistic Ranger Woody quickly realized the benefits of such a talented work force and wasted little time in taking full advantage of its incredible manpower. Although Franklin Delano Roosevelt is still criticized by some for many of his "New Deal" programs launched during the Great Depression, this was one program that worked brilliantly at a time in history when the country was at one of its lowest ebbs.

Unlike many of the wasteful and unproductive government entitlement programs of today, the "CC" boys worked hard for their money – amounting to all of one dollar per day, most of which had to be sent home at the end of every month. The long-term benefits these dedicated boys provided to the Forest Service, and the citizens of Georgia, are impossible to measure. Much of their handiwork is still evident today.

These young men virtually opened up many remote areas in the mountains by improving very poor roads that were impassable to automobiles, building new roads, and paving many of those roads with granite gravel crushed by their own hands. In Union County, the "Sultans of Suches," as they fondly referred to themselves (Camp Woody, Co. No. 1405, Project F-1, organized in 1933), planted tens of thousands of trees, fought forest fires and built at least three fire towers. They built lakes and erosion control dams, and stocked thousands of trout in remote streams. They improved the habitat in many of those streams by building fish pools and making other habitat improvements. They built rock structures and beaches at Vogel State Park and Lake Winfield Scott. (Camp Enotah, GA SP-2, 431st Co., Blairsville, also worked with Ranger Woody on a number of projects including the new fire tower at Brasstown Bald, as did the hard-working boys at Camp Robertstown, Co. 456, F-3.) They helped improve and maintain that portion of the Appalachian Trail that traverses Union and White counties, and built the Trail's historic rock shelter on Blood Mountain, a now iconic structure that hikers actually pass through.

The CC boys strung hundreds of miles of telephone wire and helped protect the forests from poachers and arsonists. They pioneered many forest improvement initiatives. They existed for a relatively short but historic span of time – less than a decade, beginning in 1933 and ending on July 1, 1942, six months after the attack on Pearl Harbor. With the advent of war, thousands of former CC workers proudly went off to serve their country, making some of the finest soldiers in the country because of their former training and experience.

Clyde Harkins Remembers

At a spry 90, Clyde Harkins of Wolf Pen Gap has a perpetual smile, an innate curiosity about life and a special twinkle in his eyes that causes you to like him immediately. He's a mountain man through and through. He possesses that tough, rugged self-confidence that can get a man through just about anything, and over the past nine decades, he's been through a lot.

Clyde has a real love of life similar to that of Ranger Woody and many other men of the mountains; it shows in everything he does. Being around him and listening to his stories is inspiring. And like practically all mountain men, he has had a lifelong taste and appreciation for the nectar of the mountains. He dearly loves to partake in a little nip of homemade corn whiskey once in a while.

For him, moonshine in its various forms has always been a sort of mountain medicine that brightens a man's life and makes him glow all over. Outsiders and flatlanders may have a hard time understanding this. To some, it simply burns going down. But to Clyde Harkins, partaking in an occasional "swaller" of white lightning is the spice of life. It's what makes life worth living!

Like Ranger Woody, Clyde comes from a long line of rugged mountaineers who settled in the headwaters of Cooper's Creek just north of Suches in Union County in the mid-1800s. The son of James (Big Jim) and Lola Harkins, and the youngest of five boys, Clyde was born in 1925. Like Ranger Woody, He grew up working on the family farm with his older brothers – plowing behind a horse and keeping track of the family's small herd of free-ranging cattle, which roamed the nearby hills. He and his brothers hunted wild hogs by day and 'coons by night. They fished for native brook trout in the crystal clear mountain streams and occasionally came across a stray deer or two that were just starting to repopulate the area. Nearby, looming over the Harkins farm, were historic Blood and Slaughter mountains where the boys eagerly spent much of their boyhood time.

The Harkins brothers were close.

"We had a saying," Clyde said. "You pick a fight with one Harkins brother, you got us all to deal with!"

At age 15, Clyde decided to join the Civilian Conservation Corps at Camp Woody in Suches during the annual enlistment in the spring of 1940. His older brother Eldo had already joined the CC and had been sent to California. Later on, Eldo served in the Army during the war and was badly wounded by shrapnel in the Philippines.

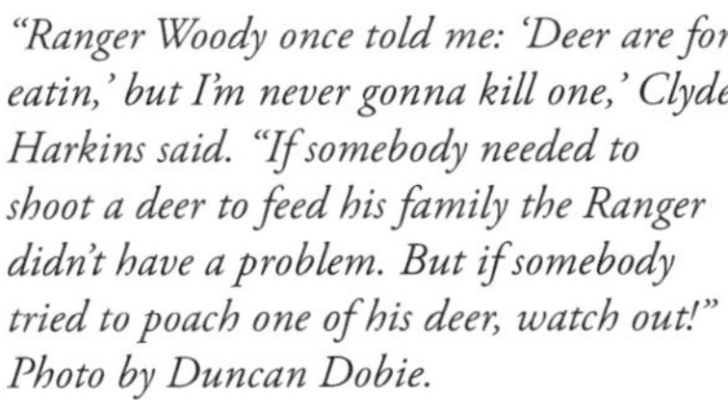

"Ranger Woody once told me: 'Deer are for eatin,' but I'm never gonna kill one,' Clyde Harkins said. "If somebody needed to shoot a deer to feed his family the Ranger didn't have a problem. But if somebody tried to poach one of his deer, watch out!" Photo by Duncan Dobie.

In 1940, Clyde knew he had a giant hurdle to overcome in order to be accepted into the CC at age 15. Giving his size and stature – he stood 5 feet, 2 inches tall and weighed about 110 pounds soaking wet – he didn't stand much of a chance. Despite his size, his mountain upbringing made him strong and agile. Since he knew the CC boys commonly engaged in considerable physical labor, he was justifiably worried that he might not pass the required physical examination. But he was determined, and on registration day, he walked from his home near Cooper's Creek down to Camp Woody in Suches to join the corps if possible (a distance of nearly 10 miles).

"Ranger Woody ran everything in Suches," Clyde said. "His sons Clyne and Walter both worked for the Forest Service during those years, and they helped their father quite a bit with his various projects. I always got along with the Ranger and both of the boys pretty good." (Camp Woody was administered by the U.S. Forest Service and as mentioned, 38-year-old Walter Woody served as Camp Project Superintendent. By 1940, 35-year-old Clyne was working for the Forest Service in Rabun County and not living in Suches.)

"You earned $30 a month with the CC," Clyde said. "When the program started in 1933, you could keep $5, but $25 had to be sent home to Momma. By the time I joined up in 1940, you could keep $8 and $22 had to be sent home.

"As soon as I got to the Suches Camp (Camp Woody), I saw Ranger Woody outside with some of the other camp officials. There were about 200 boys there that day trying to sign up. The minute he saw me, Ranger Woody singled me out. He looked over and yelled, 'What are *you* doing here, Sonny Boy?'

"'I wanna get in the CC,' I answered.

"'You'll never make it,' he said. 'Why do you wanna get in, anyway?'

"'My family needs the money,' I answered.

"'You can't make it,' he said again. "You ain't big enough."

"'You can help me get in, Ranger,' I said.

"Ranger Woody looked at me and just shook his head. Later on, while I was taking the physical, I weighed in at 109 pounds. The doctor looked at me and said, 'We've never had anyone this small in this camp.' I thought I would be going home for sure."

However, when officials started calling out names and issuing uniforms to those boys who had been accepted, Clyde's name rang out. "Talk about being surprised! I went inside and got my duffel bag of clothes that was issued to each boy. I proudly walked outside with my sea-bag duffel over my shoulder, smiling. Ranger Woody was right there. 'Well jes' look at ol' Harkins,' he yelled out so that everyone could hear. 'He made it after all!'

Clyde was beaming from ear to ear. He knew that Ranger Woody had been responsible for his acceptance. "Ranger Woody was a pretty good fellow!" Clyde said. "He helped a lot of people, but there were still some people who didn't like him. There was bad blood between the Woody's and several other families, but you're always gonna see that sort of thing in any community. He helped so many people during his ranger years, and the Forest Service people loved him to death."

During the one-year period that he served in the CC, Clyde did a variety of jobs. He helped build several of the campsites and rock grills at Lake Winfield Scott, and he helped put out sand on the beach. He worked with a crew setting out white pine saplings on Black Mountain. He also did some road work. Despite his size, he worked at "busting" rock into gravel for various road projects in the area. At the time, most of the roads in the Suches area were unpaved gravel roads, some not much more than wagon trails, and in addition to breaking up the rock, Clyde also helped spread some of the gravel

A group of CCC officials, composed of civilian and Forest Service personnel, poses at Camp Woody in Suches, circa late 1930s. Reverend Claud Boynton, who worked at the camp as a much-revered civilian supervisor and spiritual leader, stands second from right on the front row. Clyne Woody, Ranger Woody's son, stands third from left on front row, while Ranger Woody poses in the middle of the group with hat in hand. The dedicated "CC" boys, who idolized Ranger Woody, went far beyond the call of duty as they faithfully carried out many of his Forest Service and community projects. Rev. Boynton had a profound influence on Clyde Harkins' life during Clyde's one-year stint in the CCC in 1940. In later years, Rev. Boynton served as pastor for the entire Harkins family. Photo courtesy of Jean McNey.

over those unpaved roads. Busting rock was backbreaking manual work, done in those days by hand with a heavy sledge hammer. "We had a mechanized rock crusher," Clyde said, "but we crushed a lot of the small stuff by hand.

"Our local preacher, Claud Boynton, who also baptized me, trained me on fire prevention," Clyde said. "We helped put out a few small local fires during my time with the CC."

Preacher Boynton, as he was fondly known, became an institution in Union County during the late 1930s and throughout the '40s. He, like many others in Suches, had a direct link to Ranger Woody. Fresh out of college in the mid-1930s, Reverend Claud Cole Boynton had come to Lake Winfield Scott for a brief vacation with his bride, the former Annis Grace Ozmer. He had just graduated from Mercer University in Macon and was planning to attend Southern Baptist Theological Seminary in Louisville, Kentucky. After seminary, he planned to pursue a career as a church minister in a major city somewhere in the South.

But it was not to be. While staying at Lake Winfield Scott, the young minister preached several guest sermons at local churches and revivals. During one of those sermons, Ranger Woody happened to be in the congregation. Depending on how you look at it, this might have been one of the luckiest or unluckiest things that ever happened to Reverend Boynton. Ranger Woody liked what he had heard so much that he prevailed upon Reverend Boynton to remain in the mountains on a permanent basis. Once Ranger Woody set his sights on achieving an objective, nothing was going to stop him, so poor Reverend Boynton never stood much of a chance at pursuing his intended goal of running a large church in a big city some day.

Reportedly the Ranger told him, "You don't have to go away to no seminary. You'll get twice the trainin' right here in these mountains, and we need a good preacher like you in the worst way."

To sweeten the deal, Ranger Woody offered to build the preacher a house in Suches (which he did) and promised him a job working as a supervisor for the CCC at Camp Woody in Suches (which he also did), a job which helped subsidize the young couple's meager church salary and provide some badly needed income. How could the reverend refuse such an offer?

Reverend Boynton assumed leadership at Choestoe Baptist Church and started preaching part time at Mt. Lebanon Baptist Church in Suches. During the early years of his career in the mid 1930s, Preacher Boynton preached part-time on Sundays and on Wednesday nights. When he wasn't preaching, he worked with the "CC boys" at Camp Woody as chaplain, and also as a supervisor for building roads, fire towers, putting out forest fires and planting

Ranger Woody's daughter, Mae Woody, sits in front of the canoe on the left, while several friends enjoy a peaceful outing on Lake Winfield Scott, one of four lakes her father was instrumental in building. The canoes were paddled by park rangers. Photo by Kenneth Rogers, circa 1940, courtesy of Jean McNey.

trees. Serving under him, Clyde did all of those various jobs during his one-year stint.

Ranger Woody was seldom wrong with his instincts. Over the years, Reverend Boynton became an institution in the area and positively impacted many people in Union County. His career spanned nearly two decades (from the mid-1930s to 1954) in various churches within the county. Jean McNey remembered that Reverend Boynton always called her "Baby Jane." A gifted soloist who loved to sing, he once horrified Jean by making her stand up and sing by herself at Mt. Lebanon Baptist Church when she was a young girl.

This photo of Reverend Claud Boynton appeared in Outdoor Georgia magazine in 1945. At the time, the magazine had organized a fund-raising drive to solicit money from sportsmen to build a monument to honor Ranger Arthur Woody. Rev. Boynton was highly supportive of the fund and its first donor. During the two decades he spent in the North Georgia mountains, before his premature death in 1954, Rev. Boynton had an extraordinary impact on countless lives, both young and old. Photo courtesy of Outdoor Georgia magazine.

Ethelene Dyer Jones, who grew up attending Zion Baptist Church in Suches, remembers, "He was an apt teacher of the Word of God, and often led what we then called 'study courses' for members of his congregation, with the studies focused on particular books of the Bible. He was a lover of young people, and ever encouraged them to get education beyond high school. He was good at knowing how to assist them to apply for and receive scholarships for college studies. He introduced Vacation Bible Schools as part of the summer programs in every church where he served as pastor. He often liked to state of his work in the mountains: 'I came here on a vacation and spent the rest of my life serving God in these mountains.'"

Sadly, Reverend Boynton died from a sudden heart attack at age 61 on Nov. 13, 1954.

Clyde, whose nickname was "Lost John" in the CC, also did some work on the famous Rock House that stands guard over the Appalachian Trail on Blood Mountain. This is the only edifice on the entire 2,180-mile-long trail from Maine to Georgia where the trail actually passes through a manmade structure. "I got to know Charlie Elliott a little when we were working on the trail," Clyde said. "He was a good man.

"My favorite job in the CC was helping to make "fish holes" for trout down on Little Rock Creek. I loved doing that. After the war, a lot of that work was done with funds provided by the Pittman-Robertson Act. That act really paved the way for helping wildlife."

(After Ranger Woody's death in 1946, Clyde worked for the Forest Service off and on in the late 1940s. He helped build and maintain trails, worked at the trout hatchery and built and improved numerous fish holes in local streams.)

World War II Comes to the Mountains

After his one-year enlistment with the CC, Clyde returned home in 1941 at age 16. When war came later that year, all four of his older brothers eventually joined some branch of service. By this time, the Harkins boys also had been blessed with a younger sister, Stella Mae, 11 years Clyde's junior.

The oldest of the five brothers, Ira T., or I.T. as he was fondly known by his family and friends, was actually drafted into the Army in 1941 before the war started. Eldo was drafted into the Army in 1942 and saw considerable action in Guam. Twins Harley and Ralph joined the Navy in 1943. It was only a matter of time before Clyde, too, felt obliged to do his part and serve his country in some capacity.

"The Ranger was always generous about letting local people cut board trees in the forest when they needed to repair a house or a barn," Clyde said. "He believed the national forest belonged to all of the people. Once, my dad Jim Harkins needed some boards and asked Ranger Woody if he could cut a couple of trees out in the forest. A 'board tree' is a straight hardwood tree like a red oak without any knots that will produce good boards for building. After the chestnut blight hit in the 1920s, and started killing thousands of trees, we salvaged many a tree for rails and boards." Photo by Duncan Dobie.

"I tried to volunteer, even though my mother asked me not to," Clyde said. "Since I was underage, someone on the local draft board had to sign the papers. Wouldn't you know it – Ranger Woody happened to be that person! This time, he made it clear that he wasn't about to help me out."

"'That young buck ain't goin' nowhere, and I ain't signing no papers,' Ranger Woody adamantly told Clyde's parents in no uncertain terms. 'He's got enough brothers servin' the cause already. Four Harkins gone off to war is bad enough. Clyde's stayin' right here!'

Ranger Woody would not change his mind. Much of the war news being heard over the radio waves was not good. After procuring a radio for the family in the early 1940s, Arthur, June and Mae loved to listen to radio personality Gabriel Heatter at night while sitting around the fire. The popular newscaster often shared news from the battle fronts in Europe and the Pacific. By the time Clyde tried to volunteer in 1943, it's entirely possible that the Woody family had heard the devastating news about the "fighting Sullivans," five brothers from Waterloo, Iowa, who had joined the Navy together, served on the same ship, and perished on Nov. 13, 1942, after their ship the U.S.S. Juneau had been torpedoed by the Japanese. It went down near Guadalcanal in the Pacific. News of the loss arrived in the U.S. in early 1943.

Clyde was determined. As soon as he turned 18, he joined the Navy in 1944. He proudly served on the 320-foot Landing Ship Tank 284, a massive hulk of a ship that carried troops, tanks and other heavy equipment. Called an "LST" for short, Clyde made it to the coast of France just after D-Day, unloading tanks and other vehicles on the beaches of Normandy. He next saw action in Italy and eventually sailed half-way around the world to the South Pacific. Clyde was first a gunner and later a leading seaman in charge of rigging and other tackle on the ship.

"Three of my brothers saw some type of combat during the war, and Eldo was wounded pretty badly in the Philippines, but everyone came home alive," Clyde said proudly.

Because they all made it through the war alive, the five Harkins boys were treated as heroes in Union County upon their arrival home. Not to be outdone by her older brothers, a decade after the war ended, Clyde's baby sister, Stella Mae, joined the Air Force in 1956.

"Back in my CC days, we worked hard but we also had a good time," Clyde said. "The WPA, which originally stood for Roosevelt's 'Works Progress Administration' and was later changed to 'Works Projects Administration,' had a totally different meaning to us. To us it meant, 'We Piddle Around.' And we did! We tried to have a good time whenever we could. But we also did an awful lot of hard work."

I had the pleasure of meeting Clyde and interviewing him for the first time at his home near Lake Winfield Scott in July 2013. I was thrilled with the prospects of meeting an actual CC veteran and a man who personality had known Ranger Woody. I wasn't disappointed. I found Clyde to be a living, breathing witness to history, but I quickly learned that he was so much more. Like many mountaineers, I found Clyde to be a self-made man who grew up during very hard times. By necessity, he became a jack-of-all-trades, having mastered many different skills over the years in order to make a living in a very tough environment. But there were three things that really struck me about him. One was his intelligence. Clyde is a smart man. His insight into the history and the very pulse of the area was extraordinary. The second was his obvious love and reverence for the mountains where he had been raised. The third was his sense of humor. Clyde has a way of poking fun at everything in life.

Clyde has a deep abiding respect for the mountains and the wildlife that he has grown to know so well. At one point during our interview, as we were walking around his 15-acre farm, he took me up to the top of a small knoll several hundred yards behind his house so that he could show me the breathtaking view of Blood Mountain.

In some ways, Clyde might be the closest thing to a living Ranger Woody that you could ever find in the mountains in the 21st century.

Ranger Woody looks on as two unidentified men (possibly Forest Service officials) try their hand at fly fishing off a dock in one of North Georgia's most picturesque lakes, Lake Winfield Scott. The Ranger was instrumental in building the lake and stocking it with fish. Many of the rock grills in the camping areas around the lake were built by his dedicated "CC" boys. Clyde Harkins had a hand in building some of those enduring rock structures. Photo circa early 1940s, courtesy of Jean McNey.

Ranger Woody's beloved "pet" doe, Peggie, was a frequent sight around the Woody home and Ranger Station. She reportedly produced 11 fawns in 7 years during the 1930s. Photo circa late 1930s, courtesy of Jean McNey.

CHAPTER 12
Ranger Woody and His Deer

"The Ranger is awful funny about them deer a' his. Ya' better not mess with 'em, I'll tell ya' that much."

An anonymous Union County farmer, circa 1935

White-tailed deer are the most emotion stirring animals on the planet. It matters little whether you're a hunter, a non-hunter, a man, a woman, a child of nature, or a city dweller surrounded by skyscrapers that seldom gets to witness the spectacle of a full moon rising in the night sky, the sight of a deer – any deer – has a way of touching your soul. It also matters little whether you're looking at a group of deer feeding in a field, a stately buck with a huge set of "horns" breathing fire from his nostrils on a cold November day, or a sleek doe with two beautiful twin fawns in summer – *all* deer have a way of casting a magical spell over humans like no other animal on this earth can do. Without question, deer certainly had that kind of effect on a Georgia mountain boy named Arthur Woody.

Whitetails have been an integral part of American history since the first Europeans landed on our eastern shores. And just like Ranger Woody himself, whitetails are true American originals. Although some have been transplanted to other parts of the world like New Zealand and Finland, where they now thrive in large numbers, they are native only to North America (like native wild turkeys Ranger Woody so loved), and paleontologists tell us they've been around for nearly a million years.

Just as the once vast herds of buffalo in the West were the staff of life to the Plains Indians, whitetails sustained virtually all of the various tribes of Eastern Indians. Whitetails were always challenging to hunt, their delicious meat was protein-rich, and the Eastern tribes utilized every part of a deer's body. Nothing went to waste. When the Pilgrims landed on the shores of Massachusetts in 1620, local Indians generously shared venison with these people time and again to keep them from starving. Although turkeys have come to symbolize our Thanksgiving tradition in America, when those same Pilgrims celebrated their very first Thanksgiving after a deadly and harrowing winter in the New World, roast venison from the four or five deer provided by well-intentioned Indian neighbors was much more abundant at that celebrated feast than roast turkey.

The early pioneers quickly adopted the Indian tradition of hunting deer for food, making clothing out of buckskins and using other parts of the deer's body for utilitarian purposes like tools and knife handles. In the classic booklet titled *The White-Tailed Deer,* published by the Conservation Department of Olin Mathieson Chemical Company in 1961, well-known author and much-loved outdoor writer John Madson noted the following:

> America grew up eating venison and wearing buckskin.
>
> We were weaned as a nation on deer meat, took our first toddling steps in deer-hide moccasins, and came of age at King's Mountain and New Orleans when our deer-trained riflemen cut down foreign regulars in long scarlet swaths.
>
> We scraped, oiled and stretched buckskin over our cabin windows in lieu of glass. When the crops were put by, maybe we walked down the mountain to a turnpike or tavern and swapped deer hides for venomous rum we called 'The Crown's Revenge.' In early Kaintuck, when there was no flour, we gave our babies boiled venison instead of bread. Moving west, we spliced the first telegraph lines with buckskin thongs and tipped our 30-foot bullwhips with buckskin poppers. We dressed our heroes in buckskin, gloves and mukluks, and sent them off to Lundy's Lane, the Alamo, the Little Big Horn, Attu and Aachen.
>
> And we're still the people of the deer…
>
> …Anyone from the outcountry knows that a proper man looks first to his Bible, then to his buck rifle, and then to the business of deer. These things done, he has put himself in proper order to look after his nation.

John Madson (1961)

Ranger Woody and an unidentified helper bottle-feed several young fawns near the original ranger station in Ranger Woody's front yard, circa late 1920s. It is not clear whether or not these three fawns were from the original group of five, purchased in 1927, or if they were purchased a year or two later. Photo courtesy of Jean McNey.

Whitetails sustained the early white settlers and pioneers like no other animal in North America has ever done. In essence, their vital presence helped build America. Without them, many of the early pioneers and their families pushing west across the Appalachians indeed might have perished. Later, after the colonies were established, the deer hide trade became so important to the fledgling American economy up and down the Eastern seaboard that an amazing system of trade between the Indians and whites existed right up until the American Revolution and beyond. During the War for Independence, countless volunteers were sustained by the original "combat ration" – parched corn and venison jerky.

Millions of deer hides were shipped to England from the mid 1600s to the late 1700s. In Georgia, the deer-hide trade was the most valuable commodity and the No.1 means of income for the first 10 years of the colony's existence. After independence was declared in the New World and trade was broken off with England, the demand for American deer hides as an export item abruptly plummeted. It never recovered. Later on, after America became an independent nation, the steady stream of white settlers moving westward across the mountains in the early 1800s were no longer content to simply trade with the Indians for deer hides and furs. By now, fearless settlers committed to establishing homesteads had a craving for land as well, and they ultimately got what they wanted. The Cherokees were the last tribe in the Southeast to be removed in 1838 by way of the "Trail of Tears" to Oklahoma. In the late 1800s, their ancestral lands in Union County were the early "stamping" grounds of young Arthur Woody.

In most of the Eastern states, heavy market hunting for hides and venison was responsible for the whitetail's rapid decline during the latter half of the 1800s. Throughout New England and states like Ohio, New York and Pennsylvania where snow sometimes accumulated to depths of three or four feet during late winter, deer commonly "yarded" up in large groups. Herds ranging from a few animals to several dozen deer became easy pickings for market hunting riflemen. A herd of 30 or 40 whitetails "yarding" in a small, confined area where collectively they had packed down the snow, could be surrounded and wiped out by several good shooters in a matter of minutes because the deer had no means of escape. By 1900, deer in the East were absent from much of their former range. Most of the large predators were long gone as well. Large mammals like Eastern elk and buffalo, once found in sizable numbers in the East and Southeast, became extinct from their former range by the early 1700s.

After the North Georgia Mountains were opened to settlement by the Cherokee Land Lottery in 1832, whitetail numbers in the area rapidly declined over the next six decades. By 1900, when Arthur Woody was 16 years old, deer had been entirely eradicated from the region. While market hunting was responsible for the whitetail's decline in other areas, the disappearance of deer in the North Georgia Mountains was due to the fact that early settlers depended heavily on deer for food. Using large packs of well-trained dogs and fire torches at night as mentioned earlier, mountain deer were simply hunted down to the last animal by very proficient hunters. In 1895, when young Arthur Woody reportedly witnessed his father shoot the last living buck in the region, it's safe to say that whitetails had gone the way of the Eastern timber wolf, the mountain lion, the Eastern elk and the Eastern buffalo.

In his excellent book, *Game Resources of Georgia,* published in 1953, J. H. Jenkins makes an interesting observation:

> Contributing to the ease of taking deer by this method (well-trained hounds) was the open character of the forest floor. A fairly open forest floor would be expected under virgin oak-hickory forest. This was accentuated by the universal practice of burning by the early settlers and also grazing. It is well known that the Indians had been adept at burning these open mountains to create open game pastures. This was continued by the settlers particularly for cattle grazing. Ayers and Ashe (1905) remark on the open nature of the forest floor existing in 1904 before the extensive logging program began.

The Southern Deer Hunting Mystique

Mountain life was never easy and most farm families had very little time for any form of recreational activity. Because so little time was available for anything but hard work, family reunions, church socials, prayer meetings and holiday get-togethers like Christmas and Thanksgiving were much anticipated social events. Shooting contests and organized hunting trips by groups of men and their packs of dogs were especially coveted and often served as much needed diversions from long days and countless hours of backbreaking labor. As Arthur Woody often said in later life, going into the mountains for a day or two had a way of cleansing a man's soul.

Like many other mountain traditions, hunting and shooting was passed down from generation to generation. Although most mountaineers would tell you they hunted primarily out of necessity for food, and in some cases, to protect their free-roaming cattle and hogs from predators, hunting was a highly satisfying pastime that brought much enjoyment to those who participated. Yes, hunting for food served an important purpose, but it was also a significant distraction that most men dearly loved. If lucky, young boys were sometimes allowed to tag along on the hunts with their fathers.

Before being killed out by the mid 1800s, large predators like bears and "painters" (Eastern cougars or mountain lions) sometimes attacked cattle and hogs. Smaller predators like foxes, wildcats (bobcats) and even hawks and eagles occasionally preyed on chickens. Once a particular predator sinned against a farmer's livestock, its days were numbered. Farm animals were vital to a family's livelihood, and most mountaineers were crack rifle shots and expert hunters. Much like Medal of Honor recipient Sergeant Alvin C. York had done while growing up in his native Tennessee hills just north of Nashville in the early 1900s, many a mountain boy cut his teeth shooting the heads off wild turkeys with a single rifle bullet.

Mountain boys like Alvin York and Arthur Woody also grew up participating in local shooting contests; traditional old-fashioned "turkey shoots" where both turkeys and "beeves" were sometimes offered as prizes. One variation of a mountain turkey shoot in the late 1800s involved using a live turkey in a cage. The cage was protected by a wall, but an open hole in the top of the cage allowed the turkey to raise its head above the wall. Using a single-shot muzzleloader, the shooter had to aim quickly and shoot off the turkey's head while it bobbed up and down. This type of shooting required considerable skill, and if the shooter was lucky, he took home a 25-pound turkey as a prize. Later variations of the contest involved shooting paper targets at distances of 25 to 35 yards or longer. Being an expert marksman was a way of life for a young mountain boy, and Alvin York's shooting skills certainly served him well in France during World War I.

In the mid to late 1800s, a man might take off with his companions for a day or two and go a-huntin' with his long-barrelled mountain rifle. Other essential equipment included a powder horn full of powder, and a "possibles" bag filled with extra caps, or in some cases, flints; extra shot and balls; and other essential pieces of gear – matches for a fire, a sharp knife, patches, grease, a length of rope and maybe a piece of jerky to chew on. And like their Indian teachers, these rugged pioneers used every part of the deer they brought home. Little went to waste. They used deer hides for clothing and other purposes, meat for food, antlers for utensils.

Unlike today, little emphasis was placed on large antlers – the body size of a deer was much more important. But embellished stories about legendary, big-antlered stags were told around late-night campfires with great zeal. And whenever one of those fabled bucks was brought down, the antlers were usually cut up into knife handles or used for other utilitarian purposes. Occasionally

While market hunting was responsible for the whitetail's decline in other areas, the disappearance of deer in the North Georgia Mountains was due to the fact that early settlers depended heavily on deer for food. Using large packs of well-trained dogs and fire torches at night, mountain deer were simply hunted down to the last animal by very proficient hunters similar to those pictured here. Stereoview by B.W. Kilburn, 1888, Duncan Dobie collection.

large sets of antlers would be hung up in the barn or over the hearth, but very few sets of large antlers survived to present times. However, many of the much revered hunting stories soon became mountain folk tales, which were told and passed down for generations, first brought to the Georgia Mountains from Virginia and North Carolina.

Because of the scarcity of food during the harsh winter months, deer numbers were never historically as high in the North Georgia mountains as they were in other parts of the state. It took only a few generations of rugged mountain pioneers to hunt them down to the last animal by the turn of the century. Early mountaineers who had operated under the assumption that most of the Creator's abundant resources came in endless supplies soon realized this was not the case.

The Five Little Fiends of Suches

The excerpt below was taken from an article titled "How Deer Came Back to Georgia," which appeared in the Sunday magazine section of the Atlanta Constitution in the mid-1940s. (No date was attached to the clipping.) The article was written by W.W. Huber and R.M. Conarro of the U.S. Forest Service, two assistant rangers who had worked under Ranger Woody in the 1930s.

> Twenty years ago the ranger loaded his family into the new 1926 Dodge he had just bought and set out for the Pisgah National Game Preserve in North Carolina for some deer. He managed to get five fawns with the understanding he would care for them. Fawns, or baby deer, are very delicate creatures, and require as much attention as human babies. Naturally, caring for five babies at one time was quite a problem. The fawns had to be fed every six hours and their milk had to be warm. One needed a stronger formula than the others, and the ranger carefully mixed canned milk with boiled water to see that the proper diet was obtained. It was also necessary to provide bedding and cover for the young deer, as well as pens to keep them in, as a protection against dogs.
>
> These five bottle-fed babies, named Nimble, Billy, Nancy, Bessie and Bunny-Girl, are the ancestors of the deer we have today. But in their youth they were known as the five friendly "fiends." They were taken in by the Woody family to such an extent that they soon learned how to unlatch the screen door and enter the house. Dick Woody, the ranger's grandson, was

> then a sturdy lad of three, and as he would feed the deer, he soon became a favorite pal of the five "fiends." Many a noonday nap was interrupted by his four-legged friends, who could not understand why Dick wasn't playing with them, and they would walk in his bedroom and lick his face to wake him.

Judging from their names, it would appear that Nimble and Billy were buck fawns and Nancy, Bessie and Bunny Girl were doe fawns. A small pen was built next to the Woody home to house what became fondly known as the "five friendly fiends of Suches." Several published accounts claim the deer had the run of the house. They probably did enter the house once in a while but for the most part they were kept outside in a pen. Ranger Woody worried that stray dogs might come and harm the tiny deer, and they were kept up at all times until they were older. If one of the fawns got sick or needed special attention, it might have been taken inside for treatment, but the five deer never lived in the Woody home as some stories claim.

As soon as they were old enough, the beloved little fiends were transferred to a much larger holding pen inside Rock Creek Refuge. When the five deer were approximately one year old, they were released into the refuge. Once they were free-roaming, Ranger Woody let it be known to one and all that there would be a steep price to pay if anything happened to any of *his* deer.

"No deer ever lived in our house with us while I was there," Jean McNey remembered. "My grandmother would never have allowed it. And I never heard any stories about the original fawns living in the house either. We always had deer around us while I was growing up, but they always lived outside. As they got older, some of the deer learned to open the screen door and come in from time to time. I remember one time when the screen door was open and one of Papa's deer simply walked into the house, and went into a bedroom where it found one of June's fountain pens in an open dresser drawer. The deer ate the pen and ink (apparently without any negative effects). Papa had names for all of his deer and they would usually come to him when he called them. They were very smart animals and some of the does were very tame. One of his favorite deer was named Peggy. She produced 11 fawns in 7 years. Another old doe was named Bessie. She would sometimes wander into our house and look at herself in the mirror. She was later killed by one of the hunters on a 'bucks only' hunt (in 1940 or 1941). Papa was fit to be tied when she was killed because they found her out in the woods and no one 'fessed up to the deed."

Although it is entirely possible, Bessie may not have been one of the original five fawns purchased in 1927. If the deer killed had been the original Bessie, she would have been around 13 years old, an extremely old age for a wild deer. Free roaming deer can live up to 10 or 11 years in the wild, but they often die at a much younger age because of the dangers and hardships they face. Penned deer tend to live longer because they live in a less stressful environment. During the first "bucks only" firearms hunt in 1940 covered in Chapter 14, several does were shot by mistake and the hunters paid a small fine. But whoever shot Bessie refused to come forward, leaving Ranger Woody "as mad as a wet hornet."

As the Forest Service got more involved with purchasing deer from North Carolina in the late 1920s and early 1930s, those deer were put in pens near the game warden's house inside the refuge until they were old enough to be released.

Georgia stocking records indicate that Ranger Woody released four deer obtained from the Pisgah Forest in Fannin, Union and Lumpkin counties in 1928 (Rock Creek Refuge, also known as Cherokee Refuge No. 2 at the time). The following year in 1929, records indicate that 24 more deer from North Carolina were released into the refuge, but these records are sketchy at best. In all likelihood, neither the Georgia stocking records nor the Forest Service records are 100 percent accurate. The first four deer released were obviously from the original group of five fawns. It is not known what happened to the fifth fawn, if anything. In all likelihood all five fawns were released instead of four. During that same time period, Ranger Woody also reportedly acquired several additional deer from other sources and he may have released a few more deer into the refuge than records indicate.

In the continuation of "How Deer Came Back to Georgia," by W.W. Huber and R.M. Conarro, the authors go on to say:

> Ranger Woody kept buying deer and soon had placed 56 head in the mountainous region surrounding Suches, Ga. He heard of three deer left by a carnival at Cleveland, Ga., and purchased them. Later he obtained the deer at the Zimmer's Hotel in Dahlonega. One of these, a doe named Peggy, raised 11 fawns in seven years. Peggy was quite a favorite in the community as were many of the others. The Ranger made it popular for the local settlers to care for the deer, and at many farm homes one could see deer roaming at will through yards, orchards and fields.
>
> The work that Ranger Woody did to build up the deer herd in Georgia has been of much pleasure to recreationalists and sportsmen. Many Georgians have thrilled at the sight of a graceful deer jumping a fence or browsing in a clearing. Camera fans as well as hunters have shot their buck to preserve these shots for all to see.

> Ranger Woody was very proud of these deer and disapproved of the deer hunts held during the past few years (beginning in 1940). He felt that the deer herd had not yet reached its ultimate development. He also believed that to hunt them before then would be detrimental to his whole undertaking, and that his work would have been done in vain. Charlie Elliott, Wildlife Director of Georgia, and game management experts of the U.S. Forest Service, always found the Ranger ready to help protect the deer, but never ready to hunt them.
>
> Many a tiff between Woody and the "book-larned" wildlife experts would take place, when the experts, realizing that too many deer were dangerous, would suggest a hunt. One year (believed to be 1939) Woody took the wildlife inspectors around Rock Creek Lake, and knowing that one side of the lake had a lot of deer signs and the other none, routed the inspectors around the side where there were no signs of deer, while he took the other. Naturally the inspectors decided to postpone the hunt for a year.
>
> Woody was a staunch friend of all wild animals and he protected them with every ruse known. Once he found and unusually large bear track. Guarding this track, he dispatched an assistant for sand, cement, water and an iron rod. He made a cast of the bear track, using the iron rod as a handle. He carried this cast in his pickup and at strategic points, he would stop and make an imprint of the bear's track in a path, trail or road, thinking – and rightly so, that poachers would be frightened away from a spot where a large bear track had been seen. (See Chapter 7 for more on this infamous track.)
>
> He once said: "That bear track cast is as good as any three game wardens." Local people who allowed their domestic animals, mostly swine, to run at will through the mountains, upon seeing the bear track, would bring their stock in. The ranger reasoned that many a nest of grouse and turkeys had been saved from destruction by hogs through the use of the bear track. Yes, he used every ruse he could think of to protect his game.
>
> Last fall, there were three deer hunts in the Georgia Mountains (probably the 1941 hunts). The first one was attended by 60 archers from nine states. After them came two groups of 100 riflemen each of which five men were from Tennessee and the other 195 were Georgians.

Much like Bill Bergoffen (quoted in Chapter 1), who served with Ranger Woody as an assistant ranger for 14 months in the mid-1930s, W.W. Huber and Ray M. Conarro were also young foresters who worked under Ranger Woody in the mountains during the late 1930s. They, too, were smitten with his amazing abilities. Like other Forest Service employees who worked in North Georgia for a time, both of these men went on to have long distinguished careers with the Forest Service and both developed special relationships with Ranger Woody.

Most of the facts in the Huber/Conarro story are quite accurate. However, as discussed in the Prologue, it is unlikely that Ranger Woody took his entire family to North Carolina during the summer of 1927 when he acquired the five original fawns. He may have taken one of his sons along to help him, but it is doubtful that his wife and daughter went along.

"That just wouldn't have happened," said Jean McNey. "June was extremely busy at home and she never would have gone on a trip like that, and my mother (Mae) was probably busy teaching school."

Also, just to keep the record clear, several stories written about Ranger Woody in recent decades mention the fact that the three deer he acquired in Dahlonega from a leftover carnival were "Western mule deer." In truth, the carnival deer were probably large-bodied whitetails from somewhere in the Midwest. Any whitetails brought to Georgia from a Midwestern state would have been substantially larger in body size than your typical Georgia or North Carolina mountain deer, so some people often erroneously referred to them as "mule deer." If they truly had been Western mule deer, it's doubtful they would have survived in the Georgia mountains for any reasonable length of time.

The title of the story "How Deer Came Back to Georgia" was very appropriate at the time it was written. Although fair numbers of deer existed on some of Georgia's coastal islands in the late 1920s, few deer could be found in the state's interior at that time. Ranger Woody's epic trip to North Carolina

Ranger Woody's pride and joy! This young buck was photographed within the Blue Ridge WMA in 1937 by a Forest Service photographer, likely the Ranger's good friend Clint Davis. By the late 1930s, the deer herd was thriving inside the refuge and Georgia sportsmen were putting considerable pressure on the state to allow hunting. Against Ranger Woody's vehement protests, the first managed hunt took place two years later in 1940. U.S. Forest Service photo.

in 1927 definitely marked the beginning of Georgia's historic deer restoration program statewide.

Forest Service stocking records differ somewhat from the Georgia state records and appear to be closer to the actual numbers. According to those Forest Service records, four deer were released into the refuge in 1928, nine were released in 1929 and five were released in 1930. A few more were reportedly released in the early 1930s. It is believed that all of these deer were purchased from the Pisgah Reserve by Ranger Woody. During the early 1930s, the Forest Service got involved purchasing deer in larger quantities.

After the historic cooperative agreement was reached in 1936 in which the management of wildlife on Forest Service lands would be turned over to the Georgia Wildlife Resources Division (later to become the Game and Fish Commission), Forest Service records show that 46 bucks and 39 does were released in 1936, and 70 bucks and 100 does were released in 1937. It is doubtful that any of these deer were released in Rock Creek Refuge. Most were released into the other three wildlife management areas established in the mountains in 1936 and subsequently managed by the state – the 20,000-acre Chattahoochee WMA, the 30,120-acre Chestatee WMA, and the 15,000-acre Lake Burton WMA.

Along with his good friend Ranger Nick Nicholson of Clayton, it is believed that Ranger Woody was present at several, if not all, of these historic stockings. The Cohutta WMA, which eventually grew to about 95,000 acres, was established in 1937. Deer were also stocked here, and season bag limits for bucks were established. However, due to a lack of cooperation among local residents who continued hunting on a year-around basis with no regard for the law, the area was abandoned in 1960. It was reestablished in 1968 and has operated as a popular wildlife management area ever since. (Note: The historic cooperative agreement mentioned above between the Forest Service and the state of Georgia was due largely to the efforts of Ranger Woody with considerable help and support from his good friend Charlie Elliott.)

The first state-wide deer survey ever conducted in Georgia in 1932 estimated a total population of 12,452 deer (primarily found in the coastal counties and on Georgia's barrier islands). A later survey in the 1950s indicated those numbers had climbed to 33,000 deer statewide, including the mountain herd of some 3,000 to 4,000 animals that Ranger Woody had originally fostered. Today the state-wide deer population in Georgia hovers at nearly 1 million animals.

It is probably safe to say that in total, less than 100 deer were released into the Rock Creek/Blue Ridge Refuge during the late 1920s and early '30s.

By 1940, due to excellent protection, that number had mushroomed to an estimated 2,000 animals in and around the refuge.

Deer Stocking Records – Noontootly Game Management Area (Rock Creek/Blue Ridge WMA). From the U.S. Forest Service.

1928 – 4 does (by Arthur Woody, from original five fawns)

1929 – 4 bucks, 5 does (by Arthur Woody)

1930 – 2 bucks, 3 does (by Arthur Woody)

1936 – 46 bucks, 39 does (by Arthur Woody and the U.S. Forest Service).

1937 – 18 bucks, 49 does (by Arthur Woody and the U.S. Forest Service).

Total – *70 bucks, 100 does (by Arthur Woody and the U.S. Forest Service).

**All of the above deer were acquired from the Pisgah Game Reserve in North Carolina. Some were trapped in box traps as adult deer and some were caught and raised as fawns. All were cared for and released under Ranger Woody's watchful eye. This record is not complete. It is reported that Woody also bought several other deer from traveling shows and/or individuals.*

Realizing the Dream

Had the idea of bringing deer back to the North Georgia mountains really been a lifelong dream of Ranger Woody's since his boyhood or is this just another tall tale and part of the Woody Myth? Neither of Ranger Woody's granddaughters ever remembered having heard him say that he had vowed to bring deer back to the region or that he had watched his father kill the last living deer in the mountains. But they were both very young girls at the time and many aspects of the Ranger's life were probably never discussed during their childhood.

Ranger Woody did tell at least a few close friends that he had always nurtured a desire to someday have a hand in bringing deer back to the region, and that he felt a personal obligation to achieve this dream because his father

By 1938, 11 years after Ranger Woody bought his original five fawns in 1927, the "Fawn Plant" at the Pink Beds in the Pisgah National Forest was raising dozens of young fawns each year to be used for restocking purposes in the Carolinas and other states in the South. This group of three-month-old fawns eagerly gathers for "dinner." Photo by Clint Davis, U.S. Forest Service.

had been responsible for shooting the last living deer. Several credible stories written in the 1940s bear this out. By 1927, the now middle-aged Ranger Woody had finally reached a point in his career where he was ready to begin making that lifelong dream into a reality. By now, he had been a full-fledged forest ranger for almost 10 years. He had already done notable work in protecting the forests and other wildlife in his district by promoting good forestry practices and instituting remarkable fire prevention methods. For nearly 10 years, on his own initiative, he had done an incredible job of purchasing trout from out-of state sources and restocking them in some of lakes, rivers and streams in his Rock Creek Refuge and surrounding areas. Now he was ready to try to tackle one of the most imposing and important tasks in his life: to realize his lifelong dream of bringing deer back to the mountains.

The earliest written account I could find about Ranger Woody's desire to bring deer back appeared in the December 1940 issue of Outdoor Georgia magazine. The article was written by Jim McGraw shortly after the first firearms hunt of modern times was held in the Rock Creek Refuge several weeks earlier in November. During that historic hunt, 22 legal bucks, referred to as "some of the finest white-tail specimens in the country," had been taken by rifle hunters.

Several does had also been killed by mistake (as frequently happens on most typical "bucks only" hunts). (See Chapter 14, "The First Legal Firearms Deer Hunt of Modern Times in Georgia," for a full reprint of the McGraw article.) In that article, Jim McGraw goes back in time to1925 and talks about Ranger Woody reflecting on the past:

> While he stood there, the ranger's thoughts went back to the years when he was a boy in the Blue Ridge Mountains of North Georgia. In those years such things as national forests and game protection and restocking the streams with fish, were unknown. His father had killed the last deer in all that Blue Ridge country. The bears had long since gone, and big trout were things only in dreams.
>
> Perhaps someday someone would bring back the abundance of game to the land the Cherokee once knew. Perhaps someday there would be deer in the forests and big trout again in the streams. That job, like art, would be long, even after someone made a beginning. The idea suddenly dawned on Arthur Woody that perhaps no man on earth would be better qualified to make such a beginning than the ranger himself. He could have a small part in helping restore to Blue Ridge what his ancestors had helped take away.

Even though this flowery article states "the idea suddenly dawned on Arthur Woody that perhaps no man would be better qualified to make such a beginning than the ranger himself," as if he had just thought of it, the facts suggest he had been thinking about it for many years, probably since boyhood, just as the legend claims.

Several published accounts quote Charlie Elliott as saying Ranger Woody told him the story about his father killing the last deer and about his lifelong desire to bring deer back to the mountains. Shortly after Ranger Woody's death in 1946, Charlie Elliott reflected on a conversation he'd had with the Ranger. Charlie had become Director of the Georgia Game and Fish Commission in 1943, a position he held until 1949. In 1950 he became a full-time outdoor writer as the Southeast field editor for *Outdoor Life* magazine. The following quotes by Charlie Elliott come from an article written by Paul Jones in the Atlanta Constitution on Oct. 29, 1975:

> "One of the best stories about Woody I recall was the one about the deer, which he reintroduced to the mountains," said Elliott, who was Southeastern editor for *Outdoor Life* for years. "Woody told me he had

gone with his father on a hunting trip when he was a boy. He said his dad killed the last deer anywhere in the mountains.

"I vowed I would remedy that situation when I was grown," Woody told me. "He raised some money from the U.S. Forest Service. He put up a lot of his own money after he became a ranger. He went up to North Carolina and brought back a number of white-tailed deer, released them in an area near the headquarters of Rock Creek and told the people of the mountains to leave them alone.

"He named many of them. One old buck was named Old Nemo. (Charlie had come to know old Nemo well! He had an encounter with the buck in 1940 during the first-ever firearms hunt in the Blue Ridge Refuge. For more details, see Chapter 14.) He had names for others. Finally, the deer did multiply and everyone, including Woody, agreed that some of the deer ought to be taken. There were a great number of fine bucks in the tremendous herd.

"The deer season opened (in 1940) and hunters came from all around. (Because of the excitement that a hunt like this created both inside and outside of Georgia, wildlife officials decided to allow non-resident hunters to participate as well.) They took many fine trophies (22 in all as mentioned). And Woody was there at the check-out station when they started coming out of the refuge. Seeing the first big buck, Woody turned his head a little bit and the tears started streaming down his cheeks. He never shot a deer after that," said Elliott, a close and devoted friend of the old ranger (In truth, it is doubtful that Ranger Woody ever shot a deer during his entire life.)

"Today, the Blue Ridge area, which was Woody's territory – actually his domain – is one of the finest areas in the State," Elliott said.

In his 1971 report, *A Historical-Socio-Political Study of the Chattahoochee-Oconee National Forests,* Norman Bruce Alter (the Forest Ranger who took Ranger Nick Nicholson's place in the Tallulah Ranger District in Northeast Georgia upon Ranger Nick's retirement in 1952 says:

Arthur Woody, through his prodding the Forest Service and his personal efforts to have deer restored in the forest endeared himself more to sportsmen in the area than any other individual who ever worked for the service. Other efforts of the Forest Service were looked upon with more favor due to the good results of these projects. It also gave the state game officials something to work with when the Fish and Game Commission

> (should be "Game and Fish" Commission) took an active part in the game management work about 1933. Although Noontootla Game Refuge (Rock Creek/Blue Ridge Refuge) was the first in Georgia, others followed first as refuges with five-year stocking periods and later as Game Management Areas.

There can be little doubt that Ranger Woody's initiative and his almost single-handed determination to restock both trout and deer (as well as turkeys and a small number of black bears) in his beloved Rock Creek Refuge, and on other nearby National Forest lands, gave the Forest Service and the State Game and Fish Commission a tremendous jumpstart on taking the program the Ranger had initiated and expanding it into a very successful endeavor.

One can make the argument that all of this would have eventually happened anyway, sooner or later, but Ranger Woody was the catalyst for making it happen when it did. And it was no easy task. Not only did he make it happen, he often used his own money to do much of his early work in restocking deer and trout because he knew that was the only way to move his program forward.

"Come a little closer, little 'un." Arthus Woody, known simply as "the ranger," boss of the Blue Ridge District of the Chattahoochee National Forest, coaxes an almost-tame doe to come up for the tender shoot in his hand.

This newsprint photo and caption probably appeared in the Atlanta Constitution in the early 1940s. News clipping courtesy of Jean McNey.

Why would he willingly do such a thing? Because he was passionate about his mountains and he possessed an almost spiritual vision for how the mountains should be. He also had a deep understanding for what the people (the community, the taxpayers, the sportsmen of Georgia) really wanted. To him, a mountain stream or river void of fish and a vast mountain forest void of deer and turkeys was akin to building a beautiful mansion and not putting any furniture in it upon completion. Who would want to live in a house with no furniture? To him, a thriving wildlife population was as vital to his mountain paradise as gasoline was to an automobile.

As noted in the quote above, the Ranger had to continually "prod" the Forest Service to pick up the ball and run with it; that is, to actively get involved in his wildlife restoration program on his Rock Creek Refuge and on the surrounding National Forest land in general. It took a certain amount of time for this to happen. Does this mean the federal government was totally indifferent toward pursuing any sort of wildlife program? Not really.

It is important to keep in mind that this was a ground-breaking period in history. Things were happening at a rapid pace and many of the policies set up by the Forest Service involved going into uncharted territories where few precedents had been set. To a large degree, forest and wildlife management were relatively new sciences, and officials were oftentimes working on a "learn-as-you-go" basis. Mistakes were made. Even though Ranger Woody seemed to operate by the seat of his pants for much of his career, he had a knack for sensing how things should be done and in most cases things turned out just fine in the end. But it was a different story with the government. With so many other important priorities at the time that took precedence, restoring wildlife was simply not at the top of the list. Preventing fires, fighting fires once they had started, erosion control and restoring the forests and streams were of utmost concern – at first. By necessity, wildlife had to take a backseat, at least for a while.

Money was tight, and many other important issues needed attention. Looking back, it seems quite amazing that, at the time, no one at the higher levels seemed to share Ranger Woody's enthusiasm for restocking trout and deer or comprehend the significant benefits that would result from such programs. Considering the politics involved that went all the way to the highest levels in Washington D.C., it is to some degree understandable why the Forest Service couldn't see the trees for the forest; that is, until it became apparent that the public wanted wildlife restored to the mountains as much a Ranger Woody did.

The Ranger Gets His Refuge

For a variety of reasons, fire prevention and the production of timber and making a profit from that timber seemed to be the single-minded and primary focus of the Forest Service during those early days of federal ownership in the early 1900s. The goal was to make the forests self-sustaining; that is, to eventually grow enough timber so that the forests would pay their own way and not be supported by tax dollars. Aesthetics, fish and wildlife were not originally part of the program. Allowing people to enjoy the restored forests through hiking, camping, hunting and fishing were not seen as important future objectives. The federal government had expended large amounts of money into reclaiming this land and people at the highest levels including Gifford Pinchot, who served as the first Forest Service Chief from 1905 to 1910, believed first and foremost that the forest should be able to show a financial profit.

Certainly there was nothing wrong with this philosophy (Wouldn't it be nice if other government agencies strived for the same goals?), although in hindsight it did seem to be a very narrow-minded approach because there was so much more that the restored forests could offer and provide to the American people. Thank goodness Ranger Woody had the vision to understand the vast treasure trove of possibilities the forest offered to the citizens of the U.S. beyond the mere monetary value of the trees: incredible scenic splendor, hiking, camping, canoeing, hunting and fishing; studying nature, watching wildlife – the opportunities were endless. And thank goodness he had the tenacity to push the Forest Service toward the "multi-use" concept of the forests so that all of the people would benefit. After all, he had spent much of his early life doing these very same things in these very same hills, and he knew a price could not be put on them. In addition, he strongly believed the people of America actually owned the forests in the first place.

It took someone on the ground who worked in the trenches on a daily basis like Ranger Woody to blaze the trail and enlighten those who could not see the light, not some bureaucrat sitting behind a desk in Washington. And blaze the trail he did! With his constant "prodding," the Forest Service began to see the light (in conjunction with the Georgia Wildlife Resources Commission after it got involved). To its credit, the Forest Service began to make the restoration of wildlife a priority as well, and once it got involved, it did a remarkable job picking up where Ranger Woody had left off.

In an article written by Charlie Elliott in *Outdoor Life* in November 1972, titled "The Blue Ridge Hunt," Charlie said:

> Woody went quietly about stocking deer. He talked his superiors into setting aside a tract of land on Rock Creek, a remote section of the forest about 10 miles from his home, as an inviolate refuge. Fishing the mountain streams was allowed, but not hunting. A portion of this land was later set aside by Congressional action.

Later in the story he added:

> From the time the first bucks and does were released, Woody spent much of his time in the backcountry, watching the trails for humans and half-wild dogs that might molest his herd, and checking on the deer themselves. One of the original roads through the country ran up Rock Creek, but it was so rough that the few fishermen who came for the outsize rainbows (that he had stocked) had to walk miles to get to the wilderness waters.
>
> It was natural that the deer herd should multiply. It was also natural that other mountain men in the area should discover the deer. Woody put out word that these deer were his personal property and that whoever killed one would be held accountable – not only to the law, but also to Woody himself. His influence in the mountain community was so powerful that the other mountain men respected his wishes and the deer herd prospered.

Charlie goes on to talk about the coming of the Civilian Conservation Corps and the way the "CC" boys vastly improved many of the roads in the area. This was both a blessing and a curse. It was a blessing for the people of Union County, but better access brought in more outsiders, including poachers, that could be a threat to the deer population.

> Under Woody's urging, the Forest Service brass got together with the state Game Department (1936) on a protection program. The government built a house at the head of Rock Creek, and a state game warden was stationed there. Gates were placed on all roads going through the refuge, with the understanding that they would be opened and manned by a representative of either the Forest Service or the Game Department on the days that Rock Creek or its tributaries were open for trout fishing.

A few paragraphs later, Charlie noted:

After raising five young fawns in a small pen next to his home in 1927, Ranger Woody constructed larger deer pens at Hightower Gap next to the game warden's house inside Rock Creek Refuge. These young deer were likely purchased in 1928 or 1929 and were almost old enough to be released into the wild. The pipe-smoking man feeding the two deer is thought to be Charlie Elliott. Photo circa 1930, courtesy of the Charlie Elliott Wildlife Center.

Refuge" was a hallowed word. To avoid violating it, game men changed the status of Rock Creek-Noontootly region – with the exception of one block in the middle – to a Wildlife Management Area. Plans could then go ahead with the first mountain deer hunt in many decades.

Charlie Elliott's insightful reporting tells how the first wildlife management area in Georgia and the country – Blue Ridge WMA – came into existence. Without Ranger Woody's constant urging, it might never have happened.

Adaptable and Prolific

White-tailed deer are amazingly prolific animals. A relatively healthy herd with no controlled hunting and no predation is capable of doubling its numbers every two years. So a handful of deer can quickly multiply to several hundred in a very short period of time.

By all accounts, Ranger Woody's herd was well protected. All of the roads leading into the refuge were gated and locked. Roads inside the refuge were frequently patrolled. Some deer no doubt died of natural causes, but overall mortality was probably very low. Much to the Ranger's indignation, bobcats were known to have preyed on a few deer.

Other than a few bobcats, however, there were no predators in the refuge. A few of the Ranger's deer were no doubt killed by poachers over the years, but for the most part the small herd thrived in its protected sanctuary. By the late 1930s, the original 70 or 80 deer had increased to a point where many state officials started thinking in terms of conducting a managed deer hunt.

If the estimate of 2,000 deer was accurate, that would have worked out to about 35 deer per square mile inside the refuge (40,000 acres), a very high number for that area during that time period. But keep in mind the deer were not all contained inside the boundaries of the 40,000 acre refuge. They no doubt spilled out into some of the surrounding areas as well. (In the decades since 1940, deer numbers have never been as high in the mountain region as they are throughout the southern three-fourths of the state because food sources have never been as abundant or reliable, especially during the winter months. In years where the acorn crop is low, mountain deer suffer greatly. Also, by 1940, virtually tens of thousands of chestnut trees had died from the blight, causing deer, turkeys and the few bears that were present to forever lose one of their most reliable and desirable yearly food sources.)

During the height of Georgia's deer restocking program in the late 1950s and early '60s, some 2,500 deer were stocked in the piedmont and coastal plains areas of Georgia (roughly the southern two-thirds of the state). Twenty-five years later in the mid-1980s, the statewide herd had grown to an estimated 850,000 animals. Within 10 more years those numbers were well over 1 million. So it's easy to see that a few "seed" deer are capable of increasing at exponential rates if they are well protected and healthy. Interestingly enough, people often have the notion that it takes hundreds of deer to establish a herd in an area where they have been absent for many years but this is not the case. A few can turn into many in a very short time.

Ranger Woody's Greatest Dilemma

By 1900, moderate populations of native deer existed on all of Georgia's barrier islands and in a few interior areas along the coast where heavy vegetation offered good protection, but just like the mountain region, deer had been almost totally eliminated throughout much of Georgia's interior. Most of the coastal islands were privately owned by wealthy Northern industrialists and no public hunting was allowed. By the late 1930s, an ever increasing number of Georgia outdoorsmen wanted the opportunity to hunt deer legally, and news of Ranger Woody's amazing restocking program in the mountains had received considerable attention. For the time being, the mountains – and more specifically, the Blue Ridge WMA, seemed to be the only logical place where a legal hunt – the first legal hunt of the 20th century – might be viable.

Because the deer in Ranger Woody's Blue Ridge WMA were healthy and thriving, it was inevitable that wildlife officials eventually would want to plan a managed hunt to help control deer numbers and to satisfy the sportsmen who wanted to hunt them. Even though the concept of whitetail management was in its infancy, wildlife officials clearly understood that deer herds with no natural predators had to be kept in check through controlled hunting. Even Ranger Woody understood this principle better than most, although he wasn't ready to accept it. As the herd continued to expand, the idea of a controlled hunt made good sense, and sportsmen began to put pressure on the state. The state in turn put pressure on the Forest Service and on District Ranger Woody. Of course, the Ranger did everything within his power to put off the inevitable for as long as he could.

For Ranger Woody, it must have been like a dormant volcano suddenly ready to erupt. Using every means at his disposal, he did his best to postpone any type of hunt. But he knew it was coming sooner or later. This dilemma was no doubt one of the most emotional challenges he ever had to face during his long career as a Forest Ranger.

The Ranger was well into his forties when he bought the first five fawns in 1927, and they quickly captured his heart. After raising the five little fiends in 1927, and many more after that in the late 1920s and early '30s, he developed a special love and kinship with these beautiful animals. He couldn't kill one if his life depended on it. He named many of them and for years they came to him when called.

But he certainly didn't fault others who wanted to hunt deer in North Georgia. He understood why other men, both country boys like himself and city dwellers alike, enjoyed the "sport" of hunting and he gave them his full support. When it came to his special deer, however, the very same deer he had bottle fed, nurtured and agonized over for 13 years, many of which he observed on a regular basis during his daily travels, something deep inside pulled at his heartstrings. Thirteen years of taking care of these amazing animals had caused the strong-willed and tough-as-leather mountain man to grow soft. Ranger Woody's deer had touched his soul, and now he could not bear to see them killed. It was that simple. This was a problem that he grappled with right up until his death in 1946.

THE LURE OF THE CHATTAHOOCHE

By CHARLES N. ELLIOTT

A National Forest in Northern Georgia Where History and Legend Mingle and a Vast Vacation Land Awaits the Visitor

RANGER WOODY'S automobile spluttered and jerked to a stop. Beyond the steaming radiator cap the road climbed on and on, past massive boulders and fern-filled glens, under stupendous tulip trees, through glades of Lady Slipper Orchids — a rutted, two-wheel trail. For three hours we had followed that excuse for a road. Through splashing creeks we had come, across clearings where gnarled apple trees occasionally marked an old home site. And always we had climbed — up and up and up — toward the heart of a wild, virgin land. At every stream the wheezing machine had clattered to a standstill and demanded a drink, its just reward for a noble performance of duty.

Arthur Woody extracted his bulky frame from under the wheel and dug into his duffle for a bucket.

"This is the last stop," he said. "In twenty minutes we cross the divide. Refuge headquarters are a mile or two down the other side. From now on," Arthur called, "keep your eyes open for big game. During the past few years, we have released several bear and over two hundred deer on the refuge. They've spread all over the country."

The old automobile groaned and started under protest. The road grew steeper and rougher, the forest canopy thinner. Soon the narrow mountain trail broke out upon a broad highway. Arthur did not miss my look of astonishment. "I wanted you to see the road we traveled five years ago," he said; "we'll go back the new road."

The graded highway swung in a graceful curve and slid downward through tall forest trees. We passed a wire enclosure.

"An old deer pen," the ranger explained. "At first we confined deer before they were released. A couple of months ago we clipped the wings of several turkeys and turned them into this pen. A small chicken hawk, half the size of the runt gobbler, killed and ate every one before the month was out."

We moved onward with the road, gently downward in spite of the perpendicular mass of granite and earth around us. Rock Creek followed the road, pouring from ledge to ledge, swirling into huge pools, growing larger as other streams joined it from the north and south. Along the roadside were many places where deer had skidded down the steep cuts to cross the road. We stopped and examined two small artificial lakes where trout had been planted. In a few years they would be large enough to take on the quick end of a bamboo rod.

We swung left abruptly, and stopped. A neat, white bungalow sat under the trees, modern in every detail, with inside paneled walls, a white tile bathroom and electric lights.

"The Bureau of Fisheries keeps a man here," Arthur explained, "to hatch and rear all the trout we plant. Our native brook trout eggs are shipped from New

A woodland sprite — in a few short years deer have been brought back into ten thousand square miles of mountain land in northern Georgia

MAY, 1939 247

A year and a half before the first deer hunt took place on Rock Creek Refuge, Charlie Elliott wrote this story in American Forests magazine praising Ranger Arthur Woody for his work in restoring deer to the mountain region. Excerpt courtesy of American Forests, May 1939.

"I know deer are for eatin' but I'm never gonna kill one," former CCC member Clyde Harkins once heard the Ranger say.

"He couldn't ever kill a deer himself, but he had no problem with others who needed to kill an occasional deer for food," Clyde said. "Or, if a deer was doing damage to a farmer's crops, he would always tell the farmer to shoot it. A man's crop was sacred and he understood that."

Foiling a Potential Hunt in 1939

At least one somewhat humorous story did result from the Ranger's ordeal. As the deer numbers continued to increase during the late 1930s, Forest Service and State Game and Fish officials came to the refuge each year to survey the population and to discuss plans for a possible hunt. Each time this happened, Ranger Woody vehemently argued that total numbers had not yet reached huntable levels. He used every trick in the book to try to dissuade officials and put them off from year to year. Jean McNey recalled that when officials from both agencies again showed up in the spring or summer of 1939 to do their annual survey, Ranger Woody once again reached deep into his bag of tricks to win the day for his deer. He still had at least one ace up his sleeve and he played it to his advantage.

"He knew every square inch of that refuge," Jean said. "He knew all of the places where the deer could usually be found because of available food and cover as well as those places where they seldom ventured."

So what did the Ranger do?

"In an effort to make the officials think that deer numbers in the refuge were not nearly as high as they had supposed, Papa deliberately took them over to an area on the other side of Rock Creek Lake where there was almost no deer sign; no tracks, no trails, no nothing," Jean said with a smile.

"And the ploy worked!" Jean remembered. "The hunt was put off for yet another year."

Had he really fooled the wildlife experts or had it been his extraordinary power of persuasion that won the day for him and bought him another precious year? It's hard to say, but for the time being, the Ranger had dodged another bullet. He had won another round, but he knew it was temporary at best. You can't fight city hall forever. Next time he might not be so lucky. The hammer was about to fall and he was helpless to do anything about it. It happened one year later in 1940. That year game officials were not so easily duped.

North Carolina Forest Ranger Lester Schaap checks in a mountain buck at the famous Cantrell Creek Wilderness Hunt Camp in the Pisgah Game Reserve during the third annual wilderness hunt conducted in fall of 1938. The hunting camp was located in Turkey Pen Gap in the heart of the Pisgah National Forest. Because deer and bears had been protected in western North Carolina in the late 1800s and early 1900s by wealthy landowners like the Vanderbilt family, big game populations were never wiped out like they were in North Georgia where hungry pioneers and settlers hunted them down to the last animal with large packs of dogs.

Managed deer hunts at Cantrell Creek Wilderness Hunt Camp began in 1936, four years before similar hunts were conducted at Rock Creek Refuge in North Georgia. This popular hunt in western North Carolina was enjoyed by hundreds of sportsmen in the late 1930s. The camp in Turkey Pen Gap was accessible only by foot, after a five-mile hike. All provisions and equipment had to be packed in by hunters, but the Forest Service provided tents, cots and firewood. Groups of 25 sportsmen hunted the primitive area for an entire week. Bag limits included one deer or bear per hunter.

The Cantrell Creek Wilderness Hunt in North Carolina was likely the model from which Georgia wildlife officials and U.S. Forest Service personnel planned their first hunts in 1940 in the 40,000-acre Blue Ridge WMA. However, the Georgia hunt was unique in that it also included a five-day archery-only hunt, a first in the entire U.S. for bow hunters. Photo by Clint Davis, U.S. Forest Service.

Wildlife specialists were again sent up to the refuge from Atlanta in the spring of 1940 to check things out for a possible hunt later that year. Without question, surveys showed that deer numbers were strong and that plenty of mature bucks could be taken out of the herd. No does, just bucks. Some of the older bucks carried exceptional racks because of their age. The management of white-tailed deer was a relatively new science in the late 1930s, and it was considered a sin to shoot a doe at that time. It would not be until 10 years later in 1950 that noticeable over-browsing inside the refuge would lead to the legal shooting of several dozen does during the annual managed hunt. In 1950, 30 does were taken off the refuge. In 1951, 24 were shot. However, it would be many more years in Georgia before wildlife managers and sportsmen alike realized and accepted the fact that the only true way to control deer numbers in any herd was through the controlled shooting of does.

Georgia's first legal deer hunt of the 20th century was scheduled to be held in late October and early November 1940. After it became certain that a hunt would take place in the refuge, Ranger Woody argued strongly that local residents should have the first opportunity to hunt the local deer. He felt this way about fishing and using other resources as well – lakes, hiking trails and camp sites in state parks. He wanted every citizen to be able to enjoy the many outdoor activities that his mountain paradise offered, but he strongly felt that the local residents should always have the first opportunity. This turned out to be another losing battle.

Ranger Woody was forced to accept the inevitable. As time drew near for the highly publicized 1940 hunt, he publicly put on a good front. He genuinely felt affection for the hunters who were about to invade his beloved refuge, and he welcomed them with open arms. In return, those hunters grew to love and adore him. But he absolutely dreaded what was about to take place. Like it or not, he and his beloved Blue Ridge WMA were destined to make history.

A beaming Ranger Woody poses for the camera with a longbow – or "bow and arrer" as he liked to call them – during the historic archery hunt at Rock Creek Refuge in October 1940. Around 30 bowhunters from at least nine states participated in the highly-publicized event. The hunt was one of the first of its kind in the nation. Ranger Woody was happy to support this hunt because he predicted that "nary a hair'll be shaved off" any of his precious deer by bow and arrow, and he was right. He jokingly bet some of the hunters that he would gladly "eat the snout" of the first deer brought into camp. News clipping courtesy of Jean McNey.

CHAPTER 13

The "Bow and Arrer" Hunters Invade Rock Creek Refuge

The First Modern Archery Deer Hunt in Georgia, Blue Ridge WMA, 1940

"You boys with yer' bows and arrers, you be careful. I don't want none of them broadhead arrers to hit my broad bottom."

Arthur Woody, October 1940

The long-awaited announcement was big news across Georgia and it drew national headlines. As soon as word got out about the first legal deer hunt in Rock Creek/Blue Ridge Wildlife Management Area, which was scheduled to take place in late October and early November 1940, every sports writer in Georgia wanted to cover the story. Up until that point, Ranger Woody had already received quite a bit of statewide attention for his many accomplishments, but the widespread interest in this historic hunt elevated him to the status of becoming a national celebrity.

Suddenly the eyes of an entire country were upon the man who had brought deer and trout back to the North Georgia mountains. Everyone wanted to meet him: congressmen, high ranking Forest Service officials from Washington, sports writers, deer hunters, trout fishermen, politicians from Atlanta, county commissioners, and a host of other people in high positions. People from all walks of life came to Suches to meet the Ranger, and it now seemed as though June was now setting an extra plate for some special guest at suppertime a lot more frequently – almost every night. The Woody house suddenly became the family-style "Smith House" of Suches.

Thanks to excellent planning by state wildlife officials, the 1940 hunt would actually take place in two phases. A five-day archery hunt would be conducted from Oct. 29 to Nov. 2. This would be followed by two, three-day firearms hunts held Nov. 4-6 and Nov. 7-9. Each hunt generated widespread attention, but the archery hunt probably received more press because it was open to local and out-of-state hunters.

By 1940, competition archery and hunting with a longbow for big game was gaining in popularity across the nation. Although it was still considered somewhat of a novelty by many, annual deer hunts in other states like Michigan had garnered considerable interest from the news media. The same thing happened in Georgia.

Outdoor Georgia magazine, May 1940

The following excerpt is from an article written by Art Schilling and titled "Hunting Deer the Indian Way," appeared in the May 1940 issue of *Outdoor Georgia* magazine, five months before the scheduled hunt in October. Charlie Elliott, who served as Commissioner of Wildlife Resources at the time, and who had a lot to do with the planning of the history making hunts in the first place, was editor of the magazine from 1940 to 1945. During that six-year period, *Outdoor Georgia* printed numerous stories about Ranger Woody:

> The devotee of Robin Hood among Dixie nimrods will have a chance to bring down a buck with his arrow – provided he is a good enough shot – when the South's first bow-and-arrow buck deer hunt opens on October 29 on the Blue Ridge Wildlife Management Area in Georgia's Chattahoochee National Forest.
>
> Hunting is one of the last escapes of modern man from the shackles of civilization. Hunting as a sport long ago supplanted hunting as a mere means of obtaining meat. It is a happy means of getting away from desks and counters to the open freedom of the hills. And the sport of hunting reaches its zenith in thrills and zest when the bow and arrow are used. It was natural, then, that the art of archery was recognized and included in the plans for this hunt, which is the result of 14 years of cooperative restocking and protection by the United States Forest Service and the Division of Wildlife of Georgia. Deer are now plentiful, and for the first

> time since the work was initiated, sportsmen will be given as opportunity to utilize excess numbers.
>
> Game animals are a crop of the soil just as corn, timber and apple orchards. As such, game animals should be managed on sustained yield principles so that a good stock always remains to perpetuate the species. Under the same principle, the crop should be "harvested" by reducing overstocked areas to the number which the area will support.
>
> The national forests of the country are managed for "the greatest good to the largest number of people in the long run" and this managed deer hunt is an activity that will react to the benefit of Southern sportsmen.
>
> The provisions of the plan reserve the first five-day period exclusively for the archers. A second period will follow exclusively for the riflemen. This appears to be a break for the archers, but a fair one, and the arrangement was agreed on by both state and federal officials. In keeping with Southern hospitality, archers from states other than Georgia are eligible for permits to take part in this hunt. Applications and detailed information can be obtained by writing either to Charles Elliott, Director, Wildlife Division, State Capitol, Atlanta, Ga., or Supervisor William H. Fischer, Chattahoochee National Forest, Gainesville, Ga.
>
> A wilderness tent camp will be set up in the heart of the 40,000-acre area to serve as headquarters for the hunt. Here in the picturesque Southern Appalachians is the peace and tranquility of the primeval forest, as our ancestors found it when they landed on these wooded shores. The thrill of the chase today is just as keen as it was centuries ago when Robin Hood and his merry men shot the king's deer in Sherwood Forest, and those who swear allegiance to the longbow will welcome a sporting event that is rare in the United States. Even if one misses his buck, the tang of pine in the October air, the blue haze of the mountains, and the glow of campfires still beckon and call as they did in the days when the Red Man roamed the hills and bagged his game with the bow and arrow.

The article goes on to talk about the specific areas to be hunted and the dates of the archery hunt and the firearms hunt. The five-day archery hunt was limited to 50 hunters who drew permits.

Bag limits for the archery hunt and the firearms hunt were set as follows:

> Buck deer with visible antlers and hogs of both sexes may be killed. The number of buck deer which is desirable to be removed from the area is estimated at fifty. No limitation is set for the removal of hogs. Each

> permittee will be allowed to kill one buck deer and any number of hogs. Hunting cannot continue after a hunter kills one deer.

Archers drawing permits were charged a $7.50 "wilderness fee" to help defer the costs of the hunt. Georgia residents were also required to purchase a Georgia hunting license for $3.25. Non-residents paid $12.50 for a non-resident license. In addition to one antlered buck, archers could also shoot one turkey as well as unlimited numbers of raccoons, squirrels and wild hogs. Interestingly, the article also noted that:

> The District Forest Ranger will have full supervision of the hunt, and his word will be final. The supervisor will detail such forest officers that are necessary to supplement the state organization. The state will assign four Wildlife rangers to the area throughout the hunt. All state and government personnel assigned to the hunt will be under supervision of the District Forest Ranger.

The District Forest Ranger in this case was none other than Ranger Arthur Woody. At the time, Ranger Woody was not overly concerned about any of the archery hunters killing any of *his* deer. Not only did he consider hunting deer with a bow and arrow to be a complete novelty, but he correctly assumed that most of the participating archers would be short on experience when it came to hunting deer. He treated the archery hunt as a lark and he got great pleasure out of taunting the hunters. Some probably didn't appreciate his endless kidding, but it was all in good fun. Much to the displeasure of a few, he predicted that not a single deer would fall to an arrow during the hunt and he was right!

However, the Ranger knew only too well that it would be a different story with the small army of rifle hunters. For him, the events of 1940 certainly must have been like a double-edge sword. On one hand, he was a people person who welcomed the hunters with open arms. He genuinely loved the sportsmen who came to the mountains from Atlanta and other places to hunt deer and fish for trout in the streams he had stocked, and he got along with them famously. From their point of view, he was a hero and most of them worshipped the ground he walked on.

But the sharpest side of that sword involved the upcoming firearms hunt itself and it cut to the bone. Privately, the Ranger dreaded the fact that the time had come to start thinning the herd. He knew that several dozen bucks were going to die during the upcoming firearms hunt. As each day drew nearer, the emotional trauma took its toll. He was deeply troubled by the thought

During the second annual bowhunt at Rock Creek Game Refuge in early November 1941, three veteran bowmen have just finished their early morning breakfast and are preparing to head to the big woods on what the media had dubbed as "the only deer hunt organized especially for archers in the United States." From left to right are Phil Cozad of Columbus, Ohio; Dick Barbour of Atlanta (a friend of Roscoe Reams); and Lou Ribble of Richmond, Virginia. All three hunters had attended the first historic hunt the year before in 1940, a hunt in which not a single deer had been scathed by an arrow. These dedicated archers vowed to be more successful in 1941, and Lou Ribble was the only hunter in the group to actually shoot a small buck. Forest Service photo, from the Duncan Dobie collection.

of having any of his beloved deer shot by hunters. One positive aspect of the situation that could not have been predicted by anyone turned out to be the celebrity status and notoriety that came the Ranger's way as a result of that groundbreaking 1940 deer hunt. But Ranger Woody gladly would have traded all of the recognition in the world for the lives of his precious bucks. And tragically, although no one could predict the future, in hindsight it seems ironic and sad that the Ranger would not have a great deal of time to enjoy his newfound fame or the fruits of his labor. Just a few years down the road, in September 1944, he would suffer a stroke that would mark the beginning of the end for his long career and his way of life.

The following story was written by Charlie Elliott. Since Charlie served as Commissioner of Natural Resources for the State Wildlife Division, as well as editor of *Outdoor Georgia* magazine, and since he and Ranger Woody were such close friends, it stands to reason that he would want to participate in both historic hunts; first the archery hunt held in late October, and later the firearms hunt held in November. Charlie knew this was a momentous event for Ranger Woody's mountain wildlife refuge, and he wanted to witness it in person because he no doubt intended to write about it later on.

With his keen insight and magical gift for the written word, few people could have described the unfolding scene of that first wilderness deer camp nestled in the woods along Noontootly Creek as well as Charlie did. For that reason, the story is reprinted here in its entirety. The fact that Charlie was one of about 30 archery hunters makes the story that much more personal and authentic; it literally puts you around the campfire on the night before the hunt and in the woods with Charlie the next day. (Even though the state had offered 50 permits for this premier hunt, apparently only about 30 archery hunters showed up.)

The story captures both the excitement of the moment and the extreme frustration felt by most of the archers after five fruitless days due to their inexperience in hunting Ranger Woody's white-tailed deer. The article originally appeared in the December 1941 issue of *American Forests* magazine, one year after that first historic hunt took place in October 1940. Ironically, the story also happened to appear during a very significant month in American history, a month in which a previously innocent country and the world at large would forever be changed. The attack on Pearl Harbor took place on December 7.

American Forests magazine, December 1941

Modern Robin Hoods

By Charles Elliott

Don't search for Noontootly Creek on a modern road map. You won't find it there. Noontootly lies at the end of a narrow, winding mountain road and is one of the finest trout streams in the South. But this is not a story of trout.

The site for the wilderness camp was on Noontootly. Ranger Arthur Woody selected that location where Frick's Creek plunged down over the rocks and splashed against the waters of Noontootly. He said it was the one level spot "on the whole durn mount'in." So they (the Forest Service) packed in tents and blankets and cots and cut an enormous pile of wood. That was all. The camp was ready for the hunt.

The next day the hunters trooped in, twenty two of them, armed with food, personal equipment and bows and arrows. They were the first deer

American Forests Magazine

MODERN *Robin Hoods*

By CHARLES ELLIOTT

DON'T search for Noontootly Creek on a modern road map. You won't find it there. Noontootly lies at the end of a narrow, winding mountain road and is one of the finest trout streams in the South. But this is not a story of trout.

The site for the wilderness camp was on Noontootly. Ranger Arthur Woody selected that location where Frick's Creek plunged down over the rocks and splashed against the waters of Noontootly. He said it was the only level spot "on the whole durn mount'in." So they packed in tents and blankets and cots and cut an enormous pile of wood. That was all. The camp was ready for the hunt.

The next day the hunters trooped in, twenty-two of them, armed with food, personal equipment and bows and arrows. They were the first deer hunters to cross the Blue Ridge with bow and arrows in more than half a century. And they were enthusiastic. The deer were there. They had jumped big bucks out of the road on the way to camp. The United States Forest Service and the State Wildlife Division, working together, had built up a deer herd on the Chattahoochee Forest Management Area of some 2,000 animals.

I was one of the archers who had been selected for this five-day wilderness hunt. To my mind there could be no grander sport than bringing home a ten-point buck killed with an arrow. There is something about the sturdy pull of osage orange or yew, something in the music of an arrow sailing through the air, that pinches little sensations under my skin.

But my poor marksmanship with a bow is unexcelled. I doubt if I could commit suicide with my bow drawn in reverse. But such a minor detail did not tone down my enthusiasm. I was a player in this game,—once a necessity, now one of the youngest sports of the human race.

Until dusk the archers continued to arrive. When night had seeped into the laurel thickets and hemlocks of the cove, Ranger Woody built a fire in the clearing, and its blaze brought welcome light and warmth to the human circle that grew around it. Late October at an elevation of 3,000 feet, even in the southern highlands, is cold.

"What are our chances for a deer?" someone asked the ranger.

"There's plenty of big bucks a-roamin' these ridges," he replied evasively.

The hunter who had asked the question was a persistent nimrod. "Do you think we'll kill many deer?" he demanded.

Ranger Woody kicked a burning log back into the fire. "No," he said.

The talk ceased abruptly and one or two of the modern Robin Hoods thrust out their chins belligerently at the ranger. His words were a loaded challenge, cast like a powder-packed bomb into the fire.

"Why not?" three voices asked at once.

The ranger stuck a match between his lips and looked

The archer-hunter draws his seventy pound osage orange bow —power to bring down a deer or other big game animals

around the circle of hostile faces. Then he pushed his battered hat back on his head in a defiant movement. "I'll eat th' nose, raw, plumb to th' teeth, of ary deer killed by a bow n'ärrer," he stated.

He wasn't joking. The men around the campfire didn't take the statement as a joke. Dick Barbour's lean jaw muscles rippled. I saw the sinews tighten in

DECEMBER, 1941 561

Charlie Elliott's well-written article about the first-ever archery hunt at Blue Ridge WMA appeared in American Forests magazine in December 1941 (the same month Pearl Harbor was attacked). Titled "Modern Robin Hoods," the article featured a lead photo of Atlanta archer Hugh C. Thompson posed with his long bow at full draw. Courtesy of American Forests and Jean McNey.

hunters to cross the Blue Ridge with bows and arrows in more than half a century. And they were enthusiastic. The deer were there. They had jumped big bucks on the road on the way to camp. The United States Forest Service and the State Wildlife Division, working together, has built up a deer herd on the Chattahoochee Forest Management Area of some 2,000 animals. (Actually about 30 hunters participated in the hunt including several wives.)

I was one of the archers who had been selected for this five-day wilderness hunt. To my mind, there could be no grander sport than bringing home a ten-point buck killed with an arrow. There is something about the steady pull of Osage orange or yew, something in the music of the arrow sailing through the air that pinches little sensations under my skin.

But my poor marksmanship with a bow is unexcelled. I doubt if I could commit suicide with my bow drawn in reverse. But such a minor detail did not tone down my enthusiasm. I was a player in this game – once a necessity, now one of the youngest sports of the human race.

Until dusk the archers continued to arrive. When night had seeped into the laurel thickets and hemlocks of the cove, Ranger Woody built a fire in the clearing, and its blaze brought welcome light and warmth to the human circle that grew around it. Late October at an elevation of 3,000 feet, even in the Southern highlands, is cold.

"What are our chances for a deer?" someone asked the Ranger.

"There's plenty of big bucks a-roamin' these ridges," he replied evasively.

The hunter who had asked the question was a persistent nimrod. "Do you think we'll kill many deer?" he demanded.

Ranger Woody kicked a burning log into the fire. "No," he said.

The talk ceased abruptly and one or two of the modern Robin Hoods thrust out their chins belligerently at the Ranger. His words were a loaded challenge, cast like a powder-packed bomb into the fire.

"Why not?" three voices asked at once.

The Ranger stuck a match between his lips and looked around the circle of hostile faces. Then he pushed his battered hat back on his head in a defiant movement.

"I'll eat th' nose, plumb raw, to th' teeth, of ary deer killed by a bow'n arrer," he stated.

He wasn't joking. The men around the campfire didn't take the statement as a joke. Dick Barbour's lean jaw muscles rippled. I saw the sinews tighten in Otto Hart's wrist. Hart had come down with four companions from Evansville, Indiana, for the hunt. He was one of the champions of the nation and had hunted deer in Michigan with his "bow'n arrer."

That night around the campfire, Clint Davis of the southern region of the Forest Service told the archers the story of this game refuge. "Fifteen years ago," he said, "Ranger Woody bought deer with money out of his own pocket and planted them in the Rock Creek watershed. Later the Forest Service trapped deer where they were overstocked on other national forests (Pisgah Reserve) and brought them here. The original herd of 70 has grown to 2,000 in about twelve years. It proves what game management can do.

"The State Wildlife Division employs special agents to protect this management area. The mountaineers living in valleys beyond the forest boundaries have cooperated almost to the man to protect the deer. This year we opened the game refuge to the organized hunt in which you are now participating, to take off the surplus animals. The gunners will follow the Robin Hoods. We estimate that the total number of deer killed by both arrows and bullets will be around thirty."

Several of us looked toward Arthur Woody, who sat beside the fire, chewing on his match, as if to say, "There is one man who thinks we'll kill a deer." But the Ranger did not comment on the statement made by his fellow member of the Service.

The campfire had burned to amber ash, when, one by one, the men rose and sought the comfort of their blankets, for the five mile walk down from the Ranger Station had been hard on unseasoned muscles. With the grace of a 200-pound black bear, Ranger Woody rolled to his feet from where he had been lying beside the fire. (Apparently, because this was classified as a "wilderness hunt," the hunters had to hike into camp on foot.)

"Where are you going?" I asked.

"My bed's up at th' station," said the Ranger.

"Why not stay here?" I suggested.

He grinned. "Them cots is too puny," he replied, and stepping beyond the circle of light cast by the campfire, he was gone. Not more than half a dozen of us were left at the campfire.

"I was going home tomorrow," said Jack Troy, sports editor (for the Atlanta Constitution), but now I can't. I've got to stay and see the Ranger lose his bet."

"He'll lose," said Dick Hughes, one of the Hoosier archers. "Most every species of big game animal in the world has been killed by modern bows and arrows."

"The bow and arrow was used long before guns, wasn't it?" Jack asked.

Dick Barbour looked up from his task of whetting a steel arrow point to a razor edge.

"Arrow heads date back 50,000 years," he said. "The anthropologists say arrows without stone points were used long before that. The arrow was the primitive weapon of nearly every land on earth, except Australia. Gunpowder was not invented until after the year 1300. There was a lot of game killed in the 50,000 years before guns. "

"Many wars have been won with arrows, too," Jack said. "If I remember my history, William the Conqueror won the Battle of Hastings by having his Norman archers shoot their arrows into the air and drop them behind the English shields."

I reached over and took the arrow out of Dick Barbour's hand, and nicked my finger testing the sharpness of the point. "That can do some damage with a fifty-pound bow behind it," I said.

"What d' you mean, fifty?" Dick Hughes snorted. "My hunting bow has a pull of eighty pounds."

He stepped into the tent and brought out his bow, a short, thick, powerful weapon. I could hardly bend it.

"The Indians didn't have bows this strong," I said.

"The average pull of the American Indian bow was forty-five pounds," Dick said. "But bows of primitive tribes are all sizes. Some of the pigmy tribes of Africa have bows which are three or four feet long and shoot an arrow weighing less than one-fifth of an ounce. It's quite different from the bow of the Siriono Indian, the largest known. It is eight feet long and shoots an arrow the same length and an inch thick."

"Perhaps they needed powerful bows," I said, "to drive home big arrow heads into big game."

Dick Barbour grunted. "That's what most amateurs think. But the large arrow heads were chipped for small game, like rabbits and squirrels. Those very small points that most people call 'bird points' were used for game as big as deer and bear and elk because they could penetrate deep."

I had scarcely a chance to turn over in my sleeping bag before someone shook me. It was four o'clock and one of my tent mates was already pulling on his boots. I slipped into my clothes and peeped out of the tent flap. The stars were white beyond the hemlock boughs.

After breakfast we were assigned to our hunt compartments. My station was a long cove above Three Forks, almost two miles down the Noontootly from camp.

"That's a good place for a deer," the Ranger said. "Then he leaned close and whispered, "Hunt like an Indian."

When daylight came, the roar of the Noontootly was like faint thunder in the valley. I sat down on the shell of a poplar log which might have sprawled there for a hundred years. The cove below was a perfect range for deer. This year the white oak mast was heavy and acorns were a favorite food. A well-used game trail crawled along the cove floor not fifty feet away and went toward Springer Mountain, on the skyline above.

Yellow sunshine marches down the slope and spread into the canopy of leaves. While the autumn colors still were bright, I had my eyes upon the play of pigments overhead when the hard earth resounded to the ring of hooves. I pulled my bow into position for quick action as a doe and fawn came up the trail, stepping daintily among the lights and shadows. I relaxed again and the pounding of my heart slowed down.

Waiting grew monotonous. I wanted to desert the log and stalk along the trail but the Ranger's last words still rang in my ears: "Hunt like an Indian." An Indian hunted with the patience of the wilderness itself.

The forest life went on as though it were unaware of my presence. A tiny winter wren hopped upon my log, and a flock of warblers fled by. The sun swung overhead and pointed down. In the afternoon, a flock of fourteen turkeys wandered across the cove, scratching in the leaves and making little clucking noises in their throats. I could have pinned one of the big bronze birds to the ground with an arrow, but the season on turkeys had not opened.

At dusk I left my log and walked back down the trail toward camp. My luck had been the luck of all the Robin Hoods. Thompson had seen a buck that wheeled and thundered up the mountain out of range, and most of the hunters had wandered up and down their territory all day without seeing a deer. Ranger Woody heard the news in silence, though a faint smile played at the corners of his eyes.

Dick Barbour saw the smile. "I'll get a buck or break my neck trying," he swore.

The second day was a duplicate of the first, except that I did not sit still. Before the middle of the morning I left my log and spent the day ranging up and down the mountain. Once I jumped a rabbit and later on a ruffed grouse boomed up and sailed off across the slope. Coming in sight of camp at dusk, I wondered how I would lift my feet to walk the remaining short distance to the fire.

"There were no deer in my territory today," I said to Arthur Woody. "I walked over every foot of it."

"You wouldn't have seen 'em if they'd been there," he said. "Bucks can hear you and smell you before you get closer'n half a mile. You'll never kill one walkin', and with that contraption." He pointed to my "bow'n arrer."

The group of archers were the most determined men I have ever seen. They took an oath to make Arthur Woody eat that deer nose. Day after day they left camp before the east showed its first light, and night after night they dragged back again, exhausted. On the fourth day Dick Hughes fell and cut his knee. His four companions left with him for the doctor and Indiana. Almost every day some of the archers spotted bucks, but they were usually too far beyond the flight of an arrow and traveling too fast. Every man hunted hard. The deer were there. We had seen them. But no one brought in venison.

"What kind of curse have you put on this place?" Dick Barbour asked Arthur Woody.

"I ain't cursed at all," the Ranger said. "It's jest that you'uns don't know how to hunt."

The afternoon of the fifth day came, and still no one brought a deer into camp." It just goes to prove," said Thompson, as we stood around the campfire, "that a man can have as much sport without making a kill."

"Bringing home game is the least important part of any hunt," someone said, and several hunters voiced approval of the words.

"We'll take your wager next year," Thompson said to Ranger Woody.

"We'll talk about that next year," the Ranger replied.

I walked with Arthur back up the trail to the Ranger Station. "You were cocksure we wouldn't get a deer," I said. "Why?"

"I'll be cocksure the next time you see me," the Ranger grinned. "It takes more than good shootin' with a bow'n arrer to git a buck."

"What more?" I asked.

"Good woodsmanship, for one thing," he said. "The Indians were good hunters because they had to be. They laid over a trail 'til a buck came along, if'n it took a day or a week. Then they plugged him with an arrer at close range. Modern folks can't set still. They got to be a-movin' all th' time. You can't find th' deer a-movin'. You got to let th' deer find you. And plunkin' a arrer into a target settin' still at a hundred feet ain't like plunkin' it into a buck that's a-runnin' hell-for-election."

"You took a chance on having to eat a deer nose by telling me how to hunt," I said. "Remember?"

"Shore," the Ranger said, "but I was safe. I knowed you wouldn't take my advice. And I knowed you couldn't hit one of them bucks nohow, even if it was a-straddlin' you. I done seen you shoot."

The following story told by Jean McNey illustrates Ranger Woody's fun-loving sense of humor, as well as his genuine fondness for the archery hunters who had come to the mountains to participate in the first historic deer hunt. The incident likely occurred on the first night as Ranger Woody was welcoming the hunters to Rock Creek Refuge.

Spreading a Little "Mountain Cheer"

"Since the first archery hunt ever held in the game reserve was such a grand occasion, my grandfather decided to help the hunters celebrate the event by offering them a little 'mountain cheer' around the campfire," Jean McNey recalled with a smile. "A day or two before the hunt, he brought home some moonshine that he had 'confiscated.' He'd been given several empty bottles of 'bottled in bond' whiskey and he poured the moonshine into these bottles. Then he used an old trick that mountaineers are famous for. He burned some brown sugar and put it into the bottles containing the moonshine. This made the moonshine bead up just like properly aged 'bottled in bond' whiskey."

(Bottled in bond refers to American-made liquor that has been aged and bottled according to a set of legal regulations contained in the United States government's Standards of Identity for Distilled Spirits, as originally laid out in the Bottled-in-Bond Act of 1897. Why did Ranger Woody go to all this trouble to mask his mountain-made "corn likker" and make it appear to be

Ranger Arthur Woody (center) entertains the crowd of bow hunters during the much publicized five-day archery hunt in late October 1940. The nightly campfire gatherings became a ritual. In addition to sharing some much-loved tall tales, Ranger Woody added a little spice to the campfire scene by spreading a little "mountain cheer" in treating the hunters to a taste of high-octane "white lightning." The young man sitting to the Ranger's left with hat in hand is believed to be Roscoe Reams. The man kneeling to the Ranger's right is Roscoe's good friend and mentor, Hugh C. Thompson. Clint Davis stands directly behind Ranger Woody while Charlie Elliott is the third man from right (standing). Photo courtesy of Jean McNey.

legal bottle and bonded whiskey? He might well have wanted his unsuspecting victims to think it was regular whiskey, not having the potency of moonshine, and he probably didn't want the word to get out that he was distributing illegal moonshine to the hunters in the first place since the rules of the hunt clearly stated that hunters in camp could not possess any alcoholic beverages.)

"As with most gatherings of this nature, on the night before a hunt, the hunters in camp would all get together and build a roaring camp fire. They'd sit around the campfire as hunters have been doing for thousands of years and tell stories and do whatever else they do when hunters get together. So Papa took what probably amounted to several bottles or jugs of that moonshine whiskey over to the campfire and everyone drank lavishly including several Forest Service men and state game wardens who had been assigned to help out with the hunt."

This late-night campfire – with or without a supply of "white lightning" – quickly became a tradition on all of the hunts that followed and Ranger Woody usually made an appearance and told stories and joked with the men. Interestingly, the rules of the hunt as set forth by the Forest Service clearly stated that no alcoholic beverages were to be consumed during any of the hunts. But as we have seen, Ranger Woody was not one to always follow precise rules. In this case, he wanted to welcome these hunters to North Georgia on this historic occasion. To his way of thinking, there was no better way in the world to share some genuine mountain hospitality than to offer them a tasty little homemade nightcap.

It is also interesting to note that even though Ranger Woody was present at almost all of the late-night campfire get-togethers, mesmerizing the hunters with his one-of-a-kind Mark-Twain-style humor and stories and teasing them relentlessly about their obvious inexperience and lack of ability using a "bow and arrer," he was always up at the crack of dawn the next day supervising every facet of the hunt from dawn to dusk. Throughout the day, he seemed to be everywhere at once. This was true during the firearms hunt as well.

Papa's Famous Grub Call

"Whenever some unusual activity was going on in Suches like this historic deer hunt, some of the Forest Service men and other state wildlife officials would customarily sleep in the upstairs rooms in the two-story house that served as the main office at the Ranger Station across the road from our house," Jean continued. "There were no barracks or anything like that so they brought blankets and slept on cots. Since there was nowhere for these men to eat for miles around, they would come over to our house the next morning for breakfast." (The Woody house was always open to hungry Forest Service personnel and June and Mae loyally and cheerfully prepared many a pre-dawn meal over the years).

Bright and early the next morning just before 4 a.m., Ranger Woody stepped out on the front porch of his house and with a booming voice began bellowing out what would come to be known and remembered as a priceless wake-up call to the sleepy men just across the road at the station. Only a man with the Ranger's endless wit and personality could have done what he did. The excitement generated must have been much like a popular ranch cook in the far West stepping outside and ringing the traditional metal triangle to call all the hungry cowhands to a meal, only in this case the Ranger used his booming voice.

"Rise up ye long time bullies! Git your 4 o'clock whistle and yer ham and eggs! I call ya' once, I call ya' twice, I call ya' no more... the next time it'll be with a .44!"

Whether or not he ever actually used a .44 to start the action is not known, but from this day forward the Ranger's famous 4 a.m. "grub call" became a tradition any time a large activity like a managed deer hunt requiring extra manpower took place in the refuge. The men learned to love and cherish their lively breakfast call, and like many others during that time, Jean, who always helped her mother and grandmother with the cooking, had it etched in her memory forever.

And, of course, they all came! A bit sleepy eyed perhaps at first, these men learned to love and relish June and Mae's excellent cooking. Despite having told stories for hours the night before around the campfire, Ranger Woody was always up before everyone else in the mornings. This unforgettable wake-up call became a regular tradition with all of the special hunts and that took place in 1940, 1941 and 1942.

On the morning after Ranger Woody benevolently had shared his bottled mountain nectar with the two-dozen odd archery hunters around the campfire, another humorous incident took place that became etched in Jean's memory forever.

"After Papa's breakfast call, all the men came up to the house from across the road," Jean said. "One of them, I think it was a ranger named Charlie Granville, was obviously not feeling well. My mom said to him, 'Charlie, how do you want your eggs this morning?'

"He turned as white as Caspar the Friendly Ghost and he answered, 'Mae, do you have a little tomato juice?' Apparently the Ranger's white lightning consumed the night before had taken its toll on Charlie and he was nursing a severe hangover!"

Thus was the setting in the wee hours of the morning on the first day of the first historic archery hunt of the 20th Century held in Ranger Woody's beloved Rock Creek Refuge (Blue Ridge WMA) in the North Georgia mountains. Despite his misgivings about the upcoming firearms hunt that would take place in less than a week, the Ranger remained in cheerful spirits throughout the archery hunt where he continuously joked with the hunters and poked fun at their lack of experience. Despite all the good-natured fun, one thing was abundantly apparent. As the rules of the hunt plainly stated, the District Ranger – Ranger Arthur Woody – was clearly in charge.

The following article was written on location during the first day of the archery hunt on Oct. 29, 1940, by Jack Troy, a popular sports writer for the Atlanta Constitution and also an ardent admirer of Ranger Woody. Over the years, Jack wrote a number of glowing stories about the Ranger. After the Ranger's illness and death, Jack also wrote a number of heartfelt tributes.

Mr. and Mrs. Hugh C. Thompson of Atlanta had good reason to be excited about bow hunting at Rock Creek Refuge during the first hunt in 1940. One of Hugh Thompson's parents was said to be a full-blooded Cherokee Indian. Thompson was a mentor to young Roscoe Reams, who had just turned 16 when the historic archery hunt occurred. Twenty-eight years later in 1968, Thompson's son, Hugh Thompson Jr., a noted helicopter pilot in Viet Nam, gained national attention by exposing the horrors of the My Lai massacre in which hundreds of innocent Vietnamese villagers had been murdered by U.S. soldiers. Photo courtesy of Outdoor Georgia magazine, November 1940 issue.

Forest Primeval
Chattahoochee National Forest, Oct. 29 (1940)

Where Stover's Creek, Frick's Creek and Noontootly meet in a conjunction known as three forks – that's where the wilderness camp of the archery deer hunters is placed. The camp is in a small clearing by the side of the streams, in a massive hemlock grove. The rushing waters sweep under low-hanging branches of laurel and rhododendron.

This is virgin forest. In this primeval retreat, just a few miles below Winding Stair gap, the woodsman's ax has been known only to the extent of making a clearing for tents and the cook stove, and to hew a rough road in from Winding Stair gap.

The great hemlocks seem to reach halfway to the roof of the sky. After dark, they appear as great shafts extending in the deep purple night. Mr. Clint Davis assures us that so virgin is this spot of ours in the wilderness that not even the woodpecker has found it as yet. Strange then, as primeval as it really is, that the only wild and guttural sounds heard near the campfire the first night were made by starving newspapermen as they roasted whole Irish potatoes and wieners.

In the stillness of the night at lights out, the only disturbing sound is the rushing of the mountain streams. And there is the dew-kissed coolness of the mountain air. You tumble in bed with your pants on and are grateful for the warmth of the heavy blankets. Instantly the lulling mountain streams sing you to sleep.

No Shooting – For nigh unto 15 years now not a shot has been fired in the Blue Ridge Wildlife Management Area of the Chattahoochee National Forest.

The record almost was broken the other day. Ranger Arthur Woody, the old man of the mountain, and State Wildlife Ranger Clyde Wehunt apprehended a gent with a rifle and 15 cartridges.

It will cost this gent a few bucks, in more ways than one. And he didn't fire a shot.

So the deer of the area do not know the roar of a shotgun or the sharp crack of the high-powered rifle. Nor do they know the hiss of the broadhead arrow.

One should not feel too sorry of the deer however. This is one of the finest deer grounds in America. The high ridges are thick with the laurel and rhododendron and heavy with trees.

It has not rained for such a spell, too, that the deer can hear huntsmen coming blocks away. One must be expert in the ways of woodcraft to get within range.

And even the most expert find it mighty difficult. Ranger Woody, picturesque mountain character known to all who ever visited the forest, may have something there when he offer to eat the nose of every deer killed with bow and "arrer."

Ranger Woody, in a campfire chat last night, told the archers what to do in case they should get buck fever.

"Don't just stand there like the knot on a log," instructed Woody, "bite your arm. Bite it hard."

Then Woody reminded the archers again he'd eat the nose of every buck raw.

Woody's generosity came to the fore in full measure when he graciously consented for all archers killing deer to be allowed to go back up the ridges to hunt wild boar.

Lot of Fun – Today the expert archers in camp departed at daybreak on the long trek up mountainsides to the ridges where the deer and wild boar feed.

Many of them will not return until after dark. A woodsman of experience gets direction by compass. One who knows his business rarely gets lost.

They knew as they set out that the odds were greatly against them. As mentioned, the ground is dry. A deer could almost hear a pin drop in the forest. If rain comes, it will help.

Anyway, it's a great life. Whether or not they get any game, they will have had a lot of fun and exercise. And there is something odd about an appetite under such conditions. It is not only enormous but never-ending.

There never does seem to be enough mulligan stew. We'll have to speak to Cornbread Brandon, our cook about that.

Explains Gap – Ranger Woody, who is responsible for there being enough deer for two weeks of hunting, explained the term "gap."

"A gap is a low place between mountain peaks," said Woody. "It is a place both deer and humans hunt to cross mountains. Deer and hogs are just as lazy as people. They're always looking for easy places."

Fifteen years ago Woody decided to do something about this area being shot out. Bobcat and foxes abounded but the deer had disappeared.

So Woody took his own funds and purchased two doe and two bucks from a party in North Carolina. Today Woody is the toast of the forest service and the hunters of Georgia. (As has been stated many times previously, he actually purchased five young fawns from the Pisgah Game Reserve 13 years previously, not 15 years.)

He is responsible for two great hunts. A week's hunt with firearms starts next Monday from this very same wilderness camp.

Local Color – At this time of the year the mountainside is afire with the brilliant colors of autumn. Falling leaves blanket the ground in a color scheme of red, gold and burnt orange. These are the matching colors of a shirt being worn by Mr. Clint Davis, public relations expert of the United States Forest Service. In fact, when Mr. Davis stands up on the hillside there is hardly any way of telling him from a fat stump covered with leaves.

Mr. Kenneth Rogers is a bit more modest in his idea of what the well-dressed woodsmen should wear. Mr. Rogers' shirt resembles a hollyhock in full bloom. Or perhaps a peacock in high dungeon. We dwell on the aesthetic side of the hunt while waiting for reports of our fine-feathered bow and arrow allies.

(As noted, Clint Davis was a Forest Service photographer and public relations officer who worked out of the Gainesville office. He worshipped Ranger Woody and the two men were very good friends, working closely together on numerous projects over the years.

Kenneth Rogers (1907-1989) was a legendary photographer for the Atlanta Constitution from 1923-1972 who chronicled many of the photos of this historic hunt, both the archery hunt and the firearms hunt. He took many historic photos in the Atlanta area and across Georgia during his long, distinguished career. He, too, became good friends with the Ranger, and he often came to Suches to fish for trout in the refuge. The most famous photo of Ranger Woody ever taken and today one of the most familiar – sitting on a fence and waving – was the handiwork of Kenneth Rogers.)

Sportsman – Otto Hart, of Evansville, Indiana, was the first hunter to report today. He came in just before noon. A noted archer, Mr. Hart reported he had seen a doe not 10 feet away and a spiked buck which he could have shot. A spiked buck is one with its first set of horns.

"I didn't shoot at the spiked buck. I have enough trophies and I wouldn't kill a young buck."

If all the hunters felt as does Mr. Otto Hart there never would have been any game scarcity.

Making History in the Georgia Mountains

Roscoe Reams Remembers the First Blue Ridge Archery Hunt in 1940

From an interview in November 2000

During the decades of the 1950s and '60s, Atlanta native Roscoe Reams was known nationally as a trick-shooting archer who traveled the country putting on amazing demonstrations with his bow and arrow. The first time he ever picked up a longbow in his life was in preparation for the 1940 archery hunt at Blue Ridge WMA when he was 16 years old. After making a name for himself in the archery world, Roscoe shifted gears in the 1970s, '80s and '90s and became known as a nationally prominent turkey hunting expert.

He attended outdoor shows, conducted calling seminars, gave demonstrations and hunted with many of the best-known turkey hunters in the country. But his outdoor talents went far beyond simply being a passionate turkey hunter. Roscoe lived an amazing life. His outdoor career was long and varied. In many ways, he grew up to be every bit a character as his much loved mentor Arthur Woody. He first met the Ranger in 1938 when he was 14 years old.

Born in Atlanta, in 1925, Roscoe died in a car accident in September 2008 at the age of 84. As of the time of his untimely death, he was in excellent health and had slowed down very little. His love of hunting and fishing began as a boy roaming the woods and camping along the Chattahoochee River near Atlanta. He graduated from Boy's High School in Atlanta a year after World War II started, and he attended college for a time at Georgia State University.

His friendship with Ranger Woody was short-lived but life-changing. As with so many young men during this era, World War II intervened. Wanting to do his patriotic duty, Roscoe entered the Navy in 1943 at age 18. By the time he returned home after the war in the fall of 1946, Ranger Woody had passed away only a few months earlier. Roscoe deeply regretted never seeing his beloved mentor and friend again and not being able to attend his funeral service. He was able to attend a memorial service held in honor of the Ranger at Woody Gap in 1947 when the bronze plaque of Ranger Woody was dedicated (see Chapter 18).

Roscoe started hunting wild hogs in the Rock Creek Refuge with several older companions from Atlanta in 1938 when he was 14. It was during this time that he met and befriended Ranger Woody. They remained good friends and saw each other on a regular basis until Roscoe went off to war in 1943. When the first archery hunt for deer was announced in 1940, Roscoe and his close-knit group of hunting companions decided to give bow hunting a whirl.

None of these men had ever hunted with a bow and arrow before, but they all went out and acquired longbows and hunting arrows tipped with razor-sharp broadheads. This proved to be another life-changing experience for Roscoe. Little could he imagine that this chance introduction into the world of archery would propel him into a career where, in just a few short years, he would be making a very good living with his shooting skills during the decade of the 1950s.

Roscoe was a gifted archer. During the 1950s and '60s, he put on hundreds of shooting demonstrations across the country. One such demonstration took place in the ballroom of the New York Statler Hotel in New York City! He even made a TV appearance on the Tonight Show in Hollywood in the late 1950s when Steve Allen was host. For years, Roscoe put on shooting demonstrations at dozens of wildlife shows around the nation. As one of the top trick-shooting archers in the country, he was often dubbed "Atlanta's Robin Hood."

During the 1960s, Hiram Walker & Sons paid Roscoe to appear in a full page ad for its Imperial Blended Whiskey. The ad ran in several national magazines, including Life. It depicted Roscoe sampling a glass of whiskey with a quiver full of arrows on his back after a long day in the field. Ironically, in real life, Roscoe drank very little and never smoked. In 1956, Roscoe was featured in the Saturday Evening Post and several other similar publications as well as dozens of newspapers around the country shooting razor-tipped broadheads into Seiberling

After learning how to use a long bow for the first time at the historic archery hunt at Rock Creek Refuge (Blue Ridge WMA) in 1940 at age 16, Roscoe Reams went on to become a nationally-known trick archery shooter and hunter in the late 1950s and early '60s. Here Roscoe poses with a fine buck taken on Georgia's Blackbeard Island with a more-modern recurve bow. Photo courtesy of Elinor Reams.

tires, a prominent brand of automobile tires in those days. The ad was intended to demonstrate how quickly the tires resealed themselves after being punctured with razor broadheads.

Roscoe was also an avid trout fisherman, an activity he developed a passion for in North Georgia during the time he knew Ranger Woody. (See Chapter 9 for several of Roscoe's unforgettable "fish stories" involving Ranger Woody.) In April 1955, Roscoe set a record in Georgia by catching a 9-pound, 27-½ inch rainbow trout with an artificial lure at Dick's Creek near Lake Burton.

Like his mentor Ranger Woody, Roscoe grew to be a master turkey hunter and caller and for many years during his later life he was in great demand as a hunting guide and seminar speaker. He also hunted deer avidly and made hunting and fishing videos for TV in the 1980s and '90s.

Around the same time he met Arthur Woody, Roscoe was introduced to Charlie Elliott, thus beginning a close friendship that would last until Charlie's death in 2000. Roscoe and Charlie hunted and fished together for over half a century. At the time of their meeting, Charlie had recently been appointed Commissioner of Natural Resources by the state of Georgia. While working with the state and the Forest Service, Charlie had been very instrumental in establishing a statewide "Junior Ranger" program across Georgia in 1940

In this widely-circulated ad for Seiberling "puncture-proof" tires distributed nationally in the late 1950s, Roscoe Reams shoots a tire with his recurve bow. Photo courtesy of Elinor Reams.

(something he no doubt discussed in detail with Ranger Woody as plans for the program were being made).

Young Roscoe was sworn in by Charlie as a Junior Ranger, complete with shoulder patch and badge. He couldn't have been prouder. Similar to the Boy Scouts, part of a Junior Ranger's duties included engaging in some type of beneficial conservation project. At the suggestion of Ranger Woody, Roscoe's program involved stocking quail in Rock Creek Refuge. Roscoe was able to obtain some quail from the state through the efforts of Commissioner Elliott.

Roscoe always kept meticulous records on every turkey gobbler he shot, and although he never bragged about his success to outsiders, as of the spring of 2000 when I interviewed him about his friendship with Ranger Woody, he had taken a total of 586 gobblers during his long career. He was very proud of that number. I'm sure he added to it over the next eight seasons before his death.

Roscoe was returning home from a piece of property that he looked after for a friend in his old Ford Bronco after putting out some feed for the deer and turkeys in September 2008 when he was involved in a fatal accident. Perhaps it was fitting that he had been able to spend his last day on earth being outside and doing what he loved to do most of all in life.

During our interview, Roscoe shared some rare gems with me about his beloved mentor.

He Always Called Me 'Boy'

"That Arthur Woody was a mess," Roscoe said. "He was a unique individual, one of the most unique men I've ever known."

"Was he as charismatic in real life as his legend portrays?" I asked.

"No question about it," Roscoe said. "The man was a one-of-kind character. Only once or twice in a man's lifetime you get to meet someone like him if you're lucky. He was the real thing!"

"When I first met him, he was a 'federal man,' Roscoe said. "The men I hunted with in the mountains didn't like federal men so everyone was very suspicious of him at first."

At that time (1938), being a forest ranger was akin to being a game warden or revenuer, and neither was someone most average sportsmen wished to befriend. Ironically, Ranger Woody and most of the people he associated with in Suches felt the same way about all "govermunt people." Bona fide government officials were never to be trusted. Some things never change! However, as Roscoe and his companions were soon to learn, Ranger Woody never fit the mold of a true government bureaucrat. He was always pretty much just one of the boys and everyone came to respect him for his individualism.

"I met Ranger Woody through several older friends I hunted with up in Union and Fannin counties," Roscoe said. "He always called me 'Boy.' By that time, he was in his mid-50s and tubby fat. He seemed to be kind of quiet and standoffish at first, but he had a lot of personality. He would sit around the campfire with us and talk. Once you got him started, he loved to tell stories. After I got to know him a little, I really liked him a lot. We became fairly good friends during the short span of years I knew him, and I often looked him up when I was in the area.

"I was still a teenager when I began hog hunting with a very good friend named Hugh C. Thompson during the late 1930s up in the Noontootly Creek area of Fannin County," Roscoe remembers. "Back then, it was just called Rock Creek and the area around it was known as the Blue Ridge Ranger District. Later on, the refuge itself become known as Blue Ridge Wildlife Management Area, one of the state's first-ever WMAs."

For decades, domestic hogs (and cattle) had been allowed to run loose in the mountains (ever since settlement after the Cherokees had been removed

Why These Hunters Prefer Robin

IT might be a slight exaggeration to declare that every hunter who uses a bow and arrow has a different reason for choosing this particular weapon. The ranks of the arrowmen have reached such proportions that we'd probably run out of reasons before we ran out of Robin Hoods.

I've talked with many of the men who prefer an arrow to a piece of fast lead when they're stalking game, and just about all of these white Indians seem to agree on at least a couple of reasons for their preference of hunting arms. They state emphatically that a guy has to be a better hunter to kill game with a bow and arrow. They also say that the suspense is greater and with some game species, there is even an element of danger.

Ray Barnes, who prefers cold steel over hot lead, says there's a great deal more to bow hunting than most people realize.

"A rifle hunter," he insists, "sees a deer 200 yards away. He's equipped with a hunk of lead that leaves his gun barrel at speeds of up to more than half a mile per second.

Roscoe Reams perches in a tree and takes aim at a deer with his bow and arrow.

This news clipping about bow hunting on Blackbeard Island, Georgia, features a story about Roscoe Reams, circa early 1960s. Photo courtesy of Elinor Reams.

in the late 1830s.) During hog killing time (usually the first good frost in late October or early November), a group of mountaineers would go out and round up several hogs to be slaughtered. According to Roscoe, many of these hogs had belonged to homesteaders who had lost their farms during the Depression because they couldn't pay their taxes, and the hogs became feral.

As mentioned elsewhere, most of the large predators native to the mountains including wolves, mountain lions and black bears had long since been exterminated, and the hogs had no natural enemies except for an occasional bobcat. So they proliferated and multiplied. By the late 1930s, these free-roaming hogs had increased to sizable populations, and the local forestry officials wanted them out of the refuge areas because of the damage they inflicted.

"The rangers hated those hogs because they competed with the deer they were trying to restore, eating acorns and other favored deer foods," Roscoe said. "Old Arthur Woody really hated them. That's how I met him, through Hugh C. Thompson.

"At that time, they didn't allow firearms of any kind within the refuge (since there was no open deer season)," Roscoe said. "The ranger in charge (game warden) was a Mr. Sprinkle, and he liked us a lot. He actually gave us a key to the gate. Mr. Sprinkle owned some hog dogs, and he allowed us to go into the refuge with his dogs to kill some of the hogs. It was totally on the sly, since there was no legal hunting inside the refuge, and only a few people knew about it. We loved doing it and we killed a lot of hogs, but we never brought anything out. We'd always leave the meat with the ranger and go on back home.

"Ranger Woody would often come into our camp at night. We often camped at a spot known as Camp Wahsega (just southwest of Suches right above Rock Creek Lake), and he would tell stories around the campfire. He loved to tell stories and he was good at it. The area where we camped belonged to a man named C. B Langley. He had bought a parcel of land right below Cooper's Gap directly from Arthur Woody. Later on Arthur promised to sell me another piece of land nearby, and I was serious about trying to buy it. But I ended up going into the military in 1943 after the war broke out. When I returned home after the war, Arthur had died so I lost out.

"Arthur Woody was always thinking about ways he could improve the wildlife in his refuge," Roscoe continues. "He was well-known for having stocked deer and trout in the area, and he and the Forest Service were raising trout in some rearing ponds near Rock Creek Lake to put into some of the other nearby streams. He loved his trout!

Roscoe Reams shows off a mountain groundhog taken with his recurve bow in the late 1950s. Photo courtesy of Elinor Reams.

"One day when we were up there he expressed an interest in getting some quail and trying to get a bob white restocking program going. (In those days, a lot of mountain folk called bob whites 'partridges' instead of quail, not to be confused with the much larger ruffed grouse found across the mountain region of the state, which many of the locals referred to as 'pheasants.')

"Charlie Elliott had just become the new Commissioner of Natural Resources in 1938. Before that he had been director of Georgia state parks. Arthur asked me if I'd go by his office in Atlanta and make arrangements to get some quail for the refuge as part of my Junior Ranger conservation project. My father had always kept quail dogs down in Albany, and I had grown up hunting birds with him. E.D. "Ed" Rivers was the governor at the time, and with Charlie's help we got the 'partridges' that Ranger Woody wanted. Charlie and I became very good friends after that and we remained the best of friends for the next 60 years!"

Roscoe Remembers the First Week-Long Archery Deer Hunt (1940)

"When the politicians decided to conduct the first archery and gun seasons in the Blue Ridge Game Refuge in the fall of 1940 because of public pressure, Ranger Woody was adamantly against holding a firearms hunt," Roscoe said. "But everyone in our group thought both hunts were great ideas. By then we were pretty good at killing hogs with guns, so we all got ourselves longbows and decided to try to become deerslayers with bows. Many of the men I hunted with went on to become expert bow hunters. Arthur Woody was very skeptical about hunting deer with a bow. He didn't think it could be done.

"'If any of you boys can kill a deer in North Georgia with a bow and arrer – instead of using the word 'arrow' he always called arrows 'arrers' – I'll eat the asshole and all!' he boasted to us the first night in camp. (Since several newspaper and magazine writers were covering the hunt, several subsequent articles mentioned Ranger's Woody's challenge to the bow hunters and made it a big deal, but by necessity they changed the unprintable body part by going to the other end of the deer and stating that he had promised to eat the deer's "snout.")

"Well, fortunately for the ranger, we all got skunked that first season," Roscoe remembered. "One of the bow hunters did shoot a hog though. The next year, 1941, another bow hunt was held in Blue Ridge and we were all right there, raring to go. That year, Lou Ribble, a member of our group, killed the first deer up there with a bow. So we cut out the appropriate part with a knife, put it between two pieces of bread, and presented it to Arthur. Of course, Arthur never actually ate the rather delicate part like he said he would, but everyone got a big laugh out of that episode and we took several pictures of him holding the sandwich!"

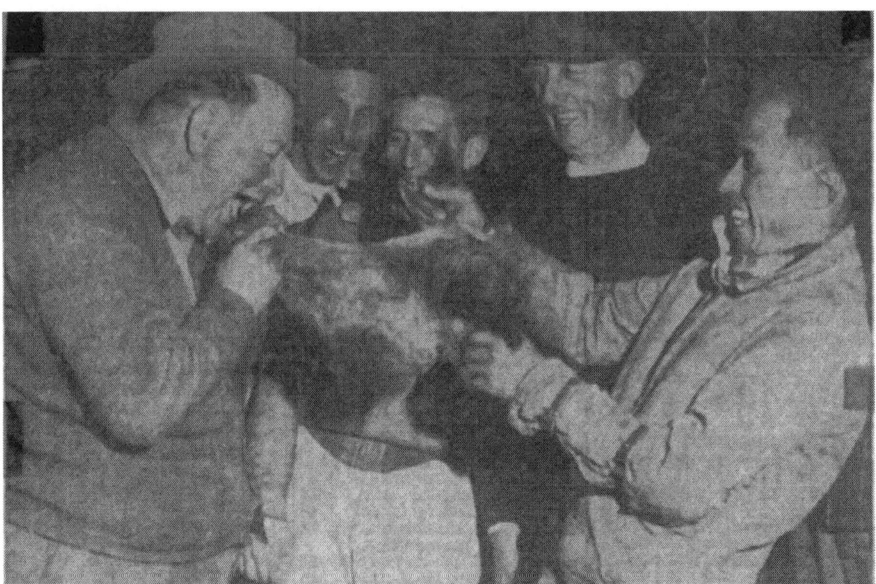

Ranger Woody "hams it up" for the camera as he pretends to eat the snout from a wild hog taken by Atlanta archer Hugh C. Thompson at the second annual archery hunt held at the Blue WMA in November 1941. One year earlier, the Ranger had jokingly mocked the bow hunters during the premier archery hunt, predicting that no one would shoot a deer with archery tackle due to lack of experience. He made a friendly wager with the hunters claiming he would "eat the snout" from any deer taken by bow and arrow, but none were. The following year, the hunters sought their revenge with the snout of a wild hog. News clipping courtesy of Jean McNey.

Mountain Tragedy Ranger Arthur Woody has often said he favored the bow and "arrar" hunters and was tempted to pay their hunting license fees himself. The idea is that they don't destroy the deer crop.

But Woody didn't realize until Tuesday that at last an archer had hit one of the deer . . . and had left it to die a painful death because it is unlawful to shoot a doe.

Some archer, on the last day of the shoot last week, shot an arrow clear through a small doe and failed to report it upon the pain of a fine and expulsion from camp.

The pain-wracked doe lingered on for a whole day, Ranger Woody calculated, and was dead for two days when found on a hillside today.

The arrow was removed intact and is plainly marked. The guilty archer is certain to be found out . . . and, in addition to paying a fine, will be subjected to a certain amount of ridicule and no little criticism in the eyes of true sportsmen.

Woody, who has so stoutly backed the archers, is sort of torn by conflicting emotions.

During the second annual archery hunt held in 1941, a dead doe was found in the woods with an arrow protruding from her body. "No one 'fessed up to the deed," Jean McNey remembered, "and the Ranger was furious." News clipping courtesy of Jean McNey.

"Originally we camped at a place called Three Forks just below Springer Mountain. Long Creek, Stover Creek and Rock Creek all come together there to form Noontootly Creek. Later we moved our camp over to Wahsega and stayed there for several years.

"When our group first started hunting up there, there was a green house up at the head of Rock Creek right above Rock Creek Lake where the ranger (game warden) lived. I remember that they had some deer fenced in next to the house and the ranger looked after them. Eventually they took down the fences and let the deer go wild. Later on, in 1940, they opened it up to outside hunting."

The following article in the Atlanta Constitution, titled "Atlanta Archers Kill Wild Hogs But No Deer in Chattahoochee," was written by John Martin and dated Nov. 11. There is no year with the article, but it appears to have been written in 1941, during the second annual hunt, when Roscoe and his companions were back for another stab at trying to shoot a buck with archery equipment. During that second annual hunt, a small buck was killed by one of Roscoe's companions as noted above.

In the article the author mentioned Roscoe's hunting companion H.C. Thompson and noted:

> Big Stomp Gap, Ga., Nov. 11 – Hatracks and rocking chairs from buck antlers were only a campfire dream here tonight as over 30 campfire disciples of Robin Hood trudged back into camp after braving sub-freezing temperatures in the coves and ridges of the Chattahoochee National Forest.
>
> Ranger Arthur Woody, pioneer mountain czar whose father reportedly killed the last big original buck in these hardwood forests, grinned as the

bowmen returned with stories of only fleeting glimpses of switching (sp) white tails as they melted into the foliage out of site (sp).

"My offer still holds good," he laughed. "I'll still eat the snout and the lights of any deer these here fellows kill with a bow and arrer."

Two Wild Hogs

Woody's scorn of the "arrer" men, however, was converted into a certain amount of respect when two Atlanta archers dragged a pair of wild hogs into camp. (Scorn was probably not a good choice of words here. Ranger Woody ridiculed the bow hunters and poked fun at them but he certainly did not scorn them.)

H.C. Thompson bagged a 162-pound sow with a steel-headed blade that bisected the heart and dropped the hog in her tracks. Charles Langley stopped a hog with an arrow that tore through a 132-pound pig and cut down several small trees on the other side. It took another dart, however, to finish the animal which turned to fight the Atlanta marksman.

Thompson's kill was immediately skinned and quartered over burning hickory embers for barbeque.

No Open Shots

Several bucks were jumped by the archers, but nobody reported an "open shot." However, Ranger Woody was showing a flashlight which he claimed was dropped by a hunter who had missed a deer within easy range.

"If they'll just admit it," he declared, "I'll have me a shirttail for keeps!"

W.R. Barbour and Wingate Short, of Atlanta, were groaning over their luck. A spike buck walked within easy shooting range and stood still – until they dropped their sandwiches and ran for their weapons.

Buck Fever

This was the first case of buck fever recorded on this second annual supervised hunt.

Some of the nation's topnotch archers were blanked on the first day. Included among them were Mr. and Mrs. H.A. Scott of Washington, and Mr. and Mrs. Phil Cozard of Columbus, Ohio.

Arrival late this afternoon of Ben Pearson, of Pine Bluff, who took a buck last year in Arkansas, boosted the hopes of the nimrods, who still insisted that Ranger Woody would be eating raw venison before the end of the week.

As seen in this photo, many of the budding archers shared the hunt with their wives during the historic five-day hunt in 1940. Ranger Woody stands to the left, while Hugh Thompson poses in the center of the photo just behind the flames of fire. Thompson's wife is sitting to his right. Photo courtesy of Jean McNey.

(Born in Arkansas in 1898, Ben Pearson (1898-1971) was a nationally known archery champion and manufacturer. He became interested in archery at an early age and won the Arkansas State Archery Championships in 1926 after placing last the year before. He later formed the Ben Pearson Company and revolutionized the archery business by mass producing archery equipment and making it affordable for the average American.)

Making National Headlines

Apparently the 1940 archery hunt at Rock Creek/Blue Ridge WMA garnered enough national attention to warrant this short piece in Time magazine. In 1940, the idea of hunting with a bow and arrow like the Indians had done during the previous century was very intriguing to many people and somewhat of a novelty as mentioned earlier, and there was little to no anti-hunting sentiment around the country like there is today. Hunting was accepted by the public as a sport, and people regarded bow hunters as unique sportsmen because of the difficulty factor.

Even those who did not hunt were intrigued by the rugged breed of outdoorsmen who went to the woods armed only with a bow and arrow. The fact that state and federal wildlife officials in Georgia had decided to allow non-resident bow hunters to participate in this widely publicized hunt created considerable interest outside of Georgia. Ranger Woody's comments at the end of the story are particularly interesting to read.

Time Magazine, Nov. 11, 1940
Under the heading: 'Sport' At Chattahoochee (National Forest, Georgia)

There are 1,500,000 archery addicts in the U.S. Most of these toxophilites are content with target shooting or flight shooting (for distance). But some 15,000 are Cock Robin killers: they want to kill something with their bows and arrows.

Fifteen years ago, bow and arrow hunting was almost extinct in the U.S. Today every state except Arizona permits hunting with bow and arrow; twelve states have special preserves for bowmen, three states (Michigan, Minnesota and Wisconsin) have separate hunting seasons for archers.

Bow and arrow hunting is encouraged by U.S. conservation authorities because kills are few and far between. A bowman must get within 75 yards of his prey before he lets fly, and even close shots often get sidetracked by a twig. In the 25 years he hunted with bow and arrow, Chicago's late Arthur Young bagged almost every species of big game on the American continent, but the U.S. has few Arthur Youngs. Last year, during Michigan's 15-day bow-and-arrow season, only four deer were shot.

(To say that a bowman must get within 75 yards of his prey before he "lets fly" is a gross exaggeration. In 1940, the very primitive long bows of the day had a limited hunting range of about 35 yards or less. Forty yards would have been stretching it, and 75 completely out of the question. Today's high-tech equipment is much more accurate at longer distances, but most whitetail hunters still consider an "ethical" shot to be within 40 yards. Some of today's hunters have the equipment and skill to accurately reach out to 50 yards and beyond, but those hunters are in a class by themselves.)

Last week, while the open season was on in Michigan, Minnesota and Wisconsin, Georgia sponsored the first organized bow and arrow deer hunt held in the U.S. since the Indians took to gunpowder.

Man behind last week's hunt in the Chattahoochee National Forest was U.S. Forest Ranger Walter Arthur Woody (should be "William Arthur Woody;" the Ranger's son was Walter), a broad-faced, broad-shouldered broad-beamed 225-pounder, known as "The Ranger" to every Georgia mountaineer. Born in the Blue Ridge District, Woody has been with the U.S. Forest Service since 1915. Fifteen years ago, when the Georgia Legislature outlawed deer hunting in its northern counties, Woody took $100 of his savings, bought two bucks and two does, turned them loose in what is now the Chattahoochee preserve. The Government followed suit, added several hundred to Woody's four. Last week, Woody figured that the Chattahoochee had 500 arrow-worthy bucks. (As mentioned previously, Ranger Woody purchased *five* fawns from the Pisgah Game Preserve in 1927, not four, but his actions had nothing to do with the Georgia Legislature. There had been no legal deer hunting in North Georgia since the turn of the century because there were no deer to hunt. The government did in fact follow suit as stated, but purchased far fewer than 100 deer in total; not several hundred as mentioned.)

The 20 expert archers (actually 22) who gathered for the five-day hunt through the Chattahoochee's forests and tangled rhododendron "hells" got lots of sage advice from Ranger Woody:

"The way to get a deer is to find a gap and then sit down and wait. A gap is a low place between mountain peaks. It is a place both deer and humans seek to cross mountains. Deer are just as lazy as humans."

"If you fire your arrow at a deer and think you've hit him, sit down, fill your pipe. Smoke it all the way through. Then get up and look for your deer. If you hit him, that will give him time to lie down and bleed. Then he can't run away."

"You boys with your bows and arrers, you be careful. I don't want any of those broadheads (arrows) to hit my broad bottom." (In truth, the Ranger probably used a little stronger language than "bottom.")

Despite these Woodycisms, last week's bowmen bagged nary a buck. One got pretty close, had his bow bent when the deer turned broadside. It was a doe.

The following story appeared in the November 1942 issue of *Outdoor Georgia* magazine. Written on the eve of the third annual archery hunt at Blue Ridge WMA, the story captures the essence of the hunt and gives interesting details about its immense popularity nationwide.

Archery "Grand Opera"

Hunters Await Opening of Regulated Hunt In Chattahoochee National Forest Area

By Joe Stearns

Bow-and-arrow experts from about 12 states will gather at Camp Wahsega this month for what is tantamount to the "Grand Opera" of archery in America. It is the third annual regulated archery hunt in the beautiful Chattahoochee National Forest, which is rapidly taking its place as one of the outstanding sporting events in the U.S.A.

State and Federal Rangers will send "Robin Hoods" into the woods in quest for wary deer for a five-day period starting November 10. The bag is not limited to deer alone. The archers may bring in wild boar, a turkey gobbler, two raccoons and ten squirrels. (Interestingly, during the premier archery hunt in 1940, "turkey gobblers" had not been on the bag list.)

This regulated archery hunt is the only one of its kind in America and has definite appeal to each and every archer. About 1700 archers (nationwide), men, women and juniors, are in what is generally considered the expert division. It is reasonable to assume that for each of these high-ranking archers, there will be 10 amateurs or near-experts, which gives some idea of the popularity of the sport. Archery has been placed on the sports schedule in hundreds of high schools. Watch this sport grow.

The setting for the hunt is magnificent. Cool, crisp Autumn days and downright cold nights will be the schedule back in mountain camp. The galaxy of colors of the trees, the crackling of dry leaves on the ground may be found over the 10,000 acres of gorgeous hunting grounds in the Blue Ridge Wildlife Management Area, a range deftly touched up by nature's magic paint brush. The herd of deer in this area has been estimated at one thousand.

Approximately 40 archers will range the woodlands for the five-day period. Then the hunt opens up for hunters with firearms. About 200 hunters will take to the woods in hopes of drawing a bead on a fine buck.

The archers have left nothing to be desired. Cooks prepare delicious meals and perhaps there will be a barbecued wild boar or venison on the menu. The hunters will stay at Camp Wahsega and of course at night there will be the gathering around the fireside to spin tales of woe and tell tall stories.

To the victor belong the spoils but also some manual labor. For example, an archer gets a wild boar weighing 175 pounds three miles from camp. All he has to do is sling it over his shoulder and lug it back to camp. At camp he will find himself the owner of weary and aching muscles, a paralyzed shoulder and probably a victim of fallen arches. He will drag his throbbing frame erect and get his picture taken and so far as he is concerned, the hunting season is an astounding success. And don't forget the barbecue.

Archers are expected from Cincinnati, Ohio; Covington, Kentucky; Glenn Allen, Virginia; Sullivan, Missouri; Washington, D.C., South Carolina and Mississippi.

The eleventh ranking archer in America will be there. He is Flight Commander A.W. Bartlebaugh, stationed in Tuscaloosa, Alabama. Mrs. Barltebaugh is listed in the hunt also and hopes fate will provide her the opportunity to show up her husband.

Archery is distinctly split into two classes. The bow and arrow man who can sock an arrow into a bull's-eye at a hundred paces and win pretty silver cups is just another fellow with soaring hopes on a hunt. Hunting down wildlife with a bow and arrow calls for a different type of skill plus quick action. Deer just won't be a still target for a steel broadhead shaft. Tommy Thompson of Atlanta, cuts loose a swift deadly arrow and has a seat at the head of the class when it comes to rough and tumble hunting in the wilderness. The chips are down on Tommy to bring in a deer – he is the lad voted most likely to succeed.

Summary

Although no one shot a deer during the premier five-day archery hunt in the Blue Ridge WMA, each of the 22 hunters who participated had a memorable time and most vowed to return to try again the following year. The Ranger had been right in his prediction, and he enjoyed rubbing it in. A few of the hunters vowed to return the next year so that they could once again take up the Ranger's challenge and turn the tables on him by making him eat the "snout" of a bow-killed deer.

In all, it had been a carefree, happy time for everyone involved – especially for Ranger Woody. But now he had a greater challenge to face and he knew the outcome would be totally different. In two short days, the firearms hunt would begin, and the Ranger knew only too well that many of these hunters would not be going home empty-handed. It was a tough pill for him to swallow.

Three Atlanta archers head off into the wilds of the Chattahoochee National Forest toward their afternoon stands with high hopes of putting a razor-sharp broadhead into a deer as they participate in the history-making, first-ever archery hunt held Oct. 29-Nov. 2, 1940, at Arthur Woody's famed Rock Creek Refuge (Blue Ridge WMA). Forest Service photo, from the Duncan Dobie collection.

Charlie Elliott (left) and Ranger Arthur Woody inspect one of 22 bucks brought into the check station during the first-ever Blue Ridge WMA firearms hunt held in November 1940. Courtesy of Outdoor Georgia magazine, October 1941, and the University of Georgia Library.

CHAPTER 14
A Nosebleed, a Media Sensation and a Lasting Legacy
The First Modern Firearms Deer Hunt in Georgia, Blue Ridge WMA, 1940

"Deer ain't thick enough yet. If they'll stop all this foolishness and give them a chance to come back, they'll soon be so plentiful that you won't have to strain the lard out of your backbone to get a buck."

Arthur Woody, 1940

Ranger Woody knew he would have to give in to the inevitable. In a conversation with Charlie Elliott, he told his friend that if some of his bucks had to die, he hoped they would die swiftly without too much suffering. He also expressed the hope that the firearms hunters would see and shoot some of the older "over-the-hill" bucks that would soon die of old age anyway. Some of these "original" bucks had reached the uncommon ages of 9 and 10 years old due to their protected environment. As a result, more than a few of these bucks carried exceptional racks.

Hunters who had drawn permits were only too happy to comply with the Ranger's wishes. Through no real hunting skills of their own – most had never hunted deer before – a number of outstanding bucks with impressive racks were taken during the 1940 hunt and in the seasons that followed.

The first archery and firearms hunts to take place in Rock Creek/Blue Ridge WMA in 1940 were pivotal in Ranger Woody's life. These events marked the pinnacle of his career – at least as far as public conception was concerned. The 1940 hunt was the first modern deer hunt held anywhere in Georgia during the 20th century. Prior to that time, deer hunting had been prohibited for many years. The hunts that followed in 1941 and 1942 were equally historic in scope, and focused considerable attention on the "wildlife paradise" found in the North Georgia mountains. They defined Ranger Arthur Woody as the man who had brought deer back to the mountains and thrust him into the spotlight – on a local level as well as nationally.

Previously the Ranger had been busily going about the business of building and protecting the deer herd, managing the forests, restocking trout and other fish, and getting roads and fire towers built at key locations in Union County. Although Kingfish had grown to be an iconic figure in his community, most of his notoriety had remained fairly localized. Now all of that was changing.

In many ways, Arthur Woody had been born to do the job of restoring deer to the mountain region. In the process, something happened that no one could have predicted. The time-hardened and crusty old mountain man who had been a hunter all his life came to love *his* deer in a special way. So when the time finally came to manage the herd through controlled hunting as he always knew it would, he could not bear the thought of seeing any of those deer killed and he agonized over the situation.

Although Ranger Woody had achieved many other important feats during his lifetime – both in conservation and in community work – his work with deer took precedent over everything else because it was so highly publicized. The now almost legendary story about raising the original "five little fiends" in Suches captured the heart of the public.

The 1940 hunt cast the die for Ranger Woody's enduring legacy in wildlife conservation – as it well should have. Tragically, that hunt also marked the beginning of the end for his long, productive career. Because of the emotional strain the hunt caused, signs of serious health issues that would only get worse in the months and years ahead began to rear their ugly head. In just a few short years, those health problems would become life-threatening. Ranger Woody's struggle with high blood pressure and heart and kidney problems over the next four years was in no way caused by his emotional reaction to the deer hunts, but the terrible stress took a heavy toll and added to the pre-existing conditions.

By the time Ranger Woody's health began to deteriorate in 1944, he had laid a solid foundation for many of his innovative conservation programs and his mark had been made. His fondest dream was to leave something good for future generations to enjoy in the mountains. By the mid-1940s, that lofty dream had become a reality. Arthur Woody possessed an uncanny ability to build and conserve for the present so that future generations could reap the benefits in later years.

A History-Making Event in Rock Creek/Blue Ridge WMA – 1940

Just like the well-publicized archery hunt, the firearms hunt also received widespread media attention. It too became a national media event. In fact, it was probably the biggest media event to ever take place in Union and Fannin counties. People were beginning to realize what an amazing job Ranger Woody had done with his deer program at Rock Creek Refuge. White-tailed deer from the Pisgah Game Reserve had also been stocked in at least four other management areas in the mountain region during the decade of the 1930s. By the early 1940s, the deer herd across the entire mountain region was expanding and well on its way to becoming a sustainable resource. In fact, the herd was doing so well that by 1943 a mountain-wide season was opened as a whole on all national forestland for the first time in the modern era.

The U.S. Forest Service and the Georgia Wildlife Division had made incredible strides in wildlife conservation. By 1940, the unprecedented cooperative "experiment" between the state of Georgia and the U.S. Forest Service signed in 1936 (to manage the wildlife resources on all national forestland in the state) was highly touted as a successful partnership between the two agencies that held much promise for the future.

The Forest Service had matured and come of age. It was no longer a fledgling organization taking baby steps into the unknown as it had been at the turn of the century. By now it had developed and implemented many creative programs. Hundreds of talented and hard-working individuals had been involved in turning those programs into shining success stories.

Turkeys and black bears had been reintroduced to several areas in the mountains and protected, the deer herd was thriving, and local streams were once again teeming with trout. Tens of thousands of acres of eroded, burned-over and clear-cut land had been reclaimed. Within a few short decades, a wasteland had been converted into new-growth, scenic young forests that would produce millions of board feet of timber for future generations. Mountain roads had been greatly improved, lakes had been built and several popular state parks had been established that were being enjoyed by untold thousands of people.

Equally important, at a time in history when jobs were so critical, untold thousands of jobs had been created within the National Forest system, the U.S. Forest Service, the CCC and various agencies within the state of Georgia. These "government" jobs were real-world jobs that utilized the services of talented and dedicated people. The foresters, wildlife rangers, surveyors, technicians, and dozens of support staff who worked at those jobs received a good day's wage for a good day's work.

It was a win-win situation for everyone involved and Ranger Woody had been in on the ground floor. He had initiated many projects on his own and had a finger in nearly every pie. Would a thriving deer herd in the North Georgia mountains have become such an amazing success story without Arthur

First camp, firearms hunt, at Rock Creek/Blue Ridge WMA, Nov. 2-5, 1940. The Forest Service provided tents and firewood, but the hunters had to hike in several miles with their own food, bedding and gear. Courtesy of Outdoor Georgia magazine, October 1941, and the University of Georgia Library.

Woody's involvement? Deer no doubt would have eventually made their way into the mountain region, but Ranger Woody's hard work and determination jump-started it decades before it might have happened otherwise.

Ironically, another young man with a vision similar to that of Ranger Woody's came to the state of Georgia as a biologist in 1947 one year after the Ranger's death. Jack Crockford, who was hired by then Game and Fish Commission Director Charlie Elliott, wasted no time in picking up where Ranger Woody had left off. By the mid-1950s, Jack had launched a state-wide deer restoration program (mostly in the southern two-thirds of Georgia but restocking continued in the mountains as well), which ultimately became as successful as Ranger Woody's program. Although Jack is today known as the "father of Georgia's deer restoration program" state wide, no one could argue that Arthur Woody was the program's "grandfather." It had all started in the North Georgia mountains.

Charlie Elliott later insisted that the most important contribution he ever made to the state as Director of the Game and Fish Commission was to hire Jack Crockford in 1947. Incidentally, Jack was a man of many talents just like Arthur Woody. While he was initiating a successful deer reintroduction program during the 1950s, he developed the now world-famous "Cap-Chur" gun used to tranquilize wild animals. Jack at first used a modified air rifle and a makeshift dart to tranquilize deer on Georgia's coastal islands for restocking in interior portions of the state.

After much trail and error, he finally developed a syringe-type aluminum dart that injected the tranquilizing agent into the deer's muscle. His prototype gun proved so successful in subduing deer that it was later patented by a young pharmaceutical salesman and mass-produced for the world-wide market. Today variations of Jack's original gun are used as a primary method for capturing wild animals in every corner of the globe.

A Last-Ditch Effort to Save Some of His Bucks

As soon as it became apparent that a managed hunt would be held in the Blue Ridge WMA in the fall of 1940, Ranger Woody went to work employing a clever tactic designed to save at least a few of his bucks.

"Papa owned 40 acres down on Rock Creek that was surrounded by the game reserve," Jean McNey remembered. "It joined that portion of the reserve area where he knew the hunters would be hunting. The property had a large field on it, so he sewed it in grain (probably oats or wheat)."

The idea was simple. As soon as the shooting started, Ranger Woody hoped to draw deer off the refuge onto his property where they would be safe. He hoped the grain would help hold them on the property until the hunt was over. Interestingly, this might well have been one of the earliest "green fields" or "food plots" ever established in Georgia especially for deer. In today's world of whitetail management, planting supplemental food plots are a common practice among game managers, hunters and landowners alike. Although most modern deer hunters believe the idea of planting grains and other nutritious foods for deer is a relatively new concept developed during the past few decades, Ranger Woody planted his special fields of grain 75 years ago!

The ploy no doubt saved the lives of a few bucks. Interestingly, not too many more years went by before the Georgia Game and Fish Commission began to make a regular practice of planting food plots in all of the wildlife management areas in the mountain region (and eventually statewide as well) to help the local deer make it through the harsh winter months when food typically becomes quite scarce. Game managers in the mountains quickly realized this food shortage was a serious problem after the acorns and browse were gone in late winter.This practice still continues today since food sources are so unpredictable in the high country during the winter months. Like so many other "firsts" in his career, Ranger Woody may have been the first deer manager in Georgia history to plant a food plot exclusively for the benefit of *his* deer.

Hunting the Ranger's Beloved Deer

Ranger Woody became so emotionally distraught during the first firearms hunt while elated hunters were bringing in their trophy bucks to the check station that he suffered the first of many severe nosebleeds. This condition occurred several times during the ensuing hunts in the early 1940s, and it continued right up until his death in 1946. Being the tough individual that he was, however, he put on a good front in the presence of hunters, reporters and all others associated with those first hunts. Family members helped keep a tight lid on the condition.

The hunters who came to Blue Ridge Refuge adored Ranger Woody and considered him a hero. He had a genuine affection for them as well. He understood their passion for deer hunting. He visited their camps, helped them check deer at the check station, and attended their late night campfires. He told stories around the campfire and graciously shared some of his beloved "mountain nectar" (white lightning) with them (even though it was against the rules to do so).

But deep down inside it tore him apart emotionally. Those who knew him best knew and understood exactly what he was going through. It was devastating for him to see the bucks he knew and loved being brought to the check station. Close friends like Charlie Elliott understood and sympathized with him. To the outside world, though, few people knew about the emotional roller coaster he was forced to navigate or just how much he actually suffered. In many ways, the deer had come to be like children to him.

After the five-day archery hunt ended on Nov. 2, two, three-day firearms hunts were held Nov. 4-6 and Nov. 7-9. Each three-day hunt was divided into two sections; a wilderness hunt and a main hunt. The separate boundaries of each hunt were specified to each group. The wilderness hunt was limited to 25 hunters per three-day period. These hunters would camp out in the refuge as the archers previously had done. The main hunt was limited to 50 hunters per three-day period. This group would stay outside the refuge and check in each morning. Most of these hunters stayed in motels in Dahlonega or camped at nearby campgrounds in the area.

In all, 150 firearms hunters had drawn permits and been approved to hunt on the refuge, but there were some no-shows. As with the archery hunt, the Forest Service and Georgia Division of Wildlife provided tents (complete with cots and mattresses) and firewood for the wilderness hunters at a specified campground. The hunters had to furnish their own food, cooking utensils and blankets. All hunting would be of the "still hunting-stalking type." No dogs were allowed to participate on any of the hunts.

The bag limit was restricted to one antlered buck per hunter. No limit was set on shooting wild hogs. Hunting hours were from 6 a.m. to 6 p.m. All bucks had to be checked in at a checking station located at Hightower Gap at the junction of Rock Creek Road and Blue Ridge Road at the south entrance to the refuge.

A Bittersweet Victory

The high-profile 1940 firearms hunt was a bittersweet victory for Ranger Woody's amazing 13-year-old deer restoration program. Although the events leading up to the hunt and certain aspects of the hunt itself no doubt made Ranger Woody very proud, it was anything but a victory for him personally.

The following story, written by Jim McGraw, appeared in the December 1940 issue of *Outdoor Georgia* magazine:

Deer Hunt
Georgia's First Supervised Shoot Produces 22 Bucks and Some of the Finest Whitetail Specimens in the Country

Fifteen years ago Ranger Arthur Woody stood on the crest of Hawk Mountain. Below him, in the cover under Hightower Gap, lay the home place of the Hawk family. A series of bold springs started there – the headwaters of famous Rock Creek. Immediately south of Hawk Mountain were the well watered slopes of Fricks Creek, and Long and Noontootly.

The panorama of forest land lay unbroken before the ranger's eyes. In the stream were native speckled trout (actually brook trout). In the forest coves and

By Beverly Wallace
Feature Editor

The thrill of a lifetime! That's what H. V. Cunningham (right), head of 4-H club work in Georgia, got when he shot the first buck on last year's controlled hunt. He and a companion are hauling the trophy to camp, something hunters won't have to do this year since packers will be available. (U. S. Forest Service photo.)

OUTDOOR GEORGIA • October 1941

First blood! Mr. G.V. Cunningham of Athens (in front), head of Georgia's 4-H Club, is credited with bringing in the first buck during the historic Blue Ridge firearms hunt held Nov. 2- 5, 1940. (Note: the magazine incorrectly listed his name as H.V. Cunningham.) Courtesy of Outdoor Georgia magazine, October 1941, and the University of Georgia Library.

on the long, gentle slopes of the hills were remnants of wild turkey flocks. A few grouse that sought the seclusion of remote coves, and gray squirrels, was the only game left in that section of the Blue Ridge.

While he stood there, the ranger's thoughts went back to the years when he was a boy in the Blue Ridge Mountains of North Georgia. In those years such things as national forests and game protection and restocking the streams with fish, were unknown. His father had killed the last deer in all that Blue Ridge country. The bears had long since gone, and big trout were things only in dreams.

Perhaps some day someone would bring back the abundance of game the land the Cherokee once knew. Perhaps some day there would be deer in the forests and big trout again in the streams. That job, like art, would be long, even after someone made a beginning. The idea suddenly dawned on Arthur Woody that perhaps no man on earth would be better qualified to make such a beginning than the ranger himself. He could have a small part in helping restore to Blue Ridge what his ancestors had helped take away.

After all titles had been cleared and the land lying generally southwest of the Toccoa River had been placed in national forests, 30,000 acres were set aside as a game sanctuary. Provisions were made for the protection of this land from poachers, a game warden was located on Rock Creek where the Hawk family had lived, and the job of rebuilding the wildlife resources on that 30,000 acres began. (Ultimately that game sanctuary expanded to 40,000 acres and became known as Rock Creek Refuge and later Blue Ridge WMA.)

Every trout fisherman in the Southeast knows the creeks Noontootly (today known as Noontootla Creek), Jones, Montgomery, Mill, Rock Creek, and Rock Creek Lake in the refuge. Many thousands of rainbow and native trout (brook trout were native, rainbow trout were non-native) have been released in those streams and in the lake. (Non-native brown trout were also released). Each year, trout fishermen eagerly await the announcement of open dates on those streams. They flock to Rock Creek Lake throughout the week-ends of summer. In countless deep pools on those creeks, the trout have grown wise and huge and hungry and only an expert fisherman can take them on flies or other artificial lures. Fifteen years of management have made this wildlife area one of the most popular trout havens in the state.

Last month, the hunters had their taste of what wildlife management can do for game. They reaped a harvest from those first big deer Ranger Arthur Woody bought from a far western state and released at the headwaters of Rock Creek, and from subsequent releases of deer trapped on over-crowded areas of the Pisgah National Forest in North Carolina. The 200 hunters who participated in the organized hunt saw how wise use of our game resources can pay dividends in very few years. They did not have to read the story or look at pictures to see the result of protection and restocking. That huge buck, startled from a thicket, or crashing down a cove, and the innumerable does and fawns, were proof enough.

The bow and arrow hunters – the Robin Hoods – led by some of the most expert archers of the southland, were the first on the hunt. Twenty of the men who drew their bows in much the same manner as those men of ancient Sherwood Forest, went into camp at Noontootly wilderness. For a week (actually five days) they ranged the hills and valleys, watching for buck signs, crouching at the sound of moving leaves, studying each thicket and ridge top with wary eyes. Many bucks were seen, and innumerable does, but none of the archers was able to get a shot.

Following the archers were the long-barrel followers of Nimrod, who were allowed to hunt only with rifles and shotguns with a single ball and without dogs. Accommodations were made in the wilderness camp for fifty of the hunters in alternate periods. The remainder of the hunters checked into the refuge each morning and were assigned stations during the day and left the management area every night.

The first buck killed was a fine eight-pointer, bagged by G.V. Cunningham of Athens, only a couple of hours after daylight the first morning. During the entire week, hunters brought in from ridges and thickets, from near the road and from miles back in the wilderness, 22 fat buck deer, ranging from spike buck to animals with 10-point heads. Some of the deer were declared by wildlife experts to be the finest white-tails ever seen in the East. One of the big bucks was said to weigh over 275 pounds.

Many interesting little stories came out of the thickets during the week the hunters roamed the ridges and slopes after bucks. One hunter brought down his kill miles away from camp. It was a big buck and as heavy as a horse. The hunter's companion walked back to camp for help to bring in the fine specimen. The companion remained in camp, but two hunters who had come in for the morning cup of coffee, went out to help. They located the hunter on top of a ridge. After an hour of struggling with the animal, one of the three returned to camp, looking for more help. This time ten hunters who had come into the campfire, volunteered. They found the deer and the two hunters on top of a ridge three miles from the wilderness camp and more than a mile from the Noontootly trail.

As they walked up, the hunter who had killed the deer raised his posterior extremity off the ground and said, "I'm glad you have come to help me. I have been out all day and am tired and hungry. You fellows bring in the deer. I'll wait for you in camp."

He turned on his heel and strode off, leaving the ten men in possession of the deer. One of those in the party, a well-known trout fisherman and writer, fumbled for his notebook and pencil and began writing.

"What are you doing?" one of the deer-tuggers inquired.

"Just making a note," he replied, "to write an article when I get home. The title of this article will be – 'A Trout Fisherman Goes Deer Hunting and Lands a Big One.'"

Another hunter shot a wild hog. When the huge black animal fell, he dropped his gun and rushed forward to his kill. He was half way there when the animal regained its feet and charged, its white tusks gleaming. The hunter reversed directions with the speed of an echo and ran on past his gun, yelling bloody murder. A timely shot from the gun of his companion saved the over-enthusiastic Nimrod much embarrassment and probably a leg.

Paul Chapman, square-shouldered dean of the state agriculture college, lost his shirt tail when he missed a buck galloping over his stand. He was followed in close succession by Charles Elliott, who brought home a patch of fur and a drop of blood on a leaf and was told that those items were inadequate. Ray Carter, well-known Atlanta sportsman, was another victim of the shirt tail act.

Everybody who attended the hunt declared it to be better sport than running deer with dogs. The early dawn, hours, the stalk, the sudden appearance of a huge buck in full flight over the brown carpeted forest floor – they said such vivid pictures come only a few times to the more fortunate sportsmen on this earth.

Many hunters came out of the woods with stories of grouse, turkeys and many squirrels. One of them vowed that he sat and held his gun on the head of a turkey gobbler while the huge bronzed bird fed up the cove and out of his sight. From the reports all game in this protected area seems to be increasing.

Officials who planned and conducted the hunt were highly pleased with the results, and said that such a hunt, barring any unusual decrease in game or unfortunate conditions of any kind, would be held again next year.

Everyone agreed that the fifteen-year dream of Ranger Arthur Woody has at last come true.

Jim McGraw's exciting and well-written account of the first modern firearms hunt in Blue Ridge WMA definitely captured the spirit of that historic event. Like many good hunting stories, it might have been somewhat embellished in certain places, but it hit a home run by capturing the true essence of Arthur Woody's incredible achievement.

The story started off by painting a serene picture of Ranger Woody standing on the crest of Hawk Mountain and looking out over his 30,000-acre domain in the late 1920s at what was then known as Blue Ridge Game District. It talked about Arthur Woody's father having killed what was said to be the last deer in the mountains back in 1895 when young Arthur was 10 years old. Bears, as well as other predators like wolves and mountain lions, had been absent form the mountains for many years before that. Most of the native brook trout had disappeared as well.

Then the author made a telling statement. He wrote, "The idea suddenly dawned on Arthur Woody that perhaps no man on earth would be better qualified to make such a beginning than the ranger himself." No truer words were ever spoken. Some 73 years have passed since Jim McGraw wrote those insightful words, and history has proven that no human being alive was better qualified to launch a modern conservation movement in the North Georgia mountains at that time and place than Arthur Woody. (Reference to the above quote was made in Chapter 11, but I thought it was important to mention it again here because of its impact.)

Two hunters admire an outstanding 10-point buck, one of the first to be brought into the check station during the first day of the historic firearms hunt at Rock Creek Refuge in November 1940. Photo courtesy of the Charlie Elliott Wildlife Center.

Photo op! Joe Kircher, regional director of the U.S. Forest Service in Atlanta, congratulates a lucky hunter who is posing for a photo with his trophy buck. Courtesy of Outdoor Georgia magazine, October 1941, and the University of Georgia Library.

The author talked about trout being restored to many native streams in the area, again largely due to Ranger Woody's pioneering efforts, and finally the story went into the nuts and bolts of the historic hunt itself; first with 20 "Robin Hood-style" bow hunters who hunted for five days and struck out completely, and finally with the rifle hunters, who were allowed to hunt in two groups in two separate areas of the refuge for two three-day periods. After all the smoke had cleared, the rifle and shotgun hunters on both combined firearms hunts had tallied up a total of 22 bucks.

Numerous photos taken during that historic hunt show Ranger Woody right in the thick of things – posing for photos with proud hunters, doing live radio interviews, and helping to supervise the hunt in every respect. Jean McNey was witness to her grandfather's blood pressure going through the ceiling and the severe nosebleed that he suffered during that first hunt, not to mention the fact that he got very little sleep during those long days and nights.

"He managed to hide his emotions during the hunt," Jean said, "But it was a different story when he got home." Few if any of the hunters present knew anything about Ranger Woody's true feelings, and he greeted and congratulated every hunter who brought in a buck with a pat on the back and a big smile on his face. But it pained him to see some of his favorite bucks – deer that he had raised in some cases and others that he had seen in the refuge and been familiar with for many years – being brought in and hung up.

The following newspaper article came out of Jean McNey's scrapbook. Although the byline, date and publication name were missing, it likely came from the outdoor section of the Atlanta Journal magazine. The somewhat humorous article gives detailed insight into the first few days of the firearms hunt.

Problem in Hunting

Hightower Gap, Chattahoochee National Forest, Nov. 6 –

Twenty chains up the old, narrow logging trail, J.D. Phillips buck lay waiting for the final haul to the wilderness camp at Three Forks.

The big 10-pronged buck, in whose veins had run the blood of the strain of the mule deer in the state of Washington, had been shot early the day before – high up in the mountains and miles away from the camp in the cove where the turbulent, rushing mountain streams converged.

A hunter is supposed to bring in his kill, but it became obvious at once to J.D. Phillips, of Atlanta, that if it were left to him to get the buck to camp, he'd never make it.

Deer hunters, however, are good sports. Relays of them worked at toting in the big buck, which had been trussed up expertly on a stout limb.

Steady, lashing rain had swelled the tumbling streams and softened the ground along the old logging trail. It had made a quagmire of the rough, twisting road into the camp from Ranger Clyde Wehunt's quarters, near Winding Star Gap.

And so finally when our party set out with the wind and the rain in our hair, the big buck was 20 chains, or a quarter of a mile away, up the winding mountain trial.

Through the cold, foam-capped mountain stream the party splashed back to camp with the kill and loaded it on a U.S. Forest Service truck, equipped with tire chains. It was then sped to Ranger Wehunt's quarters, where hunters parked their cars before beginning the three and a half mile pack into the wilderness camp.

J.D. Phillips heaved a great sigh of relief when the buck finally was securely fastened to a fender of his car.

"Never again," he said. "I'll confine my hunting hereafter to quail or dove. It's really something to get a deer out of such rough country."

And with a tired wave he headed out of the mountains toward Atlanta with his hard-earned prize.

Many Stories

There are many stories. Hugh Davis, of Gainesville, carted his big buck for miles and then floated it down the stream as far as he could. Finally it became necessary to quarter the kill in the woods. It was too big to bring in. The hooves of the buck were half as large as cows' hooves.

Bill Holcomb got his buck down to the stream and hung it on a limb for the night. It was brought in today.

The procedure was reversed in the case of Guy Perry, Clint Davis' brother-in-law. The (illegible word, possibly "rangers") brought Perry in last night.

There had been genuine alarm over Perry's absence. He had become separated from J.P. Knight and had been missing since early morning. A searching party was organized. CCC workers were about to be called out.

And while all this feverish activity was taking place in his behalf, Perry was enjoying a warm supper with June Stevens at June's place at Dial, Ga.

Told by the rangers to go downstream if he became lost, Perry had gone nine miles down the Noontootly, nine long miles, away from the wilderness camp.

It was a great relief to the campers when Stevens came into camp with Perry in tow. Clint Davis immediately apologized for having such a woodsman as a relative.

Earlier in the week an eventful occasion was kangaroo court presided over by Mr. Hugh Trotti. One of the victims was Dan Lane, who lost his shirt as well as his shirttail. It never was definitely established what Lane had shot at on his deer stand.

Favors Arrows

Head Ranger Arthur Woody, who honestly feels the loss of the deer as something personal, because he raised them, hopes there will not be a firearms hunt next year.

"They ought to call it off. The deer are too big to bring out," he says. He's right. Woody has every reason to be proud of the size of the bucks, which are larger than any to be found in the South.

He says, in jest, that in time they will produce offspring which will arrive with horns already showing. That's how robust the Chattahoochee deer are.

Woody is in favor of opening the national forest every year only to the bow and "arrar" hunters. He doesn't think they should be made to pay for the privilege. And Woody has a standing offer that he'll eat the nose of any deer killed with bow and "arrar."

"Those fellers (archery hunters) wouldn't any more than tickle them big bucks," says Woody.

It is regrettable, indeed, that the hunt has brought about the death of two does. The offending hunters were escorted to the edge of the forest, where their permits were revoked. They were fined $25 each and hastened on their way.

There's not much excuse for killing a doe. A fellow who is as quick on the trigger as that might shoot a fellow man by mistake.

Mountain Mecca

Mr. John Martin and I, spending a goodly part of the time at their quarters of State Wildlife Director Charles Elliott, have never before experiences such a variety of food as has been prepared.

We have had roast venison from the state of Washington, mallard duck liver from Canada, barbequed venison, mountain trout, hot biscuits, string beans, slaw, grits, potatoes, sorghum syrup, hot coffee, etc.

It's all native stuff we've had. Mr. Martin shot the duck and the venison was supplied by huntsmen friends. Anybody can catch fish. The vegetables came from farms, not out of cans.

Each night Mr. Martin and I have found it necessary to walk the three and a half miles into the wilderness camp – and back – for the sheer need of exercise after such a steady diet of colossal comestibles.

Game has been on the prowl at night, and it has been a thrill to pack through the wilderness unarmed and shine the eyes of nondescript animals with the strong flashlight.

This is known as roughing it.

Myth of the Mule Deer in Georgia

Several published accounts of the 1940 hunt mention mule deer, including the one above that stated J.D. Phillips of Atlanta shot a 275-pound buck "in whose veins had run the blood of the strain of the mule deer from the state of Washington." The Phillips buck was pictured in the Atlanta Constitution and was clearly a white-tailed deer, not a Western mule deer. There are no mule deer in the North Georgia mountains and it's very doubtful that Ranger Woody ever stocked any in the refuge.

As mentioned in Chapter 12, several deer that Ranger Woody acquired from a traveling carnival passing through Dahlonega in the late 1920s were reported to be mule deer. In reality, these deer were most likely whitetails from the Midwest or possibly from Washington State as noted. Because Midwestern deer are quite large in body size, as compared to Ranger Woody's much smaller North Georgia deer (which came from North Carolina), some of the sports writers of the day assumed that these large-bodied deer were mule deer.

Mule deer are a separate species only in the Western plains and the Rocky Mountain states. Even if Ranger Woody had obtained a couple of mule deer from a traveling carnival, their long-term survival in the North Georgia mountains would have been doubtful since they are not native to the area.

In 1940, whitetail hunting was new to much of the South and the sports writers of the day from Atlanta and other places were likely unaware of the distinct differences between mule deer and whitetails. To some, any large-bodied whitetail was a "mule deer." All of the photographs of bucks harvested on the Blue Ridge WMA hunt that appeared in various publications, including the ones that were referred to as "mule deer," were in fact white-tailed deer.

Charlie Elliott Loses his Shirttail

Unlike Ranger Woody who had developed a sizable midsection by 1940, Charlie Elliott was thin and agile and usually kept himself in top shape. He loved to hunt and fish whenever he was working in the mountains near Suches, and he and Ranger Woody no doubt enjoyed turkey hunting and trout fishing together whenever they could slip away for an afternoon.

Charlie loved to tell the story about the Ranger's uncanny tracking abilities. "One spring, when I was up in Union County looking for turkeys, I had gone way up a fairly steep ridge because Arthur had told me I'd see some deer and turkeys up on top. I had been up there about two hours when lo and behold, here comes Arthur, following my trail! He had tracked me up all the way up that mountain. He proceeded to tell me every spot where I had stopped to rest, where I had been sitting, and even how many pipes of tobacco I had smoked. It was uncanny! He knew everything I had done!

"He was still an expert woodsman despite his bulk, and he could read sign amazingly well. I'm sure this ability came from his long years of roaming the mountains as a boy, being observant and learning everything he could about the local plants and animals."

As noted in Chapter 12, Charlie enthusiastically attended both the archery and the firearms hunts in 1940. It was appropriate for him to be there professionally, but he wanted to be there personally as well. Being such a good friend to Ranger Woody, not to mention the fact that he was Commissioner of Wildlife Resources and editor of *Outdoor Georgia* magazine, he wouldn't have missed the historic event for anything. Earlier in the week he had camped in the wilderness camp with the archery hunters and tried his hand at bow hunting. By his own admission he later wrote, "My poor marksmanship with a bow is unexcelled. I doubt if I could commit suicide with my bow drawn in reverse."

Now, with a rifle in his hands, he felt a little more confident. Interestingly, however, despite his later fame as an outdoor writer and big-game hunter, Charlie was as green a deer hunter as most of the other sportsmen who participated in that highly publicized 1940 hunt. After all, there were few deer to hunt anywhere in Georgia at that time, and only a few of the 100-plus hunters in attendance at the Blue Ridge hunt ever had had any previous experience. As a native of Covington, Georgia, Charlie had hunted and fished all his life. But just like Ranger Woody, he had never hunted deer because there were very few deer to hunt in central Georgia while he was growing up and no legal deer season.

On November 6, the first morning of the first three-day firearms hunt, Charlie found himself high up on a ridge above Rock Creek. About mid-morning a fine buck came sneaking by his position. Charlie described the deer as "having a magnificent set of antlers, warped in such a way as to indicate an old deer past its prime." From recent conversations he'd had with Ranger Woody, he knew this was the type of deer the Ranger would most prefer to see taken out of the herd (if any deer had to be taken at all!) since this was an old buck.

"I'd brought a rifle equipped with a 4x scope for the hunt," Charlie said, "But the minute the Ranger saw it he said, 'You don't need a scope.'

Charlie asked him why and the Ranger told him that he'd probably be shooting in heavy brush at close range. 'Here, take my gun,' the Ranger said, 'and leave that thing here.' So Charlie had gone to the woods carrying the Ranger's beat up old Savage Model 99 with open sights.

As soon as the big buck presented an open shot, Charlie squeezed the trigger. "The buck staggered to one side and went down immediately," Charlie said. "But then he got back up and disappeared into the brush."

Charlie found a clump of hair and several drops of blood on a leaf where the deer had been standing. He followed a sparse blood trail for several hundred yards. Then, not trusting his own tracking skills, he decided to walk back to the check station and find Ranger Woody, who could "trail a copperhead over a rockslide."

A smiling Ranger Woody looks on as his good friend Charlie Elliott goes through the ritual of having his shirttail cut off after missing a shot at a buck earlier in the day. The photo was probably staged for publicity purposes. The ritual of losing one's shirttail after missing a deer is a longtime American tradition. Courtesy of Outdoor Georgia magazine, October 1941, and the University of Georgia Library.

An hour later, the two woodsmen were back at the blood trail. Charlie explained everything that had happened, and the Ranger started following the sparse trail.

"Arthur and I trailed that deer for 200 yards," Charlie said. "Then he stopped dead in his tracks. After studying the deer's sign for a minute or two, he proclaimed, "Why I believe this here's the track of ol' Nemo. I'd know it anywhere." Ranger Woody could read the woods like most people read the evening newspaper. "And you ain't done much more than cut hair on that ol' boy! Ya' just grazed 'im." The Ranger chuckled. "He'll live to outsmart many another tenderfoot hunter like you in these mountains 'fore one of 'em gits in a lucky shot. Why he's prob'ly back to chasin' does this very minute!"

They returned to the spot where Charlie had been sitting and examined the ground one last time. After a few minutes, the Ranger said, "Lookie here."

The Ranger pointed to a sapling that had been split by Charlie's bullet. Apparently the bullet Charlie had been shooting had hit the small tree and fragmented. One of the fragments had likely hit old Nemo and caused a flesh wound. As they were walking back down the mountain, the Ranger said, "I'm sorry you didn't get that old booger. Now he'll probably starve to death this winter."

Back at camp that evening, Charlie and at least two other hunters had to go through the "indignation" of having their shirttail cut off in front of the others for having missed a shot at a deer. The age-old tradition of cutting off a hunter's shirttail after he missed a shot was alive and well in Georgia in 1940, and most of the men in camp were only too happy to participate in the much-relished ritual. At least, as a high-profile public official representing the state, several of Charlie's companions *pretended* to cut off his shirttail in a well publicized display that was caught on camera for the Atlanta newspapers and Outdoor Georgia magazine. Since Charlie happened to be the magazine's editor, he was a favored target and the men got a big kick out of seeing him pay the price for his poor marksmanship. He later wrote several stories about the hunt.

A few days later, Ol' Nemo, as well as several other bucks that Ranger Woody knew well, were brought into the check station at Hightower Gap by other hunters. Old Nemo's luck had finally run out. A couple of large tears rolled down Ranger Woody's face as he tried to look away.

A Craving for Deer Liver

Roscoe Reams, who in the previous chapter shared some of his special memories about the five-day archery hunt in which he took part, shared yet another classic story about his friend and mentor Ranger Woody during an interview in 2000. This story was about the Ranger's acquired taste for deer liver. It's not clear when these annual incidents took place, but it is likely they took place after the managed firearms hunts were conducted in November when Roscoe and his companions were hog hunting in the refuge with special permission.

"At some point Ranger Woody developed a real liking for deer liver," Roscoe remembered. "I don't know if he ever developed a taste for venison or not, but he sure loved deer liver. By the late 1930s, he had gained so much weight that he had a hard time climbing the mountains around his home and doing much hunting on his own like he had always done most of his life. He had hunted turkeys and squirrels all his life, but I don't think he ever killed a deer in his life. He didn't have the heart for it. He loved those creatures too much.

"Some weeks after that first hunt in November 1940, I was camping over at Cooper's Gap with some of my friends. He suddenly had a craving for deer liver, and he came over to our camp looking for me. It might have been in

GEORGIANS OUTDOORS

Constitution Staff Photos--Kenneth

VENISON IS PLENTIFUL—Riflemen on the buck deer hunt in the Chattahoochee National Forest took their fill of venison last week, and a good time was had by all—needless to say. In the top photo a party of Atlantans is checking out from the Hightower Gap station with two deer. Left to right are Ranger Arthur Woody, Bill Holbrook (holding a 125-pound four-pointer), F. H. Woodcock (kneeling), W. M. Huie, H. C. Moore, W. W. Johnson, George Armstrong, of Washington, Ga., who killed the 215-pounder shown across the bumper, and H. J.

Venison was plentiful in the Blue Ridge WMA as depicted by this "Georgians Outdoors" column. Although Ranger Woody is wearing his perpetual smile, it saddened him greatly to see so many of his beloved bucks meet their fate during the historic firearms hunt. However, he was genuinely happy for the hunters and he received much acclaim for the success of the hunt. News clipping courtesy of Jean McNey.

December. I was 15 or 16 at the time. He already had a young buck picked out that he'd been watching for a while. He seemed to know most of the deer by sight and he always seemed to know where they were living. Of course, there hadn't been much deer hunting going on up there in those days, and when the season finally opened it was very short.

"He said to me, 'Boy, I've been watching this little spike-horned buck over here in such and such an area', and I want you to go shoot it. He gave me his rifle to hunt with because at the time I didn't own one of my own. I'll never forget that rifle. It was a Savage lever-action Model 99 .250 (or .250/3000, a very fast bullet that produced a velocity of over 3,000 fps), and boy was I proud to be hunting with it. (Over the years, Ranger Woody had killed countless turkeys with this rifle. Many, it was rumored, were shot on the wing after they had become airborne.)

"We headed over to the area where he knew this buck was using, and I climbed up the mountain and eventually shot it for him. Arthur then got several assistant rangers to come over and help me drag it out. He insisted on cutting out the liver himself and he wouldn't allow anyone else to do it. Then, he selected one of the rangers to take the meat down to the old folk's home in Dahlonega. For three years in a row as I remember – early 1940, 1941, and 1942 – I killed a spike buck for him and we went through that same ritual each year.

"Shortly after that, I went off to war and never saw him again. He died before I got out of the service and came home. I was not able to attend his funeral, which really upset me, but I was able to attend the dedication for him in 1947 when they put up the plaque at Woody Gap. It meant a lot to me to attend that dedication."

Aftermath of the 1940 Hunt

The first managed deer hunt in Blue Ridge WMA was an overwhelming success for the Forest Service and the Georgia Wildlife Resources Division. Plans for a similar hunt the following year were immediately set in motion. All of the hunters who had participated were thrilled and gratified at being a part of such a history-making event. Like the archery hunters, many hoped to return the following year. For most, it had been the adventure of a lifetime and few complaints were voiced.

Twenty-two bucks had been taken in six days of hunting by just over 100 rifle and shotgun hunters. Some of the bucks had exceptional trophy racks.

In addition to the 22 bucks that were legally taken by hunters during the two, five-day firearms hunts in November 1940, at least two does were shot by mistake. Holding a long-barreled lever-action Winchester rifle, this hapless hunter receives a ticket from a game warden for having committed the ultimate sin; shooting a sacred doe during a "bucks only" hunt. After paying his fine, he would have been ushered out of the refuge and sent home with no venison. Courtesy of Outdoor Georgia magazine, October 1941, and the University of Georgia Library.

As noted, one newspaper account referred to those bucks as being "some of the finest white-tail specimens in the country." In additional, at least two does had been killed by mistake. The hunters responsible had been made to pay small fines and were sent on their way. One of the does, a deer named Bessie, might have been one of the original deer purchased in 1927. If it were the same deer, she would have been 13 years old in 1940. Although unlikely, it is certainly possible since the deer inside the refuge had been so well protected over the years.

Despite much anguish and many a tear that had been shed over the killing of his deer, the destiny of Ranger Arthur Woody was now sealed forever. From this day forward, he would be known far and wide as the Forest Ranger who had brought deer back to the North Georgia mountains. After all, the historic hunt had become the biggest media event to ever take place in the Suches or North Georgia area.

An unidentified game warden poses for the camera with two outstanding bucks taken during the historic firearms hunt. Courtesy of the Kenan Research Center at the Atlanta History Center.

Ranger Woody (far right) and one of his game wardens look on as two successful hunters are interviewed on the air by well-known Atlanta radio personality and WSB Radio program director, M.K. Toalson, during the second-annual firearms hunt held in November 1941. Both the archery and firearms hunts at Blue Ridge WMA received considerable print and radio coverage due to their immense popularity. Ironically, Pearl Harbor would be attacked less than three weeks after the hunt took place. Photo courtesy of Jean McNey.

CHAPTER 15

The Roaring '40s

Other History-Making Hunts During the War Years

"The deer season opened and hunters came from all around. They took many fine trophies. And Woody was there at the check-out station when they started coming out of the refuge. Seeing the first big buck, Woody turned his head a little bit and the tears started streaming down his cheeks. He never shot a deer after that."

Charlie Elliott

The precedent had been set in 1940. The die had been cast. The Rock Creek/Blue Ridge WMA deer hunt proved so popular among hunters and so successful that similar refuge hunts were conducted in 1941 and 1942 using the same basic model; first a five-day archery hunt in mid-November followed by two, three-day firearms hunts.

The dates of the 1941 hunts were pushed back two weeks in November: the five-day archery hunt was held Nov. 11-15 and the two three-day firearms hunts were held Nov.17-19 and Nov. 20-22. The total number of firearms hunters in 1941 was increased from 150 to 200. As a safety precaution, red caps were required to be worn by all gun hunters. License fees were set at $3.25 for residents and $12.50 for non-residents. In addition, a $5 fee was charged to all regular hunters (not camping in the refuge) and a $7.50 fee was charged to archery and wilderness hunters to help defer some of the costs of setting up camp and managing the hunt.

By 1943, the entire mountain deer herd seemed to be doing so well that it was decided to open up all of the mountain counties as a whole to deer hunting, that is, on all national forestland outside of the four existing wildlife management areas then operating in the mountains. Records are sketchy, but it is believed that all four of the mountain WMAs, including Blue Ridge Refuge, were closed to deer hunting during the 1943 season. After three years of managed hunts in which just over 100 bucks were killed, Ranger Woody was no doubt elated that his beloved refuge would be closed for at least one season. (See chart below.)

In planning that mountain-wide hunt, wildlife officials made a regrettable error. Yielding to public pressure, they allowed dog hunting throughout the region. As always, the use of dogs proved all too effective in running down deer. That year, some 200 bucks were known to have been killed, far more than the desired number. In the long run, this may have been a blessing in disguise. The following summer, dog hunting in the mountain counties was outlawed by the state once and for all. Game managers quickly realized that the very same method of hunting that had been responsible for wiping out the deer in the mid to late 1800s was simply all too efficient. They knew it could happen again in the 20th century!

Deer hunts were resumed in the Blue Ridge WMA in 1944, 1945 and 1946. In 1947, for reasons unknown, the refuge was again closed to deer hunting. Hunting again resumed in 1948, 1949 and throughout the 1950s. Due to over-browsing and signs of overpopulation, a condition that Ranger Woody never had to be concerned about, the hunting of does was allowed in the refuge in 1950 and 1951.

The following chart furnished by the Georgia DNR indicates deer kill figures in the Blue Ridge WMA from 1940 to 1952. The chart is probably not 100 percent accurate. For instance, 22 bucks were known to have been killed during the 1940 hunt. Even though some of the figures may be slightly off, it does give a good picture of the kill figures for the decade of the 1940s. (As noted below, even after the refuge was officially named the "Blue Ridge WMA" in the mid-1930s, many people, including numerous wildlife officials continued to refer to it as "the Noontootly Game Management Area" or "Rock Creek Refuge.")

Deer killed in managed hunts on Noontootly Game Management Area (Rock Creek/Blue Ridge WMA)

	Rifle				Archery
Year	No. hunters	Deer Killed		Total	
		Bucks	Does		
1940	111	21	3	24	
1941	---	21	1	22	
1942	---	63	0	63	
1943	none-available (mountain wide hunt instead; refuge was probably closed)				
1944	192	36	0	36	
1945	197	24	0	24	39 hunters 1 buck
1946	197	44	4	48	53 hunters 1 buck
1947	none-available (apparently no hunts on managed areas)				
1948	246	62	0	62	
1949	391	72	0	72	3 hunters 0 deer
1950*	612	82	30	112	6 hunters 0 deer
1951*	793	62	24	86	

*Note: The first doe hunts were held in 1950 and 1951due to signs of over-browsing and over-population.

Note: The first official firearms turkey hunts in Blue Ridge WMA occurred in 1955, about 10 years after Ranger Woody's death. Interestingly, however, during the managed hunts of 1940, 1941 and 1942, archery hunters could legally kill one turkey. None were taken.

Apparently the lesson learned in 1943 was a valuable one. Fifteen years later, after Georgia had begun implementing its state-wide deer restoration program, the old Game and Fish Commission was put under a lot of pressure from some hunters and politicians to legalize dog hunting state-wide. For over a century, dog hunting had been a way of life over much of the South, especially on large plantations.

Jack Crockford, the man recognized as the father of Georgia's deer restoration program in all areas south of the mountain region, after Ranger Woody had restored deer to the mountains, was adamantly against allowing dog hunting on a state-wide basis. He knew what had happened in North Georgia in the late 1800s, and he knew what happened again in 1943. As Georgia's first graduate biologist hired by the Game and Fish Commission in 1947, he stubbornly pushed hard to limit the use of dogs when the deer program finally got some teeth in it during the late-1950s.

Eventually he won the battle, but it was hard fought and he made more than one politician very angry in the process. Dog hunting in southeast Georgia was (and still is) allowed along the coast and in the extreme southern coastal plain counties where the terrain tends to be swampy and jungle-like, and very difficult to hunt by normal means. Dog hunting is a centuries-old tradition revered by many hunters in the Deep South from Louisiana to Virginia, mostly in coastal areas as mentioned. Sadly, because of the radical changes in land ownership patterns in recent decades, it is dying a slow death, much to the distress of many old-time Southern hunters.

The following story, written by Jack Troy, well-known Sports Editor for Atlanta Constitution during 1940s, appeared in his "All in the Game" column just before the second annual hunt in the Blue Ridge WMA. Ironically, the story appeared just three weeks before Pearl Harbor was attacked.

All in the Game

By Jack Troy

Wilderness Hunt

Chattahoochee National Forest, Ga., Nov. 17. – Where the Red Man once roamed the gaps, the uplands and great valleys in a vast wooded area that has come under government supervision for preservation, paleface nimrods are engaging in the second annual wilderness deer and wild boar firearms hunt.

A permit entitles each huntsman to carry out one deer and as many boar as he can shoot. Last year more than 20 bucks fell to the unerring aim of the hunters. G.V. Cunningham, head of the state's 4-H Club, program, made the initial kill.

Ranger Arthur Woody, the man of the mountains and woodsman of whom your Uncle Sam is proud, came around to greet the firearms hunters in a rather subdued manner. It takes a lot to get the best of Old Woody. But, after all, a man who sticks his neck out is going to get it chopped off sooner or later.

Last week Woody renewed his annual promise to eat the snout of any buck or boar killed with "bow and arrar." Two boar fell to the wicked feathered darts of Atlanta archers – modern Robin Hoods who take pride in the ancient sport – and Woody was forced to go through with his bargain, in part. They made Old Woody kiss the head of each boar.

Before the firearms crowd departs, however, Woody will be his old self again. He'll be convinced then that it was sheer luck, and, by cracky, he'll be willing to make the offer again.

If the 1940 hunt marked a historic happening in Ranger Woody's beloved 40,000-acre Rock Creek Refuge, the mountain-wide hunt in 1943 marked an even greater historic event because it encompassed all of the mountain counties. Charlie Elliott wrote this timely story on the eve of that noted hunt in the June 1943 edition of *Outdoor Georgia* magazine. For the sake of simplicity, several errors in the story involving dates and numbers of deer were corrected.

Although he always hid his emotions by wearing a bright smile in public and sincerely congratulating each of the hunters who bagged a buck, Ranger Woody was an emotional wreck behind the scenes. He could never get used to seeing his beloved bucks being brought into the check station. Photo taken November 1941, courtesy of Jean McNey.

Ranger Arthur Woody…
Lives to See Game and Fish Dreams Come True in Georgia Mountains

By Charles N. Elliott
Director Game and Fish Commission

Below and beyond where we stood, the Chattahoochee National Forest was spread out like an endless relief map. Wrinkled hills, blazoned vivid with autumn colors, dropped sheer from our feet and rolled away, wave on top of wave, into the distance. The sun was up, but its yellow rays that spanned the far-flung cosmos were not warm. The wall of icy wind, pouring over and around the mountain peak, had pinched two crimson splotches on Ranger Woody's cheeks. The skin around my eyes and lips was numb.

"Tomorrer," the ranger said, "is the day I've waited fifty years fer."

I glanced sideways at this grizzled old veteran of the mountains. He was graying around the muzzle, but his steel-blue eyes were as quick and keen as the eyes of a hunting eagle. His wide mouth was friendly and humorous and the tight little lines around it had been etched there in this high country where day by day existence was not a matter of mere routine.

Started Re-stocking

"That's right," he said. "In 1928 (actually 1927), I bought six deer (actually five deer) with cash out of my own pocket and planted them down there on Rock Creek watershed. A year or two later the Forest Service bosses decided this was good deer range all through the country and brought down about 50 deer from another forest and stocked the four refuges between here and the South Carolina line. Today, in fifteen years, our herd in north Georgia has around two thousand animals in it."

"What's this about fifty years?" I asked.

The ranger jabbed a piece of yellow straw at his teeth.

"When I was a kid," he said, "my pa killed the last deer out of these mountains. I thought about that for a lot of years and made up my mind that some day, I would put back what he and the mountain men of his time took away. Last couple of years the Forest Service has held organized hunts on the refuges. Got some deer, too. But tomorrer we are opening all of north Georgia to deer hunters. Tomorrer somebody will bag the first buck that's been killed wild in these mountains in half a century."

I nodded. That was like Ranger Arthur Woody. He was one of those rare individuals who casually and without ceremony had pledged himself to a life of helping his neighbors. In his quiet, matter-of-fact way, this sixty-year-old mountaineer had brought in new ideas and prosperity to his people. And without knowing it, or even caring, he had become an institution in the cracker state.

Progress in the Hills

Among his own people, Ranger Woody is the Scattergood of the mountains. He built a new school where the children of his neighbors could go and get "book larning." He built a church. He organized Easter sunrise services which each year are broadcast at the crack of dawn from Woody Gap, above his home. Senators, Governors, statesmen from all corners of the land are known to him by the "first handles of their names." Educators seek him out in the mountain fastness to find inspiration in his homespun philosophy.

But those things are not as important to him as his job of protecting the forests from fires, or of bringing back deer and bear and wild turkeys to the woods, and trout to the swift streams of his beloved Blue Ridge.

Ever Alert

He has been the main factor in the establishment of the new deer herd. Hour after hour, he has patrolled the mountain trails, watching for poachers. Hour after hour he has waited for running dogs on the trail of a doe or a fawn. In his pickup truck, he has crunched over the gravel roads, inside and outside the refuge boundaries, watching in the dirt and sand and along the roadside for signs that tell him some intruder who has come illegally to kill game or catch his fish.

Last year he was rewarded. He has lived to see the season on deer throughout the Blue Ridge Mountains of northern Georgia.

"Didn't like it much, though," he said. "Deer ain't thick enough yet. If they'll stop all this foolishness and give them a chance to come back, they'll soon be so plentiful that you won't have to strain the lard out of your backbone to get a buck."

Principally because of his efforts, many sportsmen are looking to some day in the near future when the deer will be plentiful as they were on that morning, long ago, when the first Woody family rolled over the rugged pass at what is now Woody Gap, and picked out a beauty spot along one of the streams in the valley to build a home in the mountain wilderness.

This next story, written by well-known and gifted Atlanta Constitution writer Harold Martin, appeared in his "Dreams and Dust" column on Oct. 20, 1944. The article was written several weeks after Ranger Woody's first stroke.

Dreams and Dust

By Harold Martin
Oct. 20, 1944

Moon of the Stag

Now is the Moon of the Running Stag, as the Indians used to say, and in the cool of the morning old man Arthur Woody can step out on his back porch and hear the big bucks blowing and whistling. And sometimes, way up toward the slopes of Blood and Slaughter mountains, he can see laurel thrashing where they fight.

It makes the old ranger feel mighty good. It makes him feel so good he nearly forgets the doctor said he couldn't eat any more cream gravy and stick candy after he had that spell last summer after swimming too long in a mountain lake in the heat of a blistering day.

It makes him feel almost like a stout old stag himself again, able to hike the hills all day, his big paunch bursting through the rhododendrons, looking for fresh sign of bear and deer and turkey and wild hog.

There's a heavy mast this fall, too, and that makes old man Woody mighty proud. Just as proud as if he personally had farmed the blue hills and by his own efforts had made the oak trees drop a double crop of brown sweet acorns, and the pines shower down their cones, and the chestnuts and walnuts bear fruitfully.

Fat and Sassy Into Spring

Old man Woody loves to see a heavy mast. He knows when the mast is heavy his deer will stay fat and sleek all winter on the acorns, and the bear, who are his friends, will lie cradled in rolls of fat, and the wild hog will have some meat on their ribs, and all of the people of the woods will come into spring fat and sassy.

He knows that a heavy mast means that when spring clothes the hills in green again the fawns will be strong and healthy and nimble on their thin legs as they flash their little flags at him from the windfalls by the streams. And the yearling bucks will be husky and strong as they grow into spike-horn stags.

Yessir, old man Woody can stand out in his yard 'way up there at Woody's Gap and sniff the autumn wind and watch the play of autumn sun on the red and gold and yellow glory of Blood, and Slaughter, and Hawk, and Brasstown Bald, and know deep in his heart that men may age – even tough old rangers – but the blue hills live forever.

And if that danged young squirt of a doctor says he can't get out like he used to do, and walk the hills and speak to his deer and see where the brown bear passed, and hear the roar of the turkey's wings and see the light glint bronze on his strong back as he hurls himself toward the sun – well, he's seen it all for a long time now, and in the eye of his mind he'll see it as long as he lives.

Knew the Hills in Their Glory

For old man Woody as a boy knew the hills in all their glory. That was the time before the roads came, when a man could walk out of his cabin in the soft half-light of dawn and shoot himself a turkey before the sun had tipped the peak of the hills with gold.

Then the roads came, and hunters, and the deer were killed out and the bear moved on, and the native rainbow no longer leaped in the streams and Arthur Woody, grown and a government ranger, roamed his 150,000 acres like a man who walks through a haunted house.

But now the deer are back, and the bear are coming back, and the fish leap in the streams again and the roar of the coveys are like the firing of guns. And

Ranger Woody points to a fine Blue Ridge buck tied to the front of an automobile for the trip home as he talks to WSB Radio commentator M.K. Toalson and an unidentified man at Hightower Gap check station during the November 1941 Blue Ridge firearms hunt. Photo courtesy of Kent Kammermyer.

the hills are populated with the furred and feathered people again and old man Woody is a happy man, even though he can't eat cream gravy and roam the hills any more like an old ranger should.

(Although the author seemed to insinuate that the deer and trout disappeared after the roads came, in truth these resources had disappeared decades earlier in the late 1800s, long before any roads were improved in the mountains.)

Like dozens of other writers of the day, well-known Atlanta Constitution sports writer Jack Troy wrote many glowing stories about Ranger Woody and his work in conservation. The following column was written five months after the Ranger's death. It appeared in November 1946 just after the Blue Ridge archery hunt and just before the firearms hunt.

Atlanta Constitution November 20, 1941

Constitution Photo—Kenneth Rogers.

CHATTAHOOCHEE BUCK—Joseph C. Kircher, regional director of the United States Forest Service, weighs a buck killed by Dr. G. C. Lyda (kneeling), of Canon, Ga. Looking on the proceedings at Hightower Gap are, left to right: Ranger Arthur Woody, who launched the restocking of deer in the area; Bob Edwards, Dahlonega sportsman and caterer, and Luke Chester, holdover wildlife ranger wearing the green uniform which was abolished by the present wildlife set-up.

1941 news clipping courtesy of Jean McNey.

100 Can Gun Boar and Deer in Three-Day Hunt

by Jack Troy

In the Blue Ridge area of the Chattahoochee National Forest, 100 riflemen will be free to roam 40,000 acres in the first period of the annual deer and wild hog hunt Monday through Wednesday. An additional 100 bearers of firearms will tackle the vast acreage for the last three days.

Hunters will enter the forest at Dahlonega and will either make camp in the forest or return to Dahlonega to spend the nights. Majority will pitch their tents along Little Rock Creek.

Toccoa River bounds the northern edge of the hunting area, which will include Springer Mountain, Hawk Mountain, Hightower Gap, Winding Stair Gap and Lumpkin Ridge.

Hunters will work along Stover, Noontootly, Lovinggood, Long, Montgomery and Little Rock creeks.

The white-tailed deer and the temperamental tuskers are on the move this year, due to a shortage of food in the forest. There is a lack of acorns and other food. On the recent bow and arrow hunt, which ranged out from Camp Wahsega in the national forest, archers found the game ranging far and wide.

Archers were able to bag only one spiked deer and four wild hogs in a solid week of hunting. However, rain and fog were additional handicaps.

Archers, too, reported seeing Nellie, the canny old pet doe of the late ranger, Arthur Woody. They told of seeing Nellie limp out of the fog – the doe once suffered a broken leg – and walk between bucks and hunters until the bucks were safely out of range. They called this the spirit of Arthur Woody, for it was Woody who put the first deer in the national forest and it was his wish that they roam his beloved mountains unmolested.

Crisp, clear weather is in prospect for the firearms hunters. Game is plentiful.

Although undated, this next Atlanta Constitution column, titled "Outdoor Georgia," also written by Jack Troy, appeared shortly after the one above in the fall of 1946.

Outdoor Georgia (no date)

By Jack Troy

Some men will go to great lengths to save their face. Others, mainly deer hunters, will go all out for a shirt tail.

Frank Gross once won a stay of execution on his fancy lumberjack-style shirt tail by displaying pure mountaineer perseverance in killing a mule deer, the original species set loose in the Chattahoochee National Forest by the late Ranger Arthur Woody.

Gross admitted to having missed a deer, but he begged for another chance. His hunting companions, having a high regard for the President of the Georgia Senate, agreed.

Now Gross, of Toccoa, is one of North Georgia's leading deer hunters. He entered the forest determined that he would redeem himself. He picked a likely stand and waited.

Presently he sighted a nice rack (a pair of buck horns) among the laurel. Gross cracked down. The horns lurched. Had he hit the deer? He wasn't sure. He set out on the run. He sighted the deer. He shot again. The deer stumbled. Again he shot. The deer stumbled on. It went out of sight over a rise. Gross scrambled up the rise, reached the top and there, on the other side, was his deer. Dead. Gross, thoroughly exhausted, fell panting on the body of the mule deer.

He had saved his shirttail. It was a moment of great exuberation for the Senator from Toccoa, and he rates it as the high spot of his deer hunting experiences in Georgia.

(As previously mentioned, during the 1940s, some sports writers and hunters referred to some of the large-bodied deer found inside the refuge as "mule deer." Ranger Woody never stocked any mule deer in the Blue Ridge WMA and none were ever stocked anywhere in the mountains. Mule deer are a separate species found only on the western plains, in the Rocky Mountains and points west. The misnomer probably came about because some of the deer taken in the refuge during the managed hunts of the early 1940s were exceptionally large in body size. A few of these deer may have originally come from the Midwest, but they were all whitetails, not mule deer.)

Deer Outside Managed Area

Forester Spalding (C. K. "Lanky" Spaulding), head of the Gainesville district, escorted us on a tour of the Blue Ridge Wildlife Management Area and, on the edge of the area stopped us to chat with one of North Georgia's most genteel personalities, Junie Stephens.

Junie was one of the first forest rangers hired by Arthur Woody, the mountaineers' friend. Wise in the habits of deer, Junie reported that due to a shortage of "mass" (mast or acorn crop) in the forest, the deer were being seen in great numbers in the cornfields and bottoms outside the forest.

"Mass" is the word used for the food required by deer and wild hogs. It pertains largely to acorns. In the whole Appalachian range trees bore few acorns this year.

Deer hunters who were not drawn for the six-day hunt in the national forest may have excellent luck outside the protected areas. There are many deer this year and they are on the move.

Woody's Successor Well Liked

Ted Seely, District Forest Ranger, is a fine successor to Arthur Woody. Seely is no stranger to the Chattahoochee National Forest and mixes easily with the fine mountain people.

Woody's secret was his kindness and consideration for the people who lived in and out of the National Forest. He won their respect and admiration and, consequently, their full co-operation.

There was no poaching on his game or illegal fishing in the closed streams.

Seely has the same approach and is held in the same high regard by the residents of the district.

In other words he can sit down and visit and talk with the people and win their confidence. Above all, a district ranger must have this asset to be successful.

Post-War Restocking of Deer in Georgia

After several years of delay, the Pittman-Roberston Act was initiated in Georgia in 1944. (The delay was tied directly to politics…bad politics at that!) Two states, Nevada and Georgia, did not participate in the act until about 10 years after it had become law. Some restocking of deer occurred throughout the state in 1944 and 1945 with Pittman-Robertson funds, but for the most part, little was accomplished until after World War II had ended. In 1947, one year after Arthur Woody died, the Georgia Game and Fish Commission began to step up its restocking program with the aid of Pittman-Robertson funds, but the real concerted effort to restock deer in Georgia's interior did not begin until the late 1950s.

The Pittman-Robertson Act was designed to provide funds for wildlife management and protection. During the late 1950s, it helped fund Georgia's deer restoration program initiated by Jack Crockford. Sadly, Ranger Woody never lived to see any Pittman-Robertson funds come to his district, but he was so far ahead of the curve by the mid-1940s that he had made great strides without that money. According to Jack Crockford, "This act marked the beginning of scientific game management across the state of Georgia and the nation."

As briefly mentioned earlier, Jack Crockford has long been considered to be the father of the deer restoration program in Georgia. Ironically his incredible association with pioneering the restocking of deer in the southern 3/4 of the state did not begin until after Arthur Woody's death in 1946. Someone needed to pick up the ball and run with it, and destiny chose Jack Crockford for that job. One year after the Ranger's death in 1946, Jack Crockford was a fresh out-of-college graduate with a degree in wildlife biology from the University of Michigan (one of the first of its kind in the nation). Like so many young men his age, his college career had been interrupted by the war, where, as a pilot he had flown 328 missions in Burma.

In 1947, a young biologist and war hero from Michigan named Jack Crockford was hired by the Georgia Game and Fish Commission by wildlife department director Charlie Elliott to participate in a game survey funded by Pittman-Robertson monies. Within a few years, Jack picked up where Ranger Woody left off and began an extensive deer restocking program throughout the southern three-fourths of the state. Jack deservedly became known as the father of the deer restoration program in Georgia.

Also widely known as the man who developed the world famous "Cap-Chur" gun, Jack went on to become director of the Georgia Game and Fish Commission in the 1970s under Governor Jimmy Carter. Jack loved to trout fish and hunt grouse, and he spent much time in Ranger Woody's Blue Ridge WMA in the 1960s, '70s and '80s, one of his favorite haunts in Georgia. Pictured with his beloved German short-haired pointer "Sis," the results of a fine morning's hunt in the winter woods at Blue Ridge WMA were shared with the author. Photo circa late 1980s, by Duncan Dobie.

Ironically, Jack was hired by the State Game and Fish Commission in 1947 with a grant that came from Pittman-Robertson funds. Even more, ironical, as mentioned earlier in the book he was hired by none other than Ranger Woody's long-time friend Charlie Elliott, who had by that time taken over the helm at the Georgia Game and Fish Commission. Charlie would later state many times that his greatest achievement in conservation while heading up that department was hiring Jack Crockford.

Over the next 15 years, Jack, who had a keen interest in restocking deer throughout Georgia, would do for the rest of the state what Ranger Woody had done in North Georgia. Not only did Jack initiate a very successful state-wide restocking program, but during the process he developed the world famous Cap-Chur Gun, a modified air rifle that shot a syringe-style tranquiller dart into deer. This innovation revolutionized capturing wild animals worldwide. Jack's invention paved the way for catching hundreds of deer on some of the Georgia overpopulated coastal islands. These deer were then transported to various interior portions of the state.

A young pharmaceutical salesman named Red Palmer, who sold the drugs used for tranquilizing deer, patented Jack's innovative dart gun in the mid 1950s, naming it the "Cap-Chur Gun." Throughout the late 1950s and early 1960s, he sold thousands of dart guns across the world and became a millionaire in the process. Jack, the original designer of the gun and the revolutionary syringe-style dart, never shared in any of those profits because he was an employee of the state. Although the gun has been improved upon over the years, it still uses the same type of dart, and is built on the same principles as Jack's original prototype gun built in the early 1950s.

In 1950, a state-wide game survey estimated that about 33,000 deer existed in Georgia. By that time, the herd across North Georgia had multiplied to three or four thousand animals and the coastal region and barrier islands contained most of the balance. Deer were rare in the interior portion of the state. In some counties there were none. Due to Jack Crockford's extraordinary restocking program, every county in the state now contains sizable populations of deer and the state-wide population is well over 1 million animals.

Two beaming hunters who have bagged outstanding trophies apparently love the attention they are getting by a group of state and Forest Service officials including Ranger Arthur Woody standing second from right during the 1941 firearms hunt at Blue Ridge WMA. Courtesy of the Kenan Research Center at the Atlanta History Center.

A father and son hunting team proudly show off their incredible bounty – a fine Blue Ridge 8-point buck – as one of the refuge game wardens looks on during the 1941 firearms hunt. The father is holding a now classic rifle – a 1903 Springfield .30-06 – used by the military in World War I and soon to be used in the fast-approaching Second World War as well. Sadly, the U.S. would enter World War II only a few weeks after this photo was taken. Courtesy of the Kenan Research Center at the Atlanta History Center.

The smiles say it all as two elated hunters congratulate each other after participating in the hunt of a lifetime. Many years of hard work and time were invested by Ranger Woody and the Forest Service in protecting and growing the Blue Ridge deer herd in order to reach this high point in November 1941. Courtesy of the Kenan Research Center at the Atlanta History Center.

Several game officials help an elated hunter load his trophy buck into the back of a truck. In all, 21 bucks and one doe, shot by mistake, were taken during the 1941 firearms hunt at Blue Ridge WMA. Many of the bucks carried outstanding racks. Courtesy of the Kenan Research Center at the Atlanta History Center.

Two proud hunters wielding classic rifles smile for the camera as they show off their exceptional Blue Ridge bucks. The man on the left is holding a vintage Winchester Model 1873 lever-action (manufactured from 1873 to 1919), while his hunting partner is holding the ever-popular Remington Model 25 pump. Courtesy of the Kenan Research Center at the Atlanta History Center.

Ranger Woody loved to share his knowledge about the forest and the creatures that lived within the forest to young and old alike. Here he shows a cluster of leaves from a poplar tree to a student visiting Rock Creek Refuge with a 4-H Club group. Photo circa 1940, courtesy of Jean McNey.

Arthur Woody poses with an unknown boy. Always a man of vision who dared to "dream big," he never settled for mediocrity in his work or his life. It just so happened that a number of historic events took place in North Georgia during the first half of the 20th century, and he found himself right in the middle of them as a District Forest Ranger. Who could have imagined the mountain boy from Suches would accomplish so much during his relatively short lifetime. Photo circa 1944, courtesy of Jean McNey.

SECTION THREE – Legacy

The "Kingfish" auctions a box lunch at a fundraiser for Woody Gap School, circa 1942. In addition to his countless professional responsibilities regarding important conservation issues, Ranger Woody and his family were active in numerous civic activities in Suches and Union County. Photo courtesy of Jean McNey.

CHAPTER 16
The Beginning of the End – 1944
A Tired Old Ticker and a Worn-Out Mountain Ranger

"These mountains must be a little human. They go through periods of being dark and cold, and it looks like night will never end. But I've been watching it (the darkness) for nigh onto 60 years and it always does."

Arthur Woody

Growing up in the North Georgia mountains at a time when lakes were few and far between during the early 1900s, one has to wonder how Arthur Woody became such an accomplished swimmer. One must also wonder how he developed such a love for water during his adult life. Swimming was not a skill that the majority of hard-working mountain boys ever mastered because most had little access to deep water. But there were numerous ironies in Ranger Woody's life, and being an excellent swimmer who was at home in the water is just one of many.

We can only imagine a young Arthur Woody learning to swim in one of the deep pools from any number of streams or rivers like the Toccoa River or Rock Creek near Suches. Perhaps Granddaddy Abe taught him to swim as a boy. Perhaps he enjoyed spending a hot summer afternoon at the "old swimming hole" with other boys his age on those rare occasions when it was possible to slip away from the grueling afternoon chores.

Regardless of how it came about, Arthur Woody loved to swim and had no fear of the water. He was a strong swimmer in his later years, even after he had put on considerable weight. As soon as Woody Lake was completed in the mid-1930s, he regularly took long swims across the lake on warm summer afternoons.

"It was his way of relaxing and unwinding," said Jean McNey. "He'd often come home from the Ranger Station across the road and go for a swim late in the afternoon."

Typical of the way Arthur Woody did everything else in his life, he didn't just jump in the water and cool off. He swam from the dock behind his house all the way out to the dam and back, a distance of half a mile or more, and he did it on a frequent basis, weather permitting. Despite his bulk, this was something that very few adults his age would have ever attempted even if they had been good swimmers. As suggested in Chapter 2, this fondness for water could have been partially responsible for his famous nickname because he obviously had to take off his shoes whenever he went for a dip in the lake. Since people were used to seeing him in swimming attire, it is easy to imagine someone referring to him as the "Barefoot Ranger."

This lifelong love of being around water, that is, fishing in the lakes and streams of Union County and swimming in Woody Lake on a regular basis, was very nearly his undoing. It happened on September 18, 1944. Jean McNey remembered the events of the day as if it were yesterday:

"Papa was swimming with the wife of an assistant ranger named Brooks and they had gotten all the way across the lake to the dam when he more or less became paralysed from a sudden stroke," Jean said. "The assistant ranger's wife happened to be red-headed, and we later started kidded him unmercifully about that – swimming with the attractive red-headed wife of another man – being the real reason he'd had his stroke. But it was fortunate she was there because he might have drowned otherwise. He didn't lose consciousness, but he couldn't use his arms or legs, and she actually kept his head up and started yelling until help arrived. Some neighbors got him out of the water. Because he was partially paralyzed, they put him in a straight-back chair and took him right to the hospital."

Ranger Woody's close brush with disaster was later referred to as having been "a light stroke." In truth, it was probably much more serious. Some stories later referred to it as a heart attack. He had been experiencing symptoms of heart trouble for several years and he had been dealing with high blood pressure. His weight had not helped the situation. In fact, one of the first tell-tale symptoms of something being seriously wrong had occurred four years earlier during the firearms deer hunt in 1940 when he had experienced several severe nosebleeds.

The tough mountaineer tried to maintain his jovial spirits after the stroke, but several months went by with little sign of improvement. He was advised to go on a diet and lose at least 50 pounds in order to help control his dangerously high blood pressure. In February 1945, five months after his stroke, he was admitted to Georgia Baptist Hospital in Atlanta. Jean wrote the following heartfelt words in a special family scrapbook she assembled about the Ranger's life after her grandfather's death in 1946:

> "For the last few years the Ranger had been conscious of an unusually high blood pressure and an enlarged heart, but in spite of the doctor's warnings, it didn't seem to worry him too much until September 18, 1944, when he had a light stroke. Afterwards he became a little more concerned, even partially obeying the doctor's orders and observing his diet sheet when he felt that it didn't deny him too many of the edibles that he especially enjoyed.
>
> "Nevertheless, his health continued on the down-grade. In February 1945, he spent a couple of weeks in Georgia Baptist Hospital in order to bring his weight down and to give his doctors an opportunity to study his condition more closely. On March 22, 1946 (a year after the stroke), he suffered a severe convulsion which really seemed to be the beginning of the end. From then he spent most of the time in bed losing strength continually until June 10, when the last bit of life ebbed away."

Several years before the Ranger's stroke in September 1944, Dr. John W. Turner of Atlanta had purchased a cabin near Lake Winfield Scott in what local people termed the "flatland" area just north of Suches. Ranger Woody and Dr. Turner hit it off right away and became good friends. Like many people, Dr. Turner was quite taken with the Ranger's larger-than-life personality. Whenever the doctor and his wife spent time in the mountains, the two men often got together. Ranger Woody loved to drive Dr. Turner around and show him various parts of the game refuge or other special sights in the area.

Dr. Turner became the Ranger's primary physician shortly after the stroke. With no signs of improvement by early 1945, the good doctor found it necessary to admit his famous friend to the hospital in Atlanta so that he would be in a controlled situation where his diet could be maintained and where other tests could be completed.

Dr. Turner immediately attempted to treat his lively patient for the worrisome high blood pressure caused in part by being so overweight. After a number of tests were completed during his several week hospital stay, Ranger Woody was diagnosed with Bright's disease.

In the mid-1940s, Bright's disease was a general diagnosis that could include a wide range of kidney ailments. It was named after Dr. Richard Bright, who studied the condition in the early 19th century. A lack of understanding of how the kidneys worked at that time often resulted in this across-the-board diagnosis, when in fact there might have been a very specific cause such as acute nephritis. For that reason, the term "Bright's disease" is considered obsolete today because so many specific causes of kidney disease are known. Though certain types of kidney disease are very treatable, others result in serious, long-term, complications. In Ranger Woody's case, those complications eventually led to total kidney failure.

"Along with his high blood pressure, Papa also suffered from heart disease," Jean remembered. "The doctors said his condition was very difficult to treat because the medication he took for his kidney condition was not good for his heart condition and vice versa."

A Mountain Celebrity Comes to Atlanta

Like everything else about Ranger Woody's celebrity status in the 1940s, spending several days in an Atlanta hospital quickly turned into a highly touted media event. A picture of a beaming Arthur Woody in pajamas appeared in the Atlanta Constitution. While no mention was made of him being barefooted, he intentionally wore his trademark hat in bed for the cameras.

In his typical manner, he was quoted as saying, "I'm taking a rest, city style, because my tired ticker needs a rest."

Word quickly spread across the nation in Forest Service circles about the Ranger's hospital confinement. Cards and letters from well-wishers across Georgia and other parts of the country started pouring in. A number of heart-warming letters came from fellow Forest Service workers who had once been stationed in North Georgia, but were now working in other parts of the country. Those people who cared about Ranger Woody the most tried to make light of the situation and play it down as much as possible. But deep down inside, everyone worried about his condition.

Typical of Ranger Woody's larger-than-life persona, his two-week confinement at Georgia Baptist Hospital in Atlanta in February 1945 was regarded with much fanfare and good humor on the outside. On the inside, however, his doctors and family members were deeply concerned about his declining condition. News clipping courtesy of Jean McNey.

Constitution Staff Photo—Kenneth Rogers

WOODY RECUPERATES—Ranger Woody, famous guardian of the Chattahoochee National Forest, finally has been corraled by doctors and put to bed for a rest. Clint Davis, just back from a year of Army service in the islands, is shown above presenting his old mountain buddy a pot of flowers. Note that Woody is wearing pajamas (for the first time in his life). He is so used to wearing a hat he forgot to remove it for the picture.

The photo depicts Ranger Woody receiving a bouquet of flowers from his good friend, Forest Service photographer and PR man Sgt. Clint Davis, who was on leave from serving in the Army in the Pacific Theatre during World War II. The caption reads:

> Woody Recuperates – Ranger Woody, famous guardian of the Chattahoochee National Forest, finally has been corralled by doctors and put to bed for a rest. Clint Davis, just back from a year of Army service in the islands, is shown above presenting his old mountain buddy a pot of flowers. Note that Woody is wearing pajamas. He is so used to wearing a hat he forgot to take it off for the picture.

The accompanying story appeared in the Atlanta Constitution:

Woody Takes 'Rest Cure'

Noted State Ranger Confined to Hospital

By Sgt. Clint Davis

Tradition pictures the rugged woodsman as never pulling off his boots, but leave it to Forest Ranger Arthur Woody to upset this legend by going to bed with his hat on.

Confined to bed at Georgia Baptist Hospital, the veteran son of North Georgia's Blue Ridge country describes himself as "taking the rest cure, city fashion." He gave up the boots to please his pretty nurses, but he kept his trusty Stetson close at hand.

Woody, well-known to residents of North Georgia, and hunters and fishermen throughout the South for the past decade, has spent 35 years of his life as a forest ranger with the United States Forest Service. His bailiwick during most of this time has been the Blue Ridge district of the Chattahoochee National Forest where he serves as chief ranger.

During this long period of public service, Woody has won the respect and admiration of all who know him as a result of his conservation work in developing the forest, fish and game resources of his region. And equal to this respect on the part of thousands, has been the fear which he places in the minds of those few who would steal timber, start forest fires, or poach game and fish.

His many friends will be surprised to know that the ranger, symbol of all that is rough and rugged in the outdoors, has been forced to call a temporary halt to his strenuous activity due to what he describes as a "tired ticker that needs a little rest."

But a little illness did not prevent Woody from expressing his satisfaction over the increased numbers of deer and fish, which now abound in his forest.

Another account of Ranger Woody's hospital stay appeared in the "All in the Game" column by Atlanta Constitution Sports writer and good friend Jack Troy (late February 1945):

Ranger Woody

A most distinguished visitor from the North Georgia mountains is in our midst. Ranger Arthur Woody, famous guardian of the Chattahoochee National Forest, has got to lose a little weight to help his blood pressure so he yielded (at last) to doctor's orders to spend a period of rest in a hospital. He is at Georgia Baptist.

I'll never forget the deer hunts involving Ranger Woody. He really never approved of a one of them. After all, he stocked most of the region with deer, and he took great pride in raising them. It's legend that certain deer will meet him on his rambles through the mountains.

Anyway, he came to look on the deer as his own pets and he didn't particularly like to see them shot.

He got a great kick out of the bow and arrow hunts. And once, he offered to eat the nose off of any deer killed with an arrow.

When a visiting huntsman from another state hit a doe with an arrow and left the small, timid creature to die, Woody was beside himself with rage.

Kenneth Rogers took a picture of Woody kneeling beside the carcass. Woody was caressing the doe; and if the trace of moisture at the corner of his eyes wasn't caused by tear drops, both Rogers and I need an eye examination.

Woody never had much love for the Forest Service "technicians," as he called them. He figured, and rightly, that he probably knew more about the forest and deer than they did. So he always ranted and raved about their visits. Only a few came to know him well. And those became particular friends of his, although he never has stopped calling them "damned technicians."

I still don't know how the doctors cornered him and got him in a hospital bed – and in pajamas, too. First pair he ever wore in his life, I guess. Pink pajamas. Boy, wouldn't some of his mountain friends like to see him now!

In truth, to the hardy outdoorsman who had been the picture of health for most of his life, being admitted to an Atlanta hospital and not having command of his own destiny no doubt was a frustrating and humiliating experience. He made light of it, though, at least publicly, kidding all his friends who came to see him and constantly teasing all the nurses. If it got him down at all, he certainly tried not to let it show.

Heartfelt Letters from Special Friends

The following is one of many insightful letters written to Ranger Woody during his hospital stay in Atlanta. Dated Feb. 17, 1945, it was penned by fellow Forest Service worker R. I. Lowndes Jr., who had worked in the Ranger's district under him a year or two earlier and was now working in Lufkin, Texas.

Lowndes, who apparently was a character himself, tells it like it is!

Dear Ranger Woody,

I saw a picture of you taking a bunch of flowers from a man. What are they trying to do to my old friend? I have always thought flowers were for women folk and sissies but they did it to me once too so I guess I had better not say too much.

When Clyne was out here he told me that you had been eating too much pork and squirrel heads, but I didn't think you had over done it to where you would have to put on pink pajamas and lay in bed while pretty girls brought you chicken soup. However, you always had a way with the women, but I think that is taking advantage of 'em.

By the way, do you remember that day you showed me that the wild cats were eating one (a chicken)? Did you ever catch those cats to be sure they weren't some other kind of varmint? Somehow I always had my doubts about that.

And another thing, what happened to the bear that I put this very pen in the track of while you took a picture to show how big he was? If he is still roaming those hills I guess the pen would look like a four penny nail rather than a toothpick in the picture by now.

And that big rainbow in the pool at the crusher set, just below the rearing pools? Did anyone ever catch him? I hope he is still there because I surely would like to get a hook in his mouth.

This is a good country out here, Ranger, and a lot of good people that will treat you right as long as you stay on your side of the path, but plumb ready for a fight if you don't. Fighting is kind of cheap, too, only cost you $14.72, which you can pay in advance if you've a mind to.

Somehow there isn't any country that will take the place of those old hills about North Georgia and western North Carolina Mo. (mountains) You can't get up high and look down on the world like you can when you drive along the Blue Ridge Truck Trail. You know, just a little further out than where you met that old woman plowing an old mule. Somehow I've always missed Walter when he was out here, but maybe someday we will get together and have a good long talk about the old days when he and I were going about up there trying to get roads, dams, and other things built!

By the way, speaking of dams, I hear you got that one built down near the old veterans CCC camp that you wanted to build while I was up there (probably Lake Winfield Scott).

I guess Rock Creek Lake is so full of fish by this time, you can catch them in your hat. I know it wasn't your fault.

When the bunch comes to see you please tell them "hello" for me and that I would sure like to be up there once more.

See if you can make one of those pretty nurses write me a letter that you dictate and tell me how you are getting along and what all of the old fellows are doing.

Best of luck, but don't let 'em hand you too much soft stuff. June might have too hard a time with you when you get back home.

Yours, Lowndes

Numerous other cards and letters from friends and well-wishers reflected similar sentiments. Everyone tried to be positive, but most people no doubt suspected the long-term outlook was not good for the Ranger. This next letter also poked fun at the fact that Ranger Woody was forced to wear "pajamas." Dated February 11, 1945, it was written by H.G. Jarrard, Superintendent of Hall County Schools, in Gainesville, Georgia. Written on Hall County School board stationery, it was sent directly to Georgia Baptist Hospital:

Dear Ranger:

I saw your picture in the Atlanta Constitution yesterday and decided that I should write you. It is comforting for me to know that you are taking a rest. You are in a good place to do it. Those pretty girls will help you out. One of the things that disturbs me is that you, a mountain man, had to put on pajamas. That may not be a crime, but those things were not made for a mountain man. It is O.K. with me. However, I am insisting that you do not turn out to be a sissy. As long as you hold onto your hat you will be all right. Now, Ranger, I declare myself for the hat and flowers, but principle demands that I do not compromise with pajamas. I am a mountain man and that carries with it certain rights and privileges as well as obligations.

Now, seriously Ranger, I am interested in your getting well. If you will take it easy for a while and get off a few more pounds, you will be as good as new. We are pulling for you, and if you want us for anything, just say the word. You have been with us when we needed you and we will be with you. Just remember that. That is just what I am writing to say.

May the blessing of the Lord be upon you and yours.
Sincerely Yours,
Grady (H.G. Jarrard), CSS (County School System, Hall County, GA).

Dated March 6, 1945, the following letter is from Warren V. Woody of Chicago, Illinois (a cousin whose branch of the Woody family had left Georgia years earlier).

Dear Arthur,

Dad just forwarded a letter to me that Mae wrote to him, telling of your illness. Of course I was shocked, and certainly sympathize with you. However, in my opinion a little thing like illness will not get the ranger down. A fellow who grew up in the hills of North Georgia has to be tough… (Anyway my dad is, and I know all the Woody's are fighters.) So I know you are going to be all right. Do exactly what the doctors tell you. Stay in bed until you are 100% again, and don't get in a hurry to go home. They can treat you better there in the hospital than they can at home. However, I am sure they won't feed you as well because the meals at your house are wonderful … (I know.)

I have been very anxious to come back to Georgia for a hunt and I promise you that as soon as you are well enough to have company I will bring Dad down and we will do a little shooting. If there is anything you would like I will be glad to send it to you from Chicago.

Sincerely, Warren V. Woody

Ranger Woody returned home from his hospital stay on February 18. This next note is from a hand-written, three page letter from a Forest Service co-worker living in Missoula, Montana:

Dear Arthur,

So you fooled 'em all – Good! Am delighted to know that you are back at the ole farm-stead up on the hill top in the charming hills of North Georgia. Wish that I could drop in on you to tell you to lay off corn pone and white gravey (sp). Instead of partaking of your favorite dish, better confine your diet to some drug store vitamin pill and an apple each day. Keep down the weight – 250 are too many pounds for that old machine of yours to lug around.

What about wearing your hat to bed? Any truth to that report or were your friends just pulling a fast one on you?

You see, Woody, old boy, your behavior and your condition is well-known far beyond the confines of the Toccoa Basin. Your fame and all that goes with its remarkable record extend over beyond the Rocky Mountains and down into the valleys of the Columbia River.

I also hear that you will soon join me in retirement – fine business - you have done your share and well. Let some of the younger fellows carry the load henceforth.

After talking about some things he was doing in Montana in his own retirement, the writer closed by saying:

Arthur, can't tell you how much I am pleased to know that you are again back up home. Take care of yourself now. I know that your friend Sam will tell you all about how to do it. (Not clear who Sam is.)

Best Wishes to Mrs. Woody, Maybelle, Walter and all others of the family.

Sincerely,
Name illegible

Another hand-written note said:

Dear Arthur,

Well you are a pretty one to leave all of those fair-haired nurses in the lurch! I called up the hospital this morning to find out the visiting hours, intending to go over this afternoon. Then I called Pigeon only to learn that you had packed up and gone back to North Georgia – I think you should have stayed a week or two longer, but now that you have gone home let me urge you to take it easy and do what the doctors, Mrs. Woody and Maybelle tell you to do and what not to do.

I am very sorry that I did not get to see you this trip, but I want to come up when the weather gets warm and loaf a few days with you.

After talking about some personal things the letter closed by saying:

Hello to all the family and be good –
Name illegible

A Grateful Public Says Thanks

Shortly after Ranger Woody's stroke, the idea of dedicating a permanent monument to him and his work was first brought up during the 1944 deer hunt in Blue Ridge WMA later that year. The stroke occurred in mid-September; the hunt was held two months later in mid November. It did not take long for many of the Ranger's friends and admirers to realize that he was seriously ill and that he might not recover. Everyone wanted to do something, and some could see the writing on the wall. But most people were at a loss as to what they could do.

The following article appeared in the Game Log section of the Atlanta Constitution on January 15, 1945. It was written by Charlie Elliott in his typical eloquent and heartwarming style:

Monument Proposed For Arthur Woody

During the recent deer hunt in a management area in the Chattahoochee National Forest in North Georgia (November 1944), a worthy proposal was developed by several intimate sportsmen who were gathered from throughout the state.

"One of these days," they said, "Forest Ranger Woody will go on to the happy hunting grounds, where the Supreme Sportsman will place him in charge of a deer herd for the rest of eternity. He may be with us for another 10 or 20 years, or even longer. We all know that when he does go, a monument will be raised to the life he spent in bringing back the trout to our mountain streams and the deer and other game to our forests.

"It's all right," they said, "to erect a monument to a man after he is called from this mundane existence, but why wouldn't it be much better to remember him while he lives, so that he himself may enjoy some very small tribute to the magnificent job he has done for his fellow man?"

That thought was developed and discussed around the campfires where weary deer hunters lounged and smoked, and talked over the living moments of the day.

Human Gibraltar of Hills

If you don't know Arthur Woody, let me tell you a few simple facts about him. But this is for the very few who are not acquainted with this mountain man or with his work in the North Georgia wilderness.

Ranger Woody was born in those hills, back in the years when the wilderness there was remote, when few roads traversed the rugged passes, and when many of these mountain families rode into town for supplies only once or twice during the year. He is as much a part of the Blue Ridge as the giant hemlocks that stand in the shadows of the valleys, as the rock seams that hold the mountain sides together. The fiber of winter, the gentleness of spring, and all the color of autumn are a part of his very heart and soul.

Few woodsmen know the way of the wilderness creatures as does the Ranger. He has the eye of a hunting eagle, the tread of a catamount through the woods. He can read the signs in the leaves and earth as you and I read the type out of a book. The "dam' technicians" talk and he will listen, but there are few things they can tell him about his mountain wilderness.

Pioneer in Restocking

When Arthur Woody was a boy, he saw his father kill the last deer out of the Blue Ridge above his home. When he became a man, he pledged himself to right that wrong. With money out of his own pocket, he bought deer and placed them in the forest. That was long before the restocking programs were started by the federal government or by the state.

He bought fish eggs, raised trout, bass, muskies and turned them loose in the waters of the streams. And he talked with his mountain neighbors and they agreed to protect those creatures to give them another start, and bring hunting and fishing to them mountains. There is much more to tell. A book could be written about this man of the mountains. A book could be written on how he worked with the federal officials in helping to purchase thousands of acres that went into the building of the only national forest Georgia has. But space here prohibits the full story of his life and of his service to his fellow man.

Rock or Trees?

Now the question is – what kind of monument shall we erect to Arthur Woody? One kind of a monument is made out of stone – living rock hewed out of the mountains which have lived around him. Of course, rock is a poor substitute for the life blood and sweat and tears that a man has put in doing things for his neighbors.

Another kind of monument is a living monument of trees – some tract set aside as virgin wilderness, never to be touched by man's ax, a forest that would live and breathe and grow as a reminder of the life one man gave to his fellow Americans.

The Game Commission would like to have your suggestions. The hours of all men on this earth are numbered – we never know when we will be called by the Creator. Something should be started within the next few months, if enough hunters and fishermen and sportsmen agree with the sentiments expressed by those around the campfire on those cold December nights in the Blue Ridge.

Interestingly, Charlie Elliott offered this proposal to the sportsmen of Georgia several weeks before Ranger Woody was hospitalized in Atlanta in February 1945, and several months before he was forced to retire later that year in September 1945. Did Charlie realize from the start that this was probably one great battle his dear friend and mentor of the last two decades would never be able to win? It is very likely that he did.

OUTDOOR GEORGIA, MARCH 15, 1945 8

NATURE'S FRIEND—When Ranger Arthur Woody was a boy he saw his father kill the last whitetail deer in Georgia's Blue Ridge Mountains. Not many years ago he used his own money to start the restocking of deer in the same area. Here he offers a tidbit to Peggy, a doe that has ranged near Rock Creek and produced 11 fawns in seven years.

MAIL THIS COUPON TODAY

John Martin, Publisher, OUTDOOR GEORGIA
Corner Pryor & Auburn, Atlanta 3, Ga.

I heartily indorse OUTDOOR GEORGIA'S campaign to erect a memorial as a tribute to Ranger Arthur Woody and his great contribution to wildlife and forestry. I inclose one dollar ($1) as my share in the Arthur Woody Memorial Fund.

Name ....

Address ....

This March 1945 clipping from Outdoor Georgia magazine, published by the Ranger's good friend John Martin, shows Ranger Woody with one of his "pet" deer, a well-known doe named Peggy. After Ranger Woody's stroke in September 1944, John Martin and Charlie Elliott established a memorial fund aimed at financing some type of lasting tribute to the Ranger at Woody Gap. Sportsmen interested in making a contribution could fill out the form and send in a donation. Limited to $1 per individual, donations were received from as far away as Colorado. Ironically, this offering was made only a few weeks before the Ranger was hospitalized in Atlanta for severe heart and kidney disease. News clipping courtesy of Jean McNey.

Although several prominent people suggested establishing some type of memorial forest for Ranger Woody after his death, that idea never seemed to gain much steam. (After Ranger Woody's death, Sosebee Cove Scenic Area was fittingly dedicated as a memorial to the Ranger's life and his work in conservation.) But the idea of commissioning a bronze plaque with his likeness on it seemed to catch on very quickly. Thanks to special friends like Charlie Elliott and John Martin, the bronze plaque became a much revered reality.

Funds for the project were first solicited in the March 1945 issue of "Outdoor Georgia" magazine, edited and published at that time by John Martin. Contributions were received from as far away as Colorado. Reportedly 250 people (friends) contributed $1 each to have the 2x3-foot bronze plaque made in which the Ranger's likeness would appear with a suitable inscription. It was deliberately decided to keep contributions at $1 so that a maximum number of friends and admirers could participate.

A follow-up article about the proposed memorial appeared in the March 15, 1945 issue of Outdoor Georgia:

Dollar Limit Set on Fund for Woody
Woody's Gap

The man who has done most toward restoring deer to the mountains and trout to the cold streams of the North Georgia hills in which he was born and bred will be able to enjoy the tribute owed him by the sportsmen and citizens of Georgia.

Arthur Woody, the kingpin of the mountains and pioneer forester will live to see a living growing memorial in his honor.

It will be the north side of Black Mountain, a memorial virgin forest that no man's ax will ever scar again. A forest that will live and breathe as a reminder of the life one farseeing man of the mountain gave to his fellow Georgians and to conservation.

Originated on Hunt

Although the U.S. Forest Service has never set up a memorial to a living person, officials have consented to allow the sportsmen of the state to pay tribute to Arthur Woody.

The proposal to erect a memorial to Ranger Woody originated around the camp fire one night last winter during the managed deer hunt on the Blue Ridge area he developed. Charlie Elliott, in his "Game Log" in the January 15 (1945) issue of Outdoor Georgia, called attention to the proposal and hunters and fishermen took up the drive. Trout fishermen and deer hunters led the way.

And now everything is ready except the details. Tentative plans call for the erection of a bronze or brass plaque on a boulder located on the mountain or at Woody's Gap here. (Correct spelling is Woody Gap.)

The north side of Black Mountain will be dedicated to the veteran ranger at ceremonies attended by sportsmen, foresters, state and federal officials and citizens of Union County.

Boynton First

Sportsmen and citizens will be given the opportunity of sharing in this tribute by contributing one dollar, and only one dollar, that will go to the Arthur Woody Memorial Fund. Outdoor Georgia will accept contributions and names of contributors will be published during and after the campaign. Representative Claud G. Boynton, of Suches, also will accept the funds. (By this time, Reverend Boynton had also been elected to the Georgia legislature.)

Boynton was the first contributor. He is Union County's No. 1 double-in-brass, being a forester, preacher, school teacher and lawmaker.

If only the hunters and fishermen who know Arthur Woody personally contribute, a sizable fund is assured. Contributions are limited to one dollar to enable a large number to pay tribute to the ranger, who is recovering at his home from two recent and severe heart attacks that came close to sending him across the river.

Although the idea of setting aside a memorial forest on a portion of Black Mountain dedicated to Ranger Woody in addition to the plaque was also proposed and tentatively approved, it never came to fruition. The memorial might well have been nipped in the bud due to hostile feelings held by certain Forest Service personnel. However, the plaque did become a reality in 1947.

Well-known Atlanta artist and sculptor Steffen Thomas, who also worked on the Stone Mountain/Civil War carving of Generals Lee and Jackson and Confederate President Jefferson Davis, was commissioned to do the likeness of Ranger Woody on the plaque. It was decided that the plaque, when finished, would be placed on a large boulder taken from the side of Black Mountain and moved to a spot at the top of Woody Gap where the Woody Gap Road and the Appalachian Trail intersect. (See Chapter 18 for the dedication of this memorial to Ranger Woody.)

The following article, dated Oct. 1, 1945, was taken from a clipping in Jean's scrapbook that probably appeared in the Atlanta Constitution. A photo of Ranger Woody and his mother accompanied the article with the caption: Woodsman Woody and his Mother – Arthur Woody, North Georgia forest ranger, walks down a path with his mother, Mrs. Eliza Ingram Woody, 75, who still lives in the house in which Woody was reared. The house is about a quarter of a mile up the road from the present Blue Ridge Ranger Station.

For Rugged Old-Timer
Sportsmen Plan Plaque to Honor William Woody

Sportsmen friends of William Arthur Woody are planning a memorial for the North Georgia forest ranger who is widely esteemed as an outdoorsman, nature lover and friend of man. Because Woody is retiring after 27 years as the only ranger for the U.S. Forest Service in the Blue Ridge district of the Chattahoochee National Forest.

The memorial planned will be as simple and as rugged as the old-timer himself. It will consist of a bronze plaque embedded in a hug boulder on the north side of Black Mountain on the Blue Ridge, amidst the almost half a million acres of land that he guarded so well.

For more than a century the history of the Union County area of the Blue Ridge has been interwoven with the affairs of the Woody family. Woody Gap, a 3,300-foot-elevation pass on the shoulder of Black Mountain, connects Lumpkin and Union counties. Woody Lake lies at the mountain's foot, and the new Woody Gap School lies in the valley.

Fight Against Fires

William Arthur Woody has added new luster to the family name. A memorial to his industry and talents are the productive forests with their dwindling record of fires; increasing game in the streams and forests, and the all-weather, farm-to-market roads where once mountain people wrestled with clay and mud. One of his biggest jobs was securing the cooperation of his mountain friends in preventing wild fires.

Woody has been the instrument through which much progress has been wrought in the southern end of the Appalachian Mountains. He has been the kingpin of the Forest Service, and the Forest Service has been directly or indirectly responsible for 146 miles of roads and 88 miles of foot trails in the district. Woody advised on the location of roads and helped get right of ways.

Of all his activities, however, the one nearest his heart, and the one for which he is widely known, is game management. When he entered the Forest Service, all big game in north Georgia was gone except for a few deer. Black bears had completely abandoned the tall timber.

Population Increased

In 1927 Woody bought 14 whitetail fawns with his own money and turned them lose in the district. Later on, the Forest Service, with the State Wildlife Commission, planted 30 head of deer in the area. Seven years later the Forest Service brought 250 more whitetails to the refuge. The deer population is now estimated at between 1,500 to 2,000 and a managed hunt is permitted each year.

Black bears are still pretty scarce, but each year thousands of legal-size rainbow and brook trout are released in the swift mountain streams. Foxes and bobcats prey on desirable game – birds, rabbits, turkeys and fawns, and Woody plans to spend part of his retirement years exterminating them.

He will be succeeded by Theodore S. Seely, a graduate of the New York State College of Forestry of Syracuse University, who is now district ranger of the Talladega National Forest.

(As has been mentioned several times in previous chapters, Ranger Woody bought five fawns in 1927, not 14 as stated above. Furthermore, the Forest Service never brought 250 more whitetails to the refuge seven years later. Records show that the Forest Service was responsible for purchasing *several dozen* more deer for the refuge after about 1929, but the 250 number is an exaggeration. While other deer were stocked in other portions of the district, the entire herd in the Rock Creek Refuge stemmed from no more than 60 or 70 seed animals.)

Even though Ranger Woody was once again back home in familiar surroundings after his hospital stay, his health continued to deteriorate over the next few months. He began to drop pound after pound, but not because of any diet he was on. It was heartrending on him and those around him. By the summer of 1945, the writing was on the wall. The man who had ruled the roost in Suches for over 30 years would by necessity have to step down. He could no longer do his job.

The word "retirement" had never even been in his vocabulary. The concept was as foreign to him as traveling to the moon. But now it was a foregone conclusion that he would have to leave the job that he had been born to do and performed so well for over three decades. Suddenly he faced the most difficult challenge of his life. For reasons beyond his control, the most famous forest ranger in the nation would have to do something that went against every fiber of his being. The man with boundless energy, the man who had never given up on anything in his life, the man who always found a way to make things happen in every situation, would have to throw in the towel and give up his job. It was a tough pill for him to swallow.

With hat in hand, Arthur Woody poses for a 1945 photo on the porch of the Ranger Station office located just across the road from his house. Originally built as a home for a North Carolina forest ranger who he tried to hire, the building contained Ranger Woody's office for many years and served as the hub of Forest Service activity during the Ranger's long tenure as guardian of over 200,000 acres of national forest land. The gaunt look on the Ranger's face, due to his declining health, bares a stark contrast to the many smiling and vibrant photos of him taken just a few years earlier during happier times. Photo courtesy of Jean McNey.

CHAPTER 17
A Retirement That Nobody Wanted

"I'm glad that these hills were mine for a little while."

Arthur Woody

At 17, Jean McNey was mature beyond her years. Like her grandfather, her foresight was extraordinary. Jean wrote the touching words below in her special remembrance scrapbook that she put together shortly after the Ranger's death.

> "On September 30, 1945, the Ranger retired from public service with the Forest Service. Due to his physical condition, he felt that he was no longer able to perform the duties of his office according to his own high standards. His many friends in the service expressed their regrets in losing one who had so cheerfully and successfully given the best years of his life to their work. The Forest Service personnel honored him with a party at Woody Gap School, and there they presented him with his Forest Service badge, gold-plated, which he had proudly worn for many years." (He had worn a regular badge for many years, but this new badge had been gold-plated in his honor).

There was nothing easy or positive about Ranger Woody's forced retirement. Although he tried to keep a smile on his face, even cracking a few jokes here and there in his typical fashion, he had lost 50 to 60 pounds since his hospital stay in February. The illness from which he suffered was painful, humiliating and debilitating. By the time his retirement ceremony took place in late September, he was a mere shell of the man he had always been.

Although support from friends and co-workers was overwhelming, most were at a loss to do or say anything meaningful. A tragedy was unfolding in front of their very eyes. Some people attempted to make light of the situation by suggesting the Ranger would now have all the time in the world to devote to his beloved trout and other outdoor pursuits. But few people really believed this would happen because Ranger Woody seemed to be losing ground every day.

During one of his more light-hearted moments, the Ranger wrote this poem shortly his retirement became official:

I'M RETIRED
By W. Arthur Woody

No fires to fight; no diaries to write.
No J.F's to teach the poplar from beech (Junior Foresters).
No tools to grind; no desks to shine.
Ah, this is the life for me.

No roads to build; no fox to kill.
No lines to run for anyone.
Nobody to 'curs' if I wreck a bus.
Damn, it's good to be free!

No inspectors to fight if a scale isn't right,
Or, if I drive my car too far.
I'll back up and yell "To Hell – to hell!"
At those who used to stop me.

The rest of my life I'll stay with my wife
sit on my rear; watch those who are near
'Cause my battle is done; my race has been won.
Independent? That's what I be!

The stirring words in the last stanza "'Cause my battle is done; my race has been won," are particularly significant. Arthur Woody had indeed fought and won many battles – battles for the people in his community, and battles for his many conservation projects – and he knew in his heart that his race had indeed been well won because of the many glowing victories. He also knew in his heart that his days were numbered.

SOUTHERN OUTDOORS, July 1, 1946 . 2

GOLD FOR "THE RANGER"—This last photo of Ranger Arthur Woody was made in November, 1945 in the Woody Gap schoolyard. It shows C. K. Spaulding, supervisor of the Chattahoochee National Forest, pinning a gold honorary ranger's badge on Woody. In the group are former associates of the famous ranger, including: Ted Seely, Jerry Lethcoe, Crawford DuPree, Fritz Olander, Ed Reese, Charles Sheets and Jerry Welch.

Woody Buried

Continued from Page 1

the time of his death had a collection of fine weapons.

Once a hunter who took his share of turkeys and deer, the Ranger later became so interested in restocking the forests with whitetails that he disliked seeing a buck taken by anyone. But he was every inch a true sportsman and showed numerous riflemen stands from which they took trophy heads on supervised hunts in the Blue Ridge Management Area.

RECOVERED TWICE

Six months before he died, Woody was only a shadow of the 250-pound man who roamed the hills in any kind of weather. He partially recovered twice from severe heart attacks that would have counted out anyone with less stamina and determination.

Life was not worth living to Woody if it couldn't be in his beloved mountains. Friends once suggested that he go to Florida for his health.

"Me go down there and drink wiggle-tail water? What's the use to live if it can't be up here?"

With the Ranger gone, Woody Gap and North Georgia will never be the same to hundreds of hunters and fishermen, who agree that there was only one Arthur Woody and there'll never be another in this or any other generation.

Game Log . . .

Continued from Page 1

For Worship and Educatio

Woody's influence and kindliness
the forest. Legend are the stories
neighbors in need. His generosity
casual that many times it did not d
deed the Ranger had done.

His thinking was basic. He kne
and education, and he helped build
part in the Easter Sunrise Services
worked to bring the mountains awa
gravel roads.

Underneath it all, his first love
tures of the wilderness. I have driv
tain road, while he pointed out wh
bankment, where a gobbler had m
the tire tracks. I've never seen hi
found where two wildcats had pull
made it a personal issue between hi
to a sudden and untimely end.

Joins Vanishing Race of Pi

For the last 10 years of his life
Woody looked forward to retiring,
days in the woods and on the strea
"I know the big trout by name,"
to get 'em on a hook."

The years of hard existence too
man when the government retired hi
He had given his life to something
able to enjoy.

He has gone on to join a vanishin
the singing streams, the beauty of
earthly wilderness which were his f

A Celestial Flyrod for the

If there is a divine compensation
uncertain physical existence, I know
a happy hunting and fishing groun
heaven. It is a land for fellows lik
and turkey and squirrels and there'
hill.

In His infinite wisdom and jus
handed Arthur a celestial flyrod and
of flies. There are big trout in the
mainder of all eternity the old Ran
outwit them.

With all my heart, I hope it is tr
reward will be forever instead of fo

One of the last official photos ever made of Ranger Arthur Woody was taken in November 1945 at Woody Gap School in Suches. C.K. "Lanky" Spaulding, supervisor of the Chattahoochee National Forest from the Gainesville office, pins a gold ranger's badge on a noticeably thin and sickly Arthur Woody as a tribute to his more than 30 years of service. Sadly, one of the most famous forest rangers in the nation had been forced to retire two months earlier due to failing health. Other Forest Service officials pictured are: Ted Seely (who took Ranger Woody's place, standing behind the ranger to his left), Crawford DuPree, on left, (the accountant who Ranger Woody jokingly dubbed "Sister DuPree"), Jerry Lethcoe, Fritz Olander, Ed Reese, Charles Sheets and Jerry Welch. By November 1945, the Ranger's health was rapidly deteriorating. He died seven months later in June 1946. Photo courtesy of Jean McNey.

After his official retirement in September 1945, Ranger Woody again received cards and letters from friends, co-workers and well-wishers from across the country.

The following letter (undated) was written by the ranger's dear friend Bill Bergoffen in late 1945 near the end of the war (probably in late summer) on a Friday from his office in Washington D.C. The war ended in mid-August 1945.

As mentioned in Chapter 1, Bill Bergoffen was an old friend and protégé who had lived in the Woody house for a time and worked with Ranger Woody as an assistant ranger. In all, he spent 14 months living in Suches in the mid-1930s. Later, he rose through the ranks of the Forest Service and spent most of his career in Washington D.C. Having retired in 1976, he is best known for compiling an outstanding 200-page soft bound photo essay published by the Forest Service titled *100 Years of Federal Forestry.*

The book contains hundreds of historic photos taken around the country including one taken in 1926 where Ranger Woody is posed in front of Mt. Lebanon school, a one-room school near Suches, with the students after having given a talk about fire prevention. From several personal letters and various articles Bergoffen wrote about Ranger Woody in a monthly Forest Service publication, it's plain to see that emotions ran deep when it came to his old mentor.

Bergoffen must have been special to Ranger Woody, too, because not just anyone would have been allowed to live in the Woody house. He had a dog named Jinx that occasionally stayed in his bedroom with him on particularly cold nights. Once, when granddaughter Jean McNey came home to an empty house, Jinx got so excited that he jumped out of the upstairs bedroom window. Feeling responsible, Jean was terrified, thinking she had killed the dog. But the dog emerged from the 12- to 15-foot fall unscathed.

> (No date) Friday
> Dear Ranger,
>
> "I gotta write to him now," sez I to myself. "It don't matter that the sonuvagun never has honored any letter I've written in the past. This is extra special. I gotta write to him."
>
> So, I'm writing.
>
> It took a little time for me to become aware that you paid a little visit to the hospital. And by the time I got to see the pictures of your adventures

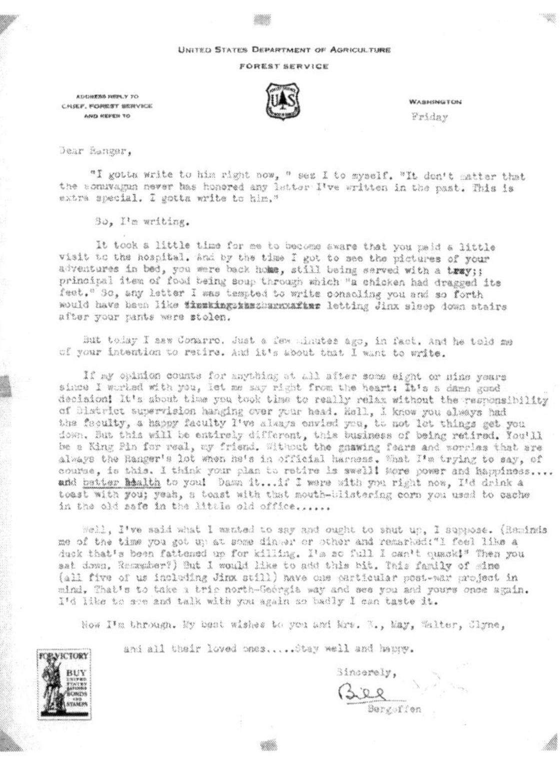

UNITED STATES DEPARTMENT OF AGRICULTURE
FOREST SERVICE

ADDRESS REPLY TO
CHIEF, FOREST SERVICE
AND REFER TO

WASHINGTON
Friday

Dear Ranger,

"I gotta write to him right now," sez I to myself. "It don't matter that the sonuvagun never has honored any letter I've written in the past. This is extra special. I gotta write to him."

So, I'm writing.

It took a little time for me to become aware that you paid a little visit to the hospital. And by the time I got to see the pictures of your adventures in bed, you were back home, still being served with a tray;; principal item of food being soup through which "a chicken had dragged its feet." So, any letter I was tempted to write consoling you and so forth would have been like letting Jinx sleep down stairs after your pants were stolen.

But today I saw Conarro. Just a few minutes ago, in fact. And he told me of your intention to retire. And it's about that I want to write.

If my opinion counts for anything at all after some eight or nine years since I worked with you, let me say right from the heart: It's a damn good decision! It's about time you took time to really relax without the responsibility of District supervision hanging over your head. Hell, I know you always had the faculty, a happy faculty I've always envied you, to not let things get you down. But this will be entirely different, this business of being retired. You'll be a King Pin for real, my friend. Without the gnawing fears and worries that are always the Ranger's lot when he's in official harness. What I'm trying to say, of course, is this. I think your plan to retire is swell! More power and happiness.... and better health to you! Damn it...if I were with you right now, I'd drink a toast with you; yeah, a toast with that mouth-blistering corn you used to cache in the old safe in the little old office......

Well, I've said what I wanted to say and ought to shut up, I suppose. (Reminds me of the time you got up at some dinner or other and remarked:"I feel like a duck that's been fattened up for killing. I'm so full I can't quack!" Then you sat down. Remember?) But I would like to add this bit. This family of mine (all five of us including Jinx still) have one particular post-war project in mind. That's to take a trip north-Georgia way and see you and yours once again. I'd like to see and talk with you again so badly I can taste it.

Now I'm through. My best wishes to you and Mrs. W., May, Walter, Clyne,

and all their loved ones.....Stay well and happy.

Sincerely,

Bill
Bergoffen

FOR VICTORY BUY UNITED STATES SAVINGS BONDS AND STAMPS

After word began to circulate that Ranger Woody's health was failing and that he would be forced to retire, this heartfelt letter from Bill Bergoffen expresses the feelings shared by many of his former assistants and other loyal Forest Service friends who had worked with him and come to love him over the years. Letter courtesy of Jean McNey.

in bed, you were back home, still being served with a tray; principal item of food being soup through which "a chicken had dragged its feet." So, any letter I was tempted to write consoling you and so forth would have been like letting Jinx sleep downstairs after your pants were stolen.

But today I saw Conarro (a fellow Forest Service friend who had also worked in the North Georgia Mountains under Ranger Woody). Just a few minutes ago, in fact, and he told me of your intention to retire. And it's about that I want to write.

If my opinion counts for anything at all after some eight or nine years since I worked with you, let me say right from the heart: It's a damn good decision! It's about time you took time to really relax without the responsibility of district supervisor hanging over your head. Hell, I know you always had the faculty, a happy faculty. I've always envied you, to not let things get you down. But this will be entirely different, this business of being retired. You'll be a King Pin for real, my friend. Without the gnawing fears and worries that are always the Ranger's lot when he's in official harness. What I'm trying to say, of course, is this. I think your plan to retire is swell. More power and happiness.... And better health to you, a toast with that mouth-blistering corn you used to cache in the old safe in the little old office.....

Well, I've said what I wanted to say and ought to shut up, I suppose. (Reminds me of the time you got up at some dinner or other and remarked; "I feel like a duck that's been fattened up for killing. I'm so full I can't quack!" Then you sat down. Remember?) But I would like to add this bit. This family of mine (all five of us including Jinx still) have one particular post-war project in mind. That's to take a trip (down) north Georgia way and see you and yours once again. I'd like to see and talk with you again so badly I can taste it.

Now I'm through. My best wishes to you and Mrs. W, May (Mae), Walter, Clyne, and all their loved ones... Stay well and happy.

Sincerely,

Bill
(Bill Bergoffen)

A second heartfelt letter from Bill Bergoffen, expressing his sentimental feelings and gratitude, was written from his Washington office several months later on November 21, 1945:

Dear Ranger,

Tomorrow is Thanksgiving Day. I've been sitting here for the past half-hour or so just thinking about tomorrow and Thanksgiving Days of years gone by.

Tomorrow is still a day off, but several Thanksgiving Days of yesteryear seem closer to me right now than tomorrow. And I am sure that tomorrow, however nice a Thanksgiving day it turns out to be, will never stay with me or come as close to my heart as a couple of Thanksgivings I spent with you and your family some years ago. All this probably sounds like a lot of double talk, but I know what I'm trying to say and I'm sure you do, too.

I've been trying to think if it was a turkey or a chicken whose head I was assigned to blow off with the shotgun one Thanksgiving. I believe it was a turkey, and how proud I was to do the honors. Other little incidents of my wonderful days and months (14 of them) I spent with you-all come crowding to my mind this afternoon. I'm not too clear about some of the things but that doesn't matter too much. You see, I remember and will never forget the sum total of your friendliness, your generosity and your sincerity toward this little "damn Yankee" who used to get more homesick and lonesome than you ever knew. Yes, all that added up to a beautiful, unforgettable experience. Just top that off with the forest and administrative education you helped me to get, and you'll understand why I shall never get over feeling grateful to you and yours… never get over being thankful for whatever Fate drew my number to be your assistant about ten years ago.

Knowing you as I did, and having you know me as you did, should excuse my indulgence in this sentiment I've tried to express above. What I'm trying to say, in effect, is "Thank You," once again, for everything!

Here in the Washington office right now are a number of men who know you and who have worked with you. I don't believe that any one of us see each other without being conscious of you, without mentioned you in one nice way or another. There's Don Clark, of course; Bill Branch, Milt Bryan and, most recently, Bill Fischer, in on detail. (Not sure what was intended here. The word "on" is probably a typo.) I hope this little bunch can get together someday soon for lunch and a bit of reminiscing which is sure to happen. Next fine day your ears burn a bit, it won't be because of any warm north Georgia sun; it'll be because a little group of men here in Washington – each one of us yearning for the good old days, though not admitting it – are talking about you.

Our little family rolls merrily along. The children are 3 and 7 respectively and as rascally as Ned (Ranger Woody's grandson) ever was, and just as lovable. Anne and I hit it off nice as you please and both look forward to that day when we can get rambling back to the Woody Gap country for a little visit. Jinx, the dog, is still with us – believe it or not.

How very often I've thought about the time your pants were stolen! I know you must have cussed me for having Jinx in bed that night and on guard like any respectable dog ought to be. But, dammit man, it gets cold in those north Georgia hills... and I never did mind the fleas for the heat Jinx afforded. By God, those were the days!

Be happy, Ranger and more power to you and your retirement! Love to all,

Bill
(Bill Bergoffen)

Another dedicated Forest Service co-worker who had worked in Suches under Ranger Woody whose name has been mentioned earlier is Ray M. Conarro, known to his friends as Connie, who in late 1945 was working out of the Atlanta office. On November 8, 1945, he wrote:

...I wanted so much to be with you on your last day of service. To be with you to swap memories of old times and thoughts of the future. I know of no place, away from home, where I feel better satisfied than I do at your place, and you must know that always I grow a bit in worldly knowledge each time I am there.

You may have received many letters from others, but, Arthur, I want you to realize that this one is from the heart. Your life has been one of usefulness; your cup runneth over for the goodness and mercy of your acts.

A letter from the Ranger's good friend of 15 years and former co-worker, Joseph C. Kircher, who by 1945 had worked his way up to the position of Regional Forester in the Atlanta office, dated September 8, 1945, reflects the much envied theme that was shared by many of the Ranger's Forest Service friends, that of the Ranger having spent an entire career in one place as opposed to being transferred around the country at various intervals. Kircher wrote:

You must get a lot of satisfaction as you look back over your accomplishments. In many ways you have been more fortunate than most of us in that you have spent your whole Forest Service career in one locality. It has given you the opportunity not only to develop that part of the Chattahoochee, but to be of tremendous service and influence in your community – among your own mountain folk. And you have taken full

> advantage in doing your part for a better "North Georgia." So you'll be able now to sit back, take it easy and look back at a job well done.

It goes without saying that the Ranger's long history of "giving back" to his community came about because of the kind of person he was, *not* because he happened to spend his entire career in one place. It is doubtful that few if any other Forest Service employees in history ever gave back to their community the way Ranger Woody did. Ranger He had no intention of ever leaving his home in the mountains and the Forest Service knew this all too well. He would have quit his job before moving to a new post.

During his prolonged illness, someone suggested that he travel to Florida and spend a few weeks in the sunshine trying to recuperate.

"'What, me go down there and drink that wiggle-tail water?' he responded. 'No thanks. I think I'll just stay right here in these mountains.'"

(The use of the term "wiggle-tail" water suggested that, unlike the superior crystal-clear, water of a mountain stream, the darkened water in Florida might have something suspicious growing in it. To Ranger Woody, nothing compared to the pure, life-giving water of a North Georgia mountain spring.)

Another very insightful letter from his special friend and co-worker, Sgt. Clint Davis, who had visited him in the hospital back in February and who had just returned stateside from his tour of duty in the Pacific with the Army during the war years, was written from the Atlanta headquarters of the Forest Service. Dated November 9, 1945, this letter attempted to be a little on the light-hearted side:

> Dear Arthur:
>
> I knew darn well that if I went into the Army and stayed out of North Georgia for a couple of years, you would get lazy and retire. Why in the hell you couldn't wait until I got back on the job is more than I can figure out. I suppose that running a ranger district interfered with your fishing and hunting, and you just couldn't let that happen, and to be truthful about it, I don't blame you.
>
> Sure sorry that I wasn't back on the job and able to get up to Suches to get a picture of you turning half of North Georgia over to Ted Seely. Since you had to give up the job, I am at least glad you waited until you could

get one of your own young bucks to turn it over to. I know Ted loves the country almost as much as you and I. It would be hard to find anyone more suited to take your place and carry on your life work as Ted Seely.

Arthur, I don't think I will ever be able to overcome the changes the war has brought about. Nothing could make me realize things have changed more than to know that Arthur Woody is not ranger on the Blue Ridge District. To me the mountains of North Georgia, with their beautiful forests, and their streams of fish and fields of deer, will always be symbolic of Arthur Woody. I am just thankful that you will continue to stay right there on the ground and keep a watchful eye over everything.

I have been very anxious to get by and see you since I returned from the Army, but not having an automobile it has been rather difficult to work out. Kenneth Rogers and I plan to drive up Sunday and spend some time shooting the bull with you. I have an idea that I will be up next week on the deer hunt also, but I am anxious to ride up on Sunday, when I have nothing to do, or anyone to nurse, and spend some time with you and the family.

While I am glad for you sake, and that of the family's, that you are retiring now in order to take it easy and get some much-needed rest, I am at the same time unable to express to you just how much I hate to see you leave the organization. During the past ten years it has been my pleasure to knock around quite a bit in the great American out-doors, and I have met hundreds of fellows who have done wonderful work in bringing back and protecting the blessings of nature, but I can frankly say that I have never found anyone who has put as much into their jobs and accomplished as much for the good of his fellow man than William Arthur Woody.

I am sure that the reason your work was such a great success is the fact that you mixed the love of your work with human kindness in dealing with one and all. Certainly no one man in our organization has succeeded as well as you in selling our work to the public. Long after you and I are both gone, your name and work will be well remembered by those who follow. What more can a man ask?

Looking forward to seeing you in the very near future, and the best of good wishes to your family, I am, as ever, your friend,

Clint Davis

Clint Davis said a mouthful when he stated that no one in the Forest Service had ever accomplished as much as his friend and mentor. Then he posed the question: *What more can a man ask for?* Certainly this reflected the feelings of dozens of Forest Service workers who had shared the privilege of working under Arthur Woody over the years. As true as these words might have been, some of Ranger Woody's supervisors and bosses in Gainesville, Atlanta and Washington D.C., would never have gone so far as to express an opinion like that. The man had simply gotten too famous, and the current leadership in the Forest Service had no intention of making a martyr out of him.

Dated November 7, 1945, the following letter was written by Lyle F. Watts, Chief of the U.S. Forest Service in Washington D.C. (Watts served as Forest Service Chief from 1943 to 1952.) It is what you might expect from a career Washington bureaucrat who was far-removed from the day-to-day workings of a District Forest Ranger – businesslike and not overly complimentary – especially in light of the fact that the man he was writing to had a long history of being a maverick ranger. Chief Lyle, too, mentioned the fact that Ranger Woody was fortunate to have spent his entire career in one place, as if that were the reason behind his incredible, never-to-be-duplicated list of accomplishments over the past 33 years:

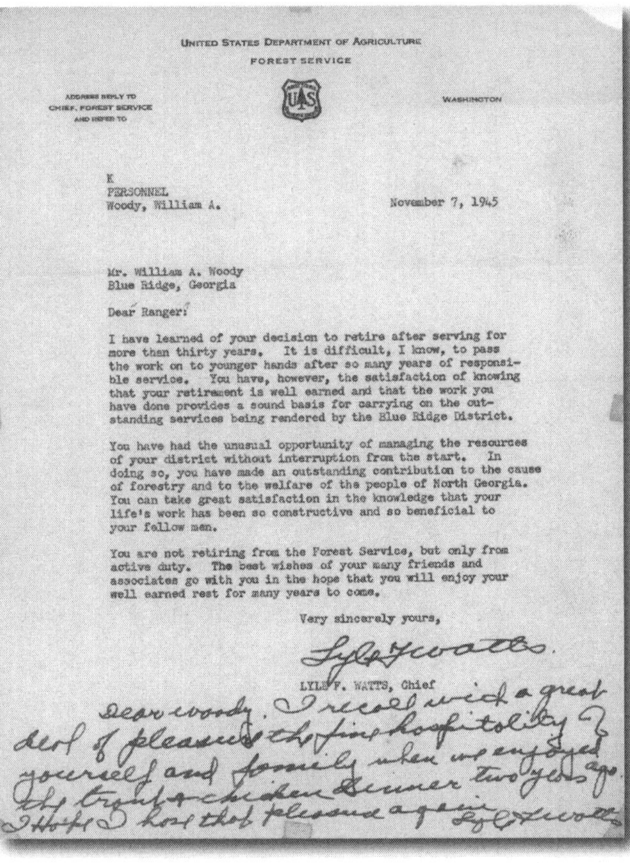

UNITED STATES DEPARTMENT OF AGRICULTURE
FOREST SERVICE

ADDRESS REPLY TO
CHIEF, FOREST SERVICE
AND REFER TO

WASHINGTON

K
PERSONNEL
Woody, William A.

November 7, 1945

Mr. William A. Woody
Blue Ridge, Georgia

Dear Ranger:

I have learned of your decision to retire after serving for more than thirty years. It is difficult, I know, to pass the work on to younger hands after so many years of responsible service. You have, however, the satisfaction of knowing that your retirement is well earned and that the work you have done provides a sound basis for carrying on the outstanding services being rendered by the Blue Ridge District.

You have had the unusual opportunity of managing the resources of your district without interruption from the start. In doing so, you have made an outstanding contribution to the cause of forestry and to the welfare of the people of North Georgia. You can take great satisfaction in the knowledge that your life's work has been so constructive and so beneficial to your fellow man.

You are not retiring from the Forest Service, but only from active duty. The best wishes of your many friends and associates go with you in the hope that you will enjoy your well earned rest for many years to come.

Very sincerely yours,

Lyle F. Watts.

LYLE F. WATTS, Chief

Dear Woody. I recall with a great deal of pleasure the fine hospitality of yourself and family when we enjoyed the trout & chicken dinner two years ago. I hope I have that pleasure again. Lyle F Watts

Letter from Lyle F. Watts, U.S. Forest Service chief from 1943 to 1952. Courtesy of Jean McNey.

Dear Ranger:

I have learned of your decision to retire after serving for more than thirty years. It is difficult, I know, to pass the work on to younger hands after so many years of responsible service. You have, however, the satisfaction of knowing that your retirement is well earned and that the work you have done provides a sound basis for carrying on the outstanding services being rendered by the Blue Ridge District.

You have had the unusual opportunity of managing the resources of your district without interruption from the start. In doing so, you have made an outstanding contribution to the cause of forestry and to the welfare of the people of North Georgia. You can take great satisfaction in the knowledge that your life's work has been so constructive and so beneficial to your fellow men.

You are not retiring from the Forest Service, but only from active duty. The best wishes of your many friends and associates go with you in the hope that you will enjoy your well earned rest for many years to come.

Very Sincerely Yours,
Lyle F. Watts, Chief

A handwritten postscript at the bottom of the typed letter added:

Dear Woody, I recall with a great deal of pleasure the fine hospitality of yourself and family when we enjoyed the trout and chicken dinner two years ago. I hope I have that pleasure again.

Lyle F. Watts

Like hundreds of other dignitaries, Forest Service workers and close friends like Charlie Elliott, Chief Watts had experienced the unforgettable thrill of being treated to a one-of-a-kind meal with the Woody family. He had never forgotten the experience.

By 1945, Ranger Woody had achieved so much and become so popular that a considerable amount of envy and jealousy existed among some of the higher-ups in Forest Service management. Among those ranks, it seemed that no one was willing to step out on a limb and give the Ranger the true amount of credit he deserved for his astounding record and his many accomplishments. People in high places simply didn't do that.

In fairness to the Chief and to the Forest Service in general, Ranger Woody had gone against the grain so many times that he had no doubt alienated some of his supervisors. Furthermore, many of his greatest achievements would not have been possible without the full support of the federal government and the timely arrival of an incredible labor force furnished by the Civilian Conservation Corps. Both entities contributed greatly to the end result, but it had never been a marriage made in heaven. Now, the end of an era was at hand. The sun was about to set on a period in history that could never be duplicated.

Ranger Arthur Woody and an unidentified boy stand in front of the Woody Gap totem pole during happier times with the Ranger's special friend, Georgia governor E.D. "Ed" Rivers, while attending an Easter Sunrise Service, circa 1939 or 1940. Commissioned by the CCC boys of Robertstown (in White County) and carved in his honor, Ranger Woody was extremely proud of the beautifully-carved pole. Photo courtesy of Jean McNey.

CHAPTER 18
End of an Era
A Grateful Public Pays Its Respects

"Courage is not having the strength to go on; it is going on when you don't have the strength."

Theodore Roosevelt

June 1946

World War II had finally ended and millions of war-weary Americans were trying their best to get back to some semblance of normalcy after four agonizing years of sacrifice and fighting. A new day was dawning in America. Millions of baby boomers would be soon clamoring to make their way in the world. National television was on the verge of invading every American household, and enthusiastic young couples were eager to buy automobiles and new houses in urban subdivisions. Americans were proud they had defeated the forces of evil and the American dream was alive and well.

In the tiny hamlet of Suches in the North Georgia mountains, there was a distinct pall in the air like a blanket of fog that would not go away. Ranger Arthur Woody, the larger-than-life character who had touched so many lives and accomplished so much during the past three decades, the man known far and wide as Kingfish or simply as "the Ranger," was fighting a desperate battle for his life, and with each passing day he was losing ground.

For the man who was so full of energy and plans for the future that he usually had two or three major projects going on at one time – it could not have been easy to face what was coming. For the first and only time in his 62 years of existence in the beloved mountain paradise he had helped create, the man who had always controlled his own destiny found himself having to yield to an overpowering and relentless foe that he was helpless to combat. To witness one's own life slipping away from a failing body must have been the ultimate challenge, an ordeal suffered by the entire family. To helplessly stand by and watch a loved one slowly waste away must have been the ultimate test of faith.

The Final Sunset

The below paragraphs reflect Jean McNey's sentiments as well as those of other close family members. Shortly after her grandfather's death, Jean was compelled to gather old photos and copies of articles and newspaper clippings and put them into a scrapbook as a permanent keepsake, and as a tribute and record of some of her grandfather's many achievements. Little did she imagine how invaluable those photos and articles inside that scrapbook would prove to be almost 70 years later during the production of this book.

> Ranger William Arthur Woody was generally known to his friends. He began his career with the Forest Service in 1912. He worked with survey crews and as a forest guard until 1918, when he received an appointment as Forest Ranger. From there until his retirement on September 30, 1945, his whole being was in his work with the Forest Service in the mountains he loved, associating with and helping his own mountain folk. He worked unceasingly to preserve forest lands, to open these mountains to the outside world by building good roads, and to replenish the mountains with fish and game. It was his life's work and he sincerely loved it.
>
> Aside from his work with the Forest Service, the Ranger was greatly interested in his community and did much to forward its improvement. He not only took part in the social gatherings of the community, as the Easter Sunrise Programs and the school entertainments, but he was earnestly interested in his fellow man and public progress. He helped to finance the building of a new church house for his church – Mt. Lebanon; he donated land on which Woody Gap School now stands for educational purposes and furnished most of the stone used in this construction. He had a big heart and used it to the advantage of his community and friends.
>
> Jean McNey, age 17

Lou Nichols remembers that her family was living in East Texas when her grandfather's condition began to worsen in 1945. She was 10 years old. Lou was born in White County in 1932 near Helen, Georgia, while her dad was working with the Forest Service in that area. Clyne started out as a water boy with the Forest Service in 1928 earning a dollar a day. He quickly worked his way up through the ranks to project manager for the CCC at Camp Woody, to forest ranger and eventually to forest engineer supervising the construction of many roads and improvements. For a number of years, he worked in Rabun County in Northeast Georgia with legendary Ranger Nick Nicholson, Georgia's first forest ranger. During World War II, Clyne was transferred to Lufkin, Texas, (in East Texas) where he supervised a German prisoner-of-war camp.

"When Papa's condition worsened and it became clear that he would probably not recover from his severe kidney condition, Daddy requested a transfer back to the southeast," Lou said. "The closest assignment he could get to Suches was in Murphy, North Carolina, where he served as a Forest Ranger. We drove back and forth quite a bit.

"Before Papa got sick, Daddy always spent his vacation time in Suches. As a young girl, I spent most of the summer with my grandparents. But unlike Jean, I spent a lot more time with my grandmother than I did my grandfather. For one thing, Papa was always out working somewhere, so I didn't get to see that much of him when I was growing up."

After his retirement ceremony in September 1945, Ranger Woody's health continued to decline for the next six months. Then, on March 22, 1946, he suffered what the family described as a severe convulsion. This might well have been another stroke or a heart attack.

"That was really the beginning of the end," Jean said. "From that time on, he was mostly bedridden and he drifted in and out of consciousness. He continued to lose strength until June 10, when the last bit of life ebbed away. During the final weeks, when Papa's kidneys were failing, we often built a roaring fire in the fireplace. We would wrap him in quilts and put his feet in a tub of hot water in an attempt to sweat out some of the poisons and impurities in his body.

"One night, about a week before he died, he'd had a particularly rough night. June and my mother took turns staying up with him all night long. The next morning he told my mother: 'Mae, I was almost gone last night. There was just a little chord holding me on. Mae, I saw it all and it was a beautiful place. But you'd be surprised at some of the people who were there. I saw people who we didn't think would ever be there, and some we thought would be there for sure were not. So you be good to everybody.'"

A haggard and hollow-eyed Ranger Woody poses with his family for the last family picture ever taken. The photo was taken in March 1945 shortly after the Ranger was released from Georgia Baptist Hospital, and a little over a year before his death. (From left to right, back row) Ned White (Jean's brother, Arthur's grandson); Mae Woody (Jean's mother, Arthur's daughter); Lou Nichols (Clyne's daughter, Arthur's granddaughter); Bill Woody (Walter's second son); Clyne (Lou's father, Arthur's second son); Dick Woody (Walter's oldest son); June Woody (Arthur's wife); Walter Woody, (Arthur's first son); Mina Woody (Walter's wife); (Front row): Ma Woody (Arthur's mother); Olene Woody (Clyne's wife, Lou's mother); Jean White McNey (Arthur's granddaughter, Mae's daughter); Arthur Woody; Barbara Woody (Clyne's daughter, Lou's sister); next to Ma Woody looking at unidentified girl. Photo courtesy of Jean McNey.

As things continued to worsen during the last few months of the Ranger's life, Dr. Turner suggested, "Try to get a little whiskey in him. It'll get his system going faster. But be careful how much you give him. In the long run, too much whiskey could cause him to become depressed."

It was a trade-off but one that Dr. Turner deemed worth the risk. Since he and Ranger Woody had enjoyed so many happy days together during better times partaking in an occasional "swaller" or two of delightful, homemade mountain dew, he knew the Ranger would not just settle for any old whiskey.

"Clyne was able to get a particularly tasty brand of corn liquor known as 'Tusquittee' from the locals where he worked in North Carolina," Jean said. "The Ranger seemed to like it. We'd give him several spoonfuls and it did seem to help."

(Tusquittee, originally spelled "Tusquitee," is a mountain community located in Clay County, North Carolina. Tusquitee is a Cherokee Indian word meaning, "Where the water-dogs laughed." A water dog, or mud-puppy, is a type of salamander found in the East that can grow over a foot long. The nearby Tusquitee Mountain Range, located inside the Nantahala National Forest, is just north of the community named for it.)

As mentioned in Chapter 9, Horace E. Shelton Jr. of Atlanta accompanied his dad on a number of fishing trips to Woody Lake when he was a small boy during the early 1940s. Horace's dad dropped by to see Ranger Woody shortly before the Ranger's death.

During the early months of 1946, my dad knew about Arthur Woody's illness and he had been keeping up with it. One day in early June, when my parents and I had driven up to the mountains to do some fishing at Lake Chatuge, Dad said, 'I think I'll drive down to Suches and see how the Ranger is getting along.' Ordinarily he would not have wanted to bother the Woody family, but for some reason, he felt compelled to go that day.

"We drove over to Suches, and dad got out and went inside the house alone. He had no idea how bad the situation really was. He was only inside for a few minutes. When he came back out and got into the car he had a somber look on his face. My mother asked him how the Ranger was. He drove off very slowly and said, 'It's bad. He didn't even know who I was.'"

One of the Ranger's last requests involved his final resting place. "I've had a good life and I've accomplished what I wanted to do," he told those closest to him. "All I ask is that you bury me so that I can see Black Mountain when I come up out of that grave on resurrection day." The wish was honored. Today, not only Ranger Woody, but June and a number of other family members are buried on the beautiful little knoll in the picturesque church cemetery that sits across the road on a picturesque hillside just above Mt. Lebanon Baptist Church. To the east, Black Mountain fills the skyline like a great, silent sentinel.

Ranger Woody died on June 10, 1946. Ironically, at the time of his death, Clyne's wife Olene had been suffering from kidney stones and had been admitted to Emory Hospital in Atlanta. The Ranger's body was kept at the house for several days until she was well enough to attend the service in Suches.

The Service

The funeral was held Thursday June 13, 1946, at 2 p.m. at Mt. Lebanon Baptist Church. Reverend Claude C. Boynton officiated. Reverend H.G. Jarrard read from the scripture, and Reverend Allyn C. Johnson led the prayers. Judge Thomas S. Candler spoke at the service. Fittingly, the pallbearers were Ted Seely, the Ranger who would be taking Ranger Woody's place, Ranger Nick

The Easter Sunrise Service at Woody Gap in April 1938 was attended by Ranger Woody's good friend, Georgia Governor E.D. "Ed" Rivers, and broadcast live on WSB radio. The young blond girl standing behind Governor Rivers is Jean White (McNey). The smaller girl to Jean's right is her cousin Lou Nichols, Clyne Woody's daughter. Note the uniformed CCC boys in the crowd. Photo courtesy of Jean McNey.

Nicholson, Mat Caldwell, Ed L. Reese, Raymond M. "Connie" Conarro of the Forest Service, A.C Shaw, and of course, Charlie Elliott.

(Judge Thomas Slaughter Candler was an influential attorney and prominent citizen from Blairsville who helped Ranger Woody with a number of important projects in Union County. Candler served as an associate justice on the Georgia Supreme Court from 1945 to 1966.)

A number of other Forest Service officials from the Gainesville and Atlanta offices were listed as Honorary Pallbearers. That list included Chattahoochee National Forest Supervisor C. K. Spaulding, Crawford DuPree (the Forest Service accountant who was forever asking the ranger to please cash his paychecks), and local Ranger Lethcoe. No doubt many of the Ranger's most dedicated friends and supporters who had interned under him at one time or another would have given a king's ransom to attend the service, but many of these Forest Service officials were by this time either in Washington D.C. or stationed in various other places around the country. Since the Ranger's illness had been so prolonged and unpredictable, few of these men were in a position to travel to North Georgia and attend the service on the spur of the moment. Although they would have liked to!

Music included "Nearer My God to Thee," "Saved by Grace," My Latest Sun," and Pearly White City." Various news reports stated that an estimated 1,500 people attended the service. Clyde Harkins, then 21, who was at the service with his family, maintained, "There were many hundreds of people in attendance, but I don't think the number reached 1,500." Whatever the exact number might have been, scores of people from all walks of life came to pay their respects to one of the greatest forest rangers, grass-roots conservationist and humanitarian of the 20th century.

Articles and Eulogies

The following story appeared in the Washington Information Digest, a weekly news bulletin sent out to Forest Service employees, on June 12, 1946. Since portions of the story were so similar to Bill Bergoffen's narrative in Chapter 1, it is a safe bet to assume that he authored this release.

Death of Ranger Arthur William Woody

At 2:15 p.m., Monday June 10 (1946), Ranger Arthur Woody of the Blue Ridge District of the Chattahoochee National Forest in Georgia passed over the great Divide. Death followed an extended illness which developed into serious complications, so serious that much of the time during the last two months "The Ranger" was in a semi-conscious condition.

Ranger Woody was born near the headquarters of the Blue Ridge District, April 1, 1884. As a boy, he tramped, hunted and fished every ridge, cove and creek of this district. On Oct. 1, 1912, he worked his first day for the Forest Service, and on July 1, 1918, he became the first Ranger in Georgia. (Actually Ranger Nick Nicholson was Georgia's first Forest Ranger. Arthur Woody was the second.) On this same job and on this same district he served faithfully for 30 years, until his retirement on September 30, 1945. On his district, one of the largest in the country, the Ranger worked constantly for improved forest resources, schools, churches, roads, medical care, and recreation. Rich and poor alike from everywhere beat a path to the door of the Ranger whose traits in real life closely resembled those of the fictional "Scattergood Bains." A pile of weather-worn boards mark the spot where the Ranger was born 62 years ago. Nearby a great granite school building stands as a monument to his generosity and labor. A living monument of silent trees with its vibrant wildlife extends for miles in every direction from his last resting place. The memory of the ranger will live on every trail, every ridge crossing, every tall fire tower, and every cool, clear trout stream on his beloved Blue Ridge District. His friends and associates deeply mourn his death.

Taken from Jean McNey's scrapbook, the credit on the following newspaper clipping reads "Constitution State News Service." (Probably the wire service arm of the Atlanta Constitution in 1946.)

Service Thursday for W.A. Woody at Mt. Lebanon

Suches, June 11 – Funeral services for William Arthur Woody, last of the old-time forest rangers and one of the most colorful characters in the entire U.S. Forest Service, will be held at 2:30 p.m. at Mt. Lebanon Church.

Ranger Woody died Monday at his home at the foot of Woody's Gap within a few miles of the area in which he had been born and raised.

He had been employed in the Chattahoochee National Forest in the Blue Ridge District since 1912. Years ago the Forestry Service began giving preference to college-trained men in their selection of rangers, and the well-known woodsman represented the last of a line of forest workers whose essential training came largely from contact with outdoor life.

His superiors in the U.S. Forest Service, however, said he had "one of the most uncanny minds for forestry and wildlife" they had ever witnessed. Young rangers, fresh out of college, whom he took under his tutelage for basic instruction in wildlife conservation, now are occupying high positions in the U. S. Forest Service councils.

Through his influence, the Federal Game Refuge was started in the North Georgia mountains. When the State Assembly outlawed deer hunting in the northern counties, Mr. Woody took his own savings, bought several deer and turned them lose in what is now the Chattahoochee National Forest.

The Woody Gap School is another project instituted through efforts of the beloved ranger. Before the school was started, Mr. Woody aided in financing the high school education of many youths in his area who had to go to other regions for their schooling because of the lack of educational facilities near their homes.

In failing health for many years, he had retired to his huge farm in the foothills of the Blue Ridge Mountains

(The "Federal Game Refuge" referred to above is the Rock Creek/Blue Ridge WMA. The reference to a "huge" farm in the foothills of the Blue Ridge Mountains owned by Ranger Woody is an exaggeration. He owned numerous parcels of real estate at the time of his death, but he never owned a "huge" farm in Suches.)

From the Gainesville Eagle,
June 13, 1946

Ranger Arthur Woody

When DEATH closed in sleep the eyes of Ranger William Arthur Woody Monday afternoon (June 10, 1946, 2:15 p.m.), it ended an era in the mountains of Northeast Georgia. Ranger Woody had spent his entire life there and the imprint of his personality, his ideals, his dreams and his determination will remain for years to come.

Arthur Woody saw a long way. Years, ago when wildlife reached its lowest ebb, in his mountains, he fought for its return, its preservation and its conservation. It was he, more than anyone else, who was responsible for the return of deer and their increase to the point where hunters might once more legally bag the game. Arthur Woody, although a U.S. Ranger, was virtually a law unto himself in that regard – he took such a personal interest in wildlife that he needed no Government regulations.

Arthur Woody saw roads through the rugged granite of the Blue Ridge. He worked for them helped promote them, and his knowledge of the terrain was happily imparted to those who would string the winding ribbons over the steep sides of dangerous cliffs.

Arthur Woody was known throughout the land among hunters and fishermen as their friend. They thought the world of him because he was interested in their world, slaved for it for 35 years and died still alert and active in its behalf. Arthur Woody will never be forgotten by these friends.

His life is a testimonial to the value of conservation. By the strength of his character and determination, he restored much of the hunting and fishing now enjoyed among his Blue Ridge Mountains. What he did, can and will be carried on because Arthur Woody was sound in his thinking and his ideals were practical.

North Georgia can be a paradise for those who love the out-of-doors. Arthur Woody knew this many years ago and he dedicated his life to helping to bring this paradise to pass. He has gone now, but his works will live after him, Arthur Woody served his fellow man.

The following story, dated July 1, 1946, appeared in Southern Outdoors, a weekly outdoor newsprint supplement that was inserted into the Atlanta Constitution.

Woody Buried; Wildlife Loses 'Best Friend'

By John Martin, editor and publisher

The end of a rich and fruitful life in the woods came to Ranger Arthur Woody on June 10 at the age of 61 and with his death the South lost its foremost native conservationist.

"The Ranger," as he was affectionately known by hosts of hunters and fishermen in Georgia and over the South, died after a lingering illness caused by a series of several heart attacks.

His death came at his North Georgia home only eight months after his retirement as District Ranger for the U.S. Forest Service. He was buried at Mt. Lebanon Church Cemetery in the shadow of Black Mountain where he was born April 1, 1885.

Funeral services for Ranger Woody were attended by a throng of over 1,500 friends from all walks of life and from all parts of Georgia.

(Actually the Ranger was 62 and born April 1, 1884.)

SOUTHERN OUTDOOR

Combined with OUTDOOR GEORGIA

Where Friends and the Outdoors Meet

SIXTH YEAR — NUMBER 24 ATLANTA, GA., JULY 1, 1946

WHEN WOODY WAS ROLLING—This picture, made by the late Walter Sparks, Atlanta news photographer, caught Ranger Arthur Woody (right) at the peak of success in wildlife restoration in the Chattahoochee National Forest. It was made in the spring of 1939 near Rock Creek Lake while Woody explained to Clint Davis, now with the Forest Service in Washington, why a brook trout is superior to the rainbow. Woody died at his home at Woody Gap June 10.

Woody Buried; Wildlife Loses 'Best Friend'

The end of a rich and fruitful life in the woods came to Ranger Arthur Woody on June 10 at the age of 61 and with his death the South lost its foremost native conservationist.

"The Ranger," as he was affectionately known by hosts of hunters and fishermen in Georgia and over the South, died after a lingering illness caused by a series of severe heart attacks.

His death came at his North Georgia home only eight months after his retirement as District Ranger for the U. S. Forest Service. He was buried at Mt. Lebanon Church Cemetery in the shadow of Black Mountain where he was born April 1, 1885.

Funeral services for Ranger Woody were attended by a throng of over 1,500 friends from all walks of life and from all parts of Georgia.

STICKLER FOR 'SPECKS'

Woody was with the Forest Service 30 years, during which he established a national record in forest fire prevention. He had won numerous citations for his work in restoration and protection of timberland.

A true woodsman and student of nature, Woody championed wildlife fundamentals. He preferred to increase and improve native species of game, leaving the exotics to the laboratory. Brook trout, which he called "specks," were his favorite fish, and the turkey was the bird for which he worked to restore in the mountains near his home at Woody Gap.

In his early years Woody was an expert rifleman and fisherman. Several times he bagged wild turkeys in full flight with his trusty rifle. He never lost his touch with rifles and guns and at

Continued on Page 2

Hunting
Fail to Su
Game Est

Results in the bag at the end
the figures in game surveys mad
in the South.

A survey recently compiled by a leading manufacturer of arms and ammunition, and consisting of figures submitted by officials of game and fish departments in 16 Southern states—including West Virginia and Oklahoma—paints a glowing picture of the abundance of rabbits, squirrels and bobwhite quail.

It takes brave souls, of course, with above-average temerity, to make a game estimate. But it takes more than youthful enthusiasm and good judgment to say that the populations of these farm game species will increase five, and again 20, years from today.

FIGURES MISLEADING

Only one of the 15 states—Georgia — reported findings that match those of the man behind the gun. The Georgia estimate was based on the reports and kills of hunters who have seen the supply of quail gradually slump during the past 20 years. While some predictions went overboard and

Pay No M

THE rod and reel racket that
was just the beginning of w
do not subscribe to the common
are suckers and will buy anythin
so starved for equipment that t
four prices for rods and reels.

These daylight holdups are
pawn shops, free lancers and ot
and other Southern cities. It sta
ceilings were abolished. The out
having a holiday at the expens
goods houses.

The black market operators
their own prices, so fantastic tha
$100 fight seats look like charita
cific, we saw a $1.90 Ocean City
$6.50. Another victim showed
made to retail for $6.50 each. H
for them.

Reputable retail sporting goo
same kind of robberies and get

GAME LOG
By Charlie Elliott

Ranger Arthur Woody

We stood where the forest flowed over the brow of the mountain and swept downward in an emerald current to the narrow river valley.

It was one of those rare days in early summer without a wisp of cloud, without a breath of air, and the valleys filled to the brim with silence.

With a simple gesture of humility, Ranger Arthur Woody took off his hat and crumpled it in his hand.

"I'm glad," he said, "that these hills were mine for a little while."

Arthur Woody was one of the few men I ever knew who had the ability of preaching great sermons in a few simple words.

Woody Left an Enduring Monument

Sports Editors

In 1946, the outdoor media practically worshipped Ranger Arthur Woody, and many special tributes like this one in Southern Outdoors were written in his honor. News clipping courtesy of Jean McNey.

Stickler for 'Specks'

Woody was with the Forest Service 30 years, during which he established a national record in forest fire prevention. He had won numerous citations for his work in restoration and protection of timberland.

A true woodsman and student of nature, Woody championed wildlife fundamentals. He preferred to increase and improve native species of game, leaving the exotics to the laboratory. Brook trout, which he called "specks," were his favorite fish, and the turkey was the bird for which he worked to restore in the mountains near his home at Woody Gap.

In his early years, Woody was an expert rifleman and fisherman. Several times he bagged wild turkeys in full flight with his trusty rifle. He never lost his touch with rifles and guns and at the time of his death had a collection of fine weapons.

Once, a hunter who took his share of turkeys and deer, the Ranger later became so interested in restocking the forests with whitetails that he disliked seeing a buck taken by anyone. But he was every inch a true sportsman and showed numerous riflemen stands from which they took trophy heads on supervised hunts in the Blue Ridge Management Area. (In truth, Ranger Woody never killed a deer, and in later life, never wanted to.)

Recovered Twice

Six months before he died, Woody was only a shadow of the 250-pound man who roamed the hills in any kind of weather. He partially recovered twice from severe heart attacks that would have counted out anyone with less stamina and determination.

Life was not worth living to Woody if it couldn't be in his beloved mountains. Friends once suggested that he go to Florida for his health.

"Me go down there and drink wiggle-tail water? What's the use to live if it can't be up here?"

With the Ranger gone, Woody Gap and North Georgia will never be the same to hundreds of hunters and fishermen, who agree that there was only one Arthur Woody and there'll never be another in this or any other generation.

Ironically, a short article that appeared just under the above tribute to Ranger Woody carried this headline:

Kirby Catches 4-Pound Brown

ROCK CREEK, Ga. – A 4-pound brown trout, largest of the season in Georgia, was taken here last week by Howard Kirby of Dial. The trout was 20 inches long and fell for a gob of red worms.

Could this have been one of the big fish Ranger Woody reportedly knew by name? If not, he no doubt sported a huge grin that day from his lofty pinnacle in the sky for this certainly seemed to be a sign from heaven!

In a continuation of the same Southern Outdoors issue dated July 1, 1946, Charlie Elliott had this to say:

SOUTHERN OUTDOORS (continued)
Where Friends and the Outdoors Meet
Atlanta, GA, July 1, 1946

GAME LOG
By Charlie Elliott

Ranger Arthur Woody

We stood where the forest flowed over the brow of the mountain and swept downward in an emerald current to the narrow river valley.

It was one of those rare days in early summer without a wisp of cloud, without a breath of air, and the valleys filled to the brim with silence.

With a simple gesture of humility, Ranger Arthur Woody took off his hat and crumpled it in his hand.

"I'm glad," he said, "that these hills were mine for a little while."

Arthur Woody was one of the few men I ever knew who had the ability of preaching great sermons in a few simple words.

Woody Left an Enduring Monument

The Ranger lived out the years of his life under the shadow of the southern Blue Ridge. He was brought up in a virgin, rugged land, where a man walked or rode horseback and followed an Indian trail from one settlement to another. The country was full of game – deer, bear, grouse, squirrels. He was with his father when the elder Woody killed the last deer in the mountains. At least a part of his life was devoted to rectifying that mistake.

He helped the United States Forest Service purchase land for what was first the Cherokee and later the Chattahoochee National Forest. He helped establish the game refuges and management areas. He bought deer with money out of his own pocket to restock the protected areas. And he was replenishing what his people before him and their neighbors had taken away.

By all the standards, Arthur Woody was a great man. They'll probably never chisel his features in marble for the Hall of Fame. He has left a more enduring monument in the hundreds of square miles of mountain hardwood forests, in the deer herds which have spread throughout the mountain counties. He has left his name in the hearts of those who love the out-of-doors, of those who follow the white water of Cooper's Creek, the Toccoa and the Chestatee with a fly rod.

By the mid 1940s when Ranger Woody's health began to deteriorate, his longtime friend of the past 20 years, Charlie Elliott, had become a "big shot" as director of the Georgia Game and Fish Commission. Always humble and down to earth, Charlie wrote several heartfelt eulogies about his beloved friend and also spoke at the Ranger's funeral service in Suches. Photo, circa late 1940s, courtesy of the Charlie Elliott Wildlife Center.

For Worship and Education

Woody's influence and kindliness reached beyond the boundaries of the forest. Legend are the stories of a helping hand he gave to his neighbors in need. His generosity was always so matter of fact, so casual that many times it did not dawn on one until later what a fine deed the Ranger had done.

His thinking was basic. He knew the need of community worship and education, and he helped build a church and a school. He took part in the Easter Sunrise Services held annually at Woody Gap. He worked to bring the mountains away from Indian trails to paved and gravel roads.

Underneath it all, his first love was the wilderness and the creatures of the wilderness. I have driven with him slowly over the mountain road, while he pointed out where a big buck slid down the embankment, where a gobbler had made V-scratches in leaves beyond the tire tracks. I've never seen him more indignant than when we found where two wildcats had pulled down a fawn in the snow. He made it a personal issue between himself and the cats until they came to a sudden and untimely end.

Joins Vanishing Race of Pioneers

For the last 10 years of his life with the Forest Service, Arthur Woody looked forward to retiring, to spending the remainder of his days in the woods and on the streams of his district.

"I know the big trout by name," he said, "and I'll have to be smart to get 'em on a hook."

The years of hard existence took their toll. He was a tired old man when the government retired him after 30 years of active service. He had given his life to something that he himself would never be able to enjoy.

He has gone on to join a vanishing race of pioneers. He left behind the singing streams, the beauty of his forests, the solitudes of an earthly wilderness which were his for so short a span of years.

A Celestial Fly Rod for the Ranger

If there is a divine compensation for the toil and privations of an uncertain physical existence, I know that the Creator has hidden away a happy hunting and fishing ground somewhere in a cranny of His heaven. It is a land for fellows like Arthur Woody. There are deer and turkey and squirrels and there'll be a grouse drumming on the hill.

In His infinite wisdom and justice, the Big Boss has already handed Arthur a celestial fly rod and line, with an amazing assortment of flies. There are big trout in the bend of the river and for the remainder of all eternity the old Ranger will be thinking of ways to outwit them.

With all my heart, I hope it is true and that Arthur Woody's just reward will be forever instead of for just a little while.

Letters of Consolation

Many of the letters received by the family mentioned the fact that Ranger Woody always thought about others and was always willing to serve his community.

"I have a satisfied faith and conviction that the Ranger now and forever will enjoy God's eternal reward for kindness and consideration to others – all our religion, our faith, our hopes – deal with our relations with our fellow man and not ourselves – the Ranger, just like any great preacher or humanitarian, fulfilled a call and will know God's just reward."

Milt, U.S. Forest Service, Washington, DC
(Milton Bryan)

"...his memory will live on with us on the Blue Ridge District in the many improvements for which he was responsible as an inspiration and a reminder of the value of good citizenship and unselfish service."

J. Herbert Stone, Regional Forester,
U.S. Forest Service, Atlanta, Georgia

"I feel that I have lost one of the best friends I have ever had and North Georgia one of its most valuable citizens."

Congressman John S. Wood,
9th District, Georgia

"Every time I see a deer or bear out in the forest or look at the rainbow trout basking and playing in the clear waters of our mountain streams, I am sure that I will see the jovial face of the Ranger, smiling on them with much satisfaction.

As he had requested, Ranger Woody was buried on a beautiful knoll above Mt. Lebanon Baptist Church, so that, in his own words, "I can see Black Mountain when I come up out of that grave on resurrection day." According to Charlie Elliott, "he never wore his religion on his shoulder like some people do in life, but he expressed his Christian upbringing and his deep faith by constantly helping others." Duncan Dobie photo.

Few men loved the birds, fishers and animals of the forest as did the ranger and none did more to see that they got a square deal. This spirit, I am sure, will live on forever."

R.I. Lowndes Jr.,
U.S. Forest Service, Cleveland, Tennessee

"I would like for you to remember that the memories of Ranger Woody will live on in the U.S. Forest Service as long as there is a National Forest in Georgia and a Blue Ridge District.

"You have the satisfaction of knowing that you married a man who did as much, if not more for conserving one of the nation's natural resources in Georgia, than anyone else."

C. Joe Galloway,
U.S. Forest Service, Alexandria, Louisiana

"I dare say there wasn't a person anywhere who had so nearly woven himself into the pattern of his community as Mr. Woody. Nor will anyone ever take his place. The story of his life would be most interesting book material."

Wanda Jones, Dahlonega, Georgia

"I want you to know that not only his friends, but the entire (Forest) Service, have lost with the passing of Arthur Woody, probably one of the most famous Rangers the Forest Service has ever had."

Frank A. Albert, Jackson, Mississippi

"We shall miss him; his cheerful greetings; his manifold acts of kindness and his genial nature will be cherished by his friends and associates."

A.R. Jordan

A Lasting Memorial for the Ranger

Dedication of the Bronze Plaque to Ranger Woody at Woody Gap

April 1947

The following story was taken from a newspaper clipping in Jean McNey's scrapbook. It is not known where the story originated.

A Great Sportsman to Be Honored Sunday

We are delighted that sportsmen and outdoorsmen will Sunday pay homage to the later Arthur Woody by unveiling a bronze bust of him on Woody's gap on Black Mountain. Arthur Woody deserves all the credit sportsmen can give him, and our only regret is that the fund to buy the bust was not raised soon enough to unveil a monument to him while he was still alive.

Arthur Woody can be called the father of forest protection and wildlife preservation in North Georgia. It was he who first imported the Virginia white-tailed deer to Georgia and turned them loose in the mountains near Grassy Gap. It was he who won the respect and friendship and cooperation of mountaineers in preserving the woods and wildlife. He paved the way and showed them how they could keep the mountains beautiful and make them a great tourist and hunter's paradise and yet yield an annual harvest of timber and game.

He showed the CCC boys where to build roads, and solicited the support of friends and neighbors in fighting forest fires that used to annually destroy millions of feet of timber, which was worth thousands of dollars.

Arthur Woody was a great man, a great sportsman and a great naturalist. The Black Mountain-Woody Gap memorial is a fitting tribute.

In a quiet but heartfelt ceremony, the bronze plaque was dedicated at Woody Gap in April 1947. The ceremony and the plaque were particularly meaningful to members of the Woody family. The 2x3-foot bronze plaque featuring the bust of Arthur Woody by well-known Atlanta artist Steffen Thomas (1906-1990) was placed on a large boulder about 4 feet tall at Woody Gap during a ceremony attended by numerous friends, family members and donors. The huge boulder was carefully chosen from a spot on the side of Black Mountain and moved to Woody Gap, a fitting tribute to the Ranger. A number of prominent people including Charlie Elliott spoke at the dedication.

This next story was also taken from a newspaper clipping in Jean's scrapbook. Although there is no byline, date or publication name with the clipping, it likely appeared in the Atlanta Constitution in early 1947.

The Woody clan was present at the bittersweet dedication of the bronze plaque on Woody Gap in April 1947. (Front row, left to right) Ma Woody, foreground with cane; June Woody; Jean White (McNey); Walter's wife, Mina Woody; Lou Woody (Nichols); Mae White; Ned White; (Back row, unknown lady and two men behind Ma Woody); Walter's son, Bill Woody; Clyne Woody; Walter Woody; Olene Woody, Clyne's wife. Several close friends including Charlie Elliott spoke at the dedication. The plaque was later stolen by vandals. Photo courtesy of Jean McNey.

Ceremonies, Bust Will Honor Woody

Sportsmen from all over the South will pay tribute to the late Arthur Woody, when a larger-than-life bust of the nationally known and loved forest ranger is unveiled at ceremonies starting at 1 o'clock next Sunday afternoon at Woody's Gap.

The famous mountaineer, a real pioneer forester who perhaps did more than any one man for the conservation and restoration of white-tailed deer and trout in the State, will be honoured by a large group including many of his mountaineer friends from Union and Towns counties.

Speeches at the ceremony on top of Black Mountain, will be made by Charlie Elliott, Director of Georgia's State Game and Fish Commission; Herbert Stone (Forest Service); Frank Gross (state senator and good friend of the ranger's); Dr. Clabus Lloyd and others. The bust based on a huge 10-ton limestone boulder from Woody's one-time favorite haunts, was done by Steffan Thomas, famous sculptor from Stone Mountain. The likeness pictures Woody wearing his favourite and well-remembered battered hat.

The bust is the first ever erected to a conservationist in the South, and is a fitting tribute to the former District Forester of the Chattahoochee game management area in North Georgia. Woody, who could neither read nor write until later in life, won national recognition for his fire prevention record, and for his unparalleled conservation work.

(Despite some stories to the contrary, Ranger Woody could read and write very proficiently. Although he was never known as a prolific writer, reading official reports and other news items was an important part of his job. Depending on who he happened to be talking to at the time, however, he might have been inclined to lead some people into believing he had a full-fledged college education, while with other individuals he was perfectly content to allow them to think he was an uneducated hillbilly who could neither read nor write.)

The following article appeared in the "So I Hear" column in the sports section of the Atlanta Constitution. Since this clipping was also pasted into Jean's scrapbook, no byline or date appeared with it.

So I Hear

Sunday April 24, (1947) a ceremony took place to honor Arthur Woody with a Bronze Bust of the Ranger wearing his always-present rumpled old hat set in a huge boulder on Black Mountain. Reportedly 250 people (friends) contributed $1 each to have the bronze made 2x3 feet in size in which his likeness appears with a suitable inscription.

The huge rock was rolled down the mountainside to a spot near the road (where the Appalachian Trail crosses the gap so that visitor's people can stop and view it.

One newspaper account: "It was a fitting tribute to a grand man who loved the mountains and all that they stand for."

Arthur Woody was a huge man physically, and the boulder will remind one of his ruggedness and the great strength of his character. He knew every crook and trail in the mountains and he never had any desire to leave them. In fact, it is my opinion that nowhere else on earth would he have been satisfied to live.

Deer Pens

He loved the wildlife of the mountains and I remember when wild turkeys ranged within a short distance of his home. When a corral was built and deer brought in to restock the area, Ranger Woody was jealous of his charges and nothing roused his ire more than for some poacher to kill one of them. He built a beautiful lake near his home which he stocked with bass and bream and it was a pleasure to him for his friends to come by and enjoy an afternoon's fishing. Nobody was as proud of the roads that the CCC boys built through the forest as Arthur Woody, and when the forest service expanded them he was highly pleased.

Deer Hunts

On the supervised deer hunts, which have been held for a number of years, except during the war period, Ranger Woody met with and joshed many hunters whom he had never seen or heard of before, all of whom admired and respected this giant of the hills.

Also taken from a cut-out clipping in Jean's scrapbook with no byline and no date or publication name, this next article probably appeared in the Atlanta Constitution just prior to the dedication ceremony in April 1947.

Sadly, the memorial plaque at Woody Gap only remained on the mountain for about 10 years. It was stolen by vandals during the late 1950s or early '60s. Bad blood runs deep in the mountains, and the bronze could have been stolen by a person or persons whose jealousy of Ranger Woody and the Woody family spanned several generations. The huge boulder on which the plaque had been attached was later moved from Woody Gap to the front yard of the old Ranger Station across from Ranger Woody's house in Suches. A new plaque (much smaller in size), honoring Ranger Woody (with no likeness, but bearing his date of birth and death), was placed on the rock where it still resides today near Highway 60.

In the Shadow of Black Mountain
Woody Family Burials

Most of Ranger Woody's immediate family including his beloved wife and three children are also buried in the hillside cemetery above Mt. Lebanon Baptist Church.

The ranger's mother, Elizabeth or "Eliza" Ingram Woody, or "Ma" Woody as she was fondly known to almost everyone, died Sept. 12, 1959 at the age of 90. She outlived her son by 13 years.

The Ranger's beloved wife, Nancy Emma Abercrombie, or June, was born Sept. 1, 1877. She died on Aug. 12, 1973 at age 96. She outlived her husband by 27 years.

Ranger Woody's eldest son, Walter "Walt" Willis Woody, was born on July 13, 1902. He died on January 25, 1986 at age 84.

Ranger Woody's second son, Clyne Woody, was born April 30, 1905. He died on December 1, 1984 at age 79. He worked for the Forest Service for 30 years.

Ranger Woody's daughter, Vella Mae Woody, was born on July 15, 1907. She died April 6, 1986, only three months after her brother Walter, at age 79.

Ranger Woody's father, Abraham Lincoln Woody or "Granddaddy Abe" as he was often called, was born in Lumpkin County on July 23, 1864. He died Sept. 5, 1919 at age 55. He was buried at Mt. Zion Baptist Church cemetery just up the road from Mt. Lebanon Baptist Church.

Ned Woody White, Jean's younger brother, born Aug. 18, 1933, died on Feb. 8, 2010. He lived just across the lake from Jean's house where the original Woody home once stood. As a boy, he too had been extremely close to his grandfather.

After the bronze plaque at Woody Gap was stolen in the late 1950s, the ceremonial boulder was relocated and placed in front of the old Ranger Station near the road across from the Woody homestead. A smaller plaque was installed. Truly, Ranger Arthur Woody was a pioneer in so many areas. Duncan Dobie photo.

Always the teacher, Georgia's most popular forest ranger takes in a splendid mountain view of the Yahoola Valley with two pretty Girl Scouts. He loved nothing better than to share his vast outdoor knowledge with youngsters and teach them about nature and conservation. The photo was made near the top of Woody Gap where the Appalachian Trail crosses what is now Highway 60 on Black Mountain. Ranger Woody was very instrumental in the building both the trail and the highway. The photo was taken several years before the Ranger's health began to fail when he was still vibrant and full of energy. Photo circa 1940, courtesy of Jean McNey.

CHAPTER 19
Last of the Old-Time Forest Rangers

"Occasionally there lives a man whose life enriches his own era and is a real heritage to the future. Simple and untutored, Arthur Woody was such a man."

Charlie Elliott, 1946

Charlie Elliott knew and understood Ranger Woody like few other men did in life. More importantly, through his great gift as a writer, Charlie recorded many facets of Ranger Woody's life and career that would have been lost forever had he not done so. Once again, I thank Charlie from the bottom of my heart for the incredible contribution he has made to this, "our" book.

In an article written in the Atlanta Constitution in his "All Outdoors" column on Oct. 26, 1957, titled, "'Public Forests, Public Trust,' Ranger Woody's Motto," Charlie made the following observations:

> He (Ranger Woody) is the "daddy" of the management area system, which has spread throughout the national forest areas of the nation. The first management area ever set up (in the nation) was at Rock Creek that flows off the north side of the Blue Ridge and into the Toccoa River.
>
> The Ranger lived by the spirit of an early Forest Service principal which declared that 'the public forests are a public trust' and should be managed for their many uses, which include hunting, fishing and other

> forms of recreation and not for timber alone. He could see far enough ahead to understand that with land being bought up by large companies, and other holdings being posted against hunting, some place must be kept inviolate for the guy who wanted to get out of doors and match his brawn and brain against the creatures of the wilderness.

Charlie mentioned the fact that Ranger Woody had bought deer with his own money and placed them in the newly created Rock Creek Refuge so that they could be protected:

> Under his watchful eye, the deer thrived and spread out along Rock Creek and Noontootly and over the mountain to the south side of the Blue Ridge. Under an agreement from the state, he put up gates on all roads leading into the refuge to keep out spotlight hunters and game goofs who would ride through the area, shoot deer from the road and let them lay.
>
> Under his system of gates and patrol, the deer multiplied so fast that within a few years after he had first stocked them, there were enough animals to allow a limited open season. I camped with Woody that first year (1940) in a massive grove of hemlocks and white pines on Noontootly Creek. It was a lovely, virgin spot with an icy, glass-clear stream, full of trout.

Today, few politicians have the vision to plan for the future and make tough decisions that will benefit the country in the decades ahead like some of our pioneers of the past. Typically we see today's crop of politicians kicking the can down the road whenever possible and putting off tough decisions with the collective attitude, "Let someone else worry about it in the future."

Every patriotic American alive today should be thankful that visionary men like Theodore Roosevelt, Arthur Woody and Charlie Elliott had the foresight and backbone to protect, preserve and conserve many of our natural and scenic sites and natural resources at a time when exploitation threatened to destroy forever what little remained of vast natural wonderlands that made up America 150 years ago – mountains, prairies, deserts, woodlands, wildlife, swamps, marshes, rivers and streams, and countless other splendid natural treasures.

Incidentally, although Charlie Elliott was much too humble to ever admit it in his 1957 column, and although he referred to Ranger Woody as the "daddy" of the management area system, he was equally instrumental in getting Georgia's first management area established as the Blue Ridge WMA by working closely with various state officials to make it happen. While Ranger

Woody prodded federal officials to establish a game refuge, Charlie worked tirelessly to get the state involved in the actual management of the fish and wildlife resources. The result was a partnership between the two agencies that has worked well in Georgia and many other states for the last 80 years.

Within a very short span of years in the late 1800s and early 1900s, attitudes turned from total exploitation – cut every tree in every forest, strip mine every acre with no thought of the damage to the soil and water incurred, kill every buffalo until the last one is gone, kill every whale in the ocean, catch every fish, shoot every passenger pigeon, pollute every river and stream – to: "You know, maybe we should take a look at what we've been doing for the past 200 years. Maybe the incredibly abundant natural resources found in America, valuable as they are, aren't so endless after all. Maybe we shouldn't kill every single buffalo or cut every tree in the forest just because they have a monetary value. Maybe some of these precious resources like giant redwood trees and white-tailed deer and bald eagles are worth more than money. If we cut every forest from Virginia to California we might just wake up one morning and find that we are living in a bomb zone." And a new word came into existence – conservation.

U. S. District Forest Ranger Arthur Woody measures a tree cut down by beavers, and stripped of bark. If you have ever whacked away on a tree this size, you know what a job it is to bring it down. Often several beavers will work on one tree as there is no such thing as a boss in the beaver world. Help Georgia protect the beavers! They're well worth it.

Ranger Woody examines a large tree felled by beavers. Photo taken from a November 1941 article in Outdoor Georgia magazine. Courtesy of the University of Georgia Library.

Ranger Arthur Woody epitomized the word. He forged his own path through the unknown wilderness of forest and wildlife management so to speak, and through his nonstop efforts, we are all better off today. Of course, he couldn't have achieved what he did without the U.S. Forest Service and the power of the federal government standing behind him.

The Forest Service deserves high praise for the amazing job it has done in the past 100-plus years. Not only did it initiate programs to prevent fires, conserve and manage forest and wildlife resources, and provide recreational resources for millions of Americans to enjoy, but during the first 30 or 40 years of its existence, the Forest Service provided countless jobs to thousands of individuals who desperately needed work during several decades of the worst economic times in American history.

For once someone got it right. For once in our nation's history, we can be proud of a government program that has not only been successful, but it has paid back many dividends to all Americans. Never again in history will we see anything like this occur. It was a one-of-a-kind happening in our nation's history. And as mentioned in Chapter 2, thank goodness the cosmic forces put a one-of-a-kind man like Arthur Woody in the right place at the right time to lead the conservation charge.

All his life, Ranger Woody loved flirting with, being around and hugging the ladies. He was truly in his element when a contingent of women admirers from a prominent Atlanta garden club drove to Suches by bus to meet the illustrious ranger in person. Note the one lady bowing down to the Kingfish in jest. Photo circa early 1940s, courtesy of Jean McNey.

While serving in various capacities with the U.S. Forest Service, the Georgia Forestry Commission, the Georgia Parks Department and the Georgia Game and Fish Commission during the 1920s, '30s and '40s, Charlie Elliott became professionally and personally connected to his dear friend and mentor Ranger Arthur Woody. The two men were involved in numerous historic projects and events in the North Georgia Mountains during those golden years of conservation. This photo was taken somewhere in the North Georgia hills, possibly on the Appalachian Trail, in the early 1930s. Several of Charlie's later articles mentioned the Ranger's dislike for wearing shoes, thus contributing to the enduring legend of the "Barefoot Ranger." Photo courtesy of the Charlie Elliott Wildlife Center.

Arthur Woody believed with his whole being that the word "conservation" meant the wise use of our resource; not no use at all. Sadly, today, and for the past few decades, when it comes to important conservation issues, spineless politicians have made decisions based on political and emotional arguments, and *not* what is best for the resource. Today the word "conservation" has almost become an obsolete term. Today the new school of preservationists and so-called environmentalism no longer believe in the wise use of our precious natural resources, many of which are renewable. For some reason, these misdirected souls argue no use at all. Never cut another tree. Never kill another deer. Allow fires to burn naturally, the way God intended.

We learned the hard way that this mentality does not work. What will the next 100 years hold?

The following story, which appeared in *Master Detective* magazine some time after Ranger Woody's death in 1946, is yet another of Charlie Elliott's eloquent tributes to the man of the mountains that he loved so much. Although a few of the classic tales told about Arthur Woody have already been related in previous chapters, it seems fitting that this last revealing and heartfelt section was also penned by his insightful and telling words.

Perennial Ranger

by Charlie Elliott

At twilight, the air was thin and like a knife. The last traces of warmth had vanished with the sun and the great oaks on the ridge rocked on their heels from the force of the wind. Just where the arm of the road cradled a tall granite cliff, the rangers had built a roaring log fire. One by one, the hunters came out of the woods, stood their rifles against the cliff and spread their fingers over the bright flames. Golden campfire light and high spirits invaded the little cove as each newcomer regaled the group with his high adventure of the day.

I leaned against the massive bole of a poplar tree, with an ear for the enthusiastic reports of who had missed and who had brought his buck deer out of this million-acre, mountain refrigerator of bleak peeks and knolls and windy valleys. I wasn't listening so much as I was thinking of a tall, gray-eyed forest ranger who had spent his life that these men might find a measure of relaxation and satisfaction in his mountain forest. I was thinking back to a spring evening when I sat in a twilight corner of Arthur Woody's front porch and listened to a neighbor's angry words.

"I'd admire ye," he said, "fer wanting' more deer, but they're coming out of th' refuge an eatin' up m' crops. I'm here t' tell ye I aim to kill every deer that jumps m' fence."

The ranger folded his hands across his stomach and looked out across the greening fields.

"Have your cows ever got into th' crops?"

The mountain man looked at him sharply.

"Yep – they have," he said slowly, after a pause.

"Didn't kill 'm did you?" Arthur asked imperturbably.

"I shot 'm in th' rump," the mountain man said, "with bird shot. Discouraged 'm kinda quick."

They sat for fully five minutes in strained silence.

"Jest don't want yuh," Arthur said, "in no trouble with the law."

The mountain farmer rose and put on his hat.

"All right ranger," he said. "I'll treat 'm like they were m' own stock. Much obliged fer th' advice."

"You didn't give Jeb any advice," I said, when the farmer had walked down the winding trail. "From where I sat, it looked like he figured that one out for himself."

The ranger grinned and explained it to me this way: "Ain't nobody," he said, "but the one who owns the itch can scratch it in th' right place."

When his neighbors brought their problems to him, they always found a sympathetic ear, seldom a word of counsel. He said that it helped a man to talk about his worries and that problems became much simpler when they were "spoke right out in th' open."

Toward his own complexities of life, Arthur had the most unusual attitude I've ever seen. He didn't think of his problems as a curse or even a cross to bear. Each was a game to be won, like checkers, or the bent nail puzzle he carried in his pocket. (Apparently the puzzle was a "brain-teaser" that he enjoyed showing people because no one could figure it out.)

Arthur was a great hulk of a man, 6 feet tall by 200 pounds. His grey eyes twinkled perennially, but behind the twinkle lay a glint like unsheathed steel. The only times I ever saw him angry was when someone had killed one of his friendly deer, or set fire to his woods. For years, he kept a bloodhound chained under his back steps to track down poachers and firebugs who came into his mountains from the outside.

He loved to eat almost as much as loved people. There was seldom a meal in the Woody house at which at least six guests didn't sit down at the table. It was an accepted fact that anyone who stopped within any mealtime would eat. June, his tiny wife, and Maybird, his daughter, kept the iron kitchen range in almost constant production with huge platters of golden biscuits, crisp cornpones, slabs of ham, fried chicken and an enormous variety of vegetables, pies, jams and jellies and homemade sauces that would have sent Duncan Hines into a rapturous tailspin. It was not a question of not being welcome around mealtime. Everybody within shouting distance of the house had to eat. Arthur's own little garden plot and the few head of stock he kept for meat were supplemented by hams, whole sides of beef, and bushel baskets of beans, potatoes, squash, corn and an assortment of fruits that his neighbors kept pouring continuously into his kitchen.

"Don't you ever sit down to a meal alone?" I asked, after one of the sybaritic banquets that would have done credit to a Roman emperor.

"Ain't got enough jars," he said, "t' put all this food in. Somebody's got t' help me eat it up, to save my waistline."

His waistline at the moment was a healthy 50 inches.

Arthur Woody, born in the early 1880s on the north side of the Blue Ridge, sprang from sturdy stock. He and many of his neighbors belonged to a race of tough pioneers who had moved into the headwaters of the Toccoa River while it was still part of the Cherokee Nation. Those hardy first settlers cleared the land of massive trees, ploughed the fertile coves, while resting rifles across their plow handles and lived on wild meat out of the forest.

In the Civil War, they favored neither the North nor South. They were Southerners by tradition but believed with the Constitution that all men should be free and that every man had a right to earn his own living by the sweat of his brow. They met and drew up a paper, deeding all their lands to the Canadian government. It is still the Canada district today and one of the few spots in solid South which votes a straight Republican ticket in every election. (Although an attempt was made to deed their land to the Canadian government, it never came about.)

When he was 14 years old, two events helped to shape the life of young Woody.

With his father, he drove an oxen team to Gainesville, forty miles away to market a load of chestnuts and apples. The boy was tremendously impressed by the smooth dirt roads and the great stone churches that he compared with the log huts where his people worshipped. His father laughed at his notion that the mountains could ever have such prosperity.

"A man does well enough," the elder Woody said, "when he takes care of his own body and soul."

Later that same fall, he saw his father track down and kill the last deer in the forests above their home.

"Huntin' jest ain't as good as it used t' be," the mountain man complained to his son.

"Who made it bad?" Arthur asked.

His father's tight-lipped silence was so embarrassing to them both that Arthur never forgot it.

Woody was still a young man when the Forest Service began to purchase land for a new national forest in the southern Blue Ridge. That was back in the "teens" of this century when a "gov'ment" man in the Georgia mountains was either a despised "revenooer" or not otherwise to be trusted. In spite of this feeling, deep rooted in his neighbors, Woody took a job with the government. He was farsighted enough to look beyond petty hatreds to roads and schools and good hunting that he wanted for his highlands.

One of his first acts when he had been sworn in as a Forest Ranger was to purchase deer with money out of his own pocket and release them on Rock Creek, the wildest part of his range. While his fire patrolmen watched over the animals, he hounded the Forest Service until they established a forty thousand acre game refuge along the creek just to shut him up and get some peace.

Twenty years after the refuge was created, Woody saw one of his dreams come true. Deer were so plentiful they had to be thinned out or allowed to starve. An organized hunt was held. When the first buck was brought out of the woods, the Ranger knelt beside it, tears running unashamedly down his cheeks.

"It's Baldy," he said, pointing to a slick scar on the buck's forehead. "I reckoned he'd have more sense than to show his spread today."

Woody's atonement of his father's sin of killing the last deer spread into a system of game management areas spread out across the United States. They are recognized as the greatest contributing factor to the astounding increase of big game in the forests of the nation.

Forest Ranger was the only job Woody ever held. Several times his supervisors, in recognition of his loyalty and ability, tried to promote him. But he always shook his head.

"I'm too old. You might train a bear cub t' set in a chair, but an old grizzly's just plain got t' have plenty of elbow room."

It was his way of saying that his home was a million acres of virgin coves, windy ridges and valleys steeped in sunshine and that he wouldn't have traded a single acre of it for the shiniest brass hat in the Service.

Woody was the most completely independent government employee I ever knew. He simply ignored rules, regulations and red tape. Getting a written report out of his activities was like pulling rocks out of a rocky hillside. When his supervisors finally assigned a clerk to his office to keep the records they required, he snorted.

"Waste of paper! Th' work's here on the ground, where anybody can see it!"

He consistently refused to wear the neat, official uniform. His favorite was a shapeless black hat and patched overalls. He owned a pair of shoes, but never wore them except when the mountain trail was rocky, when he drove into Dahlonega or Gainesville, or was expecting dignitaries.

On one occasion Ferd Silcox, then chief of the U.S. Forest Service, paid a surprise visit. He came upon a man standing by the edge of the road, shoeless and in ragged overalls.

"Where can I find Ranger Woody?" he asked.

"I be him," Arthur said.

"No!" the chief repeated. "Ranger Woody! I'm looking for Woody!"

"You're looking right at him," Arthur replied imperturbably.

Silcox sucked in his breath.

"Good God, man," he said. "Where is your uniform? And your damn shoes?"

"Don't need no shoes on," Arthur said. "I ain't goin' nowhere."

If there was ever any question about Woody's salesmanship, it vanished that evening when an immaculately dressed and amazed Forest Supervisor found his big chief and his ranger sitting on the Woody front porch, talking over the early days of the Service.

(Ferdinand A. Silcox [1882-1939], a fellow Georgian born two years before Arthur Woody, served as the 5th U.S. Forest Service Chief from 1933 to 1939. He died of a heart attack while on the job in 1939 at age 57.)

Back in the 1930s, when the federal agencies were spending vast sums of "relief" money, Arthur grumbled constantly at the waste and extravagance. But he didn't grumble too loud. The Conversation Corps was building the long dreamed of gravel roads back into every nook and cranny of his mountains, relegating to another age the sticky, bottomless mud.

Arthur stopped by the quarry on one of inspection rounds, and picked a piece of a stone that fell out of the crusher. He examined it with thoughtful eyes and dropped it in his pocket.

Later, he pointed out the road to me.

"This one," he said, "is paved with gold." He chuckled at my raised eyebrows.

"I have the gravel that went down here on the road," he said "and she run thirty dollars to the ton."

"And you didn't stop it?" I demanded. "Why?"

There wasn't another person within 30 miles of us, but he lowered his voice.

"I wanted one road up here," he confided, "that was worth what it cost t' build."

By his official connection, Arthur Woody brought many modern improvements to his little community of Suches, but it was his day by day relations with his fellow mountaineers who lived back in the coves and valleys that left his footprints deep in time's uncertain sands.

Like most mountain men, he was a trader by instinct and heritage. One of his chief pleasures in life was to get the best of a trade. By swapping cows, guns, farms and almost anything else he owned, he made a comfortable living above his salary and saved a fortune that ran high into six figures.

There was not a man living within 20 miles of him who didn't owe him money at one time or another. He held mortgages on 50 percent of the farms in his end of the county. He always kept $8,000 or $10,000 dollars in his small office safe, "jest fer tradin' purposes."

His finances overlapped into his job. If one of his neighbors on whose farm he held a mortgage refused to cooperate with his program of keeping forest fires out of the woods, or killed game out of season or on forbidden ground, he simply foreclosed and sent a truck to move the undesirable family out of the county.

On the other hand, I was in his office after we had buried one of his mountain friends. He opened his strong box, shuffled through his papers, and found a mortgage for $200 hundred dollars on the 80 acres of land his friend had left behind. He tore the paper into bits and dropped it into his wastebasket.

"I'll tell this poor widow woman," he said, "that George paid it off before he died."

Arthur Woody often said that the Lord made night for sleeping. He went to bed with the chickens and was up before the stars winked out. That hour between first light and sunup was his favorite time of day.

Sometimes he walked up the winding trail that led from his back steps to the crest of the Blue Ridge and sat on a platform rock while the world burst into celestial symphony and color with the coming of dawn.

Once, discouraged and bitter because a business failure had wiped me down to my last green fold, I was walking out the hours of the night and found him there, his hands clasped over a bulgy knee and the wind tugging at his coat. He appraised me quickly.

"You're up before ol' Massa put th' kindlin' on the sun this mornin'," he said.

I sat down beside him in the wind, where the clean fresh earth drank up new light. Beyond us the forest spilled over the brow of the mountain and swept in a dark emerald current to the river valley. The rim of the sun touched the ridge top and swelled into the sky.

"These mountains," he said, "must be a little human. They go through spells of being cold and dark, and it looks like night won't never end. But I been watchin' it for nigh on to sixty years and it always does. Now what's eatin' you?"

Posed with a group of Forest Service personnel at Vogel State Forest Park in the early 1940s, Ranger Woody was heavily involved in the construction of the Lake Trahlyta and directing the hard-working CCC boys from several local camps in the building of many of the park's amenities that still stand today as a testament to their amazing skills. Photo courtesy of Jean McNey.

When I told him, it didn't seem nearly as important. He stuck a piece of straw between his teeth and chuckled, deep inside.

"Everybody's life," he said, "is crossed up with roads. Some of them don't go nowhere. Sometimes you got to hunt around for a spell t' find one that does. Yesterday you took a wrong road, but th' sun over yonder give you a whole new day t' git on another."

That was the homespun philosophy the Ranger wore throughout his life. He never looked back on a trail over which he had come. The past died with the night and each day was a new adventure to be lived, a new problem to be solved.

Arthur Woody said that the only education he ever got was in the woods. That may have been fundamentally true. In another generation he would have been a Daniel Boone, a Davy Crockett or a Meriwether Lewis. Every mark made by claw and tooth and fang in the woods told him a story. He could trail a daintily stepping doe over the forest leaves as easily as I could follow human footprints down a muddy highway.

The Ranger spent one or more hours each day with his toes propped up at the sky and a magazine or paper in his hand. Although he had been

By the time he was a teenager, Arthur Woody knew every type of tree in the forest and the best uses for its wood. Little could he imagine that he would devote his life to restoring the mountain forests with trees and replenishing the forests and streams with abundant wildlife and fish. Photo circa 1938, courtesy of Jean McNey.

brought up in a land barren of teachers and text books, he was fully posted on current social and political problems. His thinking was basis. He knew the need of community worship and education and fulfilled the second boyhood dream when he was able to put up part of the money to help the settlement of Suches build a modern schoolhouse and church. He kept his certain and sustaining faith that his neighbors were growing with him toward a happier and more fruitful life.

Arthur was acutely aware of the nearness of man to the Sublime but he stoutly maintained that not man alone, but all earthly creatures, were made in the image of God.

Often he would point out examples of the Divine Hand right there in his mountain forest, resting his case on simple things, like the perfection of a leaf, the strength of spider silk, and how every living thing was dependent on all others for existence.

"Look long enough," he said, "and you'll find a reason and a need for every critter th' Good Lord put here on th' earth. Man, too. I'm here for a purpose. So are you. When man's time is up and his job is done, his mortal remains may turn into mould or dust, but he leaves his mark in many places that would be amazin' to him if he knew."

The years of privation and ceaseless activity finally took their toll. The Ranger was a weary old man when he retired from active service. He had given his life to redeeming a wilderness his fathers had thoughtlessly desecrated, and to improving a community he was not long privileged to enjoy.

Governors, college presidents and judges were among his friends who came from beyond the mountains to honor him a last time.

They overflowed the little church and churchyard on the hill. They mingled with the moist-eyed farmers and fishermen and forest guards. In the life of each, Arthur Woody had left some bright and cherished spot, as steadfast and eternal as the mountain that started at the church steps and climbed the tall skyline.

He had gone on to join a race of vanishing pioneers, leaving behind the singing streams, the cathedraled forests, the solitudes of an earthly wilderness that he had made so much richer and more livable that it would have been amazin' to him if he knew.

There will never be another William Arthur Woody. Truly, he was the last of the old-time forest rangers.

Blame Ranger Woody

By Elton Keith Jones

From *Mother and Child Reunion,* 1995

If a deer bolts out of the mountain's scrubby brush
And you nearly fly your car
Off a cliff into the top of a sixty-foot tulip poplar,
While you unclench your fingers from the bent
steering wheel
And will your heart back to normal place and pace
Blame Ranger Woody
He's the one.

Saw his daddy kill the last whitetail in the hills
And vowed to bring them back, and did.

If you're diving deep in a lake
And glance over your shoulder because of that eerie
not-alone feeling
Only to see too many long teeth in the too-large mouth
Of the 6-foot muskellunge inspecting your work
Blame Ranger Woody.
He's the one.

Brought barrels of trout to every little run in the hills
And muskies to the reservoirs.

Here's how he did it:
"Kiss the babies, flirt with the women, fish with the men,
and keep a big mean hound."

"If it needs done, do it, and get permission
after it's too late for them to change it."
Or build a dam so well it holds in floods
When doubting experts' supplementals wash away.

Let the road crews pave away
With ore that assays gold at thirty bucks a ton
So just for once a federal road is really worth the price.
After the farmer's funeral, tear up the note
And tell the widow it was all settled before.
Above all, don't let anybody
make you wear shoes if you don't want to.
Let your only miscalculation be
That the church you built isn't big enough
to hold the crowd for your funeral.

So when you see the fall leaves on thick forest slopes
Or hunt, fish, hike, canoe, kayak, camp or tramp
In north Georgia, look around and
Blame Ranger Woody.
He's the one.

Acknowledgements

This book has been a labor of love and I am indebted to so many special people for helping me bring Arthur Woody's amazing life to light. As noted in the Introduction, this book would never have gotten off the ground without the extraordinary help of Jean McNey, Arthur Woody's beloved granddaughter, and my dear friend Charlie Elliott, who contributed so much to Arthur Woody's story. Charlie was only too glad to share the extensive writing he did about his friend Arthur Woody. Roscoe Reams, who died in an auto accident in 2008, also shared many personal stories about his relationship with his friend and mentor Arthur Woody. Clyde Harkins, who joined the CCC in 1940 at age 15, gave me much insight into Ranger Woody's life. My deepest thanks also go to my good friend Ken Freel, a talented and professional book and copy editor, who gave me much sound advice and saved me considerable embarrassment by catching numerous mistakes and errors in my writing. Many other individuals and organizations, listed below, have gone out of their way to help me gather information and photos so that I could write about one of the greatest American conservationists in history. Thank you from the bottom of my heart.

American Forests magazine
Anne Dismukes Amerson
Atlanta Constitution
William W. Bergoffen, U.S. Forest Service
Rick Boley, Donning Graphic Designer
Bud Braddock, U.S. Forest Service
Milton M. Bryon, U.S. Forest Service
Cliff Casey
Billy Chism, publisher and editor of White County News
Mitch Cohen, U.S. Forest Service, Gainesville
Donald E. Clark, U.S. Forest Service
Jack Crockford
Melissa Cumming, Georgia DNR
Dahlonega Nugget
Clint Davis, U.S. Forest Service
The Charlie Elliott Wildlife Center
Gainesville Eagle
Rusty Garrison, Charlie Elliott Wildlife Center

Georgia Backroads
Georgia Forestry Commission
Georgia DNR
Georgia Sportsman magazine
William Gooch
Journal of Forestry
Emory Jones
Ethelene Dyer Jones
Keith Jones
Kent Kammermyer
John Kollock, gifted artist and historian
Chuck Leavell
North Georgia Journal
Outdoor Georgia magazine
Outdoor Life magazine
Rick Lavender
Harold Martin
John Martin
Master Detective magazine
The Honorable Zell Miller
Herb McClure, master turkey hunter
Lou Nichols, granddaughter of Arthur Woody
Don Pfitzer
Kenneth Rogers, one of Atlanta's great photographers
Ranger Roscoe "Nick" Nicholson
Elinor Reams
Horace E. Shelton Jr.
Southern Outdoors
Becky Bruce-Vaughters, U.S. Forest Service, Blairsville
Jack Troy, sports writer extraordinaire for the Atlanta Constitution
Susan S. Tuggle, UGA Libraries
Time magazine
Vicki Worsham, UGA Libraries
U.S. Department of the Interior
United States Fish & Wildlife Service
United States Forest Service, Gainesville, GA
Washington Information Digest
Mrs. Clyne Woody
Dr. Edward Woody, grandson of Walter Woody

Timeline –

William Arthur Woody (April 1, 1884 - June 10, 1946)

The Appalachians are among the oldest mountains in the world. White settlement began in the late 1600s and early 1700s. From the mid-1600s to the American Revolution in 1776, a mutually-beneficial association between Indians and whites exists based on the deer hide trade in the southeast and along much of the eastern seaboard.

For the first 10 years of the Georgia colony's existence (1732-1742), the sale of deer hides to England from the ports of Savannah and Charleston served as the colony's most valuable commodity and primary source of income. Indians got what they wanted – kettles, knives, beads, trade guns, blankets; and white traders got what they wanted – cash for hides. Sadly it was often a one-sided affair favoring the whites. Traders slowly push westward from the coastal areas into Indian Territory. Soon, the white man was not content to simply trade for hides. By the early 1800s, he wanted the Indian's land as well.

1828 – Gold is discovered in North Georgia. Arguments persist as to whether the first nugget was discovered in Lumpkin County or White County. One story claims a deer hunter in White County stumbled upon the first large nugget.

1832 – The Cherokee Land Lottery takes place in North Georgia. English settlers of Irish and Scottish ancestry begin moving into the mountains from coastal areas and the Carolinas. These rugged pioneers are the direct descendents of William Arthur Woody.

1838 – The Cherokee Indians are removed from North Georgia on the Trail of Tears.

1832 to 1895 – Deer disappear in the North Georgia Mountains, having been eradicated by hungry settlers using large packs of dogs. Although market hunting was responsible for the disappearance of deer in other states to the north along the eastern seaboard, deer disappeared in the Georgia mountains because highly efficient pioneers wiped them out.

1850 – As plantation life flourished in the southern two-thirds of Georgia, deer were considered a nuisance by planters and were killed indiscriminately. Like the mountain area, by the late 1800s deer were absent in many interior parts of the state. Remnant populations survived in the swampy coastal areas and barrier islands.

1880s to early 1900s – The first railroads plowed their way into the North Georgia mountains, financed by wealthy businessmen in order to tap the virgin forests. By 1910, deforestation, clear cutting, erosion, and damage from forest fires and gold mining have left behind a vast wasteland in many areas.

1884 – William Arthur Woody is born in a log cabin in Suches, Union County, Georgia, on April 1, April Fool's Day!

1895 – At 10 years of age, young Arthur reportedly witnesses his father kill one of the last living white-tailed bucks in North Georgia's Fannin County. Arthur becomes an excellent woodsman, a skilled hunter and fisherman, and loves to roam his native mountains. As he matures, he vows to someday bring deer back to the mountains where he was raised.

Early 1900s – The age of conservation has dawned and new attitudes in regard to natural resources begin to win the day. People realize that forests, wildlife and water resources are in serious trouble. Visionary conservationists understand that virgin forests are not inexhaustible. Concerned individuals like Theodore Roosevelt work hard to correct the mistakes of the past, by managing resources wisely and planning for future generations. Young Arthur Woody instinctively understands conservation principles extremely well. He is a visionary in that respect. His motto: "We should look to the forest as a source of good as well as wood."

March 1, 1911 – Congress passes the Weeks Act, initially appropriating $9 million to purchase 6 million acres of land in the eastern U.S. The U.S. Forest Service purchased 31,000 acres in the Rock Creek and Noontootly Creek area of Fannin, Gilmer, Lumpkin and Union counties from the Gennett family for $7.00 per acre. The relatively high price paid for this tract reflects the fact that much of the tract still contains valuable virgin timber due to its remote location and poor access.

Officially known as Cherokee National Game Refuge No. 2, the tract carried several other names over the next few years. Locally, Arthur Woody and others referred to it as "Rock Creek." Later still the area became fondly known as the Blue Ridge Game District, the Blue Ridge Refuge, or the Blue Ridge Ranger District. Finally, it became the Blue Ridge Wildlife Management Area, Georgia's first WMA and the first in the nation (placed under the watchful eye of Ranger Arthur Woody).

Oct. 1, 1912 – After passage of the Weeks Act, Arthur Woody, 28, begins his career with the U. S. Forest Service as an ax-man on a baseline survey crew. He soon advances to surveyor for lands acquired by the Forest Service. His uncanny knowledge of the area greatly aids the U.S. Forest Service in establishing forest boundaries. He also helps the Forest Service purchase land.

May 1, 1915 – Arthur Woody is sworn in as a forest guard with the assignment of protecting federal lands in his beloved 31,000-acre Rock Creek Refuge from fire, trespassers and poachers.

1918 – The federal government combines various local land holdings in several states (Georgia, North Carolina, South Carolina and Tennessee). On June 14, 1920, the initial land purchase becomes part of the Cherokee National Forest. A short time later, additional lands are consolidated with portions of the Cherokee being placed into the Georgia National Forest. In 1936, all of the forests in the Southeast are reorganized to follow state boundaries. That portion within the boundaries of Georgia becomes the Chattahoochee National Forest. Arthur Woody and Roscoe Nicholson serve as the first two Forest Rangers in the North Georgia mountains.

July 1, 1918 – Arthur Woody is officially sworn in as Georgia's second Forest Ranger, following Ranger Roscoe "Nick" Nicholson in Rabun County, who became Georgia's first official Forest Ranger in 1912. Ranger Woody's ever expanding federal domain, originally encompassing the 31,000 acre Rock Creek Refuge, becomes known as the Blue Ridge Ranger District. As more land is purchased by the federal government across the mountains, the Blue Ridge Ranger District eventually expands to nearly 200,000 acres. Thanks to the constant prodding of Forest Service superiors by a visionary Ranger Woody, Rock Creek Refuge becomes a managed game and wildlife reserve of 40,000 acres within that ever expanding district. The refuge eventually becomes the first "wildlife management area" in Georgia (Blue Ridge WMA) and the first in the nation.

1918 – Ranger Arthur Woody, 34, begins to restock local streams with native brook trout obtained locally and non-native rainbow trout shipped into the Gainesville train depot from Denver, Colorado. Over the next few years, Ranger Woody continues ordering rainbow trout from Colorado and brown trout from Washington State. He also orders brook trout fingerlings and eggs from New York State. Many more shipments of trout and other species are distributed in mountain streams and lakes in the area. Soon, three species of trout are thriving in the North Georgia mountains.

February 16, 1925 – Forty-one-year-old Arthur Woody negotiates the sale of 178 acres of magnificent second-growth and virgin timber from F. Alonzo Sosebee on Wolf Pen Gap Road between Vogel State Park and Suches. Known as Sosebee Cove, the tract contains one of the finest stands of mature yellow poplar found anywhere in Georgia.

1927 – Forty-three-year-old Arthur Woody travels to the Pisgah Game Reserve in western North Carolina and purchases five fawns for $20 apiece with the intention of placing them in Rock Creek Refuge as soon as they are old enough to survive in the wild.

1928 – Ranger Woody releases his one-year-old deer into the refuge near Rock Creek.

1928 and 1929 – Ranger Woody obtains several dozen more deer over the next few years from the Pisgah Game Reserve and raises them in a pen near refuge headquarters (total numbers are not clear). Later all of the deer are released into refuge.

1933 – The Civilian Conversation Corps arrives in Suches in the spring and early summer. For the next eight years, the boys of several local "CC" camps provide much needed manpower to numerous conservation and civic projects in Union County spearheaded by Ranger Woody.

July 9, 1936 – The Forest Service reorganizes federal forest lands to follow state boundaries. President Franklin Delano Roosevelt proclaims the Chattahoochee National Forest in Georgia a separate National Forest. The Chattahoochee National Forest is organized into two Ranger Districts: the Blue Ridge District managed by Ranger Arthur Woody, and the Tallulah Ranger District managed by Ranger Nick Nicholson.

1936 – Following the success of Ranger Woody's Rock Creek Refuge, later known as Blue Ridge WMA, three more WMAs are quickly established in the mountain region – the Chattahoochee, Chestatee, and Lake Burton WMAs. (Note: The first state-wide deer survey conducted in 1932 estimated a total population of 12,452 deer, located primarily in coastal counties and on coastal islands). A later survey in the 1950s estimated 33,000 deer statewide, including the mountain herd of several thousand animals started by Ranger Woody. Today the state-wide deer population exceeds one million.

1936 – An estimated 30 deer obtained from the Pisgah Game Reserve are released in Habersham, Rabun, Lumpkin and White counties of northeast Georgia. Although this occurs in portions of Ranger Nick Nicholson's district, Ranger Woody is present at several of the stocking sites.

Both rangers are extremely busy in their respective districts and they share many things in common. Both men are pioneers in the mountain region and serve during an historic time that can never be duplicated. They constantly break new ground and set the pace for the future. Both men also enjoyed exceptionally long careers in their respective ranger districts.

1936 – The U.S. Forest Service and the Georgia Wildlife Division (later to become the Georgia Game and Fish Commission) enter into an historic cooperative agreement for the management of wildlife on all U.S. Forest Service lands within the state. This is the first agreement of its kind in the nation between the federal government and a state agency. Other states soon follow suit. Over the years, a large network of state operated wildlife management areas are established nationwide on federal lands. The original concept for Georgia's first WMA (Blue Ridge) was conceived by Ranger Arthur Woody with the help and support of Charlie Elliott. Both men steadfastly believed that a thriving wildlife population should be a part of every national forest.

1937 – A state-wide bear survey estimates a total of 208 black bears, most of which are near the coast and in swampy areas of southeast Georgia. Black bears, white-tailed deer, eastern cougars and eastern wolves had disappeared from the mountain region by the early 1900s. Eastern elk and eastern buffalo had been wiped out 100 years earlier. Ranger Woody begins restocking black bears in Rock Creek Refuge.

1937 – The Pittman-Robertson Act is signed into law, eventually making federal funds available for wildlife management. According to Jack Crockford, Director of the Game and Fish Commission during the 1970s, this act made possible "the beginning of scientific game management across the country." Limited funds were appropriated for several game and fish projects in North Georgia before the U.S. was forced to enter World War II, but the program did not gain momentum until after the war in the late 1940s and early '50s.

1940 – The first deer season of modern times is held at Blue Ridge WMA – first a five-day archery hunt in late October, followed by a five-day firearms hunt for bucks only in November. Ranger Woody does not believe the herd is ready to exploit and expresses his sentiments against the hunt. Most of the 22 bucks brought in to the check station are deer he personally recognizes. Some are bucks he had raised and released. It is a traumatic moment for the Ranger.

1941, 1942 – Managed archery and firearms hunts continue at Blue Ridge WMA.

1943 – The mountain counties as a whole are opened up to deer hunting. Unfortunately, the use of dogs is allowed. At least 200 bucks are killed, far more than game managers anticipated. The following summer, dog hunting in the mountain counties is outlawed once and for all.

September 1944 – Ranger Woody suffers a stroke while swimming in Woody Lake. He suffers several more light strokes in the months following and his health began to deteriorate very rapidly.

February 1945 – Ranger Woody is hospitalized in Atlanta in an attempt to reduce his blood pressure and control his weight. He is diagnosed with heart and kidney disease.

September 1945 – Ranger Woody officially retires from the U.S. Forest Service due to failing health.

June 10, 1946 – Ranger Woody dies after a prolonged bout with kidney disease and a failing heart. His funeral is attended by many dignitaries including the governor of Georgia. Reports claim that 1,500 people come to the small mountain church to pay their respects, but that may be an exaggeration. By his request, Ranger Woody is laid to rest in the church cemetery, facing Black Mountain, so that "on the resurrection morning, I can rise up and see if my forests have been properly preserved." Most of those in attendance stayed until well after dark, sharing stories about the unforgettable character who was Ranger Arthur Woody.

2016 and beyond– The legacy of Ranger Arthur Woody, also known as "Kingfish," the "Barefoot Ranger," or simply the "Ranger," lives on in legend, tall tales and fact.

HARRY L. ROSSOLL

Index – Names, Places and Events

Appalachian Trail

The 2,186 mile-long, "Maine-to-Georgia" Appalachian Trail begins in Georgia at Springer Mountain and leaves the Peach State approximately 79 miles later at Bly Gap in North Carolina. It is the world's longest continuous trail (now part of the National Scenic Trail System) and is maintained primarily by the U. S Forest Service. All of the land it traverses in Georgia is national forest land. The trail spans 14 states from Georgia to Maine. The high point of the trail crosses Blood Mountain in Union County at 4,461 feet, while the low point crosses Dicks Creek Gap at 2,675 feet.

From its southernmost point 8 miles north of Amicalola Falls on Springer Mountain, the trail winds northeast across several mountains located in the very heart of Ranger Arthur Woody's old stamping grounds in Gilmer, Union and Towns counties – mountains with which he was intimately familiar like Black (where Woody Gap is located), Blood, Tray and Big Cedar.

After the conservation movement spearheaded by President Theodore Roosevelt began in earnest in the early 1900s, numerous proposals were made to create a "super" trail along the Appalachians. In October 1921, a Massachusetts forester named Benton McKaye published a proposal in the Journal of the American Institute of Architects titled "An Appalachian Trail: A Project in Regional Planning." The name stuck. The original proposal was for a footpath to run from the highest point in the northern Appalachians (Mt. Washington, New Hampshire) to the highest point in the southern Appalachians (Mt. Mitchell, North Carolina). Within a year work began on "America's Footpath." First completed was the section that ran from Pennsylvania to Connecticut across the new Bear Mountain Bridge.

By 1925 the overall plan began to take shape with the creation of the Appalachian Trail Conservancy. From its inception, Ranger Woody was a dedicated proponent of the trail in Georgia. The proposed route was extended to go from Maine to Georgia. However, in the original proposal, only about 20 miles of the trail would traverse Georgia. Roy Ozmer, a respected outdoorsman and close friend of Ranger Woody, was hired to explore the area from Virginia to Georgia. Both men felt that Mount

Oglethorpe, east of Jasper, was a better choice for the end of the trail than the originally proposed site further west in the Cohutta Mountains.

In 1929, Ozmer walked from Georgia to Virginia in quest of the best route across Georgia. He was aided by assistant state forester E.B. (Eddie) Stone and Stone's assistant, Charlie Elliott, also a budding friend of Ranger Woody. At the time, Elliott was an assistant district forester with the Georgia Department of Forestry. Everyone involved, including Ranger Woody, believed the trail should have a much stronger presence in the Georgia mountains than originally had been proposed. Ozmer and Stone laid out a more ambitious route that included some 79 miles of trail within the state. After the final route from Bly Gap (North Carolina) to Mount Oglethorpe was eventually agreed upon, Ranger Woody helped in many ways. He assigned Forest Service employees to assist in the construction of the trail within his ranger district which included portions of Gilmer, Union and Towns counties. Most of the early work was completed by 1931.

Charlie Elliott was given the task of setting up a network of volunteers from local hiking groups in Gainesville and other nearby areas to help with much of the work that took place on that portion of the trail traversing Blood and Black mountains. At first it was a daunting job, but he eventually recruited several volunteer groups who worked tirelessly with the Forest Service to maintain the trail, put out markers and signs and help build shelters. With the arrival of the Civilian Conservation Corps at several camps in the area in 1933, this able new labor force also did much to improve and maintain the trail in Georgia under the direction of Ranger Woody and the Forest Service. Thanks to the highly-skilled "CC" boys, the famous two-room rock shelter on Blood Mountain, built in 1937, proudly stands today as a monument to those hard-working individuals. Being the oldest shelter on the trail, it is also the only walk-through structure on the entire trail.

The Appalachian Trail was completed in 1937 with the clearing of the last 2 miles between Spaulding and Sugarloaf Mountains in Maine. At the time, the trail stretched from Mount Katahdin in Maine's Baxter State Park to Mount Oglethorpe in Georgia. Because of encroaching development around Amicalola Falls, the southernmost juncture was moved north to Springer Mountain in Gilmer County in 1958.

The trail fell into disrepair during World War II. Following Ranger Woody's death in 1946, interest in the trail was renewed in the early 1950s. The designation of the Appalachian Trail as a "National Scenic Trail" became a drawn-out political battle that lasted 15 years. In 1968, President Lyndon Johnson signed the National Trails System Act. This act, originally intended to protect the land near the Appalachian Trail, was later modified to include any footpath designated as a National Scenic Trail. Today much of "America's Trail," along with other trails in the National Scenic Trail System, is located on land that is federally protected. In Georgia, the entire 79 mile length of the Appalachian Trail remains within the protected boundaries of the Chattahoochee National Forest. Georgia is one of only three states where this is the case.

Applejack Brandy

A favorite of Ranger Arthur Woody, this apple-based "cyder spirit" was first distilled in 1698 by a Scotsman named William Laird in Monmouth County, New Jersey. In Laird's day it was known as "Jersey Lightning." Laird reportedly perfected his distilling skills in the early 1700s using apples because they were such a common commodity throughout the colonies. Applejack was a common and popular beverage made up and down the Appalachians right up through Prohibition in the early 20th century. The Ranger often kept a bottle in his safe for "special occasions."

Scattergood Baines

Scattergood Baines is a homespun fictional character created by American author Clarence Budington Kelland that first appeared in stories in the *Saturday Evening Post* in the late 1930s. Kelland based his popular character on memories from his childhood in Portland, Michigan. People often compared Ranger Arthur Woody with this larger-than-life character because of both men's mutual philanthropic activities and community involvement.

Much like Ranger Woody, Baines was described as a shrewd and jovial town leader who was involved in everything that happened in his community. As the local hardware merchant, townspeople were always coming to him with their problems and bizarre stories. He would willingly offer his down-home wisdom to anyone who would offer him a plate of food. "He was the best loved, most cussed at, and by all odds the fattest man in the modern, bustling town of Cold River."

A radio version of the character ran from 1938 to 1950, and a film version, set in the fictional New England village of Cold River and starring Guy Kibbee, appeared in 1941. Kibbee actually resembled Ranger Woody to some degree. The film was so popular that five sequels were made.

Blue Ridge Wildlife Management Area
History in the Making

With monies furnished by the Weeks Act passed in 1911, the U.S. Forest Service purchased 31,000 acres in the Rock Creek and Noontootly Creek (today known as Noontootla Creek) area of Fannin, Gilmer, Lumpkin and Union counties in the North Georgia mountains from the Gennett family for $7.00 per acre. The Gennett brothers reportedly paid around $1 acre for the tract in the early 1900s. Because of its remote location and limited access, much of the land still contained virgin timber, justifying the relatively high price paid at the time.

This tract, along with a larger tract in North Carolina purchased from the Vanderbilt family that later became part of the Pisgah Reserve, were the first two land purchases in the Southeast made by the federal government under the Weeks Act. Both tracts became part of the Cherokee National Forest in 1920 which eventually included lands in Georgia, North Carolina, South Carolina, and Tennessee. Later, each state claimed its own national forest within its boundaries and all lands inside Georgia became the Chattahoochee National Forest.

Known locally as the Noontootly National Game Refuge, the Rock Creek property officially became known as the Cherokee National Game Refuge No. 2, (Cherokee Game Refuge No. 1 included the Vanderbilt property in North Carolina). Ranger Woody usually referred to the area as Rock Creek Refuge, or simply the "game refuge," and that name stuck with local residents for many years. Later still the area became known as the Blue Ridge Game District or Blue Ridge Refuge. It was also frequently referred to as the Blue Ridge Reserve or Blue Ridge Ranger District. In 1936 it finally became Blue Ridge Wildlife Management Area, the name it still goes by today. Georgia's first official wildlife management area was also the first of its kind in the nation. Fittingly, it was placed under the watchful eye of Ranger Arthur Woody, who ultimately rose to the prestigious position of District Ranger.

Blue Ridge Refuge was later expanded to almost 39,000 acres. The refuge is incredibly significant in Forest Service history because of its many firsts – a number of which were initiated by Ranger Woody. The first rainbow and brown trout were stocked in the refuge in 1918. During the next 15 years, Ranger Woody also established trout rearing ponds on Rock Creek Lake inside the refuge. These rearing ponds were eventually taken over by the Forest Service. Today, thanks to Ranger Woody's initial efforts, Blue Ridge WMA became home to the Chattahoochee National Fish Hatchery in the mid 1930s.

Ten years after he released the first trout into Rock Creek, Ranger Woody released five deer into the refuge in 1928 (at his own expense), marking the beginning of the return of whitetails to the North Georgia mountains. The first historic deer hunt of modern times was held at Blue Ridge WMA in October and November 1940; first, a five-day archery hunt, followed by two, five-day firearms hunts. No deer were taken on the archery hunt but 22 bucks, and several does shot by mistake, were killed on the historic firearms hunt.

Over the years, Ranger Woody also reintroduced black bears and restored and protected native wild turkey populations inside the refuge. Today, the turkeys found at the Blue Ridge WMA are known for having one of the purest native bloodlines of any wild turkeys found in the mountain region, although their once-pure genetics have probably been somewhat diluted by other birds coming into the area in recent decades. Experts claim these native birds have slightly darker feathers.

Boynton, Reverend Claud Cole (1893-1954)

Reverend Claud Boynton was a beloved and well-known Baptist minister whose tenure in Union County spanned about 20 years (from the mid-1930s to 1954). Having graduated from Mercer University in Macon, Georgia, and nearing the age of 40 in the early 1930s (the exact date is not clear but it coincided with the coming of the CCC in 1933) he and his bride, the former Annis Grace Ozmer, had come to Lake Winfield Scott for a short vacation. The couple intended to continue on to Louisville, Kentucky, where Rev. Boynton planned to attend the Baptist Theological Seminary. After seminary, his goal was to pursue a preaching career in a large southern city.

While staying at Lake Winfield Scott, the young preacher happened to meet Ranger Arthur Woody. The Ranger made arrangements for him to preach several guest sermons in the Suches area. He was so well received by the people that Ranger Woody prevailed upon him to stay in Union County and pursue his preaching career in the mountains "where the people really need your style of preaching."

Despite the couple's long-term plans, Rev. Boynton didn't stand a chance. Ranger Woody not only offered to build him a house (which he did), but he also arranged a job working as a supervisor for the CCC at Camp Woody in Suches to help subsidize his meager income from preaching. Rev. Boynton was compelled to stay.

Working as both chaplain and as a supervisor improving roads, building fire towers and fighting forest fires, the young "CC" workers soon began to idol Rev. Boynton as much as they did Ranger Woody. He had a profound influence on many young lives. Rev. Boynton preached on Sundays and Wednesday nights and led his "CC" boys the remainder of the week. Over the years, he served a number of churches in the area; Choestoe Baptist Church, Zion Baptist Church and Mt. Lebanon Baptist Church in Suches. From 1944 to 1954, he served as pastor of the First Baptist Church in Blairsville.

He was always active in community affairs. He served as Union County's representative to the Georgia Legislature for several terms. He was a gifted speaker and was often invited to give guest sermons or lectures. Tragically, Rev. Boynton died in 1954 at the age of 61, following a heart attack. He is buried in the Choestoe Baptist Church Cemetery.

Brasstown Bald – Georgia's Highest Peak

Located off spur 180, just southeast of Blairsville, Georgia's highest geographic point rises to an elevation of 4,784 feet. Named after a Cherokee town and also known as Enotah Bald (from an Indian word) or Bald Mountain, Brasstown Bald resides in portions of Union and Towns counties and is surrounded by the Chattahoochee National Forest. The name "brasstown" is believed to have come from a mistranslation of a Cherokee word by early white settlers and the term "bald" usually indicates a high point in the mountains void of trees.

On a clear day, four states and the Atlanta skyline can be seen from the top of Brasstown Bald. Rabun Bald, Georgia's second highest peak stands to the northeast and Blood Mountain, which reaches a height of 4,445 feet, stands to the southwest.

The first lookout/fire tower erected on Brasstown Bald was made of wood and built in the early 1920's by the Pfister & Vogel Leather Company which owned much of the land around it at the time. The second tower was constructed in 1935, the brainchild of Ranger Arthur Woody. Knowing how popular Georgia's highest point had become to residents of the state, Ranger Woody had long dreamed about building a new lookout tower along with some type of observation deck from which people could take in the magnificent views. Despite being in the depths of the Great Depression, the opportunity to fulfill that dream came with the ready work force provided by the CCC.

Much as he did with the plans for Dockery Lake around the same time period, Ranger Woody reportedly sat at his kitchen table and drew up plans for a new stone and wooden tower. Using local rock and timber, Ranger Woody's dedicated "CC" boys camped on the Bald and completed the new structure in the summer of 1935. After World War II, the Woody Stone Tower was replaced by a steel tower in 1947. The current stone structure, which was built in 1965, sits near the location of the original tower. The Brasstown Bald museum contains a lifelike talking manikin of Arthur Woody who hosts an exhibit entitled "Man and the Mountain."

Brown, Governor Joseph Emerson (1821-1894)

Joseph E. Brown served two terms as Georgia's 42nd governor from 1857 to 1865. Later, he served as chief justice of the Supreme Court of Georgia from 1865 to 1870, and later still as a U.S. Senator from 1880 to 1891. He retired from the Senate in 1891 due to poor health.

Born in South Carolina in 1821, his family moved to Union County, Georgia, when he was a young boy. Although he grew up in an area where many of the citizens were against secession, he was an ardent believer in state's rights. After Lincoln's election in 1861, and after the secession of South Carolina, he was strongly in favor of Georgia leaving the Union as well. At the Georgia convention in January, 1861, both delegates from Union County voted against secession, but Brown was able to push it through.

However, he opposed the Confederate military draft and the taking of private property (horses and mules, supplies and slaves) by the Confederate government and soon bumped heads with Jefferson Davis. He objected strenuously to military conscription by the Confederacy and tried to keep his troops from leaving Georgia, all to no avail.

Soon after his election to the Senate in 1880, Brown became the first Georgia official to support public education for all children, something Ranger Arthur Woody would have heartily agreed with 50 years later.

Fittingly, the property in Suches, Georgia, where Governor Joe Brown grew up during the late 1820s and 1830s later became the site upon which Woody Gap School was built in 1940. Arthur Woody bought the 20 acres where Joe Brown had lived and donated it to the county for the school. Ranger Woody and his son Walter were the driving forces behind having the historic school built in Suches. Woody Gap School opened its doors in 1940.

Canada District

The "Canada District" is listed as one of 14 districts in Union County, Georgia. It is located in the southern portion of the county and takes in the small hamlet of Suches where Ranger Arthur Woody made his home. An early settlement once was located at Canada Creek near Suches. Although the exact history of the name is sketchy, it is believed to have originated during Civil War times. When war came in 1861, a number of Union County residents reportedly got together and attempted to deed their land to the Canadian government because they did not want to secede from the United States and they did not want to take sides. (A similar thing happened in extreme northwest Georgia's Dade County.) Apparently nothing came of the effort to join Canada but the name stuck.

Chattahoochee Forest National Fish Hatchery
Blue Ridge WMA, Fannin County, Georgia

Having been promoted to the respected position of Forest Ranger in 1918 by the U.S. Forest Service, one of the ground-breaking actions taken by Ranger Woody that year on his own volition was to order an unknown quantity of non-native rainbow trout from a fish hatchery in Denver, Colorado. With the help of his son Clyne, the trout were placed in Rock Creek and several other streams within the Blue Ridge Refuge (then known as Rock Creek Refuge). Thus began a very primitive trout stocking program that the Ranger continued to improve upon for the next 20 years, which included the stocking of native brook trout as well. Ranger Woody continued ordering rainbow trout in the early 1920s and also began purchasing non-native brown trout from a hatchery in Washington State. Local individuals were hired to distribute these fish throughout the area.

Ranger Woody built his first fish-rearing enclosure for his trout on the lake behind his house (Woody Lake) in the early 1920s. He later built several larger fish-rearing ponds for trout on land he owned on Rock Creek inside his Blue Ridge Refuge. In 1933, with the help of the CCC boys, he convinced the Forest Service to step up its trout stocking efforts and many lakes, stream and rivers in the North Georgia mountains were stocked with trout.

Realizing the need for a much better trout raising facility, the Chattahoochee Forest National Fish Hatchery on Rock Creek was constructed by the U.S. Forest Service in 1937. It remained under Forest Service authority for 23 years. On April 13, 1960, a cooperative agreement was signed that transferred ownership and management to the U.S. Fish and Wildlife Service. The primary responsibility of the Chattahoochee Forest National Fish Hatchery today is to raise rainbow trout, but the hatchery also raises some brook and brown trout.

Chattahoochee National Forest

The Chattahoochee National Forest, named for the river whose headwaters begin in White County in the North Georgia mountains, consists of 750,135 acres of mountain forestland acquired by the federal government in the early 1900s. Passage of the Weeks Act on March 1, 1911, provided funds for the federal government to purchase lands in the southeastern U.S. that had been ravaged by clear cutting, burning, pollution and erosion.

The first tract purchased in Georgia under the Weeks Act in 1912 by the fledgling U.S. Forest Service was the famed 31,000-acre Gennett tract that spanned portions of Fannin, Gilmer, Lumpkin and Union counties. This tract later became Ranger Arthur Woody's beloved Rock Creek Refuge (Blue Ridge WMA, the first wildlife management area in the nation). Initially all lands purchased in the southeast became part of the Cherokee National Forest. On July 9, 1936, these lands were reorganized to follow state boundaries and the North Georgia lands became the Chattahoochee National Forest.

That same year, the Chattahoochee National Forest was organized into two ranger districts, the Blue Ridge and the Tallulah districts. Longtime forest ranger Arthur Woody (who became a ranger in 1918) was named District Ranger for the Blue Ridge District, while Georgia's first forest ranger, Ranger Roscoe "Nick" Nickerson (who became a ranger in 1912), was named District Ranger for the Tallulah District.

Eventually North Georgia's Chattahoochee National Forest grew to include 750,135 acres.

Civilian Conservation Corps

The Civilian Conservation Corps (CCC) was a nationally acclaimed public work relief program initiated under President Franklin Delano Roosevelt's "New Deal" in 1933. It was designed to employ an army of unmarried young men between the ages of 18 and 25 and help their families by providing a small amount of income. Under the program the men were paid $30 per month in wages, of which $25 had to be sent home to the family. Most of the manual work performed by these young men revolved around forestry, conservation and "preserving the natural resources of these United States." Before it was dissolved in 1942 due to the war effort, the CCC had enrolled nearly three million young men working coast to coast, with up to 300,000 workers serving at any given time.

The program was a godsend to Ranger Arthur Woody and the mountains as a whole. Three local camps worked regularly with Ranger Woody on a variety of conservation projects. The boys from Camp Woody, who's Camp Project Superintendent was Arthur Woody's oldest son, Walter, were known locally as the "Satins of Suches." The Ranger also worked very closely with the boys from Camp Enotah in Blairsville and the boys from Camp Robertstown in White County.

Nicknamed "Roosevelt's Tree Army," the hard working young men from these three camps built at least three lakes, built three fire towers including the new rock and wood tower at Brasstown Bald, built camping areas and rock structures in Vogel State Park and Lake Winfield Scott, helped maintain and improve the Appalachian Trail, fought forest fires, helped apprehend arsonists, planted tens of thousands of seedlings, stocked thousands of fish in streams and rivers, improved river and stream habitat, improved dozens of roads, ran telephone lines across the mountains and engaged in numerous other important conservation initiatives.

According to Leslie Lacy, author of the *The Soil Soldiers,* published in 1976, the "Canvas Covered Convicts," (so named because they wore military style uniforms) built 3,470 fire towers and houses for the detection of fires and connected those towers with 65,100 miles of telephone line. They built roads, trails and fire breaks. They fought fires. In 1936, approximately 600 million seedlings were grown in nurseries, mostly run by the CCC, and more than half a billion seedlings were transplanted."

When the U. S. entered World War II, many of the young men who had been in the CCC were inducted into military service and the historic program was disbanded.

Crockford, Jack (1923-2011)

Hired by the state of Georgia in 1947 (two years after Arthur Woody's death), Jack Crockford has long been considered the father of the deer restoration program in Georgia. Picking up where Ranger Woody left off,

Crockford's pioneering efforts in deer restoration did for the rest of the state what Arthur Woody had done in the mountains of North Georgia.

In 1947, Jack Crockford, a fresh out-of-college graduate with a degree in wildlife biology from the University of Michigan (one of the first degrees of its kind in the nation), was hired by the state of Georgia. Like so many young men his age, his college career had been interrupted by the war, where, as a pilot, he had flown 328 missions in Burma.

Ironically, Jack was hired by the State Game and Fish Commission with a grant that came from Pittman-Robertson funds. Even more, ironical, he was hired by none other than Ranger Woody's long-time friend Charlie Elliott, who had by that time taken over the helm at the Georgia Game and Fish Commission. Charlie would later state many times that his greatest achievement while heading up that department was hiring Jack Crockford.

Not only did Crockford initiate a very successful state-wide restocking program, but during the process he developed the world famous Cap-Chur Gun, a modified air rifle that would shoot a syringe-style tranquiller dart at deer. This innovation paved the way for catching hundreds of deer on some of the Georgia coastal islands that were overpopulated for restocking in the interior portions of the state. It didn't take long before a man named Red Palmer, a drug salesman, patented Jack's innovative dart gun in the mid-1950s, naming it the "Cap-Chur Gun." Throughout the late 1950s and early 1960s, he sold thousands of dart guns around the world and became a millionaire in the process. Jack, the original designer of the gun and the revolutionary syringe-style dart, received a small royalty, but for the most part never shared in any of those profits because he was an employee of the state. Although the gun has been improved upon over the years, it still uses the same type of dart and is built on the same principles as Jack's original prototype gun built in the early 1950s.

In 1950, a state-wide game survey estimated that about 33,000 deer existed in Georgia. Today, thanks to the efforts of Jack Crockford and other hardworking individuals, Georgia now has a state-wide population that numbers well over one million animals.

Discovery of Gold in North Georgia

Several popular stories have been passed down about the discovery of gold in North Georgia in 1828 and the subsequent gold rush that took place and marked the brutal removal of the Cherokee Indians in that part of the state.

Lumpkin and White county residents have argued for years about which county actually produced the first gold nugget.

One of the most popular stories claims that a local settler named Benjamin Parks was out deer hunting near a salt lick in Lumpkin County not far from the Chestatee River in 1828 when he stumbled over a rock containing a small vein of gold that he later described as having a "deep rich yellow hue like that of an egg yolk." The site later became the famed Calhoun Mine. According to former Governor and U.S. Senator Zell Miller, who authored the classic book, *Purt Nigh Gone,* published in 2009, Parks was later interviewed by the Atlanta Constitution on his 94th birthday about his discovery.

An equally popular story maintains that one Frank Logan or his slave found gold along Duke's Creek in White County around the same time.

Yet another tale claims that a white prospector from North Carolina named Jesse Hogan acquired a small nugget of gold from a Cherokee Indian boy living along Ward's Creek near present-day Dahlonega (which at the time still belonged to the Cherokees Nation). Hogan reportedly later claimed he had found the nugget.

A fourth story credits a man named John Witheroods (or Witherow) with finding a three-ounce nugget along Duke's Creek near the present-day town of Helen in today's White County.

And a fifth tale tells us that Thomas Bowen found some gold along Duke's Creek in the roots of a tree that had blown down in a storm.

The truth will likely never be known, but we do know that after gold was discovered somewhere in the rich hills of North Georgia between the present-day towns of Dahlonega and Cleveland, the nation's first-ever gold rush soon was attracting thousands of hopeful prospectors to North Georgia.

Dockery Lake

Dockery Lake Recreational Area

Built in the mid-1930s by a CCC labor force according to specifications that Ranger Woody reportedly drew up on his kitchen table, Lake Dockery was probably built as a flood control lake. When Forest Service engineers found out Ranger Woody had authorized the building of the lake without their approval, they were said to be furious. They insisted the dam would never hold up under heavy rains. Those same engineers later built two more flood control lakes further downstream from Dockery Lake using federal guidelines. A year or so later, heavy rains washed away both government dams, while Ranger Woody's dam at Dockery Lake never faltered.

The lake was named for homesteader Andrew John Dockery. Situated on a small tributary of Waters Creek and accessible from Highway 60 just east of Suches in Lumpkin County, the 6-acre lake is stocked with trout and recreational area offers camping, hiking, picnicking and fishing. Hikers can enjoy the 3.4-mile Dockery Lake Trail, which provides access to the Appalachian Trail. Nearby Dockery Gap Scenic Overlook on Highway 60 offers a spectacular view of the mountains.

Elliott, Charlie Newton (1906-2000)

Born in Covington, Georgia, Charles Elliott briefly attended Emory University and transferred to the University of Georgia forestry school where he unexpectedly left after three years without graduating. He soon joined the Georgia Department of Forestry in 1928. Working as a forester in the North Georgia Mountains under Assistant State Forester Eddie Stone on the proposed route of the Appalachian Trail across Blood Mountain in Union County, he befriended Ranger Arthur Woody who was a staunch supporter of the trail. Ranger Woody became his close friend and mentor for the next 18 years until the Ranger's death in 1946. As a gifted writer, Elliott wrote numerous newspaper and magazine stories in the late 1930s and '40s about Ranger Woody's many achievements during those fast-paced and highly productive years.

In the early and mid-1930s, Elliott became a Regional Forester with the U.S Forest Service, continuing his close work with Ranger Woody. In 1931, he became heavily involved in the planning and building of Vogel State Park. In 1937 he became the first director of the newly organized Georgia State Parks Department. In 1938 he was appointed Commissioner of the Georgia Natural Resources Department and served as editor of Outdoor Georgia magazine, a state publication. In 1943 he became director of the Georgia Game and Fish Commission.

From 1950 until shortly before his death in 2000, he served as Southeastern field editor for Outdoor Life Magazine, distinguishing himself with his gift for the written word on many occasions. He became a well-known authority on turkey hunting and, as the "Old Professor," wrote two books on the subject. During his long career, he wrote 20 books and hundreds of newspaper and magazine articles. His dedication to conservation and wildlife was evident to those who knew him personally and those who read his many writings. He died in 2000 at age 94.

Forest Guards

As soon as large tracts of land were acquired by the federal government in the Southern Appalachians for the National Forest system after the Weeks Act was passed in 1911, fire control and fire prevention became a top priority with the U.S. Forest Service. Prior to that time, large private landowners like the Pfister & Vogel Leather Company had hired forest guards to protect their holdings from trespassers, poachers and local homesteaders who deliberately set fires. One of the early goals of the Forest Service was to practice prudent fire control and teach local landowners the merits of doing the same.

Forest guards were appointed by the Forest Service. For many years in the teens and early 1920s the job was carried out on horseback. In the early days, no lookout towers or telephone lines existed with which to communicate long distances, so locating fires and getting to them quickly was of utmost concern.

The Forest Service often hired local men to serve as forest guards and firefighters. Since burning had been such a widespread practice in the mountains for generations, forest guards helped to educate local landowners and tried to teach them that annual burning was bad for the habitat and that fire control was necessary in order to protect the forest.

Arthur Woody was sworn in as a forest guard on May 1, 1915 after serving on a survey crew for three years. His primary job was to protect federal lands within his beloved 31,000-acre Rock Creek Refuge from fire, trespassers and poachers. His salary was $50 per month, a typical forest guard's salary at that time. Three years later in 1918 Arthur Woody was promoted to the position of full-fledged Forest Ranger. At that time, he began hiring his own forest guards to help protect the ever-expanding federal lands under his supervision being purchased by the government.

Frank Gross Recreational Area

Located along the banks of Rock Creek within the Blue Ridge Wildlife Management Area of the Chattahoochee National Forest in Fannin County, Georgia, Frank Gross Recreation Area, named in honor of state senator Frank Gross who served in the late 1930s, offers a variety of recreational opportunities including hiking, camping and fishing. The nearby Appalachian Trail (accessible from Forest Road 69) and the Benton MacKaye Trail (north of the recreation area) offer hikers a chance to explore. Trout fishing has long been popular along Rock Creek and Mill Creek at Frank Gross Recreation Area, as both offer native brook trout and introduced rainbow and brown trout. The area is well known for its trout fishing and is just upstream from the national fish hatchery.

Frank Gross was an avid outdoorsman and state senator from Union County who did much for Georgia. He became close friends with Ranger Woody and Charlie Elliott. After the Ranger's death in 1946, Frank and Charlie hunted elk in Wyoming and fished for trout across the North Georgia mountains. Charlie wrote several magazine articles in *Outdoor Life* about hunts he and Frank shared in the 1950s and '60s. Frank is best remembered for his work on behalf of the local schools in Union County as well as for his support of the Forest Service. He helped set up the wildlife conservation area along Rock Creek in the Blue Ridge WMA that eventually was named in his honor.

Georgia's First Wildlife Management Area – A Cooperative Agreement Between the U.S. Forest Service and the Georgia Natural Resources Division, 1936

In March 1936 the Georgia Wildlife Division, under the leadership of Zack D. Cravey, Commissioner of Natural Resources, entered into an unprecedented cooperative agreement with the U.S. Forest Service for the management of all wildlife on National Forest land within the state. Ranger Arthur Woody had been lobbying to make his beloved Rock Creek Refuge into a game preserve for nearly 10 years, so that he could better protect the deer, turkeys and trout he had placed inside the refuge, and so that sportsmen in Georgia could ultimately hunt and fish in the refuge.

This agreement came about in part due to the tireless efforts Ranger Woody and Charlie Elliott made in bringing the state and the Forest Service together. With the official name of "Blue Ridge Wildlife Management Area," the refuge became the first wildlife management area in Georgia and the nation, as well as the first government property to be managed by a state agency.

By 1937, following the ten-plus-year success of Ranger Woody's Rock Creek Refuge (now Blue Ridge WMA), four more wildlife management areas had been established in the Chattahoochee National Forest under the direction of the Georgia Wildlife Division; the Chattahoochee WMA, the Chestatee WMA, the Cohutta WMA, and the Lake Burton WMA. Because the Georgia partnership worked so well, numerous other states soon followed suit with similar agreements. Today, the vast network of wildlife management areas found across the U.S. can trace its roots back to the vision and determination of Ranger Arthur Woody and Charlie Elliott.

Harkins, Clyde (1925-)

Born in 1925, Clyde Harkins of Wolf Pen Gap may be the last living veteran of the famed CCC Camp Woody in Suches. At age 15 in 1940, Clyde attempted to join the CCC, but he knew his small size (5 feet, 2 inches tall and 110 pounds) might be detrimental in being accepted. Thanks to Ranger Woody, who apparently used his influence, Clyde passed the physical examination and became one of the "Satins of Suches" for a 12-month stint.

Rev. Claud Boynton was Clyde's civilian supervisor. Clyde has fond memories of his year with the "CC" working on such projects as crushing granite to improve local roads, helping to build some of the rock structures and camping sites at Lake Winfield Scott and working on the famous rock house on Blood Mountain through which the Appalachian Trail runs. Clyde always felt indebted to Ranger Woody for making it possible for him to join the CCC.

Heatter, Gabriel (1890–1972)

Gabriel Heatter was a nationally prominent radio news broadcaster during the 1930s, '40s and '50s during the golden days of radio, before television became popular in the 1950s and began to eclipse the big-time radio shows. Heatter was often quoted for his words of wisdom. He was especially popular during the war years in the early 1940s when he frequently gave news about what was happening overseas. He always opened his popular show with, "There's good news tonight," although the news from the battlefronts was not always that good. The entire Woody family listened to his nightly broadcasts, especially during the war years.

Joyce Kilmer
Joyce Kilmer Memorial Forest

Joyce Kilmer was an American writer, journalist and poet from New Jersey who was killed in action in France during World War I. He reportedly was killed by a sniper's bullet at the Second Battle of the Marne in 1918. At age 31, he left behind a wife, Aline Murray, and five children. He is best remembered for a classic short poem titled "Trees," published in the collection *Trees and Other Poems* in 1914.

Today "Trees" is considered to be a national treasure. To honor his memory, a 3,800-acre stand of virgin timber was established in North Carolina in 1936 and designated as the Joyce Kilmer Memorial Forest. Charlie Elliott, who worked for the National Park Service in the early 1930s, reportedly had much to do with the establishment of the memorial forest.

Trees

I think that I shall never see
a poem lovely as a tree.
A tree whose hungry mouth is prest
Against the earth's sweet flowing breast;
A tree that looks at God all day,
And lifts her leafy arms to pray;
A tree that may in Summer wear
A nest of robins in her hair;
Upon whose bosom snow has lain;
Who intimately lives with rain.
Poems are made by fools like me,
But only God can make a tree.

Lake Winfield Scott

Lake Winfield Scott is a man-made, 18-acre high mountain lake in Union County located just north of Suches at the headwaters of Cooper Creek. At an altitude of 2,854 feet, it is one of Georgia's highest mountain lakes, resting peacefully in the shadow of historic Blood Mountain. Completed in early 1942 at the beginning of World War II, construction on the lake was begun in 1938 by the CCC boys under the direction of Arthur Woody. Ranger Woody was also personally responsible for building the road to Highway 129 at Vogel State Park that gave access to the lake. Eventually that road ran from 129 to Suches and became State Highway 180.

Lake Winfield Scott was the final CCC project in Georgia and one of the last in the nation. Because of the war effort, the CCC was discontinued in 1942. Many of its former members enlisted in the service and served their country with distinction. Today the artistic masonry of the stone buildings, walls and outdoor cooking grills in the campsites at the lake bear testament to the remarkable skills of Ranger Woody's dedicated "CC" boys.

The lake was named after General Winfield Scott, a 19th century United States Army general, diplomat, and presidential candidate. Known as "Old Fuss and Feathers," Scott was a hero of the Mexican-American War and the first American since George Washington to hold the rank of lieutenant general. At the beginning of the Civil War, Scott was temporarily placed in charge of all Union forces because of his rank.

In 1838, the local Cherokee Indians were removed from the area under the direction of General Scott and forced westward along the "Trail of Tears." Settlers later moved in, and by the early 1900s, much of the area had been heavily logged and exploited. In May 1938, the lake was opened to the public as part of the Forest Service's multiple-use plan for administering the Chattahoochee National Forest for the "greatest good for the greatest number of people." This must have made Ranger Woody very proud. He had been lobbying a somewhat single-minded Forest Service to adopt a multiple use recreational plan on all federal lands since the early-1920s. Two trailheads from Lake Winfield Scott give access to the Appalachian Trail. The lake offers excellent fishing for both stocked rainbow trout and warm water species including largemouth bass and sunfish.

Leopold, Aldo (1887-1948)

A noted American author, scientist, ecologist, forester, environmentalist, and professor at the University of Wisconsin best known for his ground-breaking book *A Sand County Almanac* (1949), which has sold more than two million copies, Rand Aldo Leopold was born in Burlington, Iowa, on January 11, 1887. Of German descent, his father frequently took the family on outdoor excursions into the woods and there instilled in young Aldo a deep love and respect for nature. Leopold spent hours in his youth studying birds and other wildlife.

In 1900, Gifford Pinchot, who had managed the vast timberland holdings for the Vanderbilt family in North Carolina, was appointed director of the newly formed Division of Forestry in the Department of Agriculture (U.S. Forest Service) under President Theodore Roosevelt. One of Pinchot's early acts was to help establish one of the nation's first forestry schools at Yale University. Hearing about the school, the teenage Leopold decided on forestry as a vocation and later attended Yale.

Leopold went on to become an ardent conservationist who emphasized wilderness conservation and preservation. By 1930, he was considered one of the nation's foremost experts on wildlife management. He advocated the scientific management of wildlife habitats by both public and private landholders.

In his 1933 book *Game Management,* Leopold defined the science of wildlife management as "the art of making land produce sustained annual crops of wild game for recreational use. Founder of the Wildlife Society in 1935, he is considered to be the father of the science of wildlife management.

Frequently quoted from his books, one of Leopold's often repeated quotes is:

"A peculiar virtue in wildlife ethics is that the hunter has no gallery to applaud or disapprove of his conduct. Whatever his acts, they are dictated by his own conscience, rather than by a mob of onlookers. It is difficult to exaggerate the importance of this fact."

While Aldo Leopold and Arthur Woody came from vastly different backgrounds, their philosophies on wildlife management, conservation and habitat improvement shared many common parallels.

Mark Trail Comic Strip

Mark Trail is a long-running newspaper comic strip created by Georgia cartoonist Ed Dodd (1902-1991). First introduced in April 1946, the popular strip centered on nature, conservation and outdoor recreational themes. When Mark Trail began, it was syndicated as a daily comic strip through the *New York Post* to 45 newspapers. Dodd, who had worked for many summers at Dan Beard's Boy Scout camp in Pennsylvania, had long been interested in nature, outdoor skills and conservation issues.

The Mark Trail character is widely believed to have been loosely based on the life and career of the pipe smoking outdoorsman Charlie Elliott (1906-2000), who worked with the U.S. Forest Service and the Georgia Natural

Resources Department in various capacities during the 1920s, '30s and '40s. Charlie and Ed Dodd were good friends. Charlie, a gifted writer, later served as a field editor for *Outdoor Life* magazine from 1950 to 1990.

In 2006, King Features syndicated the strip to nearly 175 newspapers. Over the years, the comic strip began to shift its focus to important environmental and ecological issues of the day.

Neels Gap

U.S. Highway 129 (Gaineville Highway) crosses Neels Gap approximately 2 ½ miles south of Vogel State Park. The Appalachian Trail also crosses the highway here, and weary hikers love this spot because the Mountain Crossing Walasi-Yi Center (store) and hostel are located here. The distance from Neels Gap to the top of Blood Mountain is about 4.8 miles. At 4,461 feet in elevation, Blood Mountain is the highest point on the Appalachian Trail in Georgia. The hiking distance from Neels Gap to Woody Gap is 11.4 miles.

Bonnell H.Stone, who spent most of his career managing timberland for the Pfister & Vogel Leather Company in Union County, and who today is recognized as the father of modern forestry in Georgia, was very instrumental in getting Highway 129 built across Neel's Gap in 1925. Much of the company's vast land holdings were in this area. The new highway replaced the Old Logan Turnpike across Tesnatee Gap. Highway 129 ultimately connected Gainesville and Cleveland to Blairsville and points beyond.

The New Deal (FDR, 1933)

President Franklin Delano Roosevelt's "New Deal" was a series of economic programs enacted in the United States between 1933 and 1936. Aimed at trying to help the nation recover from the Great Depression that began in October 1929, many of the programs involved presidential executive orders or laws passed by Congress during FDR's first term. The programs focused on what many people called the "3 Rs" – Relief, Recovery, and Reform: Relief for the unemployed and poor; Recovery of the economy to normal levels; and Reform of the financial system to prevent a repeat depression. Many of these programs gave new hope to mountain communities, especially in the hard hit coal mining areas of West Virginia and Kentucky.

One of the most successful programs to come out of the New Deal was the formation of the Civilian Conservation Corps in 1933. Being a lifelong Republican, Ranger Woody was very critical of most of "big government" spending programs coming out of the Roosevelt administration. But once the small army CCC boys invaded his beloved mountains, he was quick to take advantage of this ready and willing labor force. Over the next nine years, Ranger Woody's beloved "CC" boys built and improved roads, built several lakes, stocked lakes and streams with thousands of fish, built trails, built fire towers, strung miles of telephone cable, helped fight forest fires, planted tens of thousands of trees, and were engaged in numerous other conservation programs that helped the people and the forests and wildlife in the North Georgia mountains.

Nicholson, Roscoe "Nick" (1887-1959)

Much like Ranger Arthur Woody, Georgia's first official forest ranger (Ranger Woody was the second) began his career as a surveyor in the mountains of northeast Georgia. He was born and raised in Pine Mountain, an unincorporated community at the eastern edge of Rabun County, Georgia. After being appointed to the position of forest ranger in 1912, Ranger Nick, as he was fondly called, helped the U.S. Forest Service acquire much land in northeast Georgia for what would eventually become the Chattahoochee National Forest. The careers of Arthur Woody and Nick Nicholson had many parallels. Both men worked tirelessly in their respective districts to restore the forests, prevent fires, build roads, improve communications, and in general, improve the lives of the mountain people.

With the help of the "CC" boys, Ranger Nick built the first fire tower on Rabun Bald, Georgia's second highest peak (with an elevation of 4,696 feet, it is only 88 feet lower than Brasstown Bald). The "CC" boys also ran telephone lines from tree to tree up the mountain to establish communication with the tower.

Ranger "Nick" retired in 1952 after a career spanning 40 years. In 1960, the Coleman River Scenic Area near Clayton, Georgia, was dedicated to Ranger "Nick" following his 40 years of public service in honor of his promotion of conservation ideals and his many other achievements.

Ozmer, Robert Roy (1899-1969)

As a friend of Ranger Arthur Woody, Roy Ozmer was a widely-traveled and highly-eccentric outdoorsman who, upon Ranger Woody's recommendation, was hired by the Appalachian Trail Conservancy (ATC) in 1929 to physically explore and map out the best route for the trail across Georgia. Prior to 1929, Ozmer reportedly had been a well-read and well-educated actor, newspaperman and jack-of-all-trades who loved to recite poetry. While searching out the best route through Georgia, Ozmer teamed up with state forester Everett "Eddie" Stone, also a friend of Ranger Woody. With Ranger Woody's support, the two men mapped out an alternate course for the trail which spanned some 79 miles inside the state across Springer, Black, Blood and Tray mountains and into North Carolina. The new route was eventually approved and the trail was built.

During the mid-1950s, some 10 years after Ranger Woody died, Roy Ozmer became a well known "recluse" in southern Florida where he earned the nickname "the hermit of Pelican Key." He reportedly lived alone in a small shack on an island and suffered from alcoholism. He later returned to his native state of Tennessee after a hurricane destroyed his beach shack. He died in 1969.

Pinchot, Gifford (1865-1946)

Gifford Pinchot, often called the Father of American Forestry, was an American forester and politician. Born into a wealthy Connecticut family, he spent much of his life at his family's estate in Milford, Pennsylvania. After graduating from Yale, he traveled to France and studied European forestry practices. He became America's first scientifically trained forester.

Upon returning to the U.S., Pinchot became well known for advocating sound forest management and long-term sustained yields in America's forests instead of the destructive style of clear cutting which had long been the rule of the day. In 1905, Pinchot was appointed as the nation's first Chief of the U.S. Forest Service under President Theodore Roosevelt. He was instrumental in the creation of the Society of American Foresters.

In 1910 he was fired as Forest Service Chief by President William Howard Taft because the political climate concerning environmental conservation changed considerably after Roosevelt left office. The Roosevelt administration had pushed through so many federal conservation initiatives that many private interests greatly resented so much federal involvement. Under Pinchot's Forest Service leadership, millions of acres had been added to the national forests, and private interests very much resented the federal government's iron-fist control. Pinchot became a victim of those hostile feelings.

Pinchot is best known for promoting scientific forest management and emphasizing the controlled, profitable use of forests and other natural resources so they would be of maximum benefit to mankind. Some of his "preservationist" detractors took exception to this "renewable resource" philosophy. Although he was a dedicated conservationist, he also advocated managing the nation's forests so that they would be self-sustaining and pay their own way.

During the early years of Forest Service management in the Southeast, this single-minded goal did not sit well with Ranger Arthur Woody, who believed that all federal forestlands should also be managed to develop maximum fish and wildlife resources on those lands as well as a variety of outdoor recreational uses by the public. Ranger Woody pushed hard for this "multi-use" concept, but a number of years went by before this expanded philosophy became part of the Forest Service agenda.

Pinchot later served two terms as Republican governor of Pennsylvania – from 1923-26 and from 1931-34. He died of leukemia in 1946.

Pittman-Robertson Act

On September 2, 1937, Congress passed the Federal Aid to Wildlife Restoration Act, better known as the Pittman-Robertson Act (sponsored by Congressmen Key Pittman of Nevada and Willis Robertson of Virginia). The act was signed into law by President Franklin D. Roosevelt a short time later. The new law provided badly needed federal funds to state game agencies for organized wildlife restoration and management programs. It was to be funded by a 10 percent excise tax placed on all sporting arms and ammunition sold across the country. The exact amount of money to be allocated to each state would be determined by that state's size and number of paid hunting license holders. (Later on, the tax was increased to 11 percent and amended to include archery equipment as well.)

As of 2010, over $2 billion has gone into the program. In 2012, the Pittman-Robertson Act celebrated its 75th year.

After several years of delay, the Pittman-Robertson Act was initiated in Georgia in 1944. For some reason, reportedly having to do with bad politics, two states, Nevada and Georgia, did not participate in the act until several years after it had been passed. Some restocking of deer occurred throughout the state in 1944 and 1945 with P-R funds, but for the most part, little was accomplished until after World War II.

In 1947, one year after Arthur Woody died, the Georgia Game and Fish Commission began a stepped-up restocking program with aid of P-R funds. That year, Jack Crockford was hired by the state of Georgia as a biologist. Crockford, who today is widely recognized as the father of the deer restoration program in Georgia, once said, "The Pittman-Robertson Act marked the beginning of scientific game management across the state of Georgia and the nation."

Georgia receives approximately $7 million annually through the Wildlife Restoration Program and has received a total of nearly $146,000,000 since the program's inception in 1939. The Wildlife Resources Division uses these funds for a wide assortment of wildlife conservation projects.

Reams, Roscoe (1925-2008)

Born in Atlanta, in 1925, Roscoe Reams died in an auto accident in September 2008 at age 84. He graduated from Boy's High School in Atlanta and attended college for a time at Georgia State University. Roscoe started hunting wild hogs and trout fishing in the North Georgia Mountains with several older companions in 1938 when he was 14. He befriended Ranger Arthur Woody and nurtured a very close friendship for the next five years. He also developed a lifelong friendship with Charlie Elliott. In 1943, Roscoe enlisted in the Navy during World War II. By the time he returned home in 1946, Ranger Woody had passed away a few months earlier. Roscoe deeply regretted never seeing his mentor and friend again.

When the first archery season for deer was opened in Blue Ridge WMA in 1940, Roscoe and his hunting companions were part of that historic hunt. Roscoe went on to become a nationally famous trick archery shooter during the 1950s and '60s, putting on hundreds of shooting demonstrations across the country, including one in the ballroom of the Statler Hotel in New York City. He even made an appearance on the Tonight Show in Hollywood hosted at the time by Steve Allen.

In later life, Roscoe became a nationally known turkey hunting expert. He conducted seminars, judged turkey-calling contests and soften erved as a hunting guide. He and Charlie Elliott hunted turkeys and fished together for over 50 years. Roscoe once set a Georgia record by catching a 9-pound rainbow trout with an artificial lure. During the time when alligators were endangered, he was employed by the federal government to trap alligators off Blackbeard Island in Georgia so that they could be restocked in other areas.

Roscoe was often referred to as "Atlanta's Robin Hood" and a modern-day "Daniel Boone." He worked fulltime at Delta Airlines as a mechanic until his retirement in 1986. In later life, he often said that Ranger Woody had profoundly impacted his early life.

Rogers, Kenneth (1907-1989)

Kenneth Rogers was a legendary photographer for the Atlanta Constitution from 1923-1972 who chronicled many of the photos of the historic 1940 Blue Ridge WMA archery and firearms hunts. He took many historic photos in the Atlanta area and across Georgia during his long, distinguished career. He became good friends with Ranger Arthur Woody and he often traveled to Suches to fish for trout in the refuge. The most famous photo of Ranger Woody ever taken and today one of the most familiar – the Ranger sitting on a fence and waving – was the handiwork of Kenneth Rogers.

Roosevelt, Theodore (1858-1919)

Theodore "Teddy," "TR," Roosevelt was an American president, patriot, soldier, cowboy, statesman, hunter, historian, naturalist, author, and passionate conservationist who served as the 26th President of the United States from 1901 to 1909. At 42, he became the nation's youngest president in history following the assassination of President William McKinley in September 1901.

Roosevelt became a war hero serving with the Rough Riders in Cuba in 1898. Upon his return to New York, he was elected governor. Two years later he was elected Vice President under William McKinley's in 1900. On Nov. 10, 1906, Roosevelt became the first American to win a Nobel Prize for his work surrounding the Treaty of Portsmouth, which ended the Russo-Japanese War.

As an avid conservationist, Roosevelt established the U.S. Forest Service in 1905. He appointed Gifford Pinchot as the first Forest Service chief. During his term as president, he protected nearly 230,000,000 acres of public land by establishing 51 Federal Bird Reservations, four National Game Preserves, 150 National Forests and five National Parks. He used the power of the 1906 American Antiquities Act to establish 18 National Monuments.

A prolific author, Roosevelt wrote nearly 20 books. He died in his sleep from a blood clot on Jan. 6, 1919 at the age of 60. Today, a likeness of his face is cast in stone with Jefferson, Lincoln and Washington on Mt. Rushmore in South Dakota.

Silviculture

Silviculture is the scientific practice of actively controlling and managing the establishment, growth, composition, health and quality of forests to meet diverse needs and values, as opposed to simply protecting a forest and allowing it to grow naturally. The name comes from the Latin *silvi-* (forest) plus culture (as in growing). The study of forests and woods is termed silvology.

Society of American Foresters

Journal of Forestry magazine
American Forests magazine

The Society of American Foresters (SAF) is the national scientific and educational organization representing the forestry profession in the United States. Founded in 1900 by Gifford Pinchot, it is the largest professional society for foresters in the world. The mission of the Society of American Foresters is to advance the science, education, technology, and practice of forestry; to enhance the competency of its members; to establish professional excellence; and, to use the knowledge, skills, and conservation ethic of the profession to ensure the continued health and use of forest ecosystems and the present and future availability of forest resources to benefit society. SAF members include natural resource professionals in public and private settings, researchers, CEOs, administrators, educators, and students.

In print since 1902, the *Journal of Forestry* magazine has long been the official publication of the Society of American Foresters. At the height of Arthur Woody's fame in the late 1930s and early 1940s, several insightful articles about Ranger Woody appeared in the journal, written by assistant rangers who worked under him during that time period.

American Forests magazine has been in print since 1895. Charlie Elliott, who began his free-lance writing career in the late 1930s while he worked with various conservation-related organizations in the North Georgia

Mountains, wrote several very informative articles for *American Forests* about Ranger Woody in the late 1930s and early 1940s.

Sosebee Cove

Part of the Blood Mountain Wilderness, Sosebee Cove Scenic Area is a 178-acre forest preserve within the Chattahoochee National Forest located about 3 miles west of Vogel State Park on Wolf Pen Gap Road (Georgia Highway 180). On February 16, 1925, then 40-year-old Arthur Woody negotiated the sale of this magnificent tract owned by F. Alonzo Sosebee to the U.S. Forest Service. Ranger Woody often rode his horse through this tract and he knew it was unique to the mountains. He worked hard to ensure that it would be made into a forest preserve for people to enjoy well beyond his lifetime. The tract contains a rich diversity of lowland hardwoods, shrubs, and wildflowers.

Although the second growth tract of bottomland hardwood timber was cut over in the early 1900s, some of the trees remaining at the time of purchase may have been virgin trees and the tract was said to have one of the finest stands of yellow poplar found anywhere in the state of Georgia. In the spring and fall, the property is alive with numerous varieties of wildflowers. A real mountain treasure, the diverse trees and plants found within the confines of this preserve make the spot a botanist's dream. After Ranger Woody's death in 1946, Sosebee Cove Scenic Area was dedicated as a memorial to his life and his work in conservation.

The tract can be accessed by a one-half-mile-long hiking trail that consists of two linked loops. Several giant buckeye trees near the beginning of the trail are well over 100 years old.

Stone, Bonnell H.

Bonnell H. Stone is recognized as the father of forestry in Georgia. Born in Oxford, Georgia, on December 3, 1887, he spent most of his career working in Union County. That work often brought him in close contact with Ranger Arthur Woody and Charlie Elliott during the late 1920s and early 1930s.

Stone managed thousands of acres of forestland in Union County from 1913 through 1931. He received his education from Emory-at-Oxford and the University of Georgia where he majored in forestry. He took a job with the U.S. Forest Service early in his career. Later he was employed as chief forester by the Pfister & Vogel Leather Company of Milwaukee, Wisconsin, one of the largest leather producers in the country.

Prior to World War I, tannic acid from the bark of hemlock trees, chestnuts and chestnut oaks was vital to the leather-making process, and the company acquired tens of thousands of acres of forestland in the North Georgia mountains. After World War I, new tanning methods were developed, and bark from trees was no longer part of the process. As a result, Pfister & Vogel began to liquidate some of its large land holdings.

In 1927, Stone was very instrumental in helping to negotiate the donation of 223 acres of land by the company that would become Vogel State Park, one of Georgia's oldest and most popular state parks. Ranger Arthur Woody was highly supportive of the new park and the soon-to-be-built 20-acre, high mountain lake fittingly named Lake Trahlyta. He did everything he could to insure the park's successful completion.

Stone was also instrumental in getting Highway 129 built across Neels Gap in 1925. The new highway replaced the Old Logan Turnpike across Tesnatee Gap. Highway 129 ultimately connected Gainesville and Cleveland to Blairsville and points north.

In 1935, a plaque honoring Bonnell Stone was placed at Neels Gap which reads: "June, 1935. Erected to the Memory of Bonnell Stone December 3, 1887 – May 25, 1935 by The Georgia Forestry Association of which he was a founder and secretary. His public service as a trained forester merits him the distinction of being The Father of Forestry in Georgia. He inspired the donation of Vogel State Park."

Bonnell H. Stone served as chairman of the Blairsville Public Schools Board, president of the Union County Chamber of Commerce, was active in and served as an officer in the Appalachian Scenic Highway Association, was president of the Union County Good Roads Association and the Southern Good Roads Association. He was also a member of the National Council of Outdoor Recreation and the National Conference of State Parks. He was a founding member of the Georgia Forestry Association and served on the state forestry board. He served two terms in the Georgia Legislature, 1925-1926 and 1929-1931. As a representative, he worked diligently for the people in the area.

Stone, Everett "Eddie" Jr.
(no known date of birth or death)

In the mid-1920s, Eddie Stone served as Assistant State Forester of Georgia. In 1929, after proposals had been discussed for a 20-mile portion of the Appalachian Trail to extend into northwest Georgia, he took it upon himself to map out a 75-plus-mile alternate route that would begin at Mt. Oglethorpe and run in a northeasterly direction into the Nantahala Mountains in North Carolina. With considerable opposition to his plan, due mainly to the proposed location of where his route would enter North Carolina, he solicited the help of the good-natured Charlie Elliott, then serving as Assistant District Forester for the state of Georgia, to help him blaze his route and later to organize a group of Boy Scouts who would walk the trail and mark it more distinctly. This highly publicized stunt helped gain approval for his route and a compromise was reached in which most of Mr. Stone's Georgia route was approved.

Once the route had been approved, work began and the Georgia portion of the trail was completed in 1931. Eddie Stone organized the Georgia Appalachian Trail Club in 1930 to help maintain the trail. Stone was the club's first president and Charlie Elliott served as its first vice-president, secretary-treasurer and historian. With the coming of the CCC in 1933, Stone used his influence with the Forest Service and Ranger Arthur Woody to have the first shelters built on the Georgia section of the trail. Much like Ranger Woody, he was considered ahead of his time in fighting to protect the trail and make it a true wilderness experience. Stone promoted the idea of creating state forest parks in Georgia and along with Charlie Elliott and Bonnell H. Stone (no known relation), was deeply involved with the creation of Vogel State Forest Park, Georgia's second-oldest state park. In 1935, Stone took a job with the U.S. Forest Service where he drifted off into obscurity. In 2013, he was inducted into the Appalachian Trail Hall of Fame. Today Eddie Stone is considered the father of the Appalachian Trail in Georgia.

The Great Chestnut Blight

When Arthur Woody roamed the mountains as a boy in the late 1800s, giant chestnut trees reaching almost 100 feet in height grew commonly in the North Georgia Mountains. Chestnuts were one of the most dominant trees in the mountain, making up about 25 percent of all trees growing in eastern forests.

For hundreds of years before Ranger Woody's time, the Cherokees had utilized chestnuts as an important food item. Chestnuts were traditionally collected and eaten by the early settlers and used for roasting and stuffing turkeys at Thanksgiving and Christmas. Sadly, the old American tradition of "roasting chestnuts on an open fire," as immortalized in the classic song by Nat King Cole, quickly became a thing of the past in the early decades of the 1900s by a devastating blight.

A fast-spreading fungus discovered in 1904 made its way from New York to Georgia down the Appalachian chain. By 1920, thousands of trees were dying in the North Georgia mountains. By 1940, millions of chestnuts had been wiped out in the East. This sad event obviously concerned Ranger Woody deeply.

Although no one knows exactly how he went about it, photographic evidence indicates that Ranger Woody experimented with planting chestnut seedlings in the forest, probably somewhere in his beloved Rock Creek Refuge, in the late 1930s after the blight had killed millions of trees. We'll never know the details, but we can only surmise that his seedlings eventually succumbed to the blight.

Several classic photos are all that remain to bear witness to the fact that North Georgia's most famous forest ranger did his part to try to save one of his favorite tree species.

The Pisgah National Forest and Game Preserve

When northern financier George Vanderbilt constructed his massive Biltmore estate home near Ashville, North Carolina in the late 1890s, he had acquired a vast amount of mountain acreage around it (nearly 500,000 acres). Vanderbilt died unexpectedly in 1914 at age 51. The Weeks Act had been passed by congress three years earlier in 1911, paving the way for the government to purchase land in the Southeast. Knowing that her husband had always dreamed of having an undisturbed forest preserve around his mountain estate, Vanderbilt's widow initially sold 86,000 acres to the U.S. Forest Service in 1915 for $5 per acre. She went on to sell nearly 500,000 acres to the Forest Service. In 1916, the bulk of that land became the Pisgah National Forest.

The Pisgah National Game Preserve (today about 10,000 acres inside the Pisgah National Forest) was created by an act of the North Carolina legislature, an act of congress and presidential proclamation in 1916. Like many portions of the southern Appalachians, deer, black bears and turkeys had become rare in western North Carolina by the late 1800s. After acquiring his vast landholdings, Vanderbilt protected his deer and other wildlife species whose numbers had been depleted, and within a few short decades these animals had made a significant comeback. By 1927, excess deer were available for purchase in portions of the Pisgah Preserve, and Ranger Arthur Woody used some of these deer for stocking in his Rock Creek Refuge.

The Pisgah property is often referred to as the cradle of forestry in America because George Vanderbilt also had a keen interest in forest management and in making his vast land holdings self sufficient. The nation's first forestry school was established here in 1898 although it only lasted a few short years. However, Vanderbilt's school of forestry played a major role in the later creation of the U.S. Forest Service. Before his death, Vanderbilt had hired American forester Gifford Pinchot to manage the forests on his property. Much of Vanderbilt's philosophy on forest management – mainly that a forest could be managed to be self sustaining – was embodied in Pinchot's short tenure as first chief of the U.S. Forest Service. German forester Carl A. Schenck replaced Pinchot as manager of the Vanderbilt forestland holdings.

U.S. Forest Service

The U. S. Forest Service is an agency of the U.S. Department of Agriculture created by President Theodore Roosevelt in 1905. In 1876, Congress created the office of Special Agent in the Department of Agriculture to assess the existing state of all forests across the U. S. In 1881, the office was expanded into the newly formed Division of Forestry. Ten years later, the Forest Reserve Act of 1891 authorized withdrawing land from the public domain as "forest reserves," managed by the Department of the Interior. In March 1891, President Benjamin Harrison established the first forest reserve. By the end of his term in 1893, he had placed more than 13 million acres of publicly owned land in western states into the "forest reserve" category, including Yellowstone Park, the country's first national park established in 1872. In 1901, the Division of Forestry was renamed the Bureau of Forestry.

During the fast-paced Roosevelt administration, the Transfer Act of 1905 shifted the management of forest reserves from the General Land Office of the Interior Department to the Bureau of Forestry. The new agency became known as the U.S. Forest Service. Gifford Pinchot, who had served as chief forester for the vast land holdings of the Vanderbilt family in western North Carolina, became the Forest Service's first Forest Service chief.

The initial goal of the Forest Service was to restore the forests on federal lands and manage them for maximum timber production so that they could become self-sustaining and pay their own way. Today the Forest Service manages 155 national forests and 20 national grasslands, encompassing some 193 million acres.

Union County, Georgia

Union County was one of 10 counties created from the Cherokee County Territory during the Georgia Land Lottery of 1832. The original Cherokee County Territory was created from lands seized from the Cherokee Nation. In 1832, a unique lottery system involving the future counties of Bartow, Cherokee, Cobb, Floyd, Forsyth, Gilmer, Lumpkin, Murray, Paulding and Union was offered to Georgia residents. A separate lottery was also held that included 40-acre "gold districts" for $10 each in the same portions of the Cherokee Territory. Forced removal of the Cherokee Indians to Oklahoma Territory on the Trail of Tears occurred six years later in 1838. The land lottery attracted gold prospectors and settlers alike.

John Thomas is credited with giving Union County its name. A member of the Georgia House of Representatives in 1833, he reportedly wanted the county to be named Union because "none but union-like men reside in it."

With the coming of the Civil War in 1861, most Union County residents were pro Union. After Georgia left the Union, however, the majority of residents ended supporting the Confederacy. The vast majority of mountain residents also deplored slavery. Few ever owned any slaves.

Vogel State Park

Vogel State Park is Georgia's second oldest state park and one of the oldest in the nation. Located at the base of Blood Mountain in the Chattahoochee National Forest at the intersection of U.S. Highway 129 and State Route 180 (11 miles south of Blairsville), the 233-acre tract was donated to the state in 1927 by Augustus Vogel and Fred Vogel, Jr. of Milwaukee, Wisconsin. The brothers were heirs to the Pfister & Vogel Leather Company, a Wisconsin-based tannery founded by Frederick Vogel which had acquired thousands of acres of timberland in the North Georgia mountains (including most of the acreage where present-day Brasstown Bald is located, Georgia's highest point).

Prior to World War I, the bark from oak and hemlock trees was harvested and used in the leather tanning process. During the war, a synthetic tanning method was developed, making the old method obsolete. As a result, the Vogel family began to sell off much of its land holdings in North Georgia.

As chief forester for the company, University of Georgia graduate Bonnell H. Stone (today regarded as the father of modern forestry in Georgia) managed thousands of acres of forestland for Pfister & Vogel from about 1913 to 1931. Stone was very instrumental in negotiating the donation of the 233-acre tract for a state park. He was a personal and professional friend to Ranger Arthur Woody and Charlie Elliott, who were both enthusiastic supporters for having the park built. As an assistant state forester who was involved in laying out portions of the Appalachian Trail at the time, Charlie Elliott was also instrumental in helping plan some of the trails inside Vogel State Park. Ranger Woody later served on the Vogel State Park Advisory Committee.

In addition to hiking trails, cabins, miniature golf, a general store, a playground and a Civilian Conservation Corps museum, the park is highlighted by the beautiful, 20-acre Lake Trahlyta, named after a Cherokee maiden who, legend claims, is buried a few miles away at Stonepile Gap.

Rich in history, the cabins, picnic areas and camping grounds were constructed by the CCC boys stationed at Goose Creek (just north of the park) during the Great Depression. The story of the CC boys is told in the park's museum by way of exhibits, documents, photographs and other memorabilia. Ranger Woody's CC boys from Camp Woody in Suches also contributed to the building of the park.

Watts, Lyle F.

(1890-1962, Chief of Forest Service, 1943-1952)

Lyle F. Watts was born in Cerro Gordo County, Iowa, in 1890. After graduated from Iowa State College School of Forestry, he entered the Forest Service in 1913 where he served in the Rocky Mountains. In 1928, he left the Forest Service to organize the school of forestry at Utah State Agricultural College (later to become Utah State University). He reentered the Forest Service in 1929, and was later appointed regional forester in Milwaukee, Wisconsin and Portland, Oregon. In 1943, he was appointed 7th chief of the U.S. Forest Service, a position he held until 1952.

Upon Ranger Woody's retirement in September 1945, Watts wrote him a letter from Washington, D.C. commending him on his many years of dedicated service. At the end of the letter he noted that he had enjoyed a fine meal at the Woody home several months earlier. Watts was Forest Service Chief when Ranger Woody died in June 1946.

In the late 1940s, several years after Ranger Woody's death, Watts wrote: "The conservation movement...has made much headway. Today we have a splendid system of national forests making many important contributions to local communities and to the national welfare. The timber and other resources of these national forests are managed for a sustained yield, for permanent and continuing production and use in the public interest. Our national forests are furnishing an increasingly significant portion of the country's timber supply; they are protecting vitally important sources of water; their grazing lands contribute to the nation's supply of meat, wool, and leather; they afford recreational opportunities for millions of people. Their returns to the public in timber production, water supplies, flood control, livestock production, wildlife, recreation, and other services far exceed the costs of administration. It would indeed be difficult to place a dollars and cents value on many of their services and benefits...

"We need aggressive action to control unwise or destructive timber cutting– to establish certain basic rules of practice that will assure continued productivity of the forests...We need also to tighten up still more our protection of the forests from fire. We need more protection work against destructive insects and diseases...We need intensive education and other cooperative services to help forest owners improve their forests and practice real sustained yield management. We need to strengthen the public forests. We need to eliminate over-grazing and build up run-down ranges. We need to improve the condition of many watersheds. We need to replant or reseed millions of depleted acres to restore them to productivity.

"And we need to get on with these things now. Time is matching on. For a century and more this country has been taking much from the land but putting little back. We cannot keep on that way indefinitely. We have grown rich in worldly goods, but we are getting poorer in the natural resources that are the basis of those goods....Ours is a nation capable of doing things in a big way. We should aim high. Our goal should be continued abundance, not just to get by." (Journal of Forestry, Volume 48, No. 2, Feb. 1950, pages 82-83).

Ranger Woody would have heartily agreed!

Weeks Act, 1911

The Weeks Act of 1911 made it possible for the federal government to purchase land in the Southeastern United States that would eventually become part of the National Forest system administered by the U.S. Forest Service. Introduced by Massachusetts Congressman John Weeks and signed into law by William Howard Taft, Theodore Roosevelt's successor. The law made it possible to purchase private land "if the purchase was deemed necessary to protect rivers' and watersheds' headwaters in the eastern United States." Initially the Weeks Act appropriated $9 million to purchase 6 million acres of land in the eastern U.S.

Two of the first tracts purchased under the act were the Vanderbilt Tract in North Carolina that eventually became part of the Pisgah National Forest and the 31,000 acre Gennett Tract in North Georgia that eventually became Ranger Arthur Woody's beloved Rock Creek Refuge (today known as the Blue Ridge WMA, the first wildlife management area in the South and the country). Ranger Woody became the Blue Ridge District's first Forest Ranger in 1918 and ultimately had under his supervision nearly 200,000 acres of national forestland.

The Weeks Act also provided measures for a better system of cooperation between federal and state governments in regard to fire control, an endeavor in which Ranger Woody proved to be invaluable. When the Weeks Act was passed in 1911, no Southern Appalachian State had passed any fire protection laws. Georgia finally developed such a law and fire control system in 1925.

Woody Gap School

For many years, Arthur Woody and his oldest son Walter had talked about trying to initiate a better system of education for the children growing up in and around the community of Suches. After receiving support from Union County officials, plans began in 1936 to build a single school in Suches. This modern school building would consolidate the five scattered one-room, two-teacher schools of Mt. Lebanon, Mt. Zion, Cooper's Creek, Sprigg's Chapel and Valley into one central location that would offer grades K-12.

Ranger Woody and Walter made numerous trips to Blairsville (and reportedly to Atlanta as well) to get approval and work out all of the details for getting the school approved and built. At the request of the school board, Arthur Woody purchased 20 acres of land in Suches that at one time had been owned by the family of Civil War Governor Joseph Emerson Brown for the school site. Brown had grown up on the property.

The land was then donated to the county by the Woody family. The building was constructed, using native stone mined from Arthur Woody's granite mine just down the road. Arthur Woody also donated much of the lumber that went into the school. Woody Gap School was dedicated in November 1940 and the school opened its doors in January 1941, at mid-term. It was named to honor both father and son, Arthur and Walter Woody, who had worked diligently to have a school located in Suches.

Fittingly, Ranger Woody's daughter Mae White began teaching at the new school when it opened. Later, after graduating from college, his granddaughter Jean White McNey, also taught at Woody Gap School for a number of years.

Woody Gap

Woody Gap is a high mountain gap in North Georgia where Lumpkin and Union counties meet near the top of Black Mountain. Georgia Highway 60 crosses the gap and descends into the small community of Suches where it meets Highway 180. The Appalachian Trail also crosses Woody Gap at an elevation of 3,164 feet. The trail's southern end at Springer Mountain is 20 miles to the west. The northern end of the Appalachian Trail spans 2,138 miles northward from Springer Mountain and winds up at Mount Katahdin in northern Maine, Maine's highest peak.

The ridge line at Woody Gap is also the divide between the Tennessee River and Etowah River drainages. This gap in the southern Appalachian Mountains just east of Black Mountain was named in memory of the Honorable John Wesley Woody Jr., Arthur Woody's paternal grandfather, who served as postmaster of Dahlonega after the Civil War in the early 1870s.

John Wesley Woody Jr. reportedly was also one of the founders of North Georgia Agricultural College which opened its doors in 1873 (Note: the author was unable to confirm this report). A staunch Unionist like his father before him, he was chased and harassed during the early years of the Civil War by member of the Home Guard (a local group with sympathies clearly directed toward the South. John Wesley's own brother led the Guard.) In early 1864, John Wesley and his oldest son Aaron Washington Woody, then 18, traveled to Nashville and joined a cavalry division of the Union Army where father and son saw considerable action in Tennessee and northern Alabama as Sherman's Army pushed southward into Georgia. John Wesley returned home from the conflict carrying a tattered Union battle flag that he and Aaron apparently picked up during one of their many actions. Today that small Union flag, a treasured family heirloom, is still in the Woody family, residing in Wyoming with one of John Wesley's descendents.

Woody Lake

Originally an 80-acre lake, Ranger Woody built Woody Lake in early 1930s with the help of the CC boys. At the time, a creek ran through the property but much of the land was a bog. Building a lake made a lot of sense, especially since the CC boys represented a ready workforce. After the lake was built, Ranger Woody stocked it with fish and welcomed neighbors to fish in it. He also swam in the lake quite frequently during warm weather. Sadly, Woody Lake has been greatly reduced in size in recent years because of heavy siltation.

The Woody Clan

McNey, Miriam Jean White (1929 -)

Having moved in with her grandparent's at age five in 1933 with her mother Mae Woody White and brother, Ned, Jean McNey is the last living relative who knew Arthur Woody on an intimate basis. Thanks to her efforts to preserve old photos and stories about her beloved grandfather shortly after his death in 1946, and her willingness to share that information with the author, the writing of this book was made possible.

Nichols, Emmalou Woody (1934-)

Along with her first cousin Jean McNey, Lou Nichols is one of three living grandchildren of Ranger Arthur Woody. Daughter of Clyne Woody, Ranger Woody's youngest son, Lou's family did not live in Suches when she was a young girl so she did not spend as much time with her grandfather as her cousin. However, Lou did spend portions of the summer visiting her grandparents and she has been very helpful in sharing stories about both of her amazing grandparents for this book.

Ned Woody White (1933-2010)

Just like his older sister Jean McNey, Ned Woody White was very close to his beloved grandfather. Born on Aug. 18, 1933, he died in Suches on Feb. 8, 2010.

Woody, Abraham Lincoln (1864–1919)

"Granddaddy Abe," Ranger Woody's father, was born in the Yahoola Valley of Lumpkin County (just north of Dahlonega) on July 23, 1864 during the turmoil of the Civil War. By all accounts he was a maverick, but he worked hard and provided well for his family. He died as the result of a gunshot wound at age 55 on Sept. 5, 1919.

Woody, Elizabeth "Eliza" Ingram (1869-1959)

Fondly known far and wide as "Ma" Woody or "Granny" Woody, Ranger Woody's mother, was born on Sept. 1, 1868 in Wildhog (near Suches) and died on Sept. 12, 1959 in Suches at the age of 90. She outlived her husband by 40 years and her son by 13 years.

Woody, Nancy Emma Abercrombie (1877-1973)

Ranger Woody's beloved wife, fondly known to all as "June," was born on Sept. 1, 1877. She died on August 12, 1973 at the age of 96. For many years she quietly supported her husband's lifework by graciously preparing hundreds (if not thousands) of meals for Forest Service workers and dignitaries who came to Suches and by manning the home telephone line so that local firefighters could be notified, organized and sent out to fight forest fires.

Woody, Walter "Walt" Willis (1902-1986)

Ranger Woody's oldest son was born near Suches on July 13, 1902. He died in a Hall County hospital on Jan. 25, 1986. Much of his career followed that of his father, working for the U.S. Forest Service and helping his father with many of Ranger Woody's innovative programs and projects. When Camp Woody was built in Suches in 1933 (C.C.C.), he was named as civilian supervisor for the camp. Later he worked hard to ensure that Woody Gap School would become a reality in Suches (1940). Unlike his father who detested anything to do with the cattle business, Walter loved cattle and maintained a sizable cattle operation in Lumpkin County for many years.

Woody, Vella Mae (1907-1986)

Born on July 15, 1907, Ranger Woody's only daughter died on April 6, 1986. Abandoned with two young children in the early 1930s, she lived with her parents for many years, helping her mother with the endless job of preparing meals for Forest Service personnel. When Woody Gap School opened its doors in 1940, she taught grade school for a number of years.

Woody, Clyne Edward (1905-1984)

Ranger Woody's second son was born on April 30, 1905. He died on Dec. 1, 1984. Clyne had a long, distinguished career with the Forest Service, working his way up through the ranks to the position of Forest Ranger. Like his older brother Walter, Clyne was always there to help his father with many of the Ranger's outrageous projects.

Woody, Jonathan Wesley Jr. (1820-1894, married Axey Seabolt)

Records maintain that Jonathan Wesley Woody Jr. was born on July 4, 1820 in Lumpkin County (Yahoola Valley). However, since his parents did not move to the Yahoola Valley until after Indian removal in the late 1830s, John Jr. was probably born in east Georgia near Franklin in 1820 and later moved to Lumpkin County with his family. He died June 16, 1894 in Suches. A well known personality in his Yahoola community just north of Dahlonega, Ranger Woody's paternal grandfather was a controversial figure during the Civil War. He made a name for himself by remaining true to his convictions and staying loyal to the Union (as did his father, John Wesley Woody Sr.). After the war, John Jr. became postmaster of Dahlonega. Woody Gap was later named in his honor.

Woody, Axey "Axy" Seabolt (1820-1904, married Jonathan Wesley Woody Jr.)

Also a well-known figure in her community, Ranger Woody's grandmother was born on Oct. 24, 1820 in and died Feb. 9, 1904 in Suches.

Woody, Josiah Askew (1823-1899, brother of Jonathan Wesley Woody Jr.)

Josiah Askew Woody was born in Franklin, Georgia, on April 10 1823. His family moved to Lumpkin County soon after gold was discovered in the area in 1828. As a boy, he and future Georgia Civil War Governor Joseph E. Brown became close friends. A gifted speaker, Josiah became a Baptist minister before he was 20. He married Rausey M. Bryan in 1841. The couple had 15 children.

At the outbreak of the Civil War, Josiah enlisted in the Confederate Army and took part in the first Battle of Bull Run in Virginia in July 1861. Shortly after that battle, he petitioned his friend Governor Brown for an early discharge under the pretext that he was a minister of the gospel. The discharge was granted and Josiah returned to Dahlonega where he formed a group of southern loyalists known as the Home Guard. The mission of the Home Guard was to catch deserters and northern sympathizers and bring them to justice, but the Home Guard soon became a lawless renegade group.

One of those so-called deserters happened to be John Wesley Woody Jr., Josiah's older brother and Arthur Woody's grandfather. Later on, through Josiah's efforts, 81-year-old John Wesley Woody Sr. (Josiah's father) and John Jr. were captured and put on trial because of their loyalty to the Union. A guilty verdict could have meant death by hanging. Through an odd twist of events, father and son were acquitted. John Jr. later joined the Union army because he was so outraged. The split between father and son and brother against brother was never rectified. After the war, Josiah Woody moved to Crawfordville, Georgia, where he preached at a local church. He later migrated to Missouri. He died in Lincoln, Kansas, in 1899.

Woody, John Wesley Sr. (1781-1866)

Born July 16, 1781 in Surrey, North Carolina, John Wesley Sr. migrated to Lumpkin County in the early 1840s after the removal of the Cherokee Indians. He and his wife Priscilla Treadway Woody had at least 11 children, nine sons and two daughters (possibly more than two daughters. The records are unclear). When secession and Civil War came in 1861, he and his oldest son John Jr. sided with the Union. Sadly, his other eight sons sided with the Confederacy, thus causing a fracture in the family that was never rectified.

Woody, Priscilla "Precilla" Treadway (1799-1888)

Born Jan 2, 1799 in Haywood County North Carolina, Priscilla Treadway Woody died on March 13 1888 in Dahlonega. She made a name for herself as a skilled midwife, helping to deliver dozens of mountain babies over the years. After her husband's death in 1866, Priscilla moved to Dahlonega and operated a boarding house with the help of her son John Jr.

Bibliography

Books, Newspapers, Journals and Magazines

Abernathy, Perry, "Arthur Woody, the Barefoot Ranger of Suches," *Touching Home,* Daniels Publishers, 1976.

Alter, Norman Bruce, *A Historical-Socio-Political Study of the Chattahoochee-Oconee National Forests,* 1971.

Amerson, Anne Dismukes, *"I Remember Dahlonega," Memoirs of Growing Up In Lumpkin County,* Chestatee Publications, 1990.

Amerson, Anne Dismukes, *The Best of "I Remember Dahlonega," Memoirs of Lumpkin County, Georgia,* The History Press, Charleston, SC, 2006.

Appalachian Trail Journeys, November-December, 2005.

Bergoffen, William W., Bryan, Milton M., and Clark, Donald E., "WE PRESENT, William Arthur Woody: 'The Ranger,'" *Journal of Forestry* magazine, April 1946.

Bergoffen, William W., U.S. Forest Service retired, *100 Years of Federal Forestry,* United States Department of Agriculture, Agriculture Information Bulletin No. 402, 1976.

"Big Tracks in Georgia Wilds," *Outdoor Georgia* magazine, October 1940.

Brinkley, Hal E., *How Georgia Got Her Names,* privately printed, 1967 and 1973.

Davis, Sgt. Clint, (U.S. Army), "Woody Takes 'Rest Cure.' Noted State Ranger Confined to Hospital," Atlanta Constitution, no date, probably late February 1945.

Davis, Henry, *The American Wild Turkey,* Small-Arms Technical Publishing Co., 1949.

Dobie, Duncan, *Georgia's Greatest Whitetails,* Bucksnort Publishing, Marietta, GA, 1986.

Dobie, Duncan, "The Barefoot Ranger," *Georgia Sportsman,* April 1989.

Elliott, Charlie, *An Outdoor Life, the Autobiography of Charlie Elliott,* Flat Rock Press, Covington, GA, 1996.

Elliott, Charlie, *American Forests,* May, 1939.

Elliott, Charlie, "Dollar Limit Set on Fund for Woody," *Outdoor Georgia* magazine, March 15, 1945.

Elliott, Charlie, "Game Log (column)," *Southern Outdoors*, Jan. 15, 1945.

Elliott, Charlie, "Game Log (column)," *Southern Outdoors*, July 1, 1946.

Elliott, Charlie, *Gone Huntin',* Stackpole Books, 1954, pages 168-169.

Elliott, Charlie, "Hunting Deer the Indian Way," *Outdoor Georgia* magazine, May 1940.

Elliott, Charles, "Modern Day Robin Hoods," *American Forests*, December 1941.

Elliott, Charlie, "Monument Proposed For Arthur Woody," Game Log (column), Atlanta Constitution, Jan. 15, 1945.

Elliott, Charlie, *Mr. Anonymous, Robert Woodruff of Coca Cola,* Cherokee Publishing Company, Atlanta, 1982.

Elliott, Charlie, "Perennial Ranger," *Master Detective* magazine (1946 or 1947).

Elliott, Charlie, "'Public Forests, Public Trust,' Ranger Woody's Motto," the Atlanta Constitution, Oct. 26, 1957.

Elliott, Charlie, "Ranger Arthur Woody Lives to See Game and Fish Dreams Come True in Georgia Mountains," *Outdoor Life* magazine, June 1943.

Elliott, Charles N. and Mobley, M.D., *Southern Forestry,* Turner E. Smith & Company, 1938.

Elliott, Charlie, "The Blue Ridge Hunt," *Outdoor Life* magazine, November 1972.

Elliott, Charles N., "The Lure of the Chattahoochee," *American Forests* magazine, May 1939.

Experience Northeast Georgia, John Kollock's Guide to 75 special places, Sponsored by Habersham Electric Membership Corporation, 2013.

Forest Service Bulletin, (News of Arthur Woody's death), *Washington Information Digest,* June 12, 1946.

"For Rugged Old-Timer, Sportsmen Plan Plaque to Honor William Woody," author unknown, Atlanta Constitution, Oct. 1, 1945.

Frome, Michael, *Whose Woods These Are, the Story of the National Forests,* Doubleday and Company, Inc., 1962.

Georgia Backroads, summer 2005.

Grahame, Arthur, "Dixie's Game is Coming Back," *Outdoor Life* magazine, October 1941.

Geist, Valerius, *Deer of the World: Their Evolution, Behavior, and Ecology,* Stackpole Books, 1998.

Harlow, Dr. William M., *Trees of the Eastern and Central United States and Canada,* Dover Publications, New York, NY, 1957.

"Home-Grown Rangers Do Best," from the U.S. Forest Service publication: "Mountaineers and Rangers: A History of Federal Forest Management in the Southern Appalachians." No date.

Huber, W.W. and Conarro, R.M., U.S. Forest Service, "How Deer Came Back To Georgia," Atlanta Constitution, mid-1940s.

Jacobs, Jimmy, *Trout Streams of Southern Appalachia,* Backcountry Publications, 1994.

Jenkins, J. H., Project leader, *Game Resources of Georgia,* Georgia Game and Fish Commission, 1953.

Jones, Ethelene Dyer and Jones, Elton Keith, *Mother and Child Reunion,* EJ Productions, Epworth, Georgia, 1995.

Jones, Paul, column quoting Charlie Elliott, Atlanta Constitution, Oct. 29, 1975.

Kilmer, Joyce, *Trees and Other Poems,* George H. Doran Company, 1914.

Lacy, Leslie Alexander, *The Soil Soldiers, The Civilian Conservation Corps in the Great Depression,* Chilton Book Company, Radnor, PA, 1976.

Leavell, Chuck (with Mary Welch), *Forever Green, The History and Hope of the American Forest,* Evergreen Arts, Dry Branch, Georgia, 2001.

Lumsden, Thomas N., MD, *Nacoochee Valley, Its Time and Its Places,* 1989.

Madson, John, *The White-tailed Deer,* Olin Mathieson Chemical Company, 1961.

Martin, Harold, "Dreams and Dust (column)," Atlanta Constitution, Oct. 20, 1944.

Martin, Harold, "Forests Coming Back, Georgia Ranger Says," Atlanta Constitution, June 13, 1937.

Martin, John, "Atlanta Archers Kill Wild Hog But No Deer in Chattahoochee," Atlanta Constitution, November 11 (probably 1941).

Martin, John, "Woody Buried: Wildlife Loses 'Best Friend,'" *Southern Outdoors,* July 1, 1946.

McCabe, T.R. and McCabe, R.E., *White-Tailed Deer: Ecology and Management,* Stackpole Books, 1997.

McDonald, J. Scott and Miller, Karl V., *A History of White-Tailed Deer Restocking in the United States, 1878 to 2004.* Published by the Quality Deer Management Association, 1993.

McGraw, Jim, "Deer Hunt," *Outdoor Georgia* magazine, December 1940.

Miller, Zell, *Purt Nigh Gone, The Old Mountain Ways,* Stroud & Hall publishers, 2009.

Mountaineers and Rangers: A History of Federal Forest Management in the Southern Appalachians, U.S. Forest Service Publication, (no date).

Native Trees of Georgia, Georgia Forestry Commission, February 1970.

North Georgia Journal, summer 1990.

Outdoor Georgia magazine, Published by the Georgia Natural Resources Department, (later to become the Georgia Game and Fish Commission, still later to become the Georgia Department of Natural Resources): Numerous issues presented stories about Arthur Woody including May 1940, June 1940, July 1940, September 1940, October 1940, December 1940, January 1941, September 1941, October 1941, November 1941 and November 1942. Special thanks to the University of Georgia Library archives.

Pfitzer, Donald W., *Hiking Georgia,* Falcon Publishing, Inc., 1993.

"Problems in Hunting," old news clipping, no byline, likely the Atlanta Constitution, Nov. 6, 1940.

Ranger Arthur Woody (death of), Gainesville Eagle, June 13, 1946.

Rawlings, Marjorie Kinnan, *The Yearling,* Charles Scribners Sons, 1938.

Restoring America's Wildlife 1937-1987, The First 50 Years of the Federal Aid in Wildlife Restoration (Pittman-Robertson) Act, United States Department of the Interior, 1987.

Stearns, Joe, "Archery 'Grand Opera,'" *Outdoor Georgia* magazine, November 1942.

Schneider, Rachel G., *History of the Chattahoochee-Oconee National Forest* (report), no date given.

Shelton, Horace. E. Jr., "Chasing Ranger Woody's Bass," *Georgia Sportsman,* November 2009.

Time magazine, "At Chattahoochee (National Forest, Georgia)" Nov. 16, 1940.

Troy, Jack, "A Duck Hunt" (column), Atlanta Constitution, 1942 or 1943.

Troy, Jack, "All in the Game" (column), Atlanta Constitution, Nov. 17, 1940.

Troy, Jack, "Forest Primeval (column)," Atlanta Constitution, Oct. 29, 1940.

Troy, Jack, "Outdoor Georgia" (column), Atlanta Constitution, no date.

Williams, David, *The Georgia Gold Rush,* University of South Carolina Press, 1993.

About the Author

Duncan Dobie has been a full-time outdoor writer for more than 30 years. His stories and photographs have appeared in numerous books, magazines and newspapers across the country. During high school, Duncan frequently went hunting and fishing in the North Georgia mountains with several of his teachers. Here he began to discover colorful stories and legends about Ranger Arthur Woody. Those stories so impacted him that he vowed to learn more about the "Barefoot Ranger of Suches." This book, his eleventh, is the result of a lifelong quest to share Ranger Woody's remarkable story. Duncan lives in Marietta, Georgia.

This photo was taken at Sheriff Knob in Union County, Georgia in 1964 when the author was 17.

Made in the USA
Columbia, SC
06 November 2020

24084745R00280